Management: MGMT 1100

Southern Crescent Technical College

Chuck Williams

CENGAGE
Learning·

Australia • Brazil • Japan • Korea • Mexico • Singapore • Spain • United Kingdom • United States

**Management: MGMT 1100: Southern
Crescent Technical College**

MGMT 2, 2nd Edition
Chuck Williams

© 2010 Cengage Learning. All rights reserved.

Executive Editors:
 Maureen Staudt
 Michael Stranz

Senior Project Development Manager:
 Linda deStefano

Marketing Specialist:
 Courtney Sheldon

Senior Production/Manufacturing Manager:
 Donna M. Brown

Production Editorial Manager:
 Kim Fry

Sr. Rights Acquisition Account Manager:
 Todd Osborne

For product information and technology assistance, contact us at
Cengage Learning Customer & Sales Support, 1-800-354-9706

For permission to use material from this text or product,
submit all requests online at **cengage.com/permissions**
Further permissions questions can be emailed to
permissionrequest@cengage.com

This book contains select works from existing Cengage Learning resources and
was produced by Cengage Learning Custom Solutions for collegiate use. As such,
those adopting and/or contributing to this work are responsible for editorial
content accuracy, continuity and completeness.

Compilation © 2012 Cengage Learning
ISBN-13: 978-1-111-52342-8

ISBN-10: 1-111-52342-8

Cengage Learning
5191 Natorp Boulevard
Mason, Ohio 45040
USA

Cengage Learning is a leading provider of customized learning solutions with
office locations around the globe, including Singapore, the United Kingdom,
Australia, Mexico, Brazil, and Japan. Locate your local office at:
international.cengage.com/region.

Cengage Learning products are represented in Canada by Nelson Education, Ltd.
For your lifelong learning solutions, visit **www.cengage.com/custom.**
Visit our corporate website at **www.cengage.com.**

Printed in the United States of America

Brief Contents

MANAGEMENT

What Is Management?

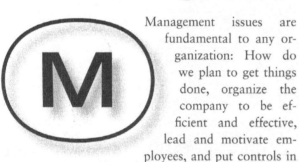

Management issues are fundamental to any organization: How do we plan to get things done, organize the company to be efficient and effective, lead and motivate employees, and put controls in place to make sure our plans are followed and our goals are met? Good management is basic to starting a business, growing a business, and maintaining a business once it has achieved some measure of success.

To understand how important *good* management is, think about mistakes like these: Mistake #1. A high-level bank manager reduces a marketing manager to tears by angrily criticizing her in front of others for a mistake that wasn't hers.[1] Mistake #2. Guidant Corporation, which makes cardiovascular medical products, waited for three years, forty-five device failures, and two patient deaths before recalling 50,000 defective heart defibrillators, 77 percent of which were already implanted in patients.[2]

Ah, bad managers and bad management. Is it any wonder that companies pay management consultants nearly $150 billion a year for advice on basic management issues such as how to lead people effectively, organize the company efficiently, and manage large-scale projects and processes?[3] This textbook will help you understand some of the basic issues that management consultants help companies resolve. (And it won't cost you billions of dollars).

After reading the next two sections, you should be able to

1 describe what management is.

2 explain the four functions of management.

Learning Outcomes

1 describe what management is.

2 explain the four functions of management.

3 describe different kinds of managers.

4 explain the major roles and subroles that managers perform in their jobs.

5 explain what companies look for in managers.

6 discuss the top mistakes that managers make in their jobs.

7 describe the transition that employees go through when they are promoted to management.

8 explain how and why companies can create competitive advantage through people.

© Mark Coffey/iStockphoto.com

1 Management Is . . .

Many of today's managers got their start welding on the factory floor, clearing dishes off tables, helping customers fit a suit, or wiping up a spill in aisle 3. Similarly, lots of you will start at the bottom and work your way up. There's no better way to get to know your competition, your customers, and your business. But whether you begin your career at the entry level or as a supervisor, your job is not to do the work but to help others do theirs. **Management** is getting work done through others. Pat Carrigan, a former elementary school principal who became a manager at a General Motors' car parts plant, says, "I've never made a part in my life, and I don't really have any plans to make one. That's not my job. My job

is to create an environment where people who do make them can make them right, can make them right the first time, can make them at a competitive cost, and can do so with some sense of responsibility and pride in what they're doing. I don't have to know how to make a part to do any of those things."[4]

Pat Carrigan's description of managerial responsibilities suggests that managers also have to be concerned with efficiency and effectiveness in the work process. **Efficiency** is getting work done with a minimum of effort,

Management getting work done through others

Efficiency getting work done with a minimum of effort, expense, or waste

expense, or waste. For example, how do millions of Girl Scouts from over 200 councils across the United States sell and deliver millions of boxes of cookies each year? In other words, what makes Girl Scouts so efficient? The national organization, Girl Scouts of America (GSA), licenses only two bakers, so when GSA changes or improves its cookie offerings, for example by adding new flavors or making healthier, sugar-free options, it can do so quickly and consistently nationwide. GSA has also designed Girl Scout cookie packages to maximize the number of boxes that can fit in a delivery truck. The national organization optimizes its overall cookie inventory by tracking sales by type of cookie and troop. Because GSA operates efficiently, 2.9 million scouts can sell and deliver over 50 million cookies in an 8-week period.[5]

Efficiency alone is not enough to ensure success. Managers must also strive for **effectiveness,** which means accomplishing tasks that help fulfill organizational objectives such as customer service and satisfaction. Wal-Mart's new computerized scheduling system is an example of efficiency and effectiveness. It typically takes a manager a full day to schedule the weekly shifts for a single store. But the computerized scheduling system calculates the schedules for Wal-Mart's 1.3 million workers in one day. The system also measures trends in store sales and customer traffic so it can have more employees on the job whenever its stores are busy. Tests in 39 stores indicated that 70 percent of customers reported improved checkout times and service using this scheduling system.[6]

2 Management Functions

Henri Fayol, who was a managing director (CEO) of a large steel company in the early 1900s, was one of the founders of the field of management. You'll learn more about Fayol and management's other key contributors when you read about the history of management in Chapter 2. Based on his 20 years of experience as a CEO, Fayol argued that "the success of an enterprise generally depends much more on the administrative ability of its leaders than on their technical ability."[7] Although Eric Schmidt, CEO of Google, has extensive expertise and experience in computer technology, Google succeeds because of his capabilities as a manager and not because of his ability to write computer code.

Effectiveness accomplishing tasks that help fulfill organizational objectives

Planning (management functions) determining organizational goals and a means for achieving them

Managers need to perform five managerial functions in order to be successful, according to Fayol: planning, organizing, coordinating, commanding, and controlling.[8] Most management textbooks today have updated this list by dropping the coordinating function and referring to Fayol's commanding function as "leading." Fayol's management functions are thus known today in this updated form as planning, organizing, leading, and controlling. Studies indicate that managers who perform these management functions well are more successful, gaining promotions for themselves and profits for their companies. One study shows that the more time CEOs spend planning, the more profitable their companies are.[9] A 25-year study at AT&T found that employees with better planning and decision-making skills were more likely to be promoted into management jobs, to be successful as managers, and to be promoted into upper levels of management.[10] The evidence is clear. Managers serve their companies well when they plan, organize, lead, and control. (That's why this book is organized around the functions of management outlined in Exhibit 1.1.)

Now let's take a closer look at each of the management functions: 2.1 planning, 2.2 organizing, 2.3 leading, and 2.4 controlling.

2.1 Planning

Planning involves determining organizational goals and a means for achieving them. As you'll learn in Chapter 5, planning is one of the best ways to improve performance. It encourages people to work harder, to work hard for extended periods, to engage in behaviors directly related to accomplishing goals, and to think of better ways to do their jobs. But most importantly, companies that plan have larger profits and faster growth than companies that don't plan.

For example, the question, "What business are we in?" is at the heart of strategic planning, which you'll

Exhibit 1.1

The Four Functions of Management

Planning Organizing

Leading Controlling

learn about in Chapter 6. If you can answer the question, "What business are you in?" in two sentences or less, chances are you have a very clear plan for your business. Exxon Mobil CEO Rex Tillerson knows precisely what business his company is in—and not in—and he'll tell you so.[11] Same for Google. Even though the company makes money selling search-based Internet advertising, Google says that it is not in the advertising business but in the business of organizing the world's information.[12] Not only can you search Google for websites, images, books and scholarly articles, and shopping opportunities, but you can also organize your personal life using Google's calendar, email, photo and document sharing, and feed reader applications. Even Google's $1.65 billion purchase of YouTube adheres to the business Google is in by helping users access and organize video content.

You'll learn more about planning in Chapter 5 on planning and decision making, Chapter 6 on organizational strategy, Chapter 7 on innovation and change, and Chapter 8 on global management.

2.2 Organizing

Organizing is deciding where decisions will be made, who will do what jobs and tasks, and who will work for whom in the company. The U.S. Department of Homeland Security has an enormous organizing challenge on its hands. The organization was formed in March 2003 to coordinate the activities of nearly two dozen federal agencies in an effort to ensure that a coordinated, efficient, and effective response could be achieved in the event of an attack or disaster. Five years later, however, the organization is still struggling with problems of, well, organization. The agencies in the Department remain housed in various locations across Washington, D.C., and the Department is answerable to over 80 Congressional committees. Even determining what tasks should be done has been a challenge. Current efforts are focused on law enforcement and security, but some leaders think focusing on preventive efforts such as intelligence and nuclear nonproliferation would be more effective. The problem: How best to organize the limited resources of money, knowledge, technology, and people to get the job done. While the Department had initial success in closing some of the biggest gaps (like airport security), the lack of adequate organization remains a major hurdle. Its former inspector general, Clark Kent Ervin, said, "It takes more than a department called Homeland Security to secure the homeland. The department has to work, and the department doesn't work."[13]

© AP Images

You'll learn more about organizing in Chapter 9 on designing organizations, Chapter 10 on managing teams, Chapter 11 on managing human resources, and Chapter 12 on managing individuals and a diverse work force.

2.3 Leading

Our third management function, **leading**, involves inspiring and motivating workers to work hard to achieve organizational goals. When Anne Mulcahy became Xerox's CEO, the company was on the brink of bankruptcy—it was $17.1 billion in debt and had only $154 million in cash. In addition, three years of steeply declining revenues and

Organizing deciding where decisions will be made, who will do what jobs and tasks, and who will work for whom

Leading inspiring and motivating workers to work hard to achieve organizational goals

increasing losses had dropped the company's stock price from $64 a share to just $4.43. Mulcahy admits that the responsibility of turning the company around frightened her: "Nothing spooked me as much as waking up in the middle of the night and thinking about 96,000 people and retirees and what would happen if this thing went south."[14] Still, she took the job.

Mulcahy, who traveled to two and sometimes three cities a day to talk to Xerox managers and employees, implored them to "save each dollar as if it were your own." And at each stop, she reminded them, "Remember, by my calculations, there are [she fills in the number] selling days left in the quarter."[15] Mulcahy said, "One of the things I care most about at Xerox is the morale and motivation at the company. I think it is absolutely critical to being able to deliver results. People have to feel engaged, motivated and feel they are making a contribution to something that is important. I spend the vast majority of my time with customers and employees, and there is nothing more important for any of us to do as leaders than communicate and engage with our two most important constituencies."[16] Today, as a result of Mulcahy's leadership and the hard work of dedicated Xerox employees, Xerox is not only back on its feet, the company is now a leading developer of new color digital printing technologies.[17]

You'll learn more about leading in Chapter 13 on motivation, Chapter 14 on leadership, and Chapter 15 on managing communication.

2.4 Controlling

The last function of management, **controlling,** is monitoring progress toward goal achievement and taking corrective action when progress isn't being made. The basic control process involves setting standards to achieve goals, comparing actual performance to those standards, and then making changes to return performance to those standards.

Needing to cut costs (the standard) to restore profitability (the goal), Continental Airlines started giving passengers small cups of their soft drinks instead of an entire can (one corrective action among many). Company spokesperson Rahsaan Johnson defended the move, saying, "Flight attendants have been telling us that the trash bags they carry were so heavy because of all the [wasted] liquid. We were pouring almost half away."[18]

Controlling monitoring progress toward goal achievement and taking corrective action when needed

Top managers executives responsible for the overall direction of the organization

Although Continental will still give entire soft drink cans to customers who request them, serving smaller drinks saves the company $100,000 a year in costs.

You'll learn more about the control function in Chapter 16 on control, Chapter 17 on managing information, and Chapter 18 on managing service and manufacturing operations.

What Do Managers Do?

Not all managerial jobs are the same. The demands and requirements placed on the CEO of Sony are significantly different from those placed on the manager of your local Wendy's restaurant.

After reading the next two sections, you should be able to

3 describe different kinds of managers.

4 explain the major roles and subroles that managers perform in their jobs.

3 Kinds of Managers

As shown in Exhibit 1.2, there are four kinds of managers, each with different jobs and responsibilities: **3.1 top managers, 3.2 middle managers, 3.3 first-line managers,** and **3.4 team leaders.**

3.1 Top Managers

Top managers hold positions like chief executive officer (CEO), chief operating officer (COO), chief financial officer (CFO), and chief information officer (CIO), and are responsible for the overall direction of the organization. Top managers have the following responsibilities.[19] First, they are responsible for creating a context for change. The CEOs of Walt Disney, Fannie Mae, Boeing, Morgan Stanley, American International Group, Merck, and Pfizer were all fired within a year's time precisely because they had not moved fast enough to bring about significant changes in their companies. Indeed, in both Europe and the United States, 35 per-

Exhibit 1.2

What the Four Kinds
of Managers Do

Jobs	Responsibilities
Top Managers CEO CIO COO Vice President CFO Corporate Heads	change commitment culture environment
Middle Managers General Manager Plant Manager Regional Manager Divisional Manager	resources objectives coordination subunit performance strategy implementation
First-Line Managers Office Manager Shift Supervisor Department Manager	nonmanagerial worker supervision teaching and training scheduling facilitation
Team Leaders Team Leader Team Contact Group Facilitator	facilitation external relationships internal relationships

cent of all CEOs are eventually fired because of their failure to successfully change their companies.[20] Creating a context for change includes forming a long-range vision or mission for the company.

Once that vision or mission is set, the second responsibility of top managers is to develop employees' commitment to and ownership of the company's performance. That is, top managers are responsible for creating employee buy-in. Third, top managers must create a positive organizational culture through language and action. Top managers impart company values, strategies, and lessons through what they do and say to others both inside and outside the company. Above all, no matter what they communicate, it's critical for CEOs to send and reinforce clear, consistent messages.[21] A former *Fortune* 500 CEO said, "I tried to [use] exactly the same words every time so that I didn't produce a lot of, 'Last time you said this, this time

you said that.' You've got to say the same thing over and over and over."[22]

Finally, top managers are responsible for monitoring their business environments. This means that top managers must closely monitor customers' needs, competitors' moves, and long-term business, economic, and social trends. You'll read more about business environments in Chapter 3.

3.2 Middle Managers

Middle managers hold positions like plant manager, regional manager, or divisional manager. They are responsible for setting objectives consistent with top management's goals and

Middle managers managers responsible for setting objectives consistent with top management's goals and for planning and implementing subunit strategies for achieving these objectives

Feats of Daring Duet

Trusting that his 61,000 employees could dramatically increase product innovation at Whirlpool appliances, CEO David Whitman told them to come up with new ideas, tell their bosses about their ideas, and, if their bosses wouldn't listen, bring their new product ideas directly to him. Employees flocked to an in-house Web site featuring a course on innovation and a list of all the new suggestions and ideas, racking up 300,000 "hits" on the site each month. Today, revenue from innovative products has quadrupled. And instead of cutting prices to maintain sales, Whirlpool's prices are now rising 5 percent per year because customers are willing to pay more for its innovative products, such as the Duet washer and dryer.[24]

Source: M. Arndt, "Creativity Overflowing," *Business Week*, 8 May 2006, 50.

for planning and implementing subunit strategies for achieving those objectives.[23] One specific middle management responsibility is to plan and allocate resources to meet objectives.

A second major responsibility is to coordinate and link groups, departments, and divisions within a company. In February 2008, a tornado destroyed a Caterpillar plant in Oxford, Mississippi, the only plant in the company that produced a particular coupling required for many of Caterpillar's machines. The disaster threatened a world-wide production shut-down. Greg Folley, a middle manager in charge of the parts division that included the plant, gave workers two weeks to restore production to pre-tornado levels. He said, "I was betting on people to get it done." He contacted new vendors, sent engineers from other Caterpillar locations to Mississippi to check for quality, and set up distribution operations in another facility. Meanwhile, Kevin Kempa, the plant manager in Oxford, moved some employees to another plant, delivered new training

First-line managers
managers who train and supervise the performance of nonmanagerial employees who are directly responsible for producing the company's products or services

to employees during the production hiatus, and oversaw reconstruction of the plant. The day before the two-week deadline, the Oxford plant was up and running and produced 8,000 parts.[24]

A third responsibility of middle management is to monitor and manage the performance of the subunits and individual managers who report to them. Graeme Betts is the manager of the Southwest region for Lloyds Pharmacy in England. While Betts works with people at all levels, from healthcare assistants to board directors, he spends most of his time with the nine area managers who report to him. He monitors and manages the performance of his area managers and, in turn, the store managers who report to them.[25]

Finally, middle managers are also responsible for implementing the changes or strategies generated by top managers. Wal-Mart's strategy reflects its mission, "Saving people money so they can live better." When Wal-Mart began selling groceries in its new 200,000-square-foot supercenters, it made purchasing manager Brian Wilson responsible for buying perishable goods more cheaply than Wal-Mart's competitors. When small produce suppliers had trouble meeting Wal-Mart's needs, Wilson worked closely with them and connected them to RetailLink, Wal-Mart's computer network, "which allows our suppliers immediate access to all information needed to help run the business." Over time, these steps helped the produce suppliers reduce costs and deliver the enormous quantities of fresh fruits and vegetables that Wal-Mart's Supercenters need.[26] They also helped Wal-Mart become the world's largest grocer.[27]

3.3 First-Line Managers

First-line managers hold positions like office manager, shift supervisor, or department manager. The primary responsibility of first-line managers is to manage the performance of the entry-level employees who are directly responsible for producing a company's goods and services. First-line managers are the only managers who don't supervise other managers. The responsibilities of first-line managers include monitoring, teaching, and short-term planning.

First-line managers encourage, monitor, and reward the performance of their workers. They also teach entry-level employees how to do their jobs. Damian Mogavero's company, Avero LLC, helps restaurants analyze sales data for each member of a restaurant's wait staff. Restaurant managers who use these data, says Mogavero, will often take their top-selling server to lunch each week as a reward. The best managers, however, will also take their poorest-selling servers out to lunch to talk about what they can do to improve their performance.[28]

First-line managers also make detailed schedules and operating plans based on middle management's intermediate-range plans. By contrast to the long-term plans of top managers (three to five years out) and the intermediate plans of middle managers (6 to 18 months out), first-line managers engage in plans and actions that typically produce results within two weeks.[29] Consider the typical convenience store manager (e.g., 7-Eleven) who starts the day by driving past competitors' stores to inspect their gasoline prices and then checks the outside of his or her store for anything that might need maintenance, such as burned-out lights or signs, or restocking, like windshield washer fluid and paper towels. Then comes an inside check, where the manager determines what needs to be done for that day. (Are there enough coffee and donuts for breakfast or enough sandwiches for lunch?) Once the day is planned, the manager turns to weekend orders. After accounting for the weather (hot or cold) and the sales trends at the same time last year, the manager makes sure the store will have enough beer, soft drinks, and Sunday papers on hand. Finally, the manager looks 7 to 10 days ahead for hiring needs. Because of strict hiring procedures (basic math tests, drug tests, and background checks), it can take that long to hire new employees. Said one convenience store manager, "I have to continually interview, even if I am fully staffed."[30]

3.4 Team Leaders

The fourth kind of manager is a team leader. This relatively new kind of management job developed as companies shifted to self-managing teams which, by definition, have no formal supervisor. In traditional management hierarchies, first-line managers are responsible for the performance of nonmanagerial employees and have the authority to hire and fire workers, make job assignments, and control resources. In this new structure, the teams themselves perform nearly all of the functions performed by first-line managers under traditional hierarchies.[31]

Getting produce to market efficiently and cheaply requires skilled execution of the four management functions.

© Photolink/Photodisc/Getty Images

Team leaders thus have a different set of responsibilities than traditional first-line managers.[32] **Team leaders** are primarily responsible for facilitating team activities toward accomplishing a goal. This doesn't mean team leaders are responsible for team performance. They aren't. The team is. Team leaders help their team members plan and schedule work, learn to solve problems, and work effectively with each other. Management consultant Franklin Jonath says, "The idea is for the team leader to be at the service of the group. It should be clear that the team members own the outcome. The leader is there to bring intellectual, emotional, and spiritual resources to the team. Through his or her actions, the leader should be able to show the others how to think about the work that they're doing in the context of their lives."[33]

Relationships among team members and between different teams are crucial to good team performance and must be well-managed by team leaders. Getting along with others is much more important in team structures because team members can't get work done without the help of other teammates. Team leaders are responsible for fostering good relationships and addressing problematic ones within their teams.

Team leaders are also responsible for managing external relationships. Team leaders act as the bridge or liaison between their teams and other teams, departments, and divisions in a company. For example, if a member of Team A complains about the quality of Team B's work, Team A's leader needs to initiate a meeting with Team B's leader. Together, these team leaders are responsible for getting members of both teams to work together to solve the problem. If it's done right, the problem is solved without involving company management or blaming members of the other team.[34]

Team leaders who fail to understand how their roles are different from those of traditional managers often struggle in their jobs. A team leader at Texas Instruments reacted with skepticism to his initial experience with teams: "I didn't buy into teams, partly because there was no clear plan on what I was supposed to do. . . . I never let the operators [team members] do any scheduling or any ordering of parts because that was mine. I figured as long as I had that, I had a job." After shifting jobs, however, he learned the difference in approach in a setting where members of the team took turns at the leadership role. He

Team leaders managers responsible for facilitating team activities toward accomplishing a goal

eventually became a consultant to help team leaders develop their skills and solve problems.[35]

You will learn more about teams in Chapter 10.

4 Managerial Roles

Although all four types of managers engage in planning, organizing, leading, and controlling, if you were to follow them around during a typical day on the job, you would probably not use these terms to describe what they actually do. Rather, what you'd see are the various roles managers play. Henry Mintzberg spent a week shadowing five American CEOs and analyzing their mail, their conversations, and their actions. He concluded that managers fulfill three major roles while performing their jobs:[36]

- interpersonal roles
- informational roles
- decisional roles

In other words, managers talk to people, gather and give information, and make decisions. Furthermore, as shown in Exhibit 1.3, these three major roles can be subdivided into 10 subroles. *Let's examine each major role—4.1 interpersonal, 4.2 informational, and 4.3 decisional roles—and their 10 subroles.*

4.1 Interpersonal Roles

More than anything else, management jobs are people-intensive. Estimates vary with the level of management,

Exhibit 1.3

Mintzberg's Managerial Roles

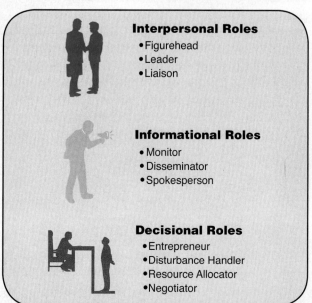

Interpersonal Roles
- Figurehead
- Leader
- Liaison

Informational Roles
- Monitor
- Disseminator
- Spokesperson

Decisional Roles
- Entrepreneur
- Disturbance Handler
- Resource Allocator
- Negotiator

but most managers spend between two-thirds and four-fifths of their time in face-to-face communication with others.[37] If you're a loner, or if you consider dealing with people a pain, then you may not be cut out for management work. In fulfilling the interpersonal role of management, managers perform three subroles: figurehead, leader, and liaison.

In the **figurehead role,** managers perform ceremonial duties like greeting company visitors, speaking at the opening of a new facility, or representing the company at a community luncheon to support local charities. In the **leader role,** managers motivate and encourage workers to accomplish organizational objectives. At Genentech, developing drugs to treat cancer and conducting research which might someday provide a cure is is enough to motivate most workers. But the culture set by Genentech's leadership helps attract and maintain the talent and passion to achieve this mission. The company offers a casual jeans-and-t-shirt work environment, employee-run clubs, onsite daycare, and sabbaticals to help employees avoid burnout. This culture, along with the company's overall success, makes Genentech, according to *Fortune* magazine, one of the best places to work in the United States.[38]

In the **liaison role,** managers deal with people outside their units. Studies consistently indicate that managers spend as much time with outsiders as they do with their own subordinates and their own bosses.[39]

4.2 Informational Roles

Not only do managers spend most of their time in face-to-face contact with others, but they spend much of it obtaining and sharing information. Indeed, Mintzberg found that the managers in his study spent 40 percent of their time giving and getting

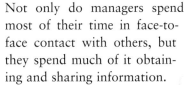

© Simon Potter/Image Source

information from others. In this regard, management can be viewed as processing information, gathering information by scanning the business environment and listening to others in face-to-face conversations, processing that information, and then sharing that information with people inside and outside the company. Mintzberg described three informational subroles: monitor, disseminator, and spokesperson.

In the **monitor role,** managers scan their environment for information, actively contact others for information, and, because of their personal contacts, receive a great deal of unsolicited information. Besides receiving firsthand information, managers monitor their environment by reading local newspapers and the *Wall Street Journal* to keep track of customers,

Figurehead role the interpersonal role managers play when they perform ceremonial duties

Leader role the interpersonal role managers play when they motivate and encourage workers to accomplish organizational objectives

Monitor role the informational role managers play when they scan their environment for information competitors, and technological changes that may affect their businesses. Now, managers can also take advantage of electronic monitoring and distribution services that track the news wires (Associated Press, Reuters, and so on) for stories related to their businesses.

Because of their numerous personal contacts and their access to subordinates, managers are often hubs for the distribution of critical information. In the **disseminator role,** managers share the information they have collected with their subordinates and others in the company. There will never be a complete substitute for face-to-face dissemination of information. Yet technology is changing how information is shared and collected. Although the primary methods of communication in large companies are email and voice mail, some managers are also beginning to use social networking technologies like Facebook and Twitter to disseminate information.[40] John Chambers, Cisco's CEO, says that 90 percent of his communication with employees is through email and voice mail. Says Chambers, "If you don't have the ability to interface with customers, employees, and suppliers, you can't manage your business."[41]

In contrast to the disseminator role, in which managers distribute information to employees inside the company, in the **spokesperson role,** managers share information with people outside their departments and companies. One of the most common ways CEOs serve as spokespeople for their companies is at annual meetings with company shareholders or the board of directors. CEOs also serve as spokespeople to the media when their companies are involved in major news stories. When Toshiba pulled the plug on its effort to position its HD-DVD technology as the dominant format for new high-definition players, ceding the market to Sony's Blu-ray, it was the company CEO Atsutoshi Nishida who explained this move to the public. Because Japanese companies value pride and tend to choose less high-profile strategies for backing out of a business deal, it was surprising that Nishida acted as the spokesperson in this situation. But Nishida emphasized, "We were in this to win," and explained Toshiba's decision to change its strategy and invest energy in alternative avenues of growth.[42]

4.3 Decisional Roles

Mintzberg found that obtaining and sharing information is not an end in itself. Obtaining and sharing information with people inside and outside the company is useful to managers because it helps them make good decisions. According to Mintzberg, managers engage in four decisional subroles: entrepreneur, disturbance handler, resource allocator, and negotiator.

In the **entrepreneur role,** managers adapt themselves, their subordinates, and their units to change. Veterans Affairs (VA) hospitals long had a reputation for red tape, inefficiency, and second class medical treatment, but today they rank as some of the best in the country. Fifteen years ago, the VA's leadership instituted a culture of accountability and change aimed at improving its entire system. Doctors, nurses, staffers, and administrators met regularly to review possible improvements. After a VA nurse noticed that rental car companies used hand-held barcode scanners to check in returned cars, she suggested using barcodes on patients' ID bracelets and their bottled medicines. Today, the VA's barcode scanners are tied to an electronic records system that prevents nurses from handing out the wrong medicines and automatically alerts the hospital pharmacy to possibly harmful drug interactions or dangerous patient allergies.[43]

In the **disturbance handler role,** managers respond to pressures and problems so severe that they demand immediate attention and action. Managers often play

Disseminator role the informational role managers play when they share information with others in their departments or companies

Spokesperson role the informational role managers play when they share information with people outside their departments or companies

Entrepreneur role the decisional role managers play when they adapt themselves, their subordinates, and their units to change

Disturbance handler role the decisional role managers play when they respond to severe problems that demand immediate action the role of disturbance handler when the board of a failing company hires a new CEO to turn the company around. After Ford Motor Company's market share shrank from 25 to 16 percent and the company lost $7 billion in nine months, Alan Mulally came from Boeing to become Ford's new CEO. Mulally quickly arranged $23.5 billion in financing to cover the losses. He plans to cut costs by reducing the number of cars Ford produces, standardizing the use of shared parts across Ford vehicles, and laying off half of Ford's 82,000 factory workers. Mulally said, "I've seen this movie before [at Boeing]. Some very good and loyal people are going to leave this company . . . , and that's going to be tough on everyone. [But,] As demoralizing as a slide down may be, the ride back up is infinitely more exhilarating."[44]

In the **resource allocator role,** managers decide who will get what resources and how much of each resource they will get. Hoping to revive sales of its luxury cars, top managers at General Motors acted as resource allocators by redirecting long-term investment of $4 billion to the company's Cadillac brand. Put in perspective, that means that executives invested nearly 10 percent of GM's total capital budget in a division that accounts for only 4 percent of GM sales.[45]

In the **negotiator role,** managers negotiate schedules, projects, goals, outcomes, resources, and employee raises. When Sprint bought Nextel (another cell phone company), the Federal Communications Commission required it to buy new radios for police and firefighters because its cell phone tower transmissions were interfering with emergency service communications in hundreds of locations. Sprint Nextel, which will spend over $3 billion to fix the problem, has been negotiating with law-enforcement agencies in Maryland and Washington to replace 35,000 radios. It took Sprint a year to negotiate a $609,000 deal with the city of Fairfax, Virginia, just to develop plans to replace its radios, and the company continues to negotiate with the FCC for extended deadlines to complete the transition.[46] Negotiating, as you can see from Sprint's dilemma, is a key to success and a basic part of managerial work.

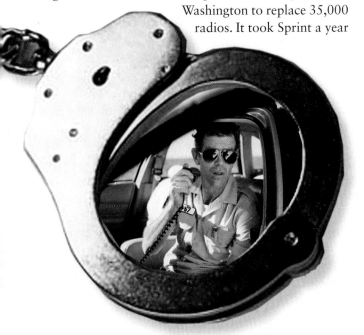

© Comstock Images/Jupiterimages

What Does It Take to Be a Manager?

I didn't have the slightest idea what my job was. I walked in giggling and laughing because I had been promoted and had no idea what principles or style to be guided by. After the first day, I felt like I had run into a brick wall. (Sales Representative #1)

Suddenly, I found myself saying, boy, I can't be responsible for getting all that revenue. I don't have the time. Suddenly you've got to go from [taking care of] yourself and say now I'm the manager, and what does a manager do? It takes a while thinking about it for it to really hit you . . . a manager gets things done through other people. That's a very, very hard transition to make. (Sales Representative #2)[47]

The statements above come from two star sales representatives, who, on the basis of their superior performance, were promoted to the position of sales manager. As their comments indicate, at first they did not feel confident about their ability to do their jobs as managers. Like most new managers, these sales managers suddenly realized that the knowledge, skills, and abilities that led to success early in their careers (and were probably responsible for their promotion into the ranks of management) would not necessarily help them succeed as managers. As sales representatives, they were responsible for managing only their own performance. But as sales managers, they were now directly responsible for supervising all of the sales representatives in their sales territories. Furthermore, they were now directly accountable for

Resource allocator role the decisional role managers play when they decide who gets what resources

Negotiator role the decisional role managers play when they negotiate schedules, projects, goals, outcomes, resources, and employee raises

whether those sales representatives achieved their sales goals.

If performance in nonmanagerial jobs doesn't necessarily prepare you for a managerial job, then what does it take to be a manager?

 After reading the next three sections, you should be able to

5 explain what companies look for in managers.

6 discuss the top mistakes that managers make in their jobs.

7 describe the transition that employees go through when they are promoted to management.

5 What Companies Look for in Managers

When companies look for employees who would be good managers, they look for individuals who have technical skills, human skills, conceptual skills, and the motivation to manage.[48] Exhibit 1.4 shows the relative importance of these four skills to the jobs of team leaders, first-line managers, middle managers, and top managers.

Technical skills are the specialized procedures, techniques, and knowledge required to get the job done. For the sales managers described above, technical skills are the ability to find new sales prospects, develop accurate sales pitches based on customer needs, and close the sale. For a nurse supervisor, technical skills include being able to insert an IV or operate a crash cart if a patient goes into cardiac arrest.

Technical skills are most important for team leaders and lower-level managers because they supervise the workers who produce products or serve customers. Team leaders and first-line managers need technical knowledge and skills to train new employees and help employees solve problems. Technical knowledge and skills are also needed to troubleshoot problems that employees can't handle. Technical skills become less important as managers rise through the managerial ranks, but they are still important.

Human skills can be summarized as the ability to work well with others. Managers with people skills work effectively within groups, encourage others to

Technical skills the specialized procedures, techniques, and knowledge required to get the job done

Human skills the ability to work well with others

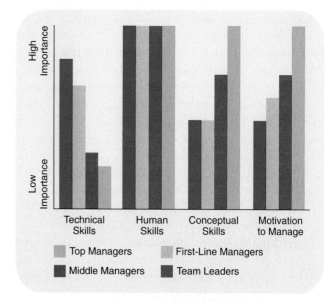

Exhibit 1.4
Management Skills

Legend:
- Top Managers
- Middle Managers
- First-Line Managers
- Team Leaders

Categories: Technical Skills, Human Skills, Conceptual Skills, Motivation to Manage

express their thoughts and feelings, are sensitive to others' needs and viewpoints, and are good listeners and communicators. Human skills are equally important at all levels of management, from first-line supervisors to CEOs. However, because lower-level managers spend much of their time solving technical problems, upper-level managers may actually spend more time dealing directly with people. On average, first-line managers spend 57 percent of their time with people, but that percentage increases to 63 percent for middle managers and 78 percent for top managers.[49]

Top Ten Mistakes Managers Make

1. Insensitive to others: abrasive, intimidating, bullying style
2. Cold, aloof, arrogant
3. Betrays trust
4. Overly ambitious: thinking of next job, playing politics
5. Specific performance problems with the business
6. Overmanaging: unable to delegate or build a team
7. Unable to staff effectively
8. Unable to think strategically
9. Unable to adapt to boss with different style
10. Overdependent on advocate or mentor

Source: M. W. McCall, Jr. and M. M. Lombardo, "What Makes a Top Executive?," *Psychology Today*, February 1983, 26–31.

Conceptual skills include the ability to see the organization as a whole, to understand how the different parts of the company affect each other, and to recognize how the company fits into or is affected by elements of its external environment such as the local community, social and economic forces, customers, and the competition. Good managers have to be able to recognize, understand, and reconcile multiple complex problems and perspectives. In other words, managers have to be smart! In fact, intelligence makes so much difference for managerial performance that managers with above-average intelligence typically outperform managers of average intelligence by approximately 48 percent.[50] Clearly, companies need to be careful to promote smart workers into management. Conceptual skills increase in importance as managers rise through the management hierarchy.

Good management involves much more than intelligence, however. For example, making the department genius a manager can be disastrous if that genius lacks technical skills, human skills, or one other factor known as the motivation to manage. **Motivation to manage** is an assessment of how motivated employees are to interact with superiors, participate in competitive situations, behave assertively toward others, tell others what to do, reward good behavior and punish poor behavior, perform actions that are highly visible to others, and handle and organize administrative tasks. Managers typically have a stronger motivation to manage than their subordinates, and managers at higher levels usually have a stronger motivation to manage than managers at lower levels. Furthermore, managers with a stronger motivation to manage are promoted faster, are rated as better managers by their employees, and earn more money than managers with a weak motivation to manage.[51]

6 Mistakes Managers Make

Another way to understand what it takes to be a manager is to look at the mistakes managers make. In other words, we can learn just as much from what managers shouldn't do as from what they should do.

Several studies of U.S. and British managers have compared "arrivers," or managers who made it all the way to the top of their companies, with "derailers," or managers who were successful early in their careers but were knocked off the fast track by the time they reached the middle to upper levels of management.[52] The researchers found that there were only a few differences between arrivers and derailers. For the most part, both groups were talented and both groups had weaknesses. But what distinguished derailers from arrivers was that derailers possessed two or more fatal flaws with respect to the way that they managed people. Although arrivers were by no means perfect, they usually had no more than one fatal flaw or had found ways to minimize the effects of their flaws on the people with whom they worked.

The number one mistake made by derailers was that they were insensitive to others by virtue of their abrasive, intimidating, and bullying management style. The authors of one study described a manager who walked into his subordinate's office and interrupted a meeting by saying, "I need to

Conceptual skills the ability to see the organization as a whole, understand how the different parts affect each other, and recognize how the company fits into or is affected by its environment

Motivation to manage an assessment of how enthusiastic employees are about managing the work of others

see you." When the subordinate tried to explain that he was not available because he was in the middle of a meeting, the manager barked, "I don't give a damn. I said I wanted to see you now."[53] Not surprisingly, only 25 percent of derailers were rated by others as being good with people compared to 75 percent of arrivers.

The second mistake was that derailers were often cold, aloof, or arrogant. Although this sounds like insensitivity to others, it has more to do with derailed managers being so smart, so expert in their areas of knowledge, that they treated others with contempt because they weren't experts, too. For example, AT&T called in an industrial psychologist to counsel its vice president of human resources because she had been blamed for ruffling too many feathers at the company.[54] Interviews with the vice president's coworkers and subordinates revealed that they thought she was brilliant. Unfortunately, these smarts were accompanied by a cold, aloof, and arrogant management style. The people she worked with complained that she does "too much too fast," treats coworkers with "disdain," "impairs teamwork," "doesn't always show her warm side," and has "burned too many bridges."

The third mistake made by derailers involved betraying a trust. Betraying a trust doesn't mean being dishonest. Instead, it means making others look bad by not doing what you said you would do when you said you would do it. That mistake, in itself, is not fatal because managers and their workers aren't machines. Tasks

go undone in every company every single business day. There's always too much to do and not enough time, people, money, or resources to do it. The fatal betrayal of trust is failing to inform others when things will not be done on time. This failure to admit mistakes, quickly inform others of the mistakes, take responsibility for the mistakes, and then fix them without blaming others distinguished the behavior of derailers from arrivers.

The fourth mistake was being overly political and ambitious. Managers who always have their eye on their next job rarely establish more than superficial relationships with peers and coworkers. In their haste to gain credit for successes that would be noticed by upper management, they make the fatal mistake of treating people as though they don't matter. An employee with an overly ambitious boss described him this way: "He gave me a new definition of shared risk: If something I did was successful, he took the credit. If it wasn't, I got the blame."[55]

The fatal mistakes of being unable to delegate, build a team, and staff effectively indicate that many derailed managers were unable to make the most basic transition to managerial work: to quit being hands-on doers and start getting work done through others. Two things go wrong when managers make these mistakes. First, when managers meddle in decisions that their subordinates should be making—when they can't stop being doers—they alienate the people who work for them. According to Richard Kilburg of Johns Hopkins University, when managers interfere with workers' decisions, "You . . . have a tendency to lose your most creative people. They're able to say, 'Screw this. I'm not staying here.'"[56] Second, because they are trying to do their subordinates' jobs in addition to their own, managers who fail to delegate will not have enough time to do anything well.

MANAGERS WHO FAIL TO DELEGATE WILL NOT HAVE ENOUGH TIME TO DO ANYTHING WELL.

Exhibit 1.5

Stages in the Transition to Management

MANAGERS' INITIAL EXPECTATIONS			AFTER SIX MONTHS AS A MANAGER			AFTER A YEAR AS A MANAGER					
JAN	FEB	MAR	APR	MAY	JUN	JUL	AUG	SEP	OCT	NOV	DEC

MANAGERS' INITIAL EXPECTATIONS	AFTER SIX MONTHS AS A MANAGER	AFTER A YEAR AS A MANAGER
⊙ Be the boss	⊙ Initial expectations were wrong	⊙ No longer "doer"
⊙ Formal authority	⊙ Fast pace	⊙ Communication, listening, & positive reinforcement
⊙ Manage tasks	⊙ Heavy workload	⊙ Learning to adapt to and control stress
⊙ Job is not managing people	⊙ Job is to be problem-solver and troubleshooter for subordinates	⊙ Job is people development

7 The Transition to Management: The First Year

In her book *Becoming a Manager: Mastery of a New Identity*, Harvard Business School professor Linda Hill followed the development of 19 people in their first year as managers. Her study found that becoming a manager produced a profound psychological transition that changed the way these managers viewed themselves and others. As shown in Exhibit 1.5, the evolution of the managers' thoughts, expectations, and realities over the course of their first year in management reveals the magnitude of the changes they experienced.

Initially, the managers in Hill's study believed that their job was to exercise formal authority and to manage tasks—basically being the boss, telling others what to do, making decisions, and getting things done. In fact, most of the new managers were attracted to management positions because they wanted to be in charge. Surprisingly, the new managers did not believe that their job was to manage people. The only aspects of people management mentioned by the new managers were hiring and firing.

After six months, most of the new managers had concluded that their initial expectations about managerial work were wrong. Management wasn't just about being the boss, making decisions, and telling others what to do. The first surprise was the fast pace and heavy workload involved. Said one manager,

Top managers spend an average of 9 minutes on a given task before having to switch to another.

"This job is much harder than you think. It is 40 to 50 percent more work than being a producer! Who would have ever guessed?" The pace of managerial work was startling, too. Another manager said, "You have eight or nine people looking for your time . . . coming into and out of your office all day long." A somewhat frustrated manager declared that management was "a job that never ended . . . a job you couldn't get your hands around."

Informal descriptions like this are consistent with studies indicating that the average first-line manager spends no more than two minutes on a task before being interrupted by a request from a subordinate, a phone call, or an email. The pace is somewhat less hurried for top managers, who spend an average of approximately nine minutes on a task before having to switch to another. In practice, this means that supervisors may perform 30 different tasks per hour, while top managers perform seven different tasks per hour, with each task typically different from the one that preceded it. A manager described this frenetic level of activity by saying, "The only time you are in control is when you shut your door, and then I feel I am not doing the job I'm supposed to be doing, which is being with the people."

The other major surprise after six months on the job was that the managers' expectations about what they should do as managers were very different from their subordinates' expectations. Initially, the

© Stockbyte/Getty Images

managers defined their jobs as helping their subordinates perform their jobs well. For the managers, who still defined themselves as doers rather than managers, assisting their subordinates meant going out on sales calls or handling customer complaints. But when the managers "assisted" in this way, their subordinates were resentful and viewed their help as interference. The subordinates wanted their managers to help them by solving problems that they couldn't solve. Once the managers realized this distinction, they embraced their role as problem-solver and troubleshooter. They could then help without interfering with their subordinates' jobs.

After a year on the job, most of the managers thought of themselves as managers and no longer as doers. In making the transition, they finally realized that people management was the most important part of their job. One manager summarized the lesson that had taken him a year to learn by saying, "As many demands as managers have on their time, I think their primary responsibility is people development. Not production, but people development." Another indication of how much their views had changed was that most of the managers now regretted the rather heavy-handed approach they had used in their early attempts to manage their subordinates. "I wasn't good at managing . . . , so I was bossy like a first-grade teacher." "Now I see that I started out as a drill sergeant. I was inflexible, just a lot of how-to's." By the end of the year, most of the managers had abandoned their authoritarian approach for one based on communication, listening, and positive reinforcement.

Finally, after beginning their year as managers in frustration, the managers came to feel comfortable with their subordinates, with the demands of their jobs, and with their emerging managerial styles. While being managers had made them acutely aware of their limitations and their need to develop as people, it also provided them with an unexpected reward of coaching and developing the people who worked for them. One manager said, "I realize now that when I accepted the position of branch manager that it is truly an exciting vocation. It is truly awesome, even at this level; it can be terribly challenging and terribly exciting."

Why Management Matters

If you walk down the aisle of the business section in your local bookstore, you'll find hundreds of books that explain precisely what companies need to do to be successful. Unfortunately, the best-selling business books tend to be faddish, changing dramatically every few years. One thing that hasn't changed, though, is the importance of good people and good management: Companies can't succeed for long without them.

After reading this section, you should be able to

8 explain how and why companies can create competitive advantage through people.

8 Competitive Advantage through People

In his books *Competitive Advantage through People* and *The Human Equation: Building Profits by Putting People First,* Stanford University business professor Jeffrey Pfeffer contends that what separates top-performing companies from their competitors is the way they treat their work forces—in other words, their management style.[57]

MGMT ≠ BOSSY

Pfeffer found that managers in top-performing companies used ideas like employment security, selective hiring, self-managed teams and decentralization, high pay contingent on company performance, extensive training, reduced status distinctions (between managers and employees), and extensive sharing of financial information to achieve financial performance that, on average, was 40 percent higher than that of other companies. These ideas, which are explained in detail in Exhibit 1.6, help organizations develop workforces that are smarter, better trained, more motivated, and more committed than their competitors' workforces. And—as indicated by the phenomenal growth and return on investment earned by these companies—smarter, better trained, and more committed workforces provide superior products and service to customers. Such customers keep buying and, by telling others about their positive experiences, bring in new customers.

According to Pfeffer, companies that invest in their people will also create long-lasting competitive advantages that are difficult for other companies to duplicate. Indeed, other studies clearly demonstrate that sound management practices can produce substantial advantages in four critical areas of organizational performance: sales revenues, profits, stock market returns, and customer satisfaction.

In terms of sales revenues and profits, a study of nearly 1,000 U.S. firms found that companies using *just some* of the ideas shown in Exhibit 1.6 had $27,044 more sales per employee and $3,814 more profit per employee than companies that didn't.[58] For a 100-person company, these differences amount to $2.7 million more in sales and nearly $400,000 more in annual profit! For a 1,000-person company, the difference grows to $27 million more in sales and $4 million more in annual profit!

Another study that considers how investing in people affects company sales found that poorly performing companies were able to improve their average return on investment

Exhibit 1.6

Competitive Advantage through People: Management Practices

1. **Employment Security**—Employment security is the ultimate form of commitment companies can make to their workers. Employees can innovate and increase company productivity without fearing the loss of their jobs.

2. **Selective Hiring**—If employees are the basis for a company's competitive advantage, and those employees have employment security, then the company needs to aggressively recruit and selectively screen applicants in order to hire the most talented employees available.

3. **Self-Managed Teams and Decentralization**—Self-managed teams are responsible for their own hiring, purchasing, job assignments, and production. Self-managed teams can often produce enormous increases in productivity through increased employee commitment and creativity. Decentralization allows employees who are closest to (and most knowledgeable about) problems, production, and customers to make timely decisions. Decentralization increases employee satisfaction and commitment.

4. **High Wages Contingent on Organizational Performance**—High wages are needed to attract and retain talented workers and to indicate that the organization values its workers. Employees, like company founders, shareholders, and managers, need to share in the financial rewards when the company is successful. Why? Because employees who have a financial stake in their companies are more likely to take a long-run view of the business and think like business owners.

5. **Training and Skill Development**—Like a high-tech company that spends millions of dollars to upgrade computers or research and development labs, a company whose competitive advantage is based on its people must invest in the training and skill development of its people.

6. **Reduction of Status Differences**—A company should treat everyone, no matter what the job, as equals. There are no reserved parking spaces. Everyone eats in the same cafeteria and has similar benefits. The result: improved communication as employees focus on problems and solutions rather than on how they are less valued than managers.

7. **Sharing Information**—If employees are to make decisions that are good for the long-run health and success of the company, they need to be given information about costs, finances, productivity, development times, and strategies that was previously known only by company managers.

Source: J. Pfeffer, *The Human Equation: Building Profits by Putting People* First (Boston: Harvard Business School Press, 1996).

In 2007, Fortune ranked Google as America's Best Company to Work for. One of the perks at the Googleplex: Free—and good—food at the cafeteria. And that includes a company sushi chef.

from 5.1 percent to 19.7 percent and increase sales by $94,000 per employee. They did this by adopting management techniques as simple as setting performance expectations and coaching, reviewing, and rewarding employee performance.[59] So, in addition to significantly improving the profitability of healthy companies, sound management practices can turn around failing companies.

To determine how investing in people affects stock market performance, researchers matched companies on *Fortune* magazine's list of "100 Best Companies to Work for in America" with companies that were similar in industry, size, and—this is key—operating performance. Both sets of companies were equally good performers; the key difference was how well they treated their employees. For both sets of companies, the researchers found that employee attitudes such as job satisfaction changed little from year to year. The people who worked for the "100 Best" companies were consistently much more satisfied with their jobs and employers year after year than were employees in the matched companies. More importantly, those stable differences in employee attitudes were strongly related to differences in stock market performance. Over

a three-year period, an investment in the "100 Best" companies would have resulted in an 82 percent cumulative stock return compared to just 37 percent for the matched companies.[60] This difference is remarkable given that both sets of companies were equally good performers at the beginning of the period.

Finally, research also indicates that managers have an important effect on customer satisfaction. Many people find this surprising. They don't understand how managers, who are largely responsible for what goes on inside the company, can affect what goes on outside the company. They wonder how managers, who often interact with customers under negative conditions (when customers are angry or dissatisfied), can actually improve customer satisfaction. It turns out that managers influence customer satisfaction through employee satisfaction. When employees are satisfied with their jobs, their bosses, and the companies they work for, they provide much better service to customers.[61] In turn, customers are more satisfied, too.

You will learn more about the service-profit chain in Chapter 18 on managing service and manufacturing operations.

It's easy to read, it outlines important topics, and it's relevant. Thanks for the good stuff on the website, I think it will **really help with tests**.

– Thomas Scholtes, Student at University of Maryland, College Park

REVIEW

HE DID

MGMT2 puts a multitude of study aids at your fingertips. After reading the chapters, check out these resources for further help:

• **Review Cards**,
  found in the back of your book, include all learning outcomes, definitions, and visual summaries for each chapter.

• **Online printable flash cards** give you three additional ways to check your comprehension of key marketing concepts.

Other great ways to help you study include **interactive management games, podcasts, audio downloads,** and **online tutorial quizzes with feedback**.

You can find it all at **4ltrpress.cengage.com/mgmt**.

HISTORY OF MANAGEMENT

In the Beginning

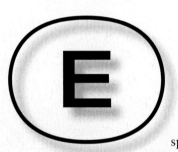

Each day, managers are asked to solve challenging problems and are given only a limited amount of time, people, or resources. Yet it's still their responsibility to get things done on time and within budget. Tell today's managers to "reward workers for improved production or performance," "set specific goals to increase motivation," or "innovate to create and sustain a competitive advantage," and they'll respond, "Duh! Who doesn't know that?" A mere 125 years ago, however, business ideas and practices were so different that today's widely accepted management ideas would have been as self-evident as space travel, cell phones, and the Internet. In fact, management jobs and management careers did not exist 125 years ago, so management was not yet a field of study. If there were no managers 125 years ago, but you can't walk down the hall today without bumping into one, where did management come from?

After reading the next section, you should be able to

1 explain the origins of management.

1 The Origins of Management

Although we can find the seeds of many of today's management ideas throughout history, not until the last two centuries did systematic changes in the nature of work and organizations create a compelling need for managers.

Learning Outcomes

1 explain the origins of management.

2 explain the history of scientific management.

3 discuss the history of bureaucratic and administrative management.

4 explain the history of human relations management.

5 discuss the history of operations, information, systems, and contingency management.

*Let's begin our discussion of the origins of management by learning about **1.1 management ideas and practice throughout history** and **1.2 why we need managers today.***

1.1 Management Ideas and Practice throughout History

Examples of management thought and practice can be found throughout history.[1] For example, the Egyptians recognized the need for planning, organizing, and controlling; for submitting written requests; and for consulting staff for advice before making decisions. The practical problems they encountered while building the great pyramids no doubt led to the development of these management ideas. The enormity of the task they faced is evident in the pyramid of King Khufu, which contains 2.3 million blocks of stone. Each block had to be quarried, cut to precise size and shape, cured (hardened in the sun), transported by boat for two to three days, moved onto the construction site, numbered to identify where it would be placed, and then shaped and smoothed so that it would fit perfectly into place. It took 20,000 workers 23 years to complete this pyramid; more than 8,000 were needed just to quarry the stones and transport them. A typical quarry expedition might include 100 army officers, 50 government and religious officials, and 200 members of the king's court to lead the expedition; 130 stone masons to cut the stones; and 5,000 soldiers, 800 foreigners, and 2,000 bond servants to transport the stones on and off the ships.[2]

It took 20,000 workers 23 years to complete this pyramid; more than 8,000 were needed just to quarry the stones and transport them.

Exhibit 2.1

Management Ideas and Practice throughout History

Time	Individual or Group	Planning	Organizing	Leading	Controlling	Contributions to Management Thought and Practice
5000 B.C.	Sumerians				√	Written record keeping.
4000 B.C. to 2000 B.C.	Egyptians	√	√		√	Planning, organizing, and controlling building the pyramids; submitting requests in writing; making decisions after consulting staff for advice.
1800 B.C.	Hammurabi				√	Controls; using witnesses in legal cases.
600 B.C.	Nebuchadnezzar	√	√			Wage incentives and production control.
500 B.C.	Sun Tzu	√		√		Strategy; identifying and attacking opponent's weaknesses.
400 B.C.	Xenophon	√	√	√	√	Management as separate art.
400 B.C.	Cyrus		√	√	√	Human relations and motion study.
175	Cato		√			Job descriptions.
284	Diocletian		√			Delegation of authority.
900	al-Farabi			√		Leadership traits.
1100	Ghazali			√		Managerial traits.
1418	Barbarigo		√			Different organizational forms/structures.
1436	Venetians				√	Numbering, standardization, and interchangeability of parts.
1500	Sir Thomas More			√		Critique of poor management and leadership.
1525	Machiavelli		√	√		Cohesiveness, power, and leadership in organizations.

Source: C. S. George, Jr., *The History of Management Thought* (Englewood Cliffs, NJ: Prentice Hall, 1972).

Exhibit 2.1 shows how other management ideas and practices throughout history relate to the management functions in the textbook.

1.2 Why We Need Managers Today

Working from 8 A.M. to 5 P.M., coffee breaks, lunch hours, crushing rush hour traffic, and punching a time clock are things we associate with today's working world. But for most of humankind's history, people didn't commute to work. Work usually occurred in homes or on farms. As recently as 1870, two-thirds of Americans earned their living from agriculture. Even most of those who didn't earn their living from agriculture didn't commute to work. Blacksmiths, furniture makers, leather-goods mak-ers, and other skilled tradesmen or crafts-men, who formed trade guilds (the historical predecessors of labor unions) in England as early as 1093, typically worked out of shops in or next to their homes.[3] Likewise, until the late 1800s, cottage workers worked with each other out of small homes that were often built in a semicircle. A family in each cottage would complete a different production step, and work passed from one cottage to the next until production was complete. With small, self-organized work groups, no commute, no bosses, and no common building, there wasn't a strong need for management.

During the Industrial Revolution (1750–1900), however, jobs and organizations changed dramatically.[4] First, the availability of power (steam engines and later electricity) enabled low-paid, unskilled laborers running machines to replace high-paid, skilled artisans who made entire goods by themselves by hand. This new mass production system was based on a division of labor: each worker, interacting with machines, performed separate, highly specialized tasks that were but a small part of all the steps required to make manufactured goods. While workers focused on their singular tasks, managers were needed to coordinate the different parts of the production system and optimize its overall performance. Productivity skyrocketed at companies that understood this. At Ford Motor Company, where the assembly line was developed, the time required to assemble a car dropped from 12.5 man hours to just 93 minutes.[5]

Accounting and the Invention of Writing

nformation management and accounting may have a common origin. Sumerian businessmen *circa* 8000-3000 B.C.E. used small clay tokens to calculate quantities of grain and livestock—and later value-added goods like perfume or pottery—they owned and traded in temples and city gates. Different shapes and sizes represented different types and quantities of goods. The tokens were also used to store data. They were kept in small clay envelopes, and the token shapes were impressed on the outside of the envelope to indicate what was inside. Eventually, someone figured out that it was easier to just write these symbols with a stylus on a tablet instead of using the tokens. In the end, the new technology of writing led to more efficient management.

Source: D. Schmandt-Besserat, *How Writing Came About* (Austin: University of Texas Press, 1997).

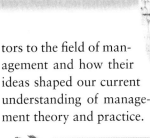
© Tom Hahn/iStockphoto.com

Second, instead of being performed in fields, homes, or small shops, jobs occurred in large, formal organizations where hundreds, if not thousands, of people worked under one roof.[6] In 1849, for example, with just 123 workers, Chicago Harvester (the predecessor of International Harvester) ran the largest factory in the United States with just 123 workers. Yet, by 1913, Henry Ford employed 12,000 employees in his Highland Park, Michigan, factory alone. With individual factories employing so many workers under one roof, companies now had a strong need for disciplinary rules to impose order and structure. For the first time, they needed managers who knew how to organize large groups, work with employees, and make good decisions.

The Evolution of Management

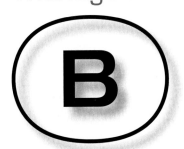

Before 1880, business educators taught only basic bookkeeping and secretarial skills, and no one published books or articles about management.[7] Today, you can turn to dozens of academic journals, hundreds of business school and practitioner journals (such as *Harvard Business Review*, *Sloan Management Review*, and the *Academy of Management Executive*), and thousands of books and articles if you have a question about management. In the next four sections, you will learn about other important contributors to the field of management and how their ideas shaped our current understanding of management theory and practice.

After reading the next four sections, which review the different schools of management thought, you should be able to

2 explain the history of scientific management.

3 discuss the history of bureaucratic and administrative management.

4 explain the history of human relations management.

5 discuss the history of operations, information, systems, and contingency management.

2 Scientific Management

Bosses, who were hired by the company owner or founder, used to make decisions by the seat of their pants—haphazardly, without any systematic study, thought, or collection of information. If the bosses decided that workers should work twice as fast, little or no thought was given to worker motivation. If workers resisted, the bosses often resorted to physical beatings to get workers to work faster, harder, or longer. With no incentives for bosses and workers to cooperate with one another, both groups played the system by trying to take advantage of each other. Moreover, each worker did the same job in his or her own way with different methods and different tools. In short, there were no procedures to standardize operations, no standards by which to judge whether performance was good or bad, and no follow-up to determine if productivity or quality actually improved when changes were made.[8]

This all changed with the advent of **scientific management,** which involved thorough study and testing of different work methods to identify the best, most efficient ways to complete a job.

*Let's find out more about scientific management by learning about **2.1 Frederick W. Taylor, the father of scientific management; 2.2 Frank and Lillian Gilbreth and motion studies;** and **2.3 Henry Gantt and his Gantt charts.***

2.1 Father of Scientific Management: Frederick W. Taylor

Frederick W. Taylor (1856–1915), the father of scientific management, began his career as a worker at Midvale Steel Company. He was later promoted to patternmaker, supervisor, and then chief engineer.

At Midvale, Taylor was deeply affected by his three-year struggle to get the men who worked for him to do, as he called it, "a fair day's work." Taylor explained that as soon as he became the boss, "the men who were working under me . . . knew that I was onto the whole game of **soldiering,** or deliberately restricting output [to one-third of what they were capable of producing]."[9] When Taylor told his workers, "I am going to try to get a bigger output," the workers responded, "We warn you, Fred, if you try to bust any of these rates [a **rate buster** was someone who worked faster than the group] we will have you over the fence in six weeks."[10]

Over the next three years, Taylor tried everything he could think of to improve output. By doing the job himself, he showed workers that it was possible to produce more output. He hired new workers and trained them himself, hoping they would produce more. But "very heavy social pressure" from the other workers kept them from doing so. Pushed by Taylor, the workers be-

gan breaking their machines so they couldn't produce. Taylor responded by fining them every time they broke a machine and for any violation of the rules, no matter how small, such as being late to work. Tensions became so severe that some of the workers threatened to shoot him.

The remedy that Taylor eventually developed was scientific management. The goal of scientific management was to use systematic study to find the optimal means of doing each task. To do that, managers had to follow the four principles shown in Exhibit 2.2. First, they had to "develop a science" for each element of work. That meant they had to study it. Analyze it. Determine the optimal means to do the work. For example, one of Taylor's controversial proposals at the time was to give rest breaks to factory workers doing physical labor. We take breaks for granted today, but factory workers in Taylor's day were expected to work without stopping.[11] Through systematic experiments, he showed that frequent rest breaks greatly increased daily output.

Second, managers had to scientifically select, train, teach, and develop workers to help them reach their full potential. Before Taylor, supervisors often hired on the basis of favoritism and nepotism. Who you knew was often more important than what you could do. By contrast, Taylor instructed supervisors to hire "first class" workers on the basis of their aptitude to do a job well. For similar reasons, he also recommended that companies train and develop their workers—a rare practice at the time.

The third principle instructed managers to cooperate with employees to ensure that the scientific principles were actually implemented. As Taylor knew from personal experience, workers and management more often than not viewed each other as enemies. Taylor said, "The majority of these men believe that the fundamental interests of employees and

© Bettmann/CORBIS

Scientific management thoroughly studying and testing different work methods to identify the best, most efficient way to complete a job

Soldiering when workers deliberately slow their pace or restrict their work outputs

Rate buster a group member whose work pace is significantly faster than the normal pace in his or her group

Want Fries with That?

Don't think scientific management has much to do with today's work life? Think again: about the last time you were at the store and the clerk said, "Have a nice day." Service providers—particularly at restaurants—use scripts to ensure that employees are following the "one best way" of interacting with the customers. McDonald's uses a speech-only script (workers must say, "May I help you, ma'am?" instead of "Can I help someone?"). At Olive Garden, workers must greet the table within thirty seconds of arrival; take the drink order within three minutes; suggest five items while taking the order; and check back with the table three minutes after the food arrives.

Source: A. Scharf, "Scripted Talk: From 'Welcome to McDonald's' to 'Paper or Plastic?' Employers Control the Speech of Service Workers," *Dollars & Sense*, September–October 2003, 35; C. McCann, "Have a Nice Day and an Icy Stare," *Marketing Week*, 2 September 2004, 27.

employers are necessarily antagonistic. Scientific management, on the contrary, is founded on the firm conviction that the true interests of the two are one and the same. Prosperity for the employer cannot exist through a long term of years unless it is accompanied by prosperity for the employee. Moreover, it is possible to give the workman what he most wants—high wages—and the employer what he wants—a low labor cost—for his manufactures."[12]

The fourth principle of scientific management was to divide the work and the responsibility equally between management and workers. Prior to Taylor, workers alone were held responsible for productivity and performance. But, said Taylor, "Almost every act of the workman should be preceded by one or more preparatory acts of the management which enable him to do his work better and quicker than he otherwise could."[13]

Above all, Taylor felt these principles could be used to determine a "fair day's work," that is, what an average worker could produce at a reasonable pace, day in and day out. Once that was determined, it was manage-

ment's responsibility to pay workers fairly for that fair day's work. In essence, Taylor was trying to align management and employees so that what was good for employees was also good for management. In this way, he felt, workers and managers could avoid the conflicts he had experienced at Midvale Steel. And one of the best ways, according to Taylor, to align management and employees was to use incentives to motivate workers. In particular, Taylor believed in piece-rate incentives in which work pay was directly tied to how much workers produced.

Although Taylor remains a controversial figure among some academics, his key ideas have stood the test of time.[14] In fact, his ideas are so well accepted and widely used that we take most of them for granted. As eminent management scholar Edwin Locke says, "The point is not, as is often claimed, that he was 'right in the context of his time' but is now outdated, but that *most of his insights are still valid today.*"[15]

2.2 Motion Studies: Frank and Lillian Gilbreth

The husband and wife team Frank and Lillian Gilbreth are best known for their use of motion studies to simplify work. Like Frederick Taylor, their early experiences significantly shaped their interests and contributions to management.

Though admitted to MIT, Frank Gilbreth (1868–1924) began his career as an apprentice bricklayer. While learning the trade, he noticed the bricklayers using three different sets of motions—one to teach others how to lay bricks, a second to work at a slow pace, and a third to work at a fast pace.[16] Wondering which was best, he studied the various approaches and began

Exhibit 2.2

Taylor's Four Principles of Scientific Management

First:	Develop a science for each element of a man's work, which replaces the old rule-of-thumb method.
Second:	Scientifically select and then train, teach, and develop the workman, whereas in the past he chose his own work and trained himself as best he could.
Third:	Heartily cooperate with the men so as to ensure all of the work being done is in accordance with the principles of the science that has been developed.
Fourth:	There is an almost equal division of the work and the responsibility between the management and the workmen. The management take over all the work for which they are better fitted than the workmen, while in the past almost all of the work and the greater part of the responsibility were thrown upon the men.

Source: F. W. Taylor, *The Principles of Scientific Management* (New York: Harper, 1911).

eliminating unnecessary motions. For example, by designing a stand that could be raised to waist height, he eliminated the need to bend over to pick up each brick. By having lower-paid workers place all the bricks with their most attractive side up, bricklayers didn't waste time turning a brick over to find it. By mixing a more consistent mortar, bricklayers no longer had to tap each brick numerous times to put it in the right position. Together, Gilbreth's improvements raised productivity from 120 to 350 bricks per hour and from 1,000 bricks to 2,700 bricks per day.

© Christine Balderas/iStockphoto.com

As a result of his experience with bricklaying, Gilbreth and his wife Lillian developed a long-term interest in using motion study to simplify work, improve productivity, and reduce the level of effort required to safely perform a job. Indeed, Frank Gilbreth said, "The greatest waste in the world comes from needless, ill-directed, and ineffective motions."[17] **Motion study** broke each task or job into separate motions and then eliminated those that were unnecessary or repetitive. Because many motions were completed very quickly, the Gilbreths used motion-picture films, a relatively new technology at the time, to analyze jobs. Most film cameras, however, were hand-cranked and thus variable in their film speed, so Frank Gilbreth invented

Motion study breaking each task or job into its separate motions and then eliminating those that are unnecessary or repetitive

Time study timing how long it takes good workers to complete each part of their jobs

the micro chronometer, a large clock that could record time to 1/2000th of a second. By placing the micro chronometer next to the worker in the camera's field of vision and attaching a flashing strobe light to the worker's hands to better identify the direction and sequence of key movements, the Gilbreths could use film to detect and precisely time even the slightest, fastest movements. Motion study typically yielded production increases of 25 to 300 percent.

Frederick W. Taylor also strove to simplify work, but he did so by managing time rather than motion.[18] Taylor developed time study to put an end to soldiering and to determine what could be considered a fair day's work. **Time study** worked by timing how long it took a "first-class man" to complete each part of his job. A standard time was established after allowing for rest periods, and a worker's pay would increase or decrease depending on whether the worker exceeded or fell below that standard.

Lillian Gilbreth (1878–1972) was an important contributor to management as well. She was the first woman to receive a Ph.D. in management as well as the first woman to become a member of the Society of Industrial Engineers and the American Society of Mechanical Engineers. When Frank died in 1924, she continued the work of their management consulting company (which they had shared for over a dozen years) on her own. Lillian was particularly concerned with the human side of work and was one of the first contributors to industrial psychology. She established ways to improve office communication, incentive programs, job satisfaction, and management training. Her work also convinced the government to enact laws regarding workplace safety, ergonomics, and child labor.

2.3 Charts: Henry Gantt

Henry Gantt (1861–1919) was first a protégé and then an associate of Frederick Taylor. Gantt is best known for the Gantt chart, but he also made significant contributions to management with respect to the training and development of workers. As shown in Exhibit 2.3, a **Gantt chart** visually indicates what tasks must be completed at which times in order to complete a project. It accomplishes this task by showing time in various units on the x-axis and tasks on the y-axis. For example, Exhibit 2.3 shows that the following tasks must be completed by the following dates: in order to start construction on a new company headquarters by the week of November 18, the architectural firm must be selected by October 7, the architectural planning done by November 4, permits obtained from the city by November 11, site preparation finished by November 18, and loans and financing finalized by November 18. Though simple and straightforward, Gantt charts were revolutionary in the era of seat-of-the-pants management because of the detailed planning information they provided to managers. Gantt said, "Such sheets show at a glance where the delays occur, and indicate what must have our attention in order to keep up the proper output." The use of Gantt charts is so widespread today that nearly all project management software and computer spreadsheets have the capability to create charts that track and visually display the progress being made on a project.

Finally, Gantt, along with Taylor, was one of the first to strongly recommend that companies train and develop their workers.[19] In his work with companies, he found that workers achieved their best performance levels if they were trained first. At the time, however, supervisors were reluctant to teach workers what they knew for fear they could lose their jobs to more knowledgeable workers. Gantt overcame the supervisors' resistance by rewarding them with bonuses for properly training all of their workers. Gantt's approach to training was straightforward: "(1) a scientific investigation in detail of each piece of work, and the determination of the best method and the shortest time in which the work can be done. (2) A teacher capable of teaching the best method and the shortest time. (3) Reward for both teacher and pupil when the latter is successful."[20]

3 Bureaucratic and Administrative Management

The field of scientific management focused on improving the efficiency of manufacturing facilities and their workers. At about the same time, equally important ideas about bureaucratic and

Gantt chart a graphic chart that shows which tasks must be completed at which times in order to complete a project or task

Exhibit 2.3

Gantt Chart for Starting Construction on a New Headquarters

Current Week					✦					
Weeks		23 Sep to 30 Sep	30 Sep to 7 Oct	7 Oct to 14 Oct	14 Oct to 21 Oct	21 Oct to 28 Oct	28 Oct to 4 Nov	4 Nov to 11 Nov	11 Nov to 18 Nov	18 Nov to 25 Nov
Tasks										
Interview and select architectural firm		Architect by October 7								
Hold weekly planning meetings with architects				Weekly planning with architects by November 4						
Obtain permits and approval from city						Permits & approval by November 11				
Begin preparing site for construction							Site preparation done by November 18			
Finalize loans and financing								Financing finalized by November 18		
Begin construction										Start building
Tasks										
Weeks		23 Sep to 30 Sep	30 Sep to 7 Oct	7 Oct to 14 Oct	14 Oct to 21 Oct	21 Oct to 28 Oct	28 Oct to 4 Nov	4 Nov to 11 Nov	11 Nov to 18 Nov	18 Nov to 25 Nov
Current Week					✦					

administrative management were developing in Europe. German sociologist Max Weber presented a new way to run entire organizations in *The Theory of Economic and Social Organization* in 1922. Henri Fayol, an experienced French CEO, published his ideas about how and what managers should do in their jobs in *General and Industrial Management* in 1916.

Let's find out more about Weber's and Fayol's contributions to management by learning about **3.1 bureaucratic management** *and* **3.2 administrative management.**

same lines, promotion within the company should no longer be based on who you knew or who you were (heredity), but on your experience or achievements. And to further limit the influence of personal connections in the promotion process, *managers* rather than organizational owners should decide who gets promoted. Third, each position or job should be viewed as part of a chain of command that clarifies who reports to whom throughout the organization. Those higher in the chain of command have the right, if they so choose,

> An organization's rules and procedures should apply to **all** members regardless of their position or status.

3.1 Bureaucratic Management: Max Weber

Today, when we hear the term *bureaucracy,* we think of inefficiency and red tape, incompetence and ineffectiveness, and rigid administrators blindly enforcing nonsensical rules. When German sociologist Max Weber (1864–1920) first proposed the idea of bureaucratic organizations, however, these problems were associated with monarchies and patriarchies rather than bureaucracies. In monarchies, where kings, queens, sultans, and emperors ruled, and patriarchies, where a council of elders, wise men, or male heads of extended families ruled, the top leaders typically achieved their positions by virtue of birthright. Likewise, promotion to prominent positions of authority was based on who you knew (politics), who you were (heredity), or traditions.

It was against this historical background that Weber proposed the then new idea of bureaucracy. According to Weber, **bureaucracy** is "the exercise of control on the basis of knowledge."[21] Rather than ruling by virtue of favoritism or personal or family connections, people in a bureaucracy would lead by virtue of their rational-legal authority—in other words, their knowledge, expertise, or experience. Furthermore, the aim of bureaucracy is not to protect authority but to achieve an organization's goals in the most efficient way possible.

Exhibit 2.4 shows the seven elements that, according to Weber, characterize bureaucracies. First, instead of hiring people because of their family or political connections or personal loyalty, they should be hired because their technical training or education qualifies them to do the job well. Second, along the

Bureaucracy the exercise of control on the basis of knowledge, expertise, or experience

to give commands, take action, and make decisions concerning activities occurring anywhere below them in the chain. Fourth, to increase efficiency and effectiveness, tasks and responsibilities should be separated and assigned to those best qualified to complete them. Fifth, an organization's rules and procedures should apply to all members regardless of their position or status. Sixth, to ensure consistency and fairness over time and across different leaders, all rules, procedures, and decisions should be recorded in writing. Finally, to reduce favoritism, "professional" managers rather than company owners should manage or supervise the organization.

When viewed in historical context, Weber's ideas about bureaucracy represent a tremendous improvement. Fairness supplanted favoritism, the goal of efficiency replaced the goal of personal gain, and logical rules and procedures took the place of traditions or arbitrary decision making.

Today, however, after more than a century of experience we recognize that bureaucracy has limitations as well. Even Weber recognized bureaucracy's limitations. He called it the "iron cage" and said, "Once fully established, bureaucracy is among those social structures which are the hardest to destroy."[22] In bureaucracies, managers are supposed to influence employee behavior by fairly rewarding or punishing employees for compliance or noncompliance with organizational policies, rules, and procedures. In reality, however, most employees would argue that bureaucratic managers emphasize punishment for noncompliance much more than reward for compliance. Ironically, bureaucratic management was created to prevent just this type of managerial behavior.

Exhibit 2.4

Elements of Bureaucratic Organizations

Qualification-based hiring:	Employees are hired on the basis of their technical training or educational background.
Merit-based promotion:	Promotion is based on experience or achievement. Managers, not organizational owners, decide who is promoted.
Chain of command:	Each job occurs within a hierarchy, the chain of command, in which each position reports and is accountable to a higher position. A grievance procedure and a right to appeal protect people in lower positions.
Division of labor:	Tasks, responsibilities, and authority are clearly divided and defined.
Impartial application of rules and procedures:	Rules and procedures apply to all members of the organization and will be applied in an impartial manner, regardless of one's position or status
Recorded in writing:	All administrative decisions, acts, rules, or procedure will be recorded in writing.
Managers separate from owners:	The owners of an organization should not manage or supervise the organization.

Source: M. Weber, *The Theory of Economic and Social Organization*, trans. A. Henderson & T. Parsons (New York: The Free Press, 1947), 329–334.

3.2 Administrative Management: Henri Fayol

Though his work was not translated and widely recognized in the United States until 1949, Frenchman Henri Fayol (1841–1925) was as important a contributor to the field of management as Frederick Taylor. Whereas Taylor's ideas changed companies from the shop floor up, Fayol's ideas, which were shaped by his experience as a managing director (CEO), generally changed companies from the board of directors down. Fayol is best known for developing five functions of managers and fourteen principles of management.

The most formative events in Fayol's business career came during his twenty-plus years as the managing director (CEO) of Compagnie de Commentry-Fourchambault-Decazeville, commonly known as Comambault, a vertically integrated steel company that owned several coal and iron ore mines and employed 10,000 to 13,000 workers. Fayol was initially hired by the board of directors to shut the "hopeless" steel company down. But, after "four months of reflection and study," he presented the board with a plan, backed by detailed facts and figures, to save the company. With little to lose, the board agreed. Fayol then began the process of turning the company around by obtaining supplies of key resources such as coal and iron ore; using research to develop new steel alloy products; carefully selecting key subordinates in research, purchasing, manufacturing, and sales and then delegating responsibility to them; and cutting costs by moving the company to a better location closer to key markets. Looking back 10 years later, Fayol attributed his and the company's success to changes in management practices. He wrote, "When I assumed the responsibility for the restoration of Decazeville, I did not rely on my technical superiority. . . . I relied on my ability as an organizer [and my] skill in handling men."[23]

Based on his experience as a CEO, Fayol argued that "the success of an enterprise generally depends much more on the administrative ability of its leaders than on their technical ability."[24] And, as you learned in Chapter 1, managers need to perform five managerial functions if they are to be successful: planning, organizing, coordinating, commanding, and controlling.[25] Because most management textbooks have dropped the coordinating function and now refer to Fayol's commanding function as "leading," these functions are widely known as planning (determining organizational goals and a means for achieving them), organizing (deciding where decisions will be made, who will do what jobs and tasks, and who will work for whom), leading (inspiring and motivating workers to work hard to achieve organizational goals), and controlling (monitoring progress toward goal achievement and taking corrective action when needed). In addition, according to Fayol, effective management is based on the fourteen principles in Exhibit 2.5.

Exhibit 2.5

Fayol's Fourteen Principles of Management

1. Division of work
Increase production by dividing work so that each worker completes smaller tasks or job elements.

2. Authority and responsibility
A manager's authority, which is the "right to give orders," should be commensurate with the manager's responsibility. However, organizations should enact controls to prevent managers from abusing their authority.

3. Discipline
Clearly defined rules and procedures are needed at all organizational levels to ensure order and proper behavior.

4. Unity of command
To avoid confusion and conflict, each employee should report to and receive orders from just one boss.

5. Unity of direction
One person and one plan should be used in deciding the activities to be used to accomplish each organizational objective.

6. Subordination of individual interests to the general interest
Employees must put the organization's interests and goals before their own.

7. Remuneration
Compensation should be fair and satisfactory to both the employees and the organization; that is, don't overpay or underpay employees.

8. Centralization
Avoid too much centralization or decentralization. Strike a balance depending on the circumstances and employees involved.

9. Scalar chain
From the top to the bottom of an organization, each position is part of a vertical chain of authority in which each worker reports to just one boss. For the sake of simplicity, communication outside normal work groups or departments should follow the vertical chain of authority.

10. Order
To avoid conflicts and confusion, order can be obtained by having a place for everyone and having everyone in his or her place; in other words, there should be no overlapping responsibilities.

11. Equity
Kind, fair, and just treatment for all will develop devotion and loyalty. This does not exclude discipline, if warranted, and consideration of the broader general interest of the organization.

12. Stability of tenure of personnel
Low turnover, meaning a stable work force with high tenure, benefits an organization by improving performance, lowering costs, and giving employees, especially managers, time to learn their jobs.

13. Initiative
Because it is a "great source of strength for business," managers should encourage the development of initiative, or the ability to develop and implement a plan, in others.

14. *Esprit de corps*
Develop a strong sense of morale and unity among workers that encourages coordination of efforts.

Sources: H. Fayol, *General and Industrial Management* (London: Pittman & Sons, 1949); M. Fells, "Fayol Stands the Test of Time," *Journal of Management History* 6 (2000): 345–360; C. Rodrigues, "Fayol's 14 Principles of Management Then and Now: A Framework for Managing Today's Organizations Effectively," *Management Decision* 39 (2001): 880–889.

4 Human Relations Management

As we have seen, scientific management focuses on improving efficiency; bureaucratic management focuses on using knowledge, fairness, and logical rules and procedures; and administrative management focuses on how and what managers should do in their jobs. The human relations approach to management focuses on people. This approach to management sees people not as just extensions of machines but as valuable organizational resources in their own right. Human relations management holds that people's needs are important and understands that their efforts, motivation, and performance are affected by the work they do and their relationships with their bosses, coworkers, and work groups. In other words, efficiency alone is not enough. Organizational success also depends on treating workers well.

Let's find out more about human relations management by learning about 4.1 Mary Parker Follett's theories of constructive conflict; 4.2 Elton Mayo's Hawthorne Studies; and 4.3 Chester Barnard's theories of cooperation and acceptance of authority.

4.1 Constructive Conflict : Mary Parker Follett

Mary Parker Follett (1868–1933) was a social worker who, after twenty-five years of working with schools and nonprofit organizations, began lecturing and writing about management and working extensively as a consultant for business and government. Many of today's "new" management ideas can be traced clearly to her work.

Follett is known for developing ideas regarding constructive conflict, also called cognitive conflict, which is discussed in Chapter 5 on decision making and Chapter 10 on teams. Unlike most people, then and now, who view conflict as bad, Follett believed that conflict could be beneficial. She said that conflict is "the appearance of difference, difference of opinions, of interests. For that is what conflict means—difference." She went on to say, "As conflict—difference—is here in this world, as we cannot avoid it, we should, I think, use it to work for us. Instead of condemning it, we should set it to work for us. Thus we shall not be afraid of conflict, but shall recognize that there is a destructive way of dealing with such moments and a constructive way." [26]

Follett believed that the best way to deal with conflict was not domination, where one side wins and the other loses, nor compromise, where each side gives up some of what they want, but integration. Said Follett,

"There is a way beginning now to be recognized at least, and even occasionally followed: when two desires are *integrated*, that means that a solution has been found in which both desires have found a place that neither side has had to sacrifice anything." So, rather than one side dominating the other or both sides compromising, the point of **integrative conflict resolution** is to have both parties indicate their preferences and then work together to find an alternative that meets the needs of both. According to Follett, "Integration involves invention, and the clever thing is to recognize this, and not to let one's thinking stay within the boundaries of two alternatives which are mutually exclusive." Indeed, Follett's ideas about the positive use of conflict and an integrative approach to conflict resolution predate accepted thinking in the negotiation and conflict resolution literature by six decades (see the best-selling book *Getting to Yes: Negotiating Agreement without Giving In* by Roger Fisher, William Ury, and Bruce Patton).

Exhibit 2.6 on the next page summarizes Follett's contributions to management in her own words. She casts power as "with" rather than "over" others. Giving orders involves discussing instructions and resentment. Authority flows from job knowledge and experience rather than position. Leadership involves setting the tone for the team rather than being aggressive and dominating, which may be harmful. Control, by contrast, should be based on facts, information, and coordination. In the end, Follett's contributions added significantly to our understanding of the human, social, and psychological sides of management. Peter Parker, the former chairman of the London School of Economics, said about Follett: "People often puzzle about who is the father of management. I don't know who the father was, but I have no doubt about who was the mother." [27]

4.2 Hawthorne Studies: Elton Mayo

Australian-born Elton Mayo (1880–1948) is best known for his role in the famous Hawthorne Studies at the Western Electric Company. The Hawthorne Studies were conducted in several stages between 1924 and 1932 at a Western Electric plant in Chicago. Although Mayo didn't join the studies until 1928, he played a significant role thereafter, writing about the results in his book, *The Human Problems of an Industrial Civilization*. [28] The first stage of the Hawthorne Studies in-

Integrative conflict resolution an approach to dealing with conflict in which both parties deal with the conflict by indicating their preferences and then working together to find an alternative that meets the needs of both

Exhibit 2.6

MARY PARKER FOLLETT SAYS...

ON CONSTRUCTIVE CONFLICT...

"As conflict—difference—is here in this world, as we cannot avoid it, we should, I think, use it to work for us. Instead of condemning it, we should set it to work for us."

ON POWER...

"It seems to me that whereas power usually means power-over, the power of some person or group over some other person or group, it is possible to develop the conception of power-with, a jointly developed power, a co-active, not a coercive power."

ON THE GIVING OF ORDERS...

"An advantage of not exacting blind obedience, of discussing your instructions with your subordinates, is that if there is any resentment, any come-back, you get it out into the open, and when it is in the open you can deal with it."

ON AUTHORITY...

"Authority should go with knowledge and experience, that is where obedience is due, no matter whether it is up the line or down."

ON LEADERSHIP...

"Of the greatest importance is the ability to grasp a total situation. . . . Out of a welter of facts, experience, desires, aims, the leader must find the unifying thread. He must see a whole, not a mere kaleidoscope of pieces. . . . The higher up you go, the more ability you have to have of this kind."

ON COORDINATION...

"The most important thing to remember about unity is—that there is no such thing. There is only unifying. You cannot get unity and expect it to last a day—or five minutes. Every man in a business should be taking part in a certain process and that process is unifying."

ON CONTROL...

"Central control is coming more and more to mean the co-relation of many controls rather than a superimposed control."

Source: Mary Parker Follett, *Mary Parker Follett—Prophet of Management: A Celebration of Writings from the 1920s*, ed. P. Graham (Boston: Harvard Business School Press, 1995).

vestigated the effects of lighting levels and incentives on employee productivity in the Relay Test Assembly Room, where workers took approximately a minute to put "together a coil, armature, contact springs, and insulators in a fixture and secure the parts by means of four machine screws."[29] Two groups of six experienced female workers, five to do the work and one to supply needed parts, were separated from the main part of the factory by a 10-foot partition and placed at a standard work bench with the necessary parts and tools. Over the next five years, the experimenters introduced various levels and combinations of lighting, financial incentives, and rest pauses (work breaks) to study the effect on productivity. Curiously, however, production levels increased whether the experimenters increased or decreased the lighting, paid workers based on individual production or group production, or increased or decreased the number and length of rest pauses. The question was: Why?

Mayo and his colleagues eventually concluded that two things accounted for the results. First, substantially more attention was paid to these workers than to workers in the rest of the plant. Mayo wrote, "Before every change of program [in the study], the group is consulted. Their comments are listened to and discussed; sometimes their objections are allowed to negate a suggestion. The group unquestionably develops a sense of participation in the critical determinations and becomes something of a social unit."[30]

For years, the Hawthorne Effect has been *incorrectly* defined as increasing productivity by paying more attention to workers.[31] But it is not simply about attention from management. This effect cannot be understood without giving equal importance to the "social units," which became intensively cohesive groups. Mayo said, "What actually happened was that six individuals became a team and the team gave itself wholeheartedly and spontaneously to cooperation in the experiment. The consequence was that they felt themselves to be participating freely and without afterthought, and were happy in the knowledge that they were working without coercion from above or limits from below."[32]

For the first time, human factors related to work were found to be more important than the physical conditions or design of the work. Together, the increased attention from management and the development of a cohesive work group led to significantly higher levels of job satisfaction and productivity. In short, the Hawthorne studies found that workers' feelings and attitudes affected their work.

The next stage of the Hawthorne Studies was conducted in the Bank Wiring Room, where "the group consisted of nine wiremen, three solderers, and two inspectors. Each of these groups performed a specific task and collaborated with the other two in completion of each unit of equipment. The task consisted of setting up the banks of terminals side-by-side on frames, wiring the corresponding terminals from bank to bank, soldering the connections, and inspecting with a test set for short circuits or breaks in the wire. One solderman serviced the work of the three wireman."[33] While productivity increased in the Relay Test Assembly Room no matter what the researchers did, productivity dropped in the Bank Wiring Room. Again, the question was: Why?

© Bettmann/CORBIS

Tough Jobs

During the early twentieth century, labor unrest, dissatisfaction, and protests (some of them violent) were widespread in the United States, Europe, and Asia. In 1919 alone, for example, more than four million American workers went on strike. Working conditions contributed to the unrest. Millions of workers in large factories toiled at boring, repetitive, unsafe jobs for low pay. Employee turnover was high and absenteeism was rampant. With employee turnover approaching 380 percent in his automobile factories, Henry Ford had to double the daily wage of his manufacturing workers from $2.50, the going wage at the time, to $5.00 to keep enough workers at their jobs. It's not surprising that Mayo's ideas became popular during this period.

Mayo and his colleagues found that different group dynamics were responsible. The workers in the Bank Wiring Room had been an existing work group for some time and had already developed strong negative norms that governed their behavior. For instance, despite a group financial incentive for production, the group members decided that they would wire only 6,000 to 6,600 connections a day (depending on the kind of equipment they were wiring), well below the production goal of 7,300 connections that management had set for them. Individual workers who worked at a faster pace were socially ostracized from the group, or "binged" (hit on the arm), until they slowed their work pace. The group's behavior was reminiscent of the soldiering that Frederick Taylor had observed.

In the end, the Hawthorne Studies demonstrated that the workplace was more complex than previously thought, that workers were not just extensions of machines, and that financial incentives weren't necessarily the most important motivator for workers. Thanks to Mayo and the Hawthorne Studies, managers better understood the effect that group social interactions, employee satisfaction, and attitudes had on individual and group performance.

4.3 Cooperation and Acceptance of Authority: Chester Barnard

Like Henri Fayol, Chester Barnard (1886–1961) had experience as a top executive that shaped his views of management. Barnard began his career in 1909 as an engineer and translator for AT&T, becoming a general manager at Pennsylvania Bell Telephone in 1922 and then president of New Jersey Bell in 1927.[34] Barnard's ideas, published in his classic book, *The Functions of the Executive*, influenced companies from the board of directors down. He is best known for his ideas about cooperation and the acceptance of authority.

Barnard proposed a comprehensive theory of cooperation in formal organizations. In fact, he defines an **organization** as a "system of consciously coordinated activities or forces of two or more persons." In other words, organization occurs whenever two people work together for some purpose, whether it be classmates working together to complete a class project, Habi-

Organization a system of consciously coordinated activities or forces created by two or more people

tat for Humanity volunteers donating their time to build a house, or managers working with subordinates to reduce costs, improve quality, or increase sales. Why did Barnard place so much emphasis on cooperation? Because cooperation is *not* the normal state of affairs: "Failure to cooperate, failure of cooperation, failure of organization, disorganization, disintegration, destruction of organization—and reorganization—are characteristic facts of human history."[35]

According to Barnard, the extent to which people willingly cooperate in an organization depends on how workers perceive executive authority and whether they're willing to accept it. Many managerial requests or directives have a *zone of indifference* in which acceptance of managerial authority is automatic. For example, if your boss asks you for a copy of the monthly inventory report, and compiling and writing that report is part of your job, you think nothing of the request and automatically send it. In general, people will be indifferent to managerial directives or orders if they (1) are understood, (2) are consistent with the purpose of the organization, (3) are compatible with the people's personal interests, and (4) can actually be carried out by those people. Acceptance of managerial authority (i.e., cooperation) is not automatic, however. Ask people to do things contrary to the organization's purpose or to their own benefit and they'll put up a fight. While many people assume that managers have the authority to do whatever they want, Barnard, referring to the "fiction of superior authority," believed that workers ultimately grant managers their authority.

5 Operations, Information, Systems, and Contingency Management

In this last section, we review four other significant historical approaches to management that have influenced how today's managers produce goods and services on a daily basis, gather and manage the information they need to understand their businesses and make good decisions, understand how the different parts of the company work together as a whole, and recognize when and where particular management practices are likely to work.

To better understand these ideas, let's learn about **5.1 operations management; 5.2 information management; 5.3 systems management;** and **5.4 contingency management**.

5.1 Operations Management

In Chapter 18, you will learn about *operations management,* which involves managing the daily production of goods and services. In general, operations management uses a quantitative or mathematical approach to find ways to increase productivity, improve quality, and manage or reduce costly inventories. The most commonly used operations management tools and methods are quality control, forecasting techniques, capacity planning, productivity measurement and improvement, linear programming, scheduling systems, inventory systems, work measurement techniques (similar to the Gilbreths' motion studies), project management (similar to Gantt's charts), and cost-benefit analysis.[36]

Today, with these tools and techniques, we take it for granted that manufactured goods will be made with standardized, interchangeable parts; that the design of those parts will be based on specific, detailed plans; and that manufacturing companies will aggressively manage inventories to keep costs low and increase productivity. These key elements of operations management have some rather strange origins: guns, geometry, and fire.

Since the 1500s, skilled craftsmen made the lock, stock, and barrel of a gun by hand. After each part was made, a skilled gun finisher assembled the parts into a complete gun. But the gun finisher did not simply screw the different parts of a gun together, as is done today. Instead, each handmade part required extensive finishing and adjusting so that it would fit together with the other handmade gun parts. Hand-fitting was necessary because, even when made by the same skilled craftsman, no two parts were alike. Today, we would say that these parts were low quality because they varied so much from part to part.

All this changed in 1791 when the U.S. government, worried about a possible war with France, ordered 40,000 muskets from private gun contractors. Because each handmade musket was unique, a replacement part had to be handcrafted if a part broke. One contractor, Eli Whitney (who is better known for his invention of the cotton gin), determined that if gun parts were made accurately enough, guns could be made with standardized, interchangeable parts. So he designed machine tools that allowed unskilled workers to make each gun part the same as the next. In 1801, he demonstrated the superiority of interchangeable parts to President-elect Thomas Jefferson by quickly and easily assembling complete muskets from randomly picked piles of musket parts. Today, most products are manufactured using standardized, interchangeable parts.

Even with Whitney's advance, manufacturers still could not produce a part unless they had seen or examined it firsthand. Thanks to Gaspard Monge, a Frenchman of modest beginnings, this soon changed. Monge's greatest achievement was his book *Descriptive Geometry*. In it, he explained techniques for drawing three-dimensional objects on paper. For the first time, precise drawings permitted manufacturers to make standardized, interchangeable parts without first examining a prototype. Today, manufacturers rely on CAD (computer-aided design) and CAM (computer-aided manufacturing) to take three-dimensional designs straight from the computer to the factory floor.

Once standardized, interchangeable parts became the norm and could be made from design drawings alone, manufacturers ran into a costly problem that they had never faced before: too much inventory. *Inventory* is the amount and number of raw materials, parts, and finished products that a company has in its possession. A solution to this problem was found in 1905 when the Oldsmobile Motor Works in Detroit burned down. Management rented a new production facility to get production up and running as quickly as possible after the fire. But because the new facility was much smaller, there was no room to store large stockpiles of inventory. Therefore, the company made do with what it called "hand-to-mouth inventories," in which each production station had only enough parts on hand to do a short production run. Since all of its parts suppliers were close by, Oldsmobile could place orders in the morning and receive them in the afternoon (even without telephones), just like today's computerized, just-in-time inventory systems. So, contrary to common belief, just-in-time inventory systems were not invented by Japanese manufacturers. Instead, they were invented out of necessity a century ago because of a fire.

5.2 Information Management

For most of recorded history, information has been costly, difficult to obtain, and slow to spread compared to modern standards. Documents were written by hand. Books and manuscripts were extremely labor-intensive and therefore expensive. Although letters and other such documents were relatively easy to produce, transporting the information in them relied on horses, foot travelers, and ships. Word of Joan of Arc's death in 1431 took 18 months to travel from France across Europe to Constantinople (now Istanbul, Turkey).

Consequently, throughout history, organizations have pushed for and quickly adopted new information technologies that reduce the cost or increase the speed with which they can acquire, retrieve, or communicate information. The first technologies to truly revolutionize the business use of information were paper and the printing press. In the 14th century, water-powered machines were created to pulverize rags into pulp to make paper. Paper prices quickly dropped by 400 percent. Less than a half-century later, Johannes Gutenberg invented the printing press, which reduced the cost and time needed to copy written information by 99.8 percent. In fifteenth-century Florence, Italy, a scribe would charge one florin (an Italian unit of money) to hand-copy one document page. By contrast, a printer would set up and print 1,025 copies of the same document for just three florins.

What Gutenberg's printing press did for publishing, the manual typewriter did for daily communication. Before 1850, most business correspondence was written by hand and copied using the letter press. With the ink still wet, the letter would be placed into a tissue paper book. A hand press would then be used to squeeze the book and copy the still-wet ink onto the tissue paper. By the 1870s, manual typewriters made it cheaper, easier, and faster to produce and copy business correspondence. Of course, in the 1980s, slightly more than a century later, typewriters were replaced by personal computers and word processing software for identical reasons.

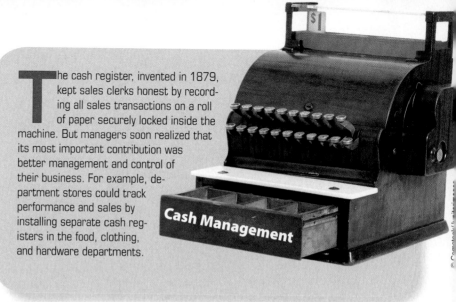

The cash register, invented in 1879, kept sales clerks honest by recording all sales transactions on a roll of paper securely locked inside the machine. But managers soon realized that its most important contribution was better management and control of their business. For example, department stores could track performance and sales by installing separate cash registers in the food, clothing, and hardware departments.

Cash Management

System a set of interrelated elements or parts that function as a whole

Subsystems smaller systems that operate within the context of a larger system

Synergy when two or more subsystems working together can produce more than they can working apart

---

Finally, businesses have always looked for information technologies that would speed access to timely information. The Medici family, which opened banks throughout Europe in the early 1400s, used posting messengers to keep in contact with their more than forty branch managers. The post messengers, who predated the U.S. Postal Service Pony Express by 400 years, could travel ninety miles per day, twice what average riders could cover, because the Medicis were willing to pay for the expense of providing them with fresh horses. The need for timely information also led companies to quickly adopt the telegraph in the 1860s, the telephone in the 1880s, and, of course, Internet technologies in the last decade.

5.3 Systems Management

Today's companies are much larger and more complex. They most likely manufacture, service, *and* finance what they sell. They also operate in complex, fast-changing, competitive, global environments that can quickly turn competitive advantages into competitive disadvantages.

How can managers make sense of this complexity both within and outside their organizations? One way to deal with organizational and environmental complexity is to take a systems view of organizations.[37] A **system** is a set of interrelated elements or parts that function as a whole. Rather than viewing one part of an organization as separate from the other parts, a systems approach encourages managers to complicate their thinking by looking for connections between the different parts of the organization. Indeed, one of the more important ideas in the systems approach to management is that organizational systems are composed of parts or **subsystems,** which are simply smaller systems within larger systems. Subsystems and their connections matter in systems theory because of the possibility for managers to create synergy. **Synergy** occurs when two or more subsystems working together can produce more than they can working apart. In other words, synergy occurs when 1 + 1 = 3.

Exhibit 2.7 illustrates how the elements of systems management work together. Whereas **closed systems** can function without interacting with their environments, nearly all organizations should be viewed as **open systems** that interact with their environments and depend on them for survival. Therefore, rather than viewing what goes on within the organization as separate from what goes on outside it, the systems approach encourages managers to look for connections between the different parts of the organization and the different parts of its environment.

A systems view of organizations offers several advantages. First, it forces managers to view their organizations as part of and subject to the competitive, economic, social, technological, and legal/regulatory forces in their environments.[38] Second, it also forces managers to be aware of how the environment affects specific parts of the organization. Third, because of the complexity and difficulty of trying to achieve synergies between different parts of the organization, the systems view encourages managers to focus on better communication and cooperation within the organization. Finally, survival also depends on making sure that the organization continues to satisfy critical environmental stakeholders such as shareholders, employees, customers, suppliers, governments, and local communities.

5.4 Contingency Management

Earlier you learned that the goal of scientific management was to use systematic study to find the one best way of doing each task and then use that one best way everywhere. The problem, as you may have gathered from reading about the various approaches to management, is that no one in management seems to agree on what that one best way is. In fact, there isn't *one* best way. More than a century of management research has shown that there are clear boundaries or limitations to most management theories and practices. None is universal. Though any theory or practice may work much of the time, none works all the time. How, then, is a manager to decide what theory to use? Well, it depends on the situation. The **contingency approach** to management clearly states that there are no universal management theories and that the most effective management theory or idea depends on the kinds of problems or situations that managers or organizations are facing at a particular time.[39]

One of the practical implications of the contingency approach is that management is much harder than it looks. In fact, because of the clarity and obviousness of management theories (OK, most of them), students and workers often wrongly assume that a company's problems would be quickly and easily solved if management would take just a few simple steps. If this were true, few companies would have problems.

A second implication of the contingency approach is that managers need to look for key contingencies that differentiate today's situation or problems from yesterday's situation or problems. Moreover, it means that managers need to spend more time analyzing problems, situations, and employees before taking action to fix them. Finally, it means that as you read this text and learn about management ideas and practices, you need to pay particular attention to qualifying phrases such as "usually," "in these situations," "for this to work," and "under these circumstances." Doing so will help you identify the key contingencies that will help you become a better manager.

Exhibit 2.7

Systems View of Organizations

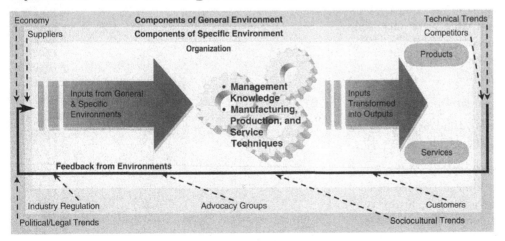

Closed systems systems that can sustain themselves without interacting with their environments

Open systems systems that can sustain themselves only by interacting with their environments, on which they depend for their survival

Contingency approach holds that there are no universal management theories and that the most effective management theory or idea depends on the kinds of problems or situations that managers are facing at a particular time and place

PLANNING AND DECISION MAKING

Even inexperienced managers know that planning and decision making are central parts of their jobs. Figure out what the problem is. Generate potential solutions or plans. Pick the best one. Make it work. Experienced managers, however, know how hard it really is to make good plans and decisions. One seasoned manager says: "I think the biggest surprises are the problems. Maybe I had never seen it before. Maybe I was protected by my management when I was in sales. Maybe I had delusions of grandeur, I don't know. I just know how disillusioning and frustrating it is to be hit with problems and conflicts all day and not be able to solve them very cleanly."[1]

Planning

Learning Outcomes

1 discuss the benefits and pitfalls of planning.

2 describe how to make a plan that works.

3 discuss how companies can use plans at all management levels, from top to bottom.

4 explain the steps and limits to rational decision making.

5 explain how group decisions and group decision-making techniques can improve decision making.

(P)

Planning is choosing a goal and developing a method or strategy to achieve that goal. In the face of tougher regulations and an industry-wide reputation for purveying junk food, General Mills sought to have 20 percent of its products meet nutrition standards. To accomplish this goal, the company had to shift its strategy from products that would be popular in the short-term to those that would meet more long-range goals. Managers had to adapt old products and develop new ones that were higher in whole grains, lower in sugar and salt, and would encourage people to eat their vegetables. Some products, like single-serving vegetables, were successful. Others, like Go-Gurt yogurt in a plastic tube, were flops. But setting clear standards for nutritional value and tying annual executive bonuses to achievement

Planning choosing a goal and developing a strategy to achieve that goal

of these goals helped General Mills meet its goal by 2006. At the end of fiscal year 2008, the company was already well on its way to the next goal: 40 percent of products meeting nutrition standards by 2010. And this with $12.4 billion in annual sales.[2]

After reading the next three sections, you should be able to

1   discuss the benefits and pitfalls of planning.

2   describe how to make a plan that works.

3   discuss how companies can use plans at all management levels, from top to bottom.

1 Benefits and Pitfalls of Planning

Are you one of those naturally organized people who always make a daily to-do list and never miss a deadline? Or are you one of those flexible, creative, go-with-the-flow people who dislike planning because it restricts their freedom? Some people are natural planners. They love it and can see only its benefits. Others dislike planning and can see only its disadvantages. It turns out that *both* views have real value.

Planning has advantages and disadvantages. Let's learn about **1.1 the benefits** and **1.2 the pitfalls of planning**.

1.1 Benefits of Planning

Planning offers four important benefits: intensified effort, persistence, direction, and creation of task strategies.[3] First, managers and employees put forth greater effort when following a plan. Take two workers. Instruct one to "do your best" to increase production. Instruct the other to achieve a 2 percent increase in production each month. Research shows that the one with the specific plan will work harder.[4]

most compelling benefit of planning is that it has been proven to work for both companies and individuals. On average, companies with plans have larger profits and grow much faster than companies that don't.[7] The same holds true for individual managers and employees: There is no better way to improve the performance of the people who work in a company than to have them set goals and develop strategies for achieving those goals.

DESPITE THE SIGNIFICANT BENEFITS ASSOCIATED WITH PLANNING, PLANNING IS NOT A CURE-ALL.

Second, planning leads to persistence, that is, working hard for long periods. In fact, planning encourages persistence even when there may be little chance of short-term success.[5] McDonald's founder Ray Kroc, a keen believer in the power of persistence, had this quotation from President Calvin Coolidge hung in all of his executives' offices: "Nothing in the world can take the place of persistence. Talent will not; nothing is more common than unsuccessful men with talent. Genius will not; unrewarded genius is almost a proverb. Education will not; the world is full of educated derelicts. Persistence and determination alone are omnipotent."

The third benefit of planning is direction. Plans encourage managers and employees to direct their persistent efforts *toward* activities that help accomplish their goals and *away* from activities that don't.[6] The fourth benefit of planning is that it encourages the development of task strategies. In other words, planning not only encourages people to work hard for extended periods and to engage in behaviors directly related to goal accomplishment, it also encourages them to think of better ways to do their jobs. Finally, perhaps the

1.2 Planning Pitfalls

Despite the significant benefits associated with planning, planning is not a cure-all. Plans won't fix all organizational problems. In fact, many management authors and consultants believe that planning can harm companies in several ways.[8]

The first pitfall of planning is that it can impede change and prevent or slow needed adaptation. Sometimes companies become so committed to achieving the goals set forth in their plans or following the strategies and tactics spelled out in them that they fail to notice when their plans aren't working or their goals need to change. When it comes to environmentally sound cars, General Motors may have missed the boat because of its "culture wedded to big cars and horsepower." GM developed experimental technology for an electric car in 2003, but dropped the project, electing to continue with its strategy of selling SUVs and fighting government fuel restrictions. Meanwhile, oil prices rose drastically, restrictions were tightened, and Toyota developed its popular Prius. Although Toyota formed its "green group" in the mid-1990s, GM only established its group dedicated to developing hybrids and electrics in 2006. They have brought the electric car idea back, but slow

Planning . . .

Working for you by:
- intensifying effort
- increasing persistence
- providing direction
- creating task strategies

Working against you by:
- impeding change
- creating a false sense of certainty
- allowing planners to plan things they don't understand how to accomplish

adaptation to new circumstances has them racing to develop the technology they need to keep the company afloat and competitive.[9]

The second pitfall is that planning can create a false sense of certainty. Planners sometimes feel that they know exactly what the future holds for their competitors, their suppliers, and their companies. However, all plans are based on assumptions. "The price of gasoline will increase by 4 percent per year." "Exports will continue to rise." For plans to work, the assumptions on which they are based must hold true. If the assumptions turn out to be false, then the plans based on them are likely to fail.

The third potential pitfall of planning is the detachment of planners. In theory, strategic planners and top-level managers are supposed to focus on the big picture and not concern themselves with the details of implementation (that is, carrying out the plan). According to management professor Henry Mintzberg, detachment leads planners to plan for things they don't understand.[10] Plans are meant to be guidelines for action, not abstract theories. Consequently, planners need to be familiar with the daily details of their businesses if they are to produce plans that can work.

2 How to Make a Plan That Works

Planning is a double-edged sword. If done right, planning brings about tremendous increases in individual and organizational performance. If planning is done wrong, however, it can have just the opposite effect and harm individual and organizational performance.

*In this section, you will learn how to make a plan that works. As depicted in Exhibit 5.1, planning consists of **2.1 setting goals, 2.2 developing commitment to the goals, 2.3 developing effective action plans, 2.4 tracking progress toward goal achievement,** and **2.5 maintaining flexibility in planning.***

2.1 Setting Goals

The first step in planning is to set goals. To direct behavior and increase effort, goals need to be specific and challenging.[11] For example, deciding to "increase sales this year" won't direct and energize workers as much as deciding to "increase North American sales by 4

Exhibit 5.1

How to Make a Plan That Works

percent in the next six months." Specific, challenging goals provide a target for which to aim and a standard against which to measure success.

One way of writing effective goals for yourself, your job, or your company is to use the S.M.A.R.T. guidelines. **S.M.A.R.T. goals** are Specific, Measurable, Attainable, Realistic, and Timely.[12] Let's see how a heating, ventilation, and air-conditioning (HVAC) company might use S.M.A.R.T. goals in its business.

The HVAC business is cyclical. It's extremely busy at the beginning of summer when homeowners find that their air-conditioning isn't working, and at the beginning of winter, when furnaces and heat pumps need repair. During these times, most HVAC companies have more business than they can handle, while at other times of year their business can be very slow. So a *Specific* goal would be to increase sales by 50 percent during the fall and spring when business is slower. This goal could be *Measured* by keeping track of the number of annual maintenance contracts sold to customers. This goal of increasing sales during the off-seasons is *Attainable* because maintenance contracts typically include spring tune-ups (air-conditioning systems) and fall tune-ups (furnace or heating systems). Moreover, a 50 percent increase in sales during the slow seasons appears to be *Realistic*. Because customers want their furnaces and air conditioners to work the first time it gets cold (or hot) each year, a well-designed pitch may make them very open to buying service contracts that ensure their equipment is in working order. Tune-up work can then be scheduled during the slow seasons, increasing sales at those times. Finally, this goal can be made

S.M.A.R.T. goals goals that are specific, measurable, attainable, realistic, and timely

Timely by asking the staff to push sales of maintenance contracts before Labor Day, the traditional end of summer, when people start thinking about the cold days ahead, and in March, when winter-weary people start longing for hot days in air-conditioned comfort. The result should be more work during the slow fall and spring seasons.

2.2 Developing Commitment to Goals

Just because a company sets a goal doesn't mean that people will try to accomplish it. If workers don't care about a goal, that goal won't encourage them to work harder or smarter. Thus, the second step in planning is to develop commitment to goals.[13]

Goal commitment is the determination to achieve a goal. Commitment to achieve a goal is not automatic. Managers and workers must choose to commit themselves to a goal. Edwin Locke, professor emeritus of management at the University of Maryland and the foremost expert on how, why, and when goals work, tells a story about an overweight friend who finally lost 75 pounds. Locke says, "I asked him how he did it, knowing how hard it was for most people to lose so much weight." His friend responded, "Actually, it was quite simple. I simply decided that I *really wanted* to do it."[14] Put another way, goal commitment is really wanting to achieve a goal.

So how can managers bring about goal commitment? The most popular approach is to set goals collectively, as a team. Rather than assigning goals to workers ("Johnson, you've got till Tuesday of next week to redesign the flux capacitor so it gives us 10 percent more output"), managers and employees choose goals together. The goals are more likely to be realistic and attainable if employees participate in setting them. Another technique for gaining commitment to a goal is to make the goal public by having individuals or work units tell others about their goals. Another way to increase goal commitment is to obtain top management's support. Top management can show support for a plan or program by providing funds, speaking publicly about the plan, or participating in the plan itself.

2.3 Developing Effective Action Plans

The third step in planning is to develop effective action plans. An **action plan** lists the specific steps (how), people (who), resources (what), and time period (when) for accomplishing a goal. Unlike most CEOs, Randy Papadellis has a unique goal that requires an extraordinary action plan. As the CEO of Ocean Spray, Papadellis has to buy all of the cranberries that his farmers produce (Ocean Spray is a farmer cooperative). His goal must be to buy the crop at the highest possible price. So he needs to figure out an action plan for how to sell the entire crop of high-cost berries. He says, "Imagine if Pepsi had to maximize the aluminum it used, and at the highest price it could afford!" Under Papadellis's direction, Ocean Spray began looking for alternative uses for cranberries beyond the traditional juice and canned products, uses that would involve new methods, people, and resources. The company invented dried-fruit Craisins by reinfusing juice into husks that used to be thrown away. Craisins have grown into a $100 million product line. Ocean Spray also developed a set of light drinks that had just 40 calories, mock berries that could be infused with other flavors (blueberry, strawberry, etc.) and used in muffins and cereals, and was the first company to introduce juice boxes. Because of these effective actions, Ocean Spray has been able to increase the price it pays its farmers over 100 percent in the past three years.[15]

2.4 Tracking Progress

The fourth step in planning is to track progress toward goal achievement. There are two accepted methods of tracking progress. The first is to set proximal goals and distal goals. **Proximal goals** are short-term goals or subgoals, whereas **distal goals** are long-term or primary goals.[16] The idea behind setting proximal goals is that achieving them may be more motivating and rewarding than waiting to reach far-off distal goals. Proxi-

---

Goal commitment the determination to achieve a goal

Action plan the specific steps, people, and resources needed to accomplish a goal

Proximal goals short-term goals or subgoals

Distal goals long-term or primary goals

Ocean Spray has been able to increase the price it pays its farmers over 100 percent in the past 3 years.

Exhibit 5.2

Effects of Goal Setting, Training, and Feedback on Safe Behavior in a Bread Factory

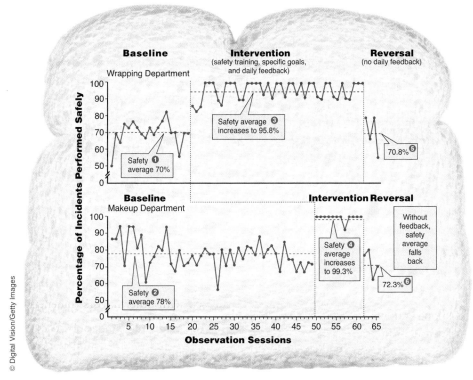

Source: Komaki, J., Barwick K. D., & Scott, L. R., "A Behavioral Approach to Occupational Safety: Pinpointing and Reinforcing Safe Performance in a Food Manufacturing Plant." *Journal of Applied Psychology* 63, (1978). Reprinted with permission of the American Psychological Association.

mal goals are less intimidating and more attainable than distal goals, which often feel like biting off more than you can chew. Proximal goals enable you to achieve a distal goal one little piece at a time.

The second method of tracking progress is to gather and provide performance feedback. Regular, frequent performance feedback allows workers and managers to track their progress toward goal achievement and make adjustments in effort, direction, and strategies.[17]

Proper action on performance feedback can keep you from failing to adapt, one of the pitfalls of planning. Exhibit 5.2 shows the impact of feedback on safety behavior at a large bakery company. During the baseline period, workers in the wrapping department, who measure and mix ingredients, roll the bread dough, and put it into baking pans, performed their jobs safely about 70 percent of the time (see dialogue box 1 in Exhibit 5.2). The baseline safety record for workers in the makeup department, who bag and seal baked bread and assemble, pack, and tape cardboard cartons for shipping, was somewhat better at 78 percent (see dialogue box 2). The company then gave workers 30 minutes of safety training, set a goal of 90 percent safe behavior, and then provided daily feedback (such as a chart similar to Exhibit 5.2). Performance improved dramatically. During the intervention period, safely-performed behaviors rose to an average of 95.8 percent for wrapping workers (see dialogue box 3) and 99.3 percent for workers in the makeup department (see dialogue box 4), and never fell below 83 percent. In this instance, the combination of training, a challenging goal, and feedback led to a dramatic increase in performance.

The importance of feedback can be seen in the reversal stage, when the company quit posting daily feedback on safe behavior. Without daily feedback, the percentage of safely-performed behavior returned to baseline levels, 70.8 percent for the wrapping department (see dialogue box 5) and 72.3 percent for the makeup department (see dialogue box 6). For planning to be effective, workers need both a specific, challenging goal and regular feedback to track their progress. Indeed, further research indicates that the effectiveness of goal setting can be doubled by the addition of feedback.[18]

2.5 Maintaining Flexibility

Because action plans are sometimes poorly conceived and goals sometimes turn out not to be achievable, the last step in developing an effective plan is to maintain

Exhibit 5.3

Planning from Top to Bottom

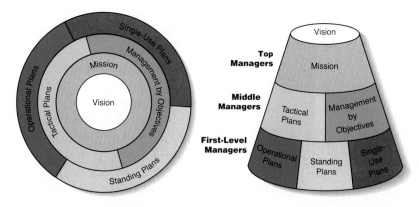

the same direction. Exhibit 5.3 illustrates this planning continuity, beginning at the top with a clear definition of the company vision and ending at the bottom with the execution of operational plans.

*Let's see how **3.1 top managers create the organizational vision and mission, 3.2 middle managers develop tactical plans and use management by objectives to motivate employee efforts toward the overall vision and mission,** and **3.3 first-level managers use operational, single-use, and standing plans to implement the tactical plans**.*

flexibility. One method of maintaining flexibility while planning is to adopt an options-based approach.[19] The goal of **options-based planning** is to keep options open by making small, simultaneous investments in many alternative plans. Then, when one or a few of these plans emerge as likely winners, you invest even more in these plans while discontinuing or reducing investment in the others. In part, options-based planning is the opposite of traditional planning. Whereas the purpose of an action plan is to commit people and resources to a particular course of action, the purpose of options-based planning is to leave those commitments open by maintaining **slack resources,** that is, a cushion of resources such as extra time, people, money, or production capacity, that can be used to address and adapt to unanticipated changes, problems, or opportunities.[20] Holding options open gives you choices. And choices, combined with slack resources, give you flexibility.

3 Planning from Top to Bottom

Planning works best when the goals and action plans at the bottom and middle of the organization support the goals and action plans at the top of the organization. In other words, planning works best when everybody pulls in

Options-based planning maintaining flexibility by making small, simultaneous investments in many alternative plans

Slack resources a cushion of extra resources that can be used with options-based planning to adapt to unanticipated change, problems, or opportunities

Strategic plans overall company plans that clarify how the company will serve customers and position itself against competitors over the next two to five years

Vision a statement of a company's purpose or reason for existing

3.1 Starting at the Top

Top management is responsible for developing long-term **strategic plans** that make clear how the company will serve customers and position itself against competitors in the next two to five years. Strategic planning begins with the creation of an organizational vision and an organizational mission.

A **vision** is a statement of a company's purpose or reason for existing.[21] Vision statements should be brief—no more than two sentences. They should also be enduring, inspirational, clear, and consistent with widely shared company beliefs and values. An excellent example of a well-crafted vision statement is that of Avon, the cosmetics company: To be the company that best understands and satisfies the product, service, and self-fulfillment needs of women—globally. That statement guides everyone in the organization and provides a focal point for the delivery of beauty products and services to the customer, women around the world. The vision is the same whether Avon is selling lipstick to women in India, shampoo packets to women in the Amazon, or jewelry to women in the United States. Despite these regional differences in specific strategy, the overall goal—understanding the needs of women globally—does not change. Furthermore, Avon's vision is clear, inspirational, and consistent with Avon's company values and the principles that guide the company. Other ex-

Dreams on the Back of a Napkin

Company mission statements are often a source of frustration for members of a committee charged with writing one. Employees often read a cliché mission statement like "We continually revolutionize business data to allow us to quickly integrate unique solutions to stay competitive in tomorrow's world" with glazed eyes. Such documents often get shoved in a drawer and make little impact on how people work. The process of plugging nouns and verbs into a formula, combined with a desire for it to be all-encompassing, can make a mission statement uninspiring and meaningless. According to Carmine Gallo, what makes a real difference in the work of an organization is not a bulky mission statement, but a concise and inspiring vision that can fit on the back of a napkin. It'll stick. It'll inspire members of the organization to be creative, and it'll motivate them to invest their energies into a shared dream.

Source: Gallo, C., "The Napkin Test; Why it's time to replace your company's bulky mission statement with a vision concise enough to fit on the back of a napkin." *BusinessWeek Online*,10 December 2007, available online at http://www.business-week.com/smallbiz/content/dec2007/sb2007127_010305.htm?chan=search [accessed 28 July 2008].

amples of organizational visions that have been particularly effective include Walt Disney Company's "to make people happy" and Schlage Lock Company's "to make the world more secure."[22]

The **mission,** which flows from the vision, is a more specific goal that unifies company-wide efforts, stretches and challenges the organization, and possesses a finish line and a time frame. For example, in 1961, President John F. Kennedy established an organizational mission for NASA with this simple statement: "Achieving the goal, before this decade is out, of landing a man on the moon and returning him safely to earth."[23] NASA achieved this goal on July 20, 1969, when astronaut Neil Armstrong walked on the moon. Once a mission has been accomplished, a new one should be chosen. Again, however, the new mission must grow out of the organization's vision, which does not change significantly over time. NASA's new mission, in line with its vision "to improve life here, to extend life there, to find life beyond," is to return to the moon "as early as 2015 and no later than 2020" and to use the moon "as a stepping stone for more ambitious missions to Mars and beyond."[24]

3.2 Bending in the Middle

Middle management is responsible for developing and carrying out tactical plans to accomplish the organization's mission. **Tactical plans** specify how a company will use resources, budgets, and people to accomplish specific goals within its mission. Whereas strategic plans and objectives are used to focus company efforts over the next two to five years, tactical plans and objectives are used to direct behavior, efforts, and attention over the next six months to two years. For example,

Craig Knouf, CEO of Associated Business Systems, a 110-person business that sells office equipment in Portland, Oregon, reviews his company's 30-page business plan monthly to compare the company's actual performance with the goals set forth in the plan. He is especially focused at the six- and twelve-month markers. When Knouf noticed that the company had sold more high-volume scanners over a six-month period than before, he changed his business plan to put more emphasis on scanners and scanning software. As a result, sales of scanning products, which will double this year over last, now account for one-third of all sales. Working without his business plan, says Knouf, "would be like driving a car with no steering wheel."[25]

Management by objectives is a management technique often used to develop and carry out tactical plans. **Management by objectives,** or MBO, is a four-step process in which managers and their employees (1) discuss possible goals; (2) collectively select goals that are challenging, attainable, and consistent with the company's overall goals; (3) jointly develop tactical plans that lead to the accomplishment of tactical goals and objectives; and

Mission a statement of a company's overall goal that unifies company-wide efforts toward its vision, stretches and challenges the organization, and possesses a finish line and a time frame

Tactical plans plans created and implemented by middle managers that specify how the company will use resources, budgets, and people over the next six months to two years to accomplish specific goals within its mission

Management by objectives (MBO) a four-step process in which managers and employees discuss and select goals, develop tactical plans, and meet regularly to review progress toward goal accomplishment

(4) meet regularly to review progress toward accomplishment of those goals.

3.3 Finishing at the Bottom

Lower-level managers are responsible for developing and carrying out **operational plans,** which are the day-to-day plans for producing or delivering the organization's products and services. Operational plans direct the behavior, efforts, and priorities of operative employees for periods ranging from 30 days to six months. There are three kinds of operational plans: single-use plans, standing plans, and budgets.

Single-use plans deal with unique, one-time-only events. For example, Industrial Motion, Inc., a small international procurement service, relocated from California to North Carolina in order to reduce its operating expenses. The company had to come up with a plan for everything from managing business data, moving key employees and hiring new ones, and buying furniture to improvising in unforeseen situations.[26] The move will happen once; it requires a single-use plan.

Unlike single-use plans that are created, carried out, and then never used again, **standing plans** can be used repeatedly to handle frequently recurring events. If you encounter a problem that you've seen before, someone in your company has probably written a standing plan that explains how to address it. Using this plan rather than reinventing the wheel will save you time. There are three kinds of standing plans: policies, procedures, and rules and regulations.

Policies indicate the general course of action that company managers should take in response to a particular event or situation. A well-written policy will also specify why the policy exists and what outcome the policy is intended to produce. Be-

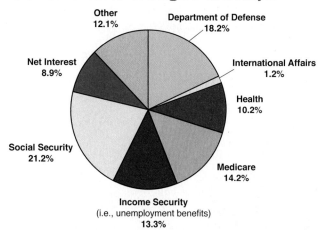

2007 U.S. Federal Government Budget Outlays

Other 12.1%
Department of Defense 18.2%
Net Interest 8.9%
International Affairs 1.2%
Health 10.2%
Social Security 21.2%
Medicare 14.2%
Income Security (i.e., unemployment benefits) 13.3%

Source: Economic Report of the President, *Federal Receipts and Outlays, by Major Category, and Surplus or Deficit, Fiscal Years 1940 -2007*, 2006 Report Spreadsheet Tables, B60, available online at http://a257.g.akamaitech.net/7/257/24222/15feb20061000/www.gpoaccess.gov/eop/2006/B80.xls.

cause the average employee surfs the Internet 11.1 hours per week, many companies have policies of either monitoring or blocking access to non-work-related Web sites. After its monitoring policy failed, Chaparral Energy, an oil and gas company, switched to software that blocks access to religious, political, or sexually oriented Web sites. Employee Web surfing has now dropped from an hour to less than fifteen minutes a day.[27]

Procedures are more specific than policies because they indicate the series of steps that should be taken in response to a particular event. A manufacturer's procedure for handling defective products might include the following steps. Step 1: Rejected material is locked in a secure area with "reject" documentation attached. Step 2: Material Review Board (MRB) identifies the defect and how far outside the standard the rejected products are. Step 3: MRB determines the disposition of the defective product as either scrap or as rework. Step 4: Scrap is either discarded or recycled, and rework is sent back through the production line to be fixed. Step 5: If delays in delivery will result, MRB member notifies customer.[28]

Rules and regulations are even more specific than procedures because they specify what must or must not happen. They describe precisely how a particular action should be performed. For instance, many companies have rules and regulations forbidding managers from writing job reference letters for employees who have worked at their firms because a negative reference may prompt a former employee to sue for defamation of character.[29]

After single-use plans and standing plans, budgets are the third kind of operational plan. **Budgeting** is quantitative planning because it forces managers to decide how to allocate available money to best accomplish

Operational plans day-to-day plans, developed and implemented by lower-level managers, for producing or delivering the organization's products and services over a 30-day to six-month period

Single-use plans plans that cover unique, one-time-only events

Standing plans plans used repeatedly to handle frequently recurring events

Policy a standing plan that indicates the general course of action that should be taken in response to a particular event or situation

Procedure a standing plan that indicates the specific steps that should be taken in response to a particular event

Rules and regulations standing plans that describe how a particular action should be performed or what must happen or not happen in response to a particular event

Budgeting quantitative planning through which managers decide how to allocate available money to best accomplish company goals company goals. According to Jan King, author of *Business Plans to Game Plans,* "Money sends a clear message about your priorities. Budgets act as a language for communicating your goals to others."

What Is Rational Decision Making?

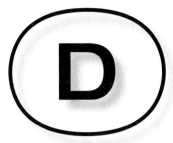

Decision making is the process of choosing a solution from available alternatives.[30] **Rational decision making** is a systematic process in which managers define problems, evaluate alternatives, and choose optimal solutions that provide maximum benefits to their organizations.

After reading the next two sections, you should be able to

4 explain the steps and limits to rational decision making.

5 explain how group decisions and group decision-making techniques can improve decision making.

4 Steps and Limits to Rational Decision Making

There are six steps in the rational decision-making process: 4.1 define the problem, 4.2 identify decision criteria, 4.3 weight the criteria, 4.4 generate alternative courses of action, 4.5 evaluate each alternative, and 4.6 compute the optimal decision. Then we'll consider 4.7 limits to rational decision making.

Steps of the Rational Decision-Making Process

1. Define the Problem
2. Identify Decision Criteria
3. Weight the Criteria
4. Generate Alternative Courses of Action
5. Evaluate Each Alternative
6. Compute the Optimal Decision

4.1 Define the Problem

The first step in decision making is to identify and define the problem. A **problem** exists when there is a gap between a desired state (what is wanted) and an existing state (the situation you are actually facing). Women want to look good and feel comfortable in clothes that fit properly, but sizes are not universal. There are no industry standards, which means it's hard for a woman to know her size as she could in the past. Today's sizes vary from brand to brand and don't take into account body type. As a result, women either leave the store without purchasing anything because they can't find a perfect fit, or purchase an imperfectly fitting garment, discard it after a couple of wears, and decide not to buy the brand again. Either way, garment companies lose customers.

The presence of a gap between an existing state and a desired state is no guarantee that managers will make decisions to solve problems. Two things must occur for this to happen.[31] First, managers have to be aware of the gap. But that isn't enough. Managers also have to be motivated to reduce the gap. In other words, managers have to know there is a problem and *want* to solve it. Finally, it's not enough to be aware of a problem and be motivated to solve it. Managers must also have the knowledge, skills, abilities, and resources to fix the problem. Cricket Lee has tried to solve the sizing problem in the women's clothing industry by developing Fitlogic, a simple siz-

Decision making the process of choosing a solution from available alternatives

Rational decision making a systematic process of defining problems, evaluating alternatives, and choosing optimal solutions

Problem a gap between a desired state and an existing state

ing standard that takes account of body type and is not intimidating for larger women. Although she lacked name recognition, she recruited help in licensing her system to Jones Apparel for one line of pants sold on a home shopping-network. She has so far met with limited success in selling Fitlogic, but has influenced the industry as more companies start accounting for body shape, as Banana Republic does by assigning different names to pants with different fit.[32]

4.2 Identify Decision Criteria

Decision criteria are the standards used to guide judgments and decisions. Typically, the more criteria a potential solution meets, the better that solution will be.

Imagine that your boss asks for a recommendation on outfitting the sales force, many of whom travel regularly, with new computers. What general factors would be important when purchasing these computers? Reliability, price, warranty, on-site service, and compatibility with existing software, printers, and computers would all be important, but you must also consider the technical details. With technology changing so quickly, you'll probably want to buy laptops with as much capability and flexibility as you can afford. What are your options? Well, laptops come in four distinct model types. There are budget models that are good for routine office work but are usually saddled with a slower processor; workhorse models that are not lightweight, but have everything included; slim models for traveling but that usually require an external drive to read/write to a DVD/CD; and tablet models that include extra features like handwriting-recognition software.[33] But what will the sales force really need? Will they need to burn CDs and DVDs or just read them? How much memory will the users need? How many files and programs will they need to store on their hard drives? Answering questions like these will help you identify the criteria that will guide the purchase of the new equipment.

4.3 Weight the Criteria

After identifying decision criteria, the next step is deciding which criteria are more or less important. Although there are numerous mathematical models for weighting decision criteria, all require the decision

Exhibit 5.4

Absolute Weighting of Decision Criteria for a Car Purchase

5 critically important **4 important** **3 somewhat important** **2 not very important** **1 completely unimportant**					
1. Predicted reliability	1	2	3	4	(5)
2. Owner satisfaction	1	(2)	3	4	5
3. Predicted depreciation	(1)	2	3	4	5
4. Avoiding accidents	1	2	3	(4)	5
5. Fuel economy	1	2	3	4	(5)
6. Crash protection	1	2	3	(4)	5
7. Acceleration	(1)	2	3	4	5
8. Ride	1	2	(3)	4	5
9. Front seat comfort	1	2	3	4	(5)

maker to provide an initial ranking of the criteria. Some use **absolute comparisons**, in which each criterion is compared to a standard or ranked on its own merits. Someone who would like to purchase a new car might consider the following criteria: predicted reliability, previous owners' satisfaction, predicted depreciation (the price you could expect if you sold the car), ability to avoid an accident, fuel economy, crash protection, acceleration, ride, and front seat comfort.

Different individuals will rank these criteria differently, depending on what they value or require in a car. Exhibit 5.4 shows the absolute weights that someone buying a car might use. Because these weights are absolute, each criterion is judged on its own importance, using a five-point scale, with "5" representing "critically important" and "1" representing "completely unimportant." In this instance, predicted reliability, fuel economy, and front seat comfort were rated most important, and acceleration and predicted depreciation were rated least important.

Another method uses **relative comparisons**, in which each criterion is compared directly to every other criterion.[34] Exhibit 5.5 shows six criteria that someone might use when buying a house. Moving across the first row, we see that the time of the daily commute has been rated more important ($+1$) than school system quality; less important (-1) than having an inground pool, sun room, or a quiet street, and just as important as the house being brand new (0). Total weights, which are obtained by summing the scores in each column, indicate that the daily commute and school system quality are the most important factors to this home buyer, while an inground pool, sun room, and a quiet street are the least important.

4.4 Generate Alternative Courses of Action

After identifying and weighting the criteria that will guide the decision-making process, the next step is to identify possible courses of action that could solve the problem. The idea is to generate as many alternatives as possible. Let's assume that you're trying to select a city in Europe to be the location of a major office. After meeting with your staff, you generate a list of possible alternatives: Amsterdam, the Netherlands; Barcelona or Madrid, Spain; Berlin or Frankfurt, Germany; Brussels, Belgium; London, England; Milan, Italy; Paris, France; and Zurich, Switzerland.

4.5 Evaluate Each Alternative

The next step is to systematically evaluate each alternative against each criterion. Because of the amount of information that must be collected, this step can take much longer and be much more expensive than other steps in the decision-making process. When selecting a European city for your office, you could contact economic development offices in each city, systematically interview businesspeople or executives who operate there, retrieve and use published government

And the winner is . . . London. When all the weights are calculated and compared, London is the best city in Europe for business.

© Jason Walton/iStockphoto.com

data on each location, or rely on published studies such as Cushman & Wakefield's *European Cities Monitor*, which conducts an annual survey of more than 500 senior European executives who rate 33 European cities on twelve business-related criteria.[35]

No matter how you gather the information, the key is to use that information to systematically evaluate each alternative against each criterion once you have it. Exhibit 5.6 on the next page shows how each of the 10 cities on your staff's list fared on each of the 12 criteria (higher scores are better), from qualified staff to freedom from pollution. Although London is the easiest place to get to and from work, it is also one of the most polluted cities on the list. Although telecommunications in Barcelona might not be optimal, it offers your employees the highest quality of life. Paris offers excellent access to markets and clients, but if your staff is multilingual, Amsterdam may be a better choice.

4.6 Compute the Optimal Decision

The final step in the decision-making process is to compute the optimal decision by determining the optimal value of each alternative. This is done by multiplying the rating for each criterion (Step 4.5) by the weight for that criterion (Step 4.3), and then summing those scores for each alternative course of action that you generated (Step 4.4). The 500 executives participating in Cushman & Wakefield's survey of the best European cities for business rated the 12 decision criteria in terms of importance, as shown in the first line of Exhibit 5.6 on the next page. Access to quality staff was deemed most important. Freedom from pollution, on the other hand, while a concern, was not high on the

Exhibit 5.5

Relative Comparison of Home Characteristics

HOME CHARACTERISTICS	L	SSQ	IP	SR	QS	NBH
Daily commute (L)		+1	−1	−1	−1	0
School system quality (SSQ)	−1		−1	−1	−1	−1
Inground pool (IP)	+1	+1		0	0	+1
Sun room (SR)	+1	+1	0		0	0
Quiet street (QS)	+1	+1	0	0		0
Newly built house (NBH)	0	+1	−1	0	0	
Total weight	+2	+5	−3	−2	−2	0

Exhibit 5.6

Criteria Ratings Used to Determine the Best Locations for a New Office

	Qualified Staff	Access to Markets	Communications	Intercity Transport	Staff Cost	Languages	Government Climate	Office Value	Office Availability	Intracity Transport	Quality of Life	Pollution	Ranking
Weights	62%	58%	55%	52%	36%	29%	27%	26%	26%	24%	21%	16%	
Amsterdam	0.38	0.60	0.34	0.71	0.25	1.05	0.37	0.42	0.28	0.50	0.43	0.49	5
Barcelona	0.29	0.26	0.17	0.28	0.54	0.26	0.47	0.50	0.38	0.48	1.16	0.43	4
Berlin	0.41	0.30	0.56	0.24	0.30	0.39	0.36	0.63	0.75	0.64	0.36	0.24	8
Brussels	0.32	0.43	0.30	0.45	0.15	0.95	0.36	0.33	0.36	0.30	0.32	0.26	6
Frankfurt	0.54	0.65	0.61	1.04	0.18	0.51	0.16	0.26	0.38	0.32	0.12	0.17	3
London	1.44	1.41	1.39	1.75	0.13	1.41	0.60	0.28	0.57	1.20	0.40	0.08	1
Madrid	0.24	0.31	0.25	0.41	0.49	0.21	0.38	0.43	0.44	0.40	0.62	0.14	7
Milan	0.31	0.33	0.14	0.22	0.26	0.25	0.13	0.20	0.17	0.19	0.28	0.06	10
Paris	0.78	1.02	0.84	1.30	0.19	0.50	0.27	0.32	0.41	0.96	0.59	0.13	2
Zurich	0.27	0.19	0.22	0.24	0.04	0.50	0.42	0.10	0.18	0.37	0.48	0.72	13

Source: "European Cities Monitor 2007," Cushman & Wakefield, available at http://www.berlin-partner.de/fileadmin/chefredaktion/documents/pdf_Presse/European_Investment_Monitor_2007.pdf, accessed 2 October 2008.

list of priorities. To calculate the optimal value for Paris, its score in each category is multiplied by the weight for each category (.78 x .62 in the qualified staff category, for example). Then all of these scores are added together to produce the optimal value, as follows:

$$(.78 \times .62) + (1.02 \times .58) + (.84 \times .55) +$$
$$(1.30 \times .52) + (.19 \times .36) + (.5 \times .29) +$$
$$(.27 \times .27) + (.32 \times .26) + (.41 \times .26) +$$
$$(.96 \times .24) + (.59 \times .21) + (.13 \times .16) = 3.06$$

Since London has a weighted average of 4.6 compared to 3.06 for Paris and 2.14 for Frankfurt, London clearly ranks as the best location for your company's new European office because of its large number of qualified staff; easy access to markets; outstanding ease of travel to, from, and within the city; excellent telecommunications; and top-notch business climate.

4.7 Limits to Rational Decision Making

In general, managers who diligently complete all six steps of the rational decision-making model will make better decisions than those who don't. So, when they can, managers should try to follow the steps in the rational decision-making model, especially for big decisions with long-range consequences.

To make perfect rational decisions, managers have to operate in a perfect world with no real-world constraints. Of course, it never actually works like that in the real world. Managers face time and money constraints. They often don't have time to make extensive lists of decision criteria. And they often don't have the resources to test all possible solutions against all possible criteria.

In theory, fully rational decision makers **maximize** decisions by choosing the optimal solution. In practice, however, limited resources along with attention, memory, and expertise problems make it nearly impossible for managers to maximize decisions. Consequently, most managers don't maximize—they satisfice. Whereas maximizing is choosing the best alternative, **satisficing** is choosing a "good enough" alternative. In reality, however, the manager's limited time, money, and expertise mean that only a few alternatives will be assessed against a few decision criteria. In practice, the manager will visit two or three computer or electronic stores, read a few recent computer reviews, and get bids from Dell, Lenovo, Gateway, and Hewlett-Packard. The

Maximizing choosing the best alternative

Satisficing choosing a "good enough" alternative

decision will be complete when the manager finds a good enough laptop computer that meets a few decision criteria.

5 Using Groups to Improve Decision Making

According to a study reported in *Fortune* magazine, 91 percent of U.S. companies use teams and groups to solve specific problems (i.e., make decisions).[36] Why so many? When done properly, group decision making can lead to much better decisions than those typically made by individuals. In fact, numerous studies show that groups consistently outperform individuals on complex tasks.

*Let's explore the **5.1 advantages and pitfalls of group decision making** and see how the following group decision-making methods—**5.2 structured conflict, 5.3 the nominal group technique, 5.4 the Delphi technique.***

5.1 Advantages and Pitfalls of Group Decision Making

Groups can do a much better job than individuals in two important steps of the decision-making process: defining the problem and generating alternative solutions.

Still, group decision making is subject to some pitfalls that can quickly erase these gains. One possible pitfall is groupthink. **Groupthink** occurs in highly cohesive groups when group members feel intense pressure to agree with each other so that the group can approve a proposed solution.[37] Because groupthink leads to consideration of a limited number of solutions and restricts discussion of any considered solutions, it usually results in poor decisions. Groupthink is most likely to occur under the following conditions:

- The group is insulated from others with different perspectives.
- The group leader begins by expressing a strong preference for a particular decision.
- The group has no established procedure for systematically defining problems and exploring alternatives.
- Group members have similar backgrounds and experiences.[38]

Groupthink is thought to have contributed to the explosion of the space shuttle Columbia in February 2003. Foam used to insulate the shuttle frequently causes damage to the wing during a shuttle's launch. When Columbia re-entered the atmosphere, wing damage allowed superhot gas to enter the wing, which caused the shuttle to explode. Previous shuttle missions made the possibility of this problem known, and dam-

age on this particular mission was suspected. However, NASA's culture does not allow individuals to be wrong, and its dependence on public and political support for its existence can influence decisions in favor of keeping missions on schedule even when delay would allow such problems to be investigated. Managers were reluctant to be the first to point out the problem, and requests for satellite images of the damage to Columbia during flight were ignored. The result? Loss of lives and a negative reputation for NASA, consequences worse than those that would have resulted from a delay to investigate the problems.[39]

A second potential problem with group decision making is that it takes considerable time. Reconciling schedules so that group members can meet takes time. Furthermore, it's a rare group that consistently holds productive task-oriented meetings to work through the decision process effectively. Some of the most common complaints about meetings (and thus decision making) are that the meeting's purpose is unclear, participants are unprepared, critical people are absent or late, conversation doesn't stay focused on the problem, and no one follows up on the decisions that were made. As Google's vice president of search products and user experience, Marissa Mayer, holds over 70 meetings a week and is the last executive to hear a pitch be-

Groupthink a barrier to good decision making caused by pressure within a group for members to agree with each other

fore it is made to the cofounders. To keep meetings on track, Mayer has set down six guidelines. Meetings must (1) have a firm agenda and (2) an assigned note-taker. Meetings must occur (3) during established office hours, and (4) preferably in short, ten-minute micromeetings. Those running the meeting should (5) discourage office politics and rely on data, and above all, they should (6) stick to the clock. Mayer's guidelines help meetings stay focused and productive.[40]

Strong-willed group members can constitute a third possible pitfall to group decision making. Such an individual, whether the boss or a vocal group member, dominates group discussion and puts limits on how the problem is defined and what the solutions can be. Another potential problem is group members may not feel accountable for the decisions made and actions taken by the group unless they are personally responsible for some aspect of carrying out those decisions.

Although these pitfalls can lead to poor decision making, this doesn't mean that managers should avoid using groups to make decisions. When facilitated well, group decision making can lead to much better decisions. The pitfalls of group decision making are not inevitable. Managers can overcome most of them by using the various techniques described next.

5.2 Structured Conflict

Most people view conflict negatively. Yet the right kind of conflict can lead to much better group decision making. **C-type conflict,** or "cognitive conflict," focuses on problem- and issue-related differences of opinion.[41] In c-type conflict, group members disagree because their different experiences and expertise lead them to view the problem and its potential solutions differently. C-type conflict is also characterized by a willingness to examine, compare, and reconcile those differences to produce the best possible solution. Alteon WebSystems, now a division of Nortel Networks, makes critical use of c-type conflict. Top manager Dominic Orr described Alteon's c-type conflict this way:

> **C-type conflict (cognitive conflict)** disagreement that focuses on problem- and issue-related differences of opinion

> **A-type conflict (affective conflict)** disagreement that focuses on individual or personal issues

> **Devil's advocacy** a decision-making method in which an individual or a subgroup is assigned the role of a critic

After an idea is presented, we open the floor to objective, and often withering, critiques. And if the idea collapses under scrutiny, we move on to another: no hard feelings. We're judging the idea, not the person. At the same time, we don't really try to regulate emotions. Passionate conflict means that we're getting somewhere, not that the discussion is out of control. But one person does act as referee—by asking basic questions like "Is this good for the customer?" or "Does it keep our time-to-market advantage intact?" By focusing relentlessly on the facts, we're able to see the strengths and weaknesses of an idea clearly and quickly.[42]

By contrast, **a-type conflict,** meaning "affective conflict," refers to the emotional reactions that can occur when disagreements become personal rather than professional. A-type conflict often results in hostility, anger, resentment, distrust, cynicism, and apathy. Unlike c-type conflict, a-type conflict undermines team effectiveness by preventing teams from engaging in the activities characteristic of c-type conflict that are critical to team effectiveness. Examples of a-type conflict statements are "your idea," "our idea," "my department," "you don't know what you are talking about," or "you don't understand our situation." Rather than focusing on issues and ideas, these statements focus on individuals.[43]

The **devil's advocacy** approach can be used to create c-type conflict by assigning an individual or a subgroup the role of critic. The following five steps establish a devil's advocacy program:

1. Generate a potential solution.
2. Assign a devil's advocate to criticize and question the solution.
3. Present the critique of the potential solution to key decision makers.
4. Gather additional relevant information.
5. Decide whether to use, change, or not use the originally proposed solution.[44]

When properly used, the devil's advocacy approach introduces c-type conflict into the decision-making process. Contrary to the common belief that conflict is bad, studies show that structured conflict leads to less a-type conflict, improved decision quality, and greater acceptance of decisions once they have been made.[45]

5.3 Nominal Group Technique

Nominal means "in name only." Accordingly, the **nominal group technique** received its name because it begins with a quiet time in which group members independently write down as many problem definitions and alternative solutions as possible. In other words, the nominal group technique begins by having group members act as individuals. After the quiet time the group leader asks each group member to share one idea at a time with the group. As they are read aloud, ideas are posted on flipcharts or wallboards for all to see. This step continues until all ideas have been shared. In the next step, the group discusses the advantages and disadvantages of the ideas. The nominal group technique closes with a second quiet time in which group members independently rank the ideas presented. Group members then read their rankings aloud, and the idea with the highest average rank is selected.[46]

The nominal group technique improves group decision making by decreasing a-type conflict. But it also restricts c-type conflict. Consequently, the nominal group technique typically produces poorer decisions than does the devil's advocacy approach. Nonetheless, more than 80 studies have found that nominal groups produce better ideas than those produced by traditional groups.[47]

5.4 Delphi Technique

In the **Delphi technique,** the members of a panel of experts respond to questions and to each other until reaching agreement on an issue. The first step is to assemble a panel of experts. Unlike other approaches to group decision making, however, it isn't necessary to bring the panel members together in one place. Because the Delphi technique does not require the experts to leave their offices or disrupt their schedules, they are more likely to participate.

The second step is to create a questionnaire consisting of a series of open-ended questions for the experts. In the third step, the panel members' written responses are analyzed, summarized, and fed back to the panel for reactions until the members reach agreement. Asking the members why they agree or disagree is important because it helps uncover their unstated assumptions and beliefs. Again, this process of summarizing panel feedback and obtaining reactions to that feedback continues until the panel members reach agreement.

5.5 Electronic Brainstorming

Brainstorming, in which group members build on others' ideas, is a technique for generating a large number of alternative solutions. Brainstorming has four rules:

1. The more ideas, the better.
2. All ideas are acceptable, no matter how wild or crazy they might seem.
3. Other group members' ideas should be used to come up with even more ideas.
4. Criticism or evaluation of ideas is not allowed.

Though brainstorming is great fun and can help managers generate a large number of alternative solutions, it does have a number of disadvantages. Fortunately, **electronic brainstorming,** in which group members use computers to communicate and generate alternative solutions, overcomes the disadvantages associated with face-to-face brainstorming.[48]

The first disadvantage that electronic brainstorming overcomes is **production blocking,** which occurs when you have an idea but have to wait to share it because someone else is already presenting an idea to the group. During this short delay, you may forget your idea or decide that it really wasn't worth sharing. Production blocking doesn't happen with electronic brainstorming. All group members are seated at computers, so everyone can type in ideas whenever they occur. There's no waiting your turn to be heard by the group.

The second disadvantage that electronic brainstorming overcomes is **evaluation apprehension,** that is, being afraid of what others will think of your ideas. With electronic brainstorming, all ideas are anonymous. When you type in an idea and hit the Enter key to share it with the group, group members

---

Nominal group technique a decision-making method that begins and ends by having group members quietly write down and evaluate ideas to be shared with the group

Delphi technique a decision-making method in which members of a panel of experts respond to questions and to each other until reaching agreement on an issue

Brainstorming a decision-making method in which group members build on each others' ideas to generate as many alternative solutions as possible

Electronic brainstorming a decision-making method in which group members use computers to build on each others' ideas and generate many alternative solutions

Production blocking a disadvantage of face-to-face brainstorming in which a group member must wait to share an idea because another member is presenting an idea

Evaluation apprehension fear of what others will think of your ideas

see only the idea. Furthermore, many brainstorming software programs also protect anonymity by displaying ideas in random order. So, if you laugh maniacally when you type "Cut top management's pay by 50 percent!" and then hit the Enter key, it won't show up immediately on everyone's screen. This makes it doubly difficult to determine who is responsible for which comments.

In the typical layout for electronic brainstorming, all participants sit in front of computers around a U-shaped table. This configuration allows them to see their computer screens, the other participants, a large main screen, and a meeting leader or facilitator. Step 1 in electronic brainstorming is to anonymously generate as many ideas as possible. Groups commonly generate 100 ideas in a half-hour period. Step 2 is to edit the generated ideas, categorize them, and eliminate redundancies. Step 3 involves ranking the categorized ideas in terms of quality. Step 4, the last step, has three parts: generate a series of action steps, decide the best order for accomplishing these steps, and identify who is responsible for each step. All four steps are accomplished with computers and electronic brainstorming software.[49]

Studies show that electronic brainstorming is much more productive than face-to-face brainstorming. Four-person electronic brainstorming groups produce 25 to 50 percent more ideas than four-person regular brain-storming groups, and twelve-person electronic brainstorming groups produce 200 percent more ideas than regular groups of the same size! In fact, because production blocking (i.e., waiting your turn) is not a problem for electronic brainstorming, the number and quality of ideas generally increase with group size.[50]

Even though it works much better than traditional brainstorming, electronic brainstorming has disadvantages, too. An obvious problem is the expense of computers, networks, software, and other equipment. As these costs continue to drop, however, electronic brainstorming will become a viable option for more groups.

Another problem is that the anonymity of ideas may bother people who are used to having their ideas accepted by virtue of their position (i.e., the boss). On the other hand, one CEO said, "Because the process is anonymous, the sky's the limit in terms of what you can say, and as a result it is more thought-provoking. As a CEO, you'll probably discover things you might not want to hear but need to be aware of."[51]

A third disadvantage is that outgoing individuals who are more comfortable expressing themselves verbally may find it difficult to express themselves in writing. Finally, the most obvious problem is that participants have to be able to type. Those who can't type, or who type slowly, may be easily frustrated and find themselves at a disadvantage to experienced typists.

Avoiding Blamestorming and Coblabberation

Without serious planning and adherence to brainstorming guidelines and procedures, brainstorming can quickly degenerate into blamestorming (where zero progress is made) or coblabberation (settling for an unimaginative solution just to get the session over with). Indeed, Professor Paul Paulus of the University of Texas at Arlington conducted a study comparing the number and quality of ideas of four people brainstorming versus four individuals working alone. Results: the brainstormers were only half as effective as the solo thinkers. Professor David Perkins of Harvard is not surprised. He prefers having people write down their ideas then bring them in. That way, you get diversity without all the politicking.

Source: Sandberg, J., "Brainstorming Works Best If People Scramble for Ideas on Their Own," *Wall Street Journal*, 13 June 2006, B1.

INNOVATION AND CHANGE

Organizational Innovation

Sometimes the solution to a problem causes another problem. Jernhusen AB, a Swedish property-administration firm, is building a new office and retail building near Stockholm's Central Station. How should they heat it? Problem number two: How should they get rid of excess heat in the train station, generated by the 250,000 people who pass through it every day? As Karl Sundholm, representative of Jernhusen, puts it, "All people produce heat, and that heat is in fact fairly difficult to get rid of. Instead of opening windows and letting all that heat go to waste we want to harness it through the ventilation system." The innovative solution to both problems? Convert the heat in the station to hot water and pump it through the heating system of the new building using pipes that connect the building to the station. Sundholm estimates the system will cost about 300,000 kronor (32,000 Euros; US$47,000) to install, and it is likely to reduce energy consumption by 15 percent. Per Berggren, Jernhusen's managing director notes, "It's more like thinking out of the box, being environmentally smart."[1]

Learning Outcomes

1. explain why innovation matters to companies.

2. discuss the different methods that managers can use to effectively manage innovation in their organizations.

3. discuss why not changing can lead to organizational decline.

4. discuss the different methods that managers can use to better manage change as it occurs.

Organizational innovation the successful implementation of creative ideas in organizations

Creativity the production of novel and useful ideas

Organizational innovation is the successful implementation of creative ideas in an organization.[2] **Creativity,** which is a form of organizational innovation, is the production of novel and useful ideas.[3] In the first part of this chapter, you will

© Jochen Tack/Alamy

learn why innovation matters and how to manage innovation to create and sustain a competitive advantage. In the second part, you will learn about **organizational change,** which is a difference in the form, quality, or condition of an organization over time.[4] You will also learn about the risk of not changing and the ways in which companies can manage change. But first, let's deal with organizational innovations like using body heat to warm buildings.[5]

After reading the next two sections on organizational innovation, you should be able to

1 explain why innovation matters to companies.

2 discuss the different methods that managers can use to effectively manage innovation in their organizations.

1 Why Innovation Matters

We can only guess what changes technological innovations will bring in the next twenty years. It is likely that many of us will carry computers in our pockets. But will our printer send a message to the supplier when it's out of ink? Will the Internet make movie theaters and televisions obsolete? Will we

> **Organizational change** a difference in the form, quality, or condition of an organization over time

edit our own news?[6] Who knows? The only thing we do know for sure about the next twenty years is that innovation will continue to change our lives.

*Let's begin our discussion of innovation by learning about: **1.1 technology cycles** and **1.2 innovation streams.***

1.1 Technology Cycles

In Chapter 3, you learned that *technology* consists of the knowledge, tools, and techniques used to transform inputs (raw materials, information, etc.) into outputs (products and services). A **technology cycle** begins with the birth of a new technology and ends when that technology reaches its limits and dies as it is replaced by a newer, substantially better technology.[7] For example, technology cycles occurred when air-conditioning supplanted fans, when Henry Ford's Model T replaced horse-drawn carriages, and when planes replaced trains as a means of cross-country travel.

From Gutenberg's invention of the printing press in the 1400s to the rapid advance of the Internet, studies of hundreds of technological innovations have shown that nearly all technology cycles follow the typical **S-curve pattern of innovation** shown in Exhibit 7.1.[8] Early in a technology cycle, there is still much to learn, so progress is slow, as depicted by point A on the S-curve. The flat slope indicates that increased effort (i.e., money, research and development) brings only small improvements in technological performance. Fortunately, as the new technology matures, researchers figure out how to get better performance from it. This is represented by point B of the S-curve in Exhibit 7.1. The steeper slope indicates that small amounts of effort will result in significant increases in performance. At point C, the flat slope again indicates that further efforts to develop this particular technology will result in only small increases in per-

Technology cycle a cycle that begins with the birth of a new technology and ends when that technology reaches its limits and is replaced by a newer, substantially better technology

S-curve pattern of innovation a pattern of technological innovation characterized by slow initial progress, then rapid progress, and then slow progress again as a technology matures and reaches its limits

Exhibit 7.1

S-Curves and Technological Innovation

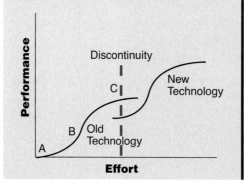

Source: R. N. Foster, *Innovation: The Attacker's Advantage* (New York: Summitt, 1986).

formance. More importantly, however, point C indicates that the performance limits of that particular technology are being reached. In other words, additional significant improvements in performance are highly unlikely.

Intel's technology cycles have followed this pattern. Intel spends billions to develop new computer chips and to build new production facilities to produce them. Intel has found that the technology cycle for its integrated circuits is about three years. In each three-year cycle, Intel spends billions to introduce a new chip, improves the chip by making it a little bit faster each year, and then replaces that chip at the end of the cycle with a brand new, different chip that is substantially faster than the old chip. At first, though (point A), the billions Intel spends typically produce only small improvements in performance. But after six months to a year with a new chip design, Intel's engineering and production people typically figure out how to make the new chips much faster than they were initially (point B). Yet, despite impressive gains in performance, Intel is unable to make a particular computer chip run any faster because the chip reaches its design limits.

After a technology has reached its limits at the top of the S-curve, significant improvements in performance usually come from radical new designs or new performance-enhancing materials (point C). In Exhibit 7.1, that new technology is represented by the second S-curve. The changeover or discontinuity between the old and new technologies is represented by the dotted line. At first, the old and new technologies will likely coexist. Eventually,

Joseph Balgazette designed the first interceptor sewers to carry London's sewage down the banks of the Thames to be dumped into the estuary.

© Otto Herschan/Hulton Archive/Getty Images

however, the new technology will replace the old technology. When that happens, the old technology cycle will be complete, and a new one will have started. The changeover between Intel's newer and older computer chip designs typically takes about one year. Over time, improving existing technology (tweaking the performance of the current technology cycle), combined with replacing old technology with new technology cycles (i.e., new, faster computer chip designs replacing older ones), has increased the speed of Intel's computer processors by a factor of 70 in just nineteen years.

Though the evolution of Intel's Pentium chips has been used to illustrate S-curves and technology cycles, it's important to note that technology cycles and technological innovation don't necessarily involve faster computer chips or cleaner-burning automobile engines. Remember, *technology* is simply the knowledge, tools, and techniques used to transform inputs into outputs. So a technology cycle occurs whenever there are major advances or changes in the *knowledge, tools,* and *techniques* of a field or discipline, whatever they may be. For example, one of the most important technology cycles in the history of civilization occurred in 1859, when 1,300 miles of central sewer line were constructed throughout London to carry human waste to the sea more than eleven miles away. This sewer system replaced the practice of dumping raw sewage into streets where it drained into public wells that supplied drinking water. Preventing waste runoff from contaminating water supplies stopped the spread of cholera that had killed millions of people for centuries in cities throughout the world.[9] Indeed, the water you drink today is safe thanks to this technological breakthrough. So, when you think about technology cycles, don't automatically think "high technology." Instead, broaden your perspective by considering advances or changes in any kind of knowledge, tools, and techniques.

Patent #4,131,919

1.2 Innovation Streams

In Chapter 6, you learned that organizations can create *competitive advantage* for themselves if they have a *distinctive competence* that allows them to make, do, or perform something better than their competitors. A competitive advantage becomes sustainable if other companies cannot duplicate the benefits obtained from that distinctive competence. Technological innovation can enable competitors to duplicate the benefits obtained from a company's distinctive advantage. It can also quickly turn a company's competitive advantage into a competitive disadvantage. For more than 110 years, Eastman Kodak was the dominant producer of photographic film worldwide. That is, until Kodak invented the digital camera (patent 4,131,919). But Kodak itself was unprepared for the rapid acceptance of its new technology, and its managers watched film quickly become obsolete for the majority of camera users. Technological innovation turned Kodak's competitive advantage into a competitive disadvantage.[10]

As the Kodak example shows, companies that want to sustain a competitive advantage must understand and protect themselves from the strategic threats of innovation. Over the long run, the best way for a company to do that is to create a stream of its own innovative ideas and products year after year. Consequently, we define **innovation streams** as patterns of innovation over time that can create sustainable competitive advantage.[11] Exhibit 7.2 on the next page shows a typical innovation consisting of a series of technology cycles. Recall that a technol-

Innovation streams
patterns of innovation over time that can create sustainable competitive advantage

ogy cycle begins with a new technology and ends when that technology is replaced by a newer, substantially better technology. The innovation stream in Exhibit 7.2 shows three such technology cycles.

An innovation stream begins with a **technological discontinuity,** in which a scientific advance or a unique combination of existing technologies creates a significant breakthrough in performance or function. Technological discontinuities are followed by a **discontinuous change,** which is characterized by technological substitution and design competition. **Technological substitution** occurs when customers then purchase new technologies to replace older technologies.

Discontinuous change is also characterized by **design competition,** in which the old technology and several different new technologies compete to establish a new technological standard or dominant design. For example, Toshiba and Sony competed for dominance in a new standard format for home video, Toshiba with its HD DVD technology and Sony with Blu-ray. Because of large investments in old technology, and because the new and old technologies are often incompatible with each other, companies and consumers are reluctant to switch to a different technology during a design competition. Toshiba lost the design competition because Warner Bros., which had been using both technologies, decided to go exclusively with Blu-ray. Retailers followed suit, announcing intentions to focus on Blu-ray equipment and videos. Some "early adopters" of HD DVD will continue to use the technology for their collections, but most people will eventually use Blu-ray because it will dominate the market.[12] In addition, during design competition, the older technology usually improves significantly in response to the competitive threat from the new technologies; this response also slows the changeover from older to newer technologies.

Exhibit 7.2

Innovation Streams: Technology Cycles over Time

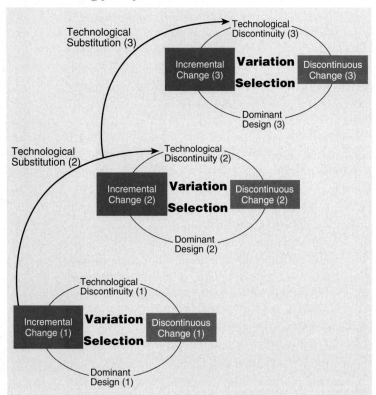

Source: Adapted from M. L. Tushman, P. C. Anderson, & C. O'Reilly, "Technology Cycles, Innovation Streams, and Ambidextrous Organizations," in *Managing Strategic Innovation and Change,* ed. M. L. Tushman & P. Anderson (1997), 3–23. © 1997 by Oxford University Press, Inc. Used by permission of Oxford University Press, Inc.

Discontinuous change is followed by the emergence of a **dominant design,** which becomes the new accepted market standard for technology.[13] Dominant designs emerge in several ways. The best technology doesn't always become the dominant design because a number of other factors come into play. One is critical mass, meaning that a particular technology can become the dominant design simply because most people use it. As of April 2008, Blu-ray held 64 percent of the market share while HD DVD had only 36 percent.[13] Toshiba dropped HD DVD in part because, with a critical mass of Blu-ray adopters, Blu-ray had become the dominant design.

A design can also become dominant if it solves a practical problem. For example, the QWERTY keyboard (named for the top left line of letters) became the dominant design for typewriters because it slowed typists who caused mechanical typewriter keys to jam because they typed too fast. Though computers can easily be switched to the DVORAK keyboard layout, which doubles typing speed and cuts typing errors by half, QWERTY lives on as the standard keyboard. In this instance, the QWERTY keyboard solved a problem that, with computers, is no longer relevant. Yet it remains the dominant technology because most people learned to type that way and continue to use it.

Dominant designs can also emerge through independent standards bodies. The International Telecommunications Union (**http://www.itu.ch**) is an independent organization that establishes standards for the communications industry. The ITU was founded in Paris in 1865 because European countries all had different telegraph systems that could not communicate with each other. After three months of negotiations, twenty countries signed the International Telegraph Convention, which standardized equipment and instructions, enabling telegraph messages to flow seamlessly from country to country. Today, as in 1865, various standards are proposed, discussed, negotiated, and changed until agreement is reached on a final set of standards that communication industries (i.e., Internet, telephone, satellites, radio, etc.) will follow worldwide.

A recent energy bill requires automakers to produce cars that meet a Corporate Average Fuel Economy (CAFE) standard of 35 miles per gallon by 2020. Automakers are pursuing alternative fuel technologies such as ethanol and diesel in an effort to increase fuel economy and meet the legal standard. Although research into alternative fuel technologies tends to be adopted in a climate of high oil prices and abandoned when they fall, it is not impossible to envision a future in which gasoline-burning engines are no longer the dominant technology on the road.[14]

No matter how it happens, the emergence of a dominant design is a key event in an innovation stream. First, the emergence of a dominant design indicates that there are winners and losers. Technological innovation both enhances and destroys competence. Companies that bet on the now-dominant design usually prosper. In contrast, when companies bet on the wrong design or the old technology, they may experience **technological lockout,** which occurs when a new dominant design (i.e., a significantly better technology) prevents a company from competitively

selling its products or makes it difficult to do so.[15] Toshiba has now stopped producing HD DVD players. It will continue to make spare parts for existing machines and may apply the technology to downloading videos online. But it will shift its business strategy to other sectors, such as flash drives, which are beginning to replace hard drives in computers.[16] In fact, more companies are likely to go out of business in a time of discontinuous change and changing standards than in an economic recession or slowdown.

Second, the emergence of a dominant design signals a shift from design experimentation and competition to **incremental change,** a phase in which companies innovate by lowering the cost and improving the functioning and performance of the dominant design. For example, manufacturing efficiencies enable Intel

Protecting Innovation

One of the risks in coming up with great new ideas is that someone might steal them. Published work, such as books and magazine articles, are protected by copyrights, while designs for new devices such as the iPhone are protected by patents. But what about business methods? Amazon.com developed a "1-Click" method to make shopping at the site easier: once you enter your information, you can select and purchase items with a single click. Barnes and Noble used a similar process and called it "Express Checkout," but Amazon filed suit, accusing Barnes and Noble of patent infringement. Can such a business process be patented, too? In October 2008, a federal appeals court ruled that patents should apply only to "physical objects or substances" and not "abstractions" like the energy cost risk-hedging strategy of a bank which had been denied a patent by the Board of Patent Appeals.

Source: M. Leone, "Patents Under Pressure," *CFO* (May 2008) 64-69. "The End of Business Process Patents," *Portfolio.com* (30 October 2008). Available at http://www.portfolio.com/news-markets/top-5/2008/10/30/Business-Process-Patents-Overturned/

Technological lockout when a new dominant design (i.e., a significantly better technology) prevents a company from competitively selling its products or makes it difficult to do so

Incremental change the phase of a technology cycle in which companies innovate by lowering costs and improving the functioning and performance of the dominant technological design

© Frank Wing/Photodisc/Getty Images

© iStockphoto.com

to cut the cost of its chips by one-half to two-thirds during a technology cycle, while doubling or tripling their speed. This focus on improving the dominant design continues until the next technological discontinuity occurs.

2 Managing Innovation

One consequence of technology cycles and innovation streams is that managers must be equally good at managing innovation in two very different circumstances. First, during discontinuous change, companies must find a way to anticipate and survive the technological changes that can suddenly transform industry leaders into losers and industry unknowns into powerhouses. Companies that can't manage innovation following technological discontinuities risk quick organizational decline and dissolution. Second, after a new dominant design emerges following discontinuous change, companies must manage the very different process of incremental improvement and innovation. Companies that can't manage incremental innovation slowly deteriorate as they fall farther behind industry leaders.

Unfortunately, what works well when managing innovation during discontinuous change doesn't work well when managing innovation during periods of incremental change (and vice versa). Consequently, to successfully manage innovation streams, companies need to be good at three things: **2.1 managing sources of innovation, 2.2 managing innovation during discontinuous change,** and **2.3 managing innovation during incremental change.**

2.1 Managing Sources of Innovation

Innovation comes from great ideas. So a starting point for managing innovation is to manage the sources of innovation, that is, where new ideas come from. One place that new ideas originate is

brilliant inventors. But only a few companies have the likes of an Edison, Marconi, or Graham Bell working for them. Given that great thinkers and inventors are in short supply, what might companies do to ensure a steady flow of good ideas?

Well, when we say that innovation begins with great ideas, we're really saying that innovation begins with creativity. As we defined it at the beginning of this chapter, creativity is the production of novel and useful ideas.[17] Although companies can't command employees to be creative ("You *will* be more creative!"), they can jump-start innovation by building **creative work environments** in which workers perceive that creative thoughts and ideas are welcomed and valued. As Exhibit 7.3 shows, creative work environments have six components that encourage creativity: challenging work, organizational encouragement, supervisory encouragement, work group encouragement, freedom, and a lack of organizational impediments.[18]

Work is *challenging* when it requires effort, demands attention and focus, and is perceived as important to others in the organization. According to researcher Mihaly Csikszentmihalyi (pronounced ME-high-ee CHICK-sent-me-high-ee), challenging work promotes creativity because it creates a rewarding psychological experience known as "flow." **Flow** is a psychological state of effortlessness, in which you become completely absorbed in what you're doing and time seems to fly.[19] A key part of creating flow experiences, and thus creative work environments, is to achieve a balance between skills and task challenge. When workers can do more than is required of them, they become bored, and when their skills aren't sufficient to accomplish a task, they become anxious. When skills and task challenge are balanced, however, flow and creativity can occur.

Creative work environments workplace cultures in which workers perceive that new ideas are welcomed, valued, and encouraged

Flow a psychological state of effortlessness, in which you become completely absorbed in what you're doing and time seems to pass quickly

Exhibit 7.3
Components of Creative Work Environments

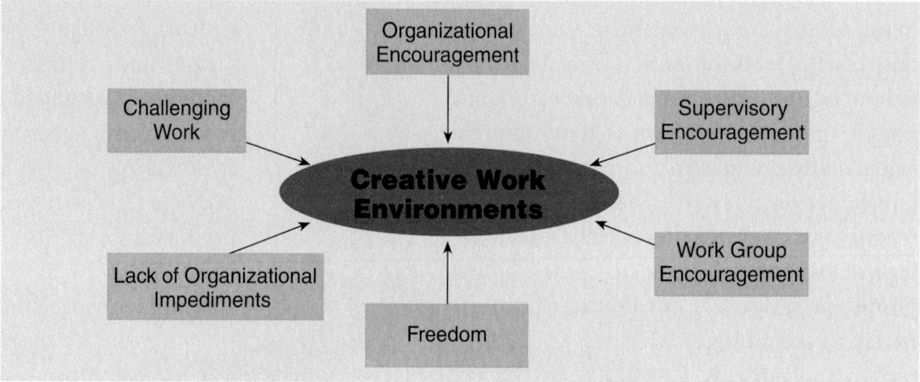

Sources: T. M. Amabile, R. Conti, H. Coon, J. Lazenby, and M. Herron, "Assessing the Work Environment for Creativity," *Academy of Management Journal* 39 (1996): 1154–1184.

A creative work environment requires three kinds of encouragement: organizational, supervisory, and work group encouragement. *Organizational encouragement* of creativity occurs when management encourages risk taking and new ideas, supports and fairly evaluates new ideas, rewards and recognizes creativity, and encourages the sharing of new ideas throughout different parts of the company. Many companies keep technology on a tight leash. But Douglas Merrill, chief information officer at Google, allows employees to use whatever hardware, operating systems, and software helps them be creative and get the job done efficiently, whether Google or another company designed them.[20] *Supervisory encouragement* of creativity occurs when supervisors provide clear goals, encourage open interaction with subordinates, and actively support development teams' work and ideas. *Work group encouragement* occurs when group members have diverse experience, education, and backgrounds and the group fosters mutual openness to ideas; positive, constructive challenge to ideas; and shared commitment to ideas.

An example of organizational and supervisory encouragement can be found at Adobe, which builds software for business and publishing. Every quarter, Adobe hosts the Idea Champion Showcase, an American Idol-style "ideathon" in which six presenters get ten minutes each to pitch a new business idea involving product concept, packaging, technology, whatever. Top executives are not invited to the showcase because their tendency to be cautious makes them want to "hurl rocks" at nascent ideas before they have a chance to develop. Rick Bess is an idea mentor at Adobe. He developed the showcase after an internal study showed that too many roadblocks were being thrown in front of new ideas, keeping them from penetrating the organizational hierarchy.[21]

Freedom means having autonomy over one's day-to-day work and a sense of ownership and control over one's ideas. Numerous studies have indicated that creative ideas thrive under conditions of freedom. At Royal Philips Electronics (Philips), all groups within the company have been given complete freedom to rethink every product with the goal of making it simpler for the end user to install and use.[22]

To foster creativity, companies may also have to *remove impediments* to creativity from their work environments. Internal conflict and power struggles, rigid management structures, and a conservative bias toward the status quo can all discourage creativity. They create the perception that others in the organization will decide which ideas are acceptable and deserve support.

2.2 Experiential Approach: Managing Innovation during Discontinuous Change

A study of 72 product-development projects (i.e., innovation) in 36 computer companies across the United States, Europe, and Asia sheds light on how to manage innovation. Companies that succeeded in periods of discontinuous change (characterized by technological substitution and design competition, as described earlier) typically followed an experiential approach to innovation.[23] The **experiential approach to innovation** assumes that innovation is occurring within a highly uncertain environment and that the key to fast product innovation is to use intuition, flexible options, and hands-on experience to reduce uncertainty and accelerate learning and understanding. The experiential approach to innovation has five aspects: design iterations, testing, milestones, multifunctional teams, and powerful leaders.[24]

An "iteration" is a repetition. So a **design iteration** is a cycle of repetition in which a company tests a prototype of a new product or service, improves on the design, and then builds and tests the improved product or service prototype. A **product prototype** is a full-scale working model that is being tested for design, function, and reliability. **Testing** is a systematic comparison of different product designs or design iterations. Companies that want to create a new dominant design following a technological discontinuity quickly build, test, improve, and retest a series of different product prototypes. Rickster Powell has jumped from an airplane 20,000 times in order to test parachute designs. He and a partner strap cameras to their bodies to film the chute's deployment, which

Experiential approach to innovation an approach to innovation that assumes a highly uncertain environment and uses intuition, flexible options, and hands-on experience to reduce uncertainty and accelerate learning and understanding

Design iteration a cycle of repetition in which a company tests a prototype of a new product or service, improves on that design, and then builds and tests the improved prototype

Product prototype a full-scale, working model that is being tested for design, function, and reliability

Testing the systematic comparison of different product designs or design iterations

Facilitating Idea Flow

Doug Hall hosts "Brain Brew," a radio show that features new business ideas and answers questions from callers looking for advice on how to develop or market theirs. Hall's newest innovation is Planet Eureka (http://www.planeteureka.com), a website that aims to be an innovation marketplace, bringing together independent researchers and inventors, small businesses, and big businesses. The goal? Get new ideas into the marketplace by bringing people together. Big businesses can be slow at innovation but have the resources to produce and market the idea. Inventors have freedom to think and tend to be quick about innovation but often lack access to big business. Planet Eureka uses a job-hunt site model, where inventors can post their ideas and companies both large and small can search the site for the next "Eureka!"

Source: A. Cordeiro, "Online Market Lets Companies Buy and Sell Ideas," *The Wall Street Journal,* **22 April 2008, B7.**

mgmt trend

enables the manufacturers to look for problems. Only nine out of 50 designs he's tested have actually been produced. Needless to say, he always wears a spare chute. [25]

By trying a number of very different designs or making successive improvements and changes in the same design, frequent design iterations reduce uncertainty and improve understanding. Simply put, the more prototypes you build, the more likely you are to learn what works and what doesn't. Also, when designers and engineers build a number of prototypes, they are less likely to fall in love with a particular prototype. Instead, they'll be more concerned with improving the product or technology as much as they can. Testing speeds up and improves the innovation process, too. When two very different design prototypes are tested against each other or the new design iteration is tested against the previous iteration, product design strengths and weaknesses quickly become apparent. Likewise, testing uncovers errors early in the design process when they are easiest to correct. Finally, testing accelerates learning and understanding by forcing engineers and product designers to examine hard data about product performance. When there's hard evidence that prototypes are testing well, the confidence of the design team grows. Also, personal conflict between design team members is less likely when testing focuses on hard measurements and facts rather than personal hunches and preferences.

Milestones are formal project review points used to assess progress and performance. For example, a company that has put itself on a 12-month schedule to complete a project might schedule milestones at the 3-month, 6-month, and 9-month points on the schedule. By making people regularly assess what they're doing, how well they're performing, and whether they need to take corrective action, milestones provide structure to the general chaos that follows technological discontinuities. Milestones also shorten the innovation process by creating a sense of urgency that keeps everyone on task.

Multifunctional teams are work teams composed of people from different departments. Multifunctional teams accelerate learning and understanding by mixing and integrating technical, marketing, and manufacturing activities. By involving all key departments in development from the start, multifunctional teams speed innovation through early identification of new ideas or problems that would typically not have been generated or addressed until much later.

Powerful leaders provide the vision, discipline, and motivation to keep the innovation process focused, on time, and on target. Powerful leaders are able to get resources when they are needed, are typically more experienced, have high status in the company, and are held directly responsible for the product's success or failure. On average, powerful leaders can get innovation-related projects done nine months faster than leaders with little power or influence. One such powerful leader was Phil Martens, the former head of Ford's product development. With a year to go before introduction and Ford's hybrid Escape months behind schedule, he told the team, "We are going to deliver on time. . . . Anything you need you'll get." [26] Despite daily inquiries "from above," he promised no interruptions or interference from anyone—even top management. And, when the team members needed something, they got it without waiting.

Milestones formal project review points used to assess progress and performance

Multifunctional teams work teams composed of people from different departments

2.3 Compression Approach: Managing Innovation during Incremental Change

Whereas the experiential approach is used to manage innovation in highly uncertain environments during periods of discontinuous change, the compression approach is used to manage innovation in more certain environments during periods of incremental change. Whereas the goals of the experiential approach are significant improvements in performance and the establishment of a *new* dominant design, the goals of the compression approach are lower costs and incremental improvements in the performance and function of the *existing* dominant design.

The general strategies in each approach are different, too. With the experiential approach, the general strategy is to build something new, different, and substantially better. Because there's so much uncertainty—no one knows which technology will become the market leader—companies adopt a winner-take-all approach by trying to create the market-leading, dominant design. With the compression approach, the general strategy is to compress the time and steps needed to bring about small, consistent improvements in performance and functionality. Because a dominant technology design already exists, the general strategy is to continue improving the existing technology as rapidly as possible.

In short, a **compression approach to innovation** assumes that innovation is a predictable process, that incremental innovation can be planned using a series of steps, and that compressing the time it takes to complete those steps can speed up innovation. The compression approach to innovation has five aspects: planning, supplier involvement, shortening the time of individual steps, overlapping steps, and multifunctional teams.[27]

In Chapter 5, *planning* was defined as choosing a goal and a method or strategy to achieve that goal. When *planning for incremental innovation,* the goal is to squeeze or compress development time as much as possible, and the general strategy is to create a series of planned steps to accomplish that goal. Planning for incremental innovation helps avoid unnecessary steps and enables developers to sequence steps in the right order to avoid wasted time and delays between steps. Planning also reduces misunderstandings and improves coordination.

Most planning for incremental innovation is based on the idea of generational change. **Generational change** occurs when incremental improvements are made to a dominant technological design such that the improved version of the technology is fully backward

Extreme Makeover

Standing in front of her mirror, Hana Zalal, the president of Cargo Cosmetics, was holding a tube of lipstick and wondering how to redesign it. Then came a packaging epiphany: make it completely biodegradable. An alumna of the University of Toronto's civil engineering program, she went to the university for help. Professor Mohini Sain took up the project and worked with Cargo and a local injection-molding company for two years to figure out how to form corn into a lipstick tube at a "fast and cheap commercial rate." They succeeded. Not only does the new PlantLove lipstick tube decompose in 47 days with composting, the box it comes in is embedded with wildflower seeds and can be planted instead of discarded. And as you would expect, the lipstick itself is environmentally friendly and uses no mineral or petroleum oils or derivatives.

Source: S. Bhattacharya, "Cosmetics Company Cargo Takes Green and Floral Path," *Toronto Star,* 16 January 2007; "Lipstick Maker Goes Green with Biodegradable Tube," *CBC Canada,* 20 April 2007, available online at http://www.cbc.ca.

© Susan Van Etten

compatible with the older version.[28] Software is backward compatible if a new version of the software will work with files created by older versions. Likewise, one of the important features of gaming machines, like the Xbox 360 and the Nintendo Wii, is their ability to play games purchased for earlier machines. In fact, the latest Game Boy can play games originally purchased more than 20 years ago.

Because the compression approach assumes that innovation can follow a series of preplanned steps, one of the ways to shorten development time is *supplier involvement.* Delegating some of the preplanned steps in the innovation process to outside suppliers reduces the amount of work that internal development

Compression approach to innovation
an approach to innovation that assumes that incremental innovation can be planned using a series of steps and that compressing those steps can speed innovation

Generational change
change based on incremental improvements to a dominant technological design such that the improved technology is fully backward compatible with the older technology

teams must do. Plus, suppliers provide an alternative source of ideas and expertise that can lead to better designs. Rowmark produces thin plastic sheets that can be engraved or shaped by a thermoforming process. In an effort to improve the performance of their product, lower the cost of raw materials, and avoid disruptions in supply, it recruits the companies who supply its resin and additives to participate in the product design and manufacturing processes. Suppliers have knowledge that can help Rowmark put out a better product at lower cost. Loyalty and flexibility is important, as is cultural fit between the supplier and the manufacturer, because they are effectively becoming a single team. Eric Hausserman, Rowmark's vice president for manufacturing and technology, points out, "We see our suppliers as partners in every sense of the term."[29] In general, the earlier suppliers are involved, the quicker they catch and prevent future problems, such as unrealistic designs or mismatched product specifications.

Another way to shorten development time is simply to *shorten the time of individual steps* in the innovation process. A common way to do that is through computer-aided design (CAD). CAD speeds up the design process by allowing designers and engineers to make and test design changes using computer models rather than physically testing expensive prototypes. CAD also speeds innovation by making it easy to see how design changes affect engineering, purchasing, and production.

In a sequential design process, each step must be completed before the next step begins. But sometimes multiple development steps can be performed at the same time. *Overlapping steps* shorten the development process by reducing delays or waiting time between steps. Warner Bros. is using overlapping steps to reduce the time it takes to make the entire series of seven *Harry Potter* films—one for each of the seven books in J.K. Rowling's series. Because the actors were aging and would soon resemble adults more than high school students, Warner Bros. used new directors and new production teams for each of the movies in the *Harry Potter* series so it could begin shooting the next film while the previous one was in post production and the one prior to that was in the theaters.[30]

Organizational Change

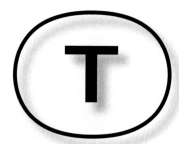

The idea was simple. Build a series of electronics superstores and watch the customers and profits pour in. For a while, it seemed to work. Sales at Incredible Universe grew to $725 million in less than four years as the company grew to seventeen stores, each of which stocked an average of 85,000 products in a 185,000-square-foot building. That's more than four times the size of Circuit City stores, a rival at the time. Yet, because of the size, inventory, and extras, the breakeven point for each store was $70 million in sales per year. So despite rapid growth, the company was losing money at record rates. Managers were unable to change the store concept quickly enough to reverse the situation, so the parent company, Tandy Corporation, closed Incredible Universe just four years after its founding. Businesses operate in a constantly changing environment. Recognizing and adapting to internal and external changes can mean the difference between continued success and going out of business. Companies that fail to change run the risk of organizational decline.[31]

Beating a Sluggish Economy

Starbucks, the ubiquitous coffee shop that popularized gourmet coffee, posted its first ever loss in July 2008. What's got them down? Overexpansion, increase in the price of commodities, competition from companies like McDonald's, which are making improved (and less expensive) coffee, and an overall slower economy. CEO Howard Schultz aimed to give the company a jolt in early 2008 by introducing the new Pike Place roast, among other tactics. But even a venti strategy couldn't wake up the company, which announced plans to close 600 stores in the U.S. and trim management in an effort to weather the storm. But you still probably won't have to walk far to get your next caffeine fix.

Source: L. Gunnison, "Black and Brew," Portfolio.com, available online at http://www.portfolio.com/news-markets/top-5/2008/07/30/Starbucks-Loss [accessed 5 August 2008]

After reading the next two sections on organizational change, you should be able to

3   discuss why not changing can lead to organizational decline.

4   discuss the different methods that managers can use to better manage change as it occurs.

3 Organizational Decline: The Risk of Not Changing

Businesses operate in a constantly changing environment. Recognizing and adapting to internal and external changes can mean the difference between continued success and going out of business. Companies that fail to change run the risk of organizational decline.[32]

Organizational decline occurs when companies don't anticipate, recognize, neutralize, or adapt to the internal or external pressures that threaten their survival.[33] In other words, decline occurs when organizations don't recognize the need for change. General Motors' loss of market share in the automobile industry is an example of organizational decline. There are five stages of organizational decline: blinded, inaction, faulty action, crisis, and dissolution.[34]

In the *blinded stage*, decline begins because key managers fail to recognize the internal or external changes that will harm their organizations. This "blindness" may be due to a simple lack of awareness about changes or an inability to understand their significance. It may also come from the overconfidence that can develop when a company has been successful.

In the *inaction stage*, as organizational performance problems become more visible, management may recognize the need to change but still take no action. The managers may be waiting to see if the problems will correct themselves. Or, they may find it difficult to change the practices and policies that previously led to success. Possibly, too, they wrongly assume that they can easily correct the problems, so they don't feel the situation is urgent.

In the *faulty action stage*, faced with rising costs and decreasing profits and market share, management will announce "belt-tightening" plans designed to cut costs, increase efficiency, and restore profits. In other words, rather than recognizing the need for fundamental changes, managers assume that if they just run a tighter ship, company performance will return to previous levels.

In the *crisis stage*, bankruptcy or dissolution (i.e., breaking up the company and selling its parts) is likely to occur unless the company completely reorganizes the way it does business. At this point, however, companies typically lack the resources to fully change how they run their businesses. Cutbacks and layoffs will have reduced the level of talent among employees. Furthermore, talented managers who were savvy enough to see the crisis coming will have found jobs with other companies, often with competitors.

In the *dissolution stage*, after failing to make the changes needed to sustain the organization, the company is dissolved through bankruptcy proceedings or by selling assets in order to pay suppliers, banks, and creditors. At this point, a new CEO may be brought in to oversee the closing of stores, offices, and manufacturing facilities, the final layoff of managers and employees, and the sale of assets.

Because decline is reversible at each of the first four stages, not all companies in decline reach final dissolution. For example, GM is trying to aggressively cut costs, stabilize its shrinking market share, and use innovative production techniques in an effort to reverse a decline that has lasted nearly a decade and resulted in all-time low stock prices.

4 Managing Change

According to social psychologist Kurt Lewin, change is a function of the forces that promote change and the opposing forces that slow or resist change.[35] **Change forces** lead to differences in the form, quality, or condition of an organization over time.

By contrast, **resistance forces** support the status quo, that is, the existing conditions in organizations. Change is difficult under any circumstances. In a study of heart bypass patients, doctors told participants straightforwardly to change their eating and health habits or they would die. Unbelievably, a full 90 percent of participants did *not* change their habits at all![36] This fierce resistance to change also applies to organizations.

Resistance to change is caused by self-interest, misunderstanding and distrust, and a general intolerance for change.[37] People resist change

---

Organizational decline a large decrease in organizational performance that occurs when companies don't anticipate, recognize, neutralize, or adapt to the internal or external pressures that threaten their survival

Change forces forces that produce differences in the form, quality, or condition of an organization over time

Resistance forces forces that support the existing state of conditions in organizations

Resistance to change opposition to change resulting from self-interest, misunderstanding and distrust, and a general intolerance for change

© Dennis Kitchen/Stone/Getty Images

out of *self-interest* because they fear that change will cost or deprive them of something they value. For example, resistance might stem from a fear that the changes will result in a loss of pay, power, responsibility or even perhaps one's job. People also resist change because of *misunderstanding and distrust;* they don't understand the change or the reasons for it, or they distrust the people—typically management—behind the change. Resistance isn't always visible at first, however. Some of the strongest resisters may initially support the changes in public, nodding and smiling their agreement, but then ignore the changes in private and do their jobs as they always have. Management consultant Michael Hammer calls this deadly form of resistance the "Kiss of Yes."[38]

Unfreezing getting the people affected by change to believe that change is needed

Change intervention the process used to get workers and managers to change their behavior and work practices

Refreezing supporting and reinforcing new changes so that they stick

Resistance may also come from a generally low tolerance for change. Some people are simply less capable of handling change than others. People with a *low tolerance for change* feel threatened by the uncertainty associated with change and worry that they won't be able to learn the new skills and behaviors needed to successfully negotiate change in their companies.

Because resistance to change is inevitable, successful change efforts require careful management. In this section you will learn about **4.1 managing resistance to change, 4.2 what not to do when leading organizational change,** and **4.3 different change tools and techniques.**

4.1 Managing Resistance to Change

According to Kurt Lewin, managing organizational change is a basic process of unfreezing, change intervention, and refreezing. **Unfreezing** is getting the people affected by change to believe that change is needed. During the **change intervention** itself, workers and managers change their behavior and work practices. **Refreezing** is supporting and reinforcing the new changes so that they stick.

Resistance to change is an example of frozen behavior. Given the choice between changing and not changing, most people would rather not change. Because resistance to change is natural and inevitable, managers need to unfreeze resistance to change to create successful change programs. The following methods can be used to manage resistance to change: education and communication, participation, negotiation, top management support, and coercion.[39]

When resistance to change is based on insufficient, incorrect, or misleading information, managers should *educate* employees about the need for change and *communicate* change-related information to them. Managers must also supply the information and funding or other support employees need to make changes. For example, resistance to change can be particularly strong when one company buys another company. New York-Presbyterian Healthcare System reduced resistance to change by designating mentors to coach individuals, groups, and departments in newly acquired companies about its procedures and practices. New York Presbyterian's Diane Iorfida said, "Keeping employees informed every step of the way is so important. It's also important to tell the truth, whatever you do. If you don't know, say you don't know."[40]

Another way to reduce resistance to change is to have those affected by the change *participate in planning and implementing the change process.* Employees who participate have a better understanding of the change and the need for it. Furthermore, employee concerns about change can be addressed as they occur if employees participate in the planning and implementa-

What to Do When Employees Resist Change

UNFREEZING

- **Share reasons** Share the reasons for change with employees.
- **Empathize** Be empathetic to the difficulties that change will create for managers and employees.
- **Communicate** Communicate the details simply, clearly, extensively, verbally, and in writing.

CHANGE

- **Explain** Explain the benefits, "what's in it for them."
- **Champion** Identify a highly respected manager to manage the change effort.
- **Create opportunities for feedback** Allow the people who will be affected by change to express their needs and offer their input.
- **Time it right** Don't begin change at a bad time, for example, during the busiest part of the year or month.
- **Offer security** If possible, maintain employees' job security to minimize fear of change.
- **Educate** Offer training to ensure that employees are both confident and competent to handle new requirements.
- **Don't rush** Change at a manageable pace.

Source: G. J. Iskat and J. Liebowitz, "What to Do When Employees Resist Change," *Supervision*, 1 August 1996.

GOOD TIP!

tion process. CEO A. G. Lafley turned around Procter & Gamble by refocusing the company on its billion-dollar brands (e.g., Tide, Pantene). Martin Nuechtern, then chief of global hair care, said, "A. G. made things very clear: Make sure you focus on Pantene."[41] While Lafley clearly shifted the focus to P&G's best brands, the strategies to reenergize those brands were generated through employee participation. At an informal luncheon with midlevel managers, Lafley said, "I don't have a speech planned. I thought we could talk. I'm searching for meaty issues. Give me some meaty issues."[42] Then, he listened to their ideas.

Employees are also less likely to resist change if they are allowed to discuss and agree on who will do what after change occurs. Resistance to change also decreases when change efforts receive *significant managerial sup-*

port. Managers must do more than talk about the importance of change, though. They must provide the training, resources, and autonomy needed to make change happen. For example, with a distinguished 70-year history of hand-drawing Hollywood's most successful animated films (*Snow White, Bambi, The Little Mermaid, Beauty and the Beast*), animators at Walt Disney Company naturally resisted the move to computer-generated (CG) animation. So Disney supported the difficult change by putting all of its animators through a six-month "CG Boot Camp," where they learned how to draw animated characters with computers.[43]

Finally, resistance to change can be managed through **coercion,** or the use of formal power and authority to force others to change. Because of the intense negative reactions it can create (e.g., fear, stress, resentment, sabotage of company products), coercion should be used only when a crisis exists or when all other attempts to reduce resistance to change have failed.

4.2 What *Not* to Do When Leading Change

So far, you've learned how to execute a basic change process (unfreezing, change, refreezing) and how to manage resistance to change. Harvard Business School professor John Kotter argues that knowing what *not* to do is just as important as knowing what to do when it comes to achieving successful organizational change.[44]

Managers commonly make certain errors when they lead change. The first two errors occur during the unfreezing phase, when managers try to get the people affected by change to believe that change is really needed. The first and potentially most serious error is *not establishing a great enough sense of urgency.* Indeed, Kotter estimates that more than half of all change efforts fail because the people affected are not convinced that change is necessary. People will feel a greater sense of urgency if a leader in the company makes a public, candid assessment of the company's problems and weaknesses.

The second mistake that occurs in the unfreezing process is *not creating a powerful enough coalition.* Change often starts with one or two people. But change has to be supported by a critical and growing group of people to build enough momentum to change an entire department, division, or company. Besides top management, Kotter recommends that key employees, managers, board members, customers, and even union leaders be members of a *core change coalition* which

Coercion using formal power and authority to force others to change

guides and supports organizational change. Procter & Gamble's CEO A. G. Lafley says, "If you are going to make a significant change, you have to declare where are we going and why are we going there. Then you have to put together this guiding coalition. You have to put the true disciples together—the prophets who believe in it as passionately as you do. And they help you to carry the organization, because you can't carry a 100,000-person organization spread across 80 to 100 countries by yourself."

The next four errors that managers make occur during the change phase, when a change intervention is used to try to get workers and managers to change their behavior and work practices. *Lacking a vision* for change is a significant error at this point. As you learned in Chapter 5, a *vision* is a statement of a company's purpose or reason for existing. A vision for change makes clear where a company or department is headed and why the change is occurring. Change efforts that lack vision tend to be confused, chaotic, and contradictory. By contrast, change efforts guided by visions are clear and easy to understand and can be effectively explained in five minutes or less.

Undercommunicating the vision by a factor of ten is another mistake in the change phase. According to Kotter, companies mistakenly hold just one meeting to announce the vision. Or, if the new vision receives heavy emphasis in executive speeches or company newsletters, senior management then undercuts the vision by behaving in ways contrary to it. Successful communication of the vision requires that top managers link everything the company does to the new vision and that they "walk the talk" by behaving in ways consistent with the vision.

Furthermore, even companies that begin change with a clear vision sometimes make the mistake of *not removing obstacles to the new vision.* They leave formidable barriers to change in place by failing to redesign jobs, pay plans, and technology to support the new way of doing things.

Another error in the change phase is *not systematically planning for and creating short-term wins.* Most people don't have the discipline and patience to wait two years to see if the new change effort works. Change is threatening and uncomfortable, so people need to see an immediate payoff if they are to continue to support it. Kotter recommends that managers create short-term wins by actively picking people and projects that are likely to work extremely well early in the change process.

The last two errors that managers make occur during the refreezing phase, when attempts are made to support and reinforce changes so that they stick. *Declaring victory too soon* is a tempting mistake in the refreezing phase. Managers typically declare victory right after the first large-scale success in the change process. Declaring success too early has the same effect as draining the gasoline out of a car: it stops change efforts dead in their tracks. With success declared, supporters of the change process stop pushing to make change happen.

CHANGE EFFORTS THAT LACK VISION TEND TO BE CONFUSED, CHAOTIC, AND CONTRADICTORY.

Beyond Chicken Noodle

Your grandmother's old standby may cure your cold and heal your soul, but it isn't good enough to revive Campbell Soup Co.'s downturn or achieve its goal of expanding into global markets. CEO Douglas Conant is charged with the task of making sure the famous red label remains the leader in soup. But that will mean change. Chicken soup may be food for the soul in the United States . . .

. . . but not so much for the Chinese. The company must learn the ins and outs of soup in different cultures and establish strategies for breaking into those markets. Conant offers some tips for transformation: All things are possible. See the situation straight. Have high standards and follow through. Take the time to get it right.

Source: J. Jargon, "Campbell's Chief Looks for Splash of Innovation," *The Wall Street Journal*, 30 May 2008, 88

© PRNewsFoto/via Bloomberg News/Landov / Courtesy of Chapel House Photography

After all, why push when success has been achieved? Rather than declaring victory, managers should use the momentum from short-term wins to push for even bigger or faster changes. This maintains urgency and prevents change supporters from slacking off before the changes are frozen into the company's culture.

The last mistake that managers make is *not anchoring changes in the corporation's culture.* An *organization's culture* is the set of key values, beliefs, and attitudes shared by organizational members that determines the "accepted way of doing things" in a company. As you learned in Chapter 3, changing cultures is extremely difficult and slow. According to Kotter, two things help anchor changes in a corporation's culture. The first is directly showing people that the changes have actually improved performance. The second is to make sure that the people who get promoted fit the new culture. If they don't, it's a clear sign that the changes were only temporary.

4.3 Change Tools and Techniques

Imagine your boss came to you and said, "All right, genius, you wanted it. You're in charge of turning around the division." How would you start? Where would you begin? How would you encourage change-resistant managers to change? What would you do to include others in the change process? How would you get the change process off to a quick start? Finally, what approach would you use to promote long-term effectiveness and performance? Results-driven change, the General Electric workout, and organizational development are three change tools and techniques that can be used to address these issues.

One of the reasons that organizational change efforts fail is that they are activity-oriented rather than results-oriented. In other words, they focus primarily on changing company procedures, management philosophy, or employee behavior. Typically, there is much buildup and preparation as consultants are brought in, presentations are made, books are read, and employees and managers are trained. There's a tremendous emphasis on "doing things the new way." But, with all the focus on "doing," almost no attention is paid to results, to seeing if all this activity has actually made a difference.

By contrast, **results-driven change** supplants the emphasis on activity with a laser-like focus on quickly measuring and improving results.[46] For example, top managers at Hyundai knew that if they were to compete successfully against the likes of Honda and Toyota, they would have to substantially improve the quality of their cars. So top managers guided the company's results-driven change process by increasing the number of quality teams from 100 to 865. Then, all employees were required to attend seminars on quality improvement and use the results of industry quality studies, like those published annually by J.D. Power and Associates, as their benchmark. Before the change, a new Hyundai averaged 23.4 initial quality problems; after the results-driven change efforts, that number dropped to 9.6.[47]

Another advantage of results-driven change is that managers introduce changes in procedures, philosophy, or behavior only if they are likely to improve measured performance. In other words, changes are tested to see whether they actually make a difference. Consistent with this approach, Chairman Chung invested $30 million in a test center where cars were subjected to a sequence of extremely

> **Results-driven change** change created quickly by focusing on the measurement and improvement of results

Exhibit 7.4

How to Create a Results-Driven Change Program

1. Set measurable, short-term goals to improve performance.
2. Make sure your action steps are likely to improve measured performance.
3. Stress the importance of immediate improvements.
4. Solicit help from consultants and staffers to achieve quick improvements in performance.
5. Test action steps to see if they actually yield improvements. If they don't, discard them and establish new ones.
6. Use resources you have or that can be easily required. It doesn't take much.

Source: R. H. Schaffer & H. A. Thomson, J.D, "Successful Change Programs Begin with Results," *Harvard Business Review on Change* (Boston: Harvard Business School Press, 1998), 189–213.

harsh conditions to allow engineers to pinpoint defects and fix problems.[48]

A third advantage of results-driven change is that quick, visible improvements motivate employees to continue to make additional changes to improve measured performance. Exhibit 7.4 describes the basic steps of results-driven change.

The **General Electric workout** is a special kind of results-driven change. The "workout" involves a three-day meeting that brings together managers and employees from different levels and parts of an organization to quickly generate and act on solutions to specific business problems.[49] On the first morning, the boss discusses the agenda and targets specific business problems that the group will solve. The boss then leaves, and an outside facilitator breaks the group (typically 30 to 40 people) into five or six teams and helps them spend the next day and a half discussing and debating solutions. On day three, in what GE calls a "town meeting," the teams present specific solutions to their boss, who has been gone since day one. As each team's spokesperson makes specific suggestions, the boss has only three options: agree on the spot, say no, or ask for more information so that a decision can be made by a specific, agreed-on date.[50]

Organizational development is a philosophy and collection of planned change interventions designed to improve an organization's long-term health and performance. Organizational development takes a long-range approach to change; assumes that top management support is necessary for change to succeed; creates change by educating workers and managers to change ideas, beliefs, and behaviors so that problems can be solved in new ways; and emphasizes employee participation in diagnosing, solving, and evaluating problems.[51] As shown in Exhibit 7.5, organizational development interventions begin with the recognition of a problem. Then, the company designates a **change agent** to be formally

General Electric workout a three-day meeting in which managers and employees from different levels and parts of an organization quickly generate and act on solutions to specific business problems

Organizational development a philosophy and collection of planned change interventions designed to improve an organization's long-term health and performance

Change agent the person formally in charge of guiding a change effort

Exhibit 7.5

General Steps for Organizational Development Interventions

1. **Entry**	A problem is discovered and the need for change becomes apparent. A search begins for someone to deal with the problem and facilitate change.
2. **Startup**	A change agent enters the picture and works to clarify the problem and gain commitment to a change effort.
3. **Assessment & feedback**	The change agent gathers information about the problem and provides feedback about it to decision makers and those affected by it.
4. **Action planning**	The change agent works with decision makers to develop an action plan.
5. **Intervention**	The action plan, or organizational development intervention, is carried out.
6. **Evaluation**	The change agent helps decision makers assess the effectiveness of the intervention.
7. **Adoption**	Organizational members accept ownership and responsibility for the change, which is then carried out through the entire organization.
8. **Separation**	The change agent leaves the organization after first ensuring that the change intervention will continue to work.

Source: W. J. Rothwell, R. Sullivan, and G. M. McLean, *Practicing Organizational Development: A Guide for Consultants* (San Diego: Pfeiffer & Co., 1995).

in charge of guiding the change effort. This person can be someone from the company or a professional consultant. The change agent clarifies the problem, gathers information, works with decision makers to create and implement an action plan, helps to evaluate the plan's effectiveness, implements the plan throughout the company, and then leaves (if from outside the company) after making sure the change intervention will continue to work.

Organizational development interventions are aimed at changing large systems, small groups, or people.[52]

More specifically, the purpose of *large system interventions* is to change the character and performance of an organization, business unit, or department. *Small group intervention* focuses on assessing how a group functions and helping it work more effectively to accomplish its goals. *Person-focused intervention* is intended to increase interpersonal effectiveness by helping people become aware of their attitudes and behaviors and acquire new skills and knowledge. Exhibit 7.6 describes the most frequently used organizational development interventions for large systems, small groups, and people.

Exhibit 7.6

Different Kinds of Organizational Development Interventions

LARGE SYSTEM INTERVENTIONS	
Sociotechnical systems	An intervention designed to improve how well employees use and adjust to the work technology used in an organization.
Survey feedback	An intervention that uses surveys to collect information from the members, reports the results of that survey to the members, and then uses those results to develop action plans for improvement.
SMALL GROUP INTERVENTIONS	
Team building	An intervention designed to increase the cohesion and cooperation of work group members.
Unit goal setting	An intervention designed to help a work group establish short- and long-term goals.
PERSON-FOCUSED INTERVENTIONS	
Counseling/coaching	An intervention designed so that a formal helper or coach listens to managers or employees and advises them on how to deal with work or interpersonal problems.
Training	An intervention designed to provide individuals with the knowledge, skills, or attitudes they need to become more effective at their jobs.

Source: W. J. Rothwell, R. Sullivan, and G. M. McLean, *Practicing Organizational Development: A Guide for Consultants* (San Diego: Pfeiffer & Co., 1995).

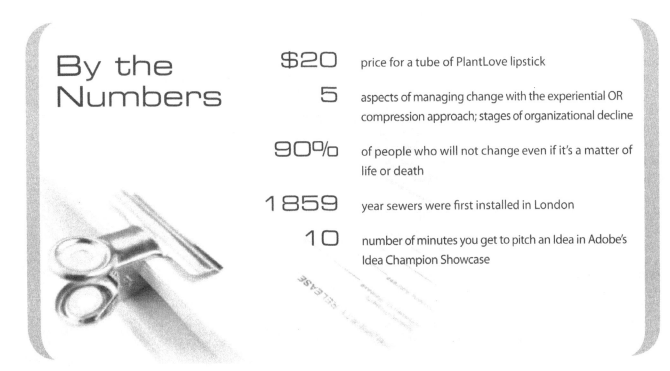

By the Numbers

$20	price for a tube of PlantLove lipstick
5	aspects of managing change with the experiential OR compression approach; stages of organizational decline
90%	of people who will not change even if it's a matter of life or death
1859	year sewers were first installed in London
10	number of minutes you get to pitch an Idea in Adobe's Idea Champion Showcase

DESIGNING ADAPTIVE ORGANIZATIONS

Structure and Process

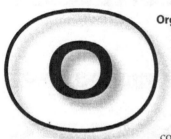

Organizational structure is the vertical and horizontal configuration of departments, authority, and jobs within a company. Organizational structure is concerned with vertical questions such as "Who reports to whom?" as well as horizontal questions such as "Who does what?" and "Where is the work done?" For example, Sony Corporation of America is headed by Howard Stringer, Chairman and CEO, who is based in New York City. But Sony has a number of divisions to handle different sectors of the company's business, each headed by its own President or CEO. PlayStation is developed and managed in Foster City, California by Sony Computer Entertainment. Sony camcorders, home theater equipment, LCD screens, VAIO computers, Blu-ray disc players, and the Walkman are handled in San Diego by Sony Electronics. The Spider-Man films and "Seinfeld" are brought to you by Sony Pictures, a division of Sony Entertainment in Culver City, California, while the music of Justin Timberlake and Avril Lavigne comes courtesy of Sony/BMG in New York City.[1] Companies like Sony use organizational structure to set up departments and relationships among employees in order to make business happen. You can see Sony's organizational structure in Exhibit 9.1.

An **organizational process** is the collection of activities that transform in-

Organizational structure the vertical and horizontal configuration of departments, authority, and jobs within a company

Organizational process the collection of activities that transform inputs into outputs that customers value

Learning Outcomes

1 describe the departmentalization approach to organizational structure.

2 explain organizational authority.

3 discuss the different methods for job design.

4 explain the methods that companies are using to redesign internal organizational processes (i.e., intraorganizational processes).

5 describe the methods that companies are using to redesign external organizational processes (i.e., interorganizational processes).

© iStockphoto.com

Exhibit 9.1

Sony Corporation's Organizational Chart

Electronics Business								Sony Ericsson Mobile Communications	Game Business Group	Entertainment Business Group	Sony Financial Holdings Group
Semiconductor & Component Group				Consumer Products Group							
Semiconductor Business Group	Electronic Devices Business Group	Chemical & Energy Business Group	B2B Solutions Business Group	VAIO Business Group	Digital Imaging Business Group	Audio & Video Business Group	TV Business Group				

Headquarters / Corporate R&D

The organizational chart displays Sony's horizontal and vertical dimensions.

Source: Sony Organizational Chart available online at http://www.sony.net/SonyInfo/CorporateInfo/Data/organization.html, [accessed 10 September 2008].

Exhibit 9.2

Process View of Microsoft's Organization

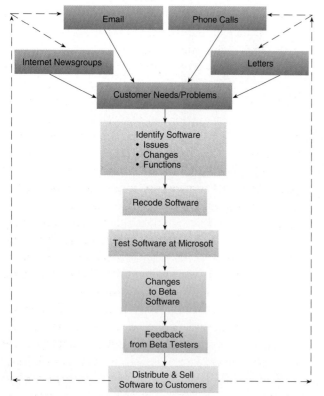

puts into outputs that customers value.[2] Organizational process asks: How do things get done? For example, Microsoft uses basic internal and external processes to write computer software, shown in Exhibit 9.2. The process starts when Microsoft gets external feedback from customers through Internet newsgroups, email, phone calls, or letters. This information helps Microsoft understand customers' needs and problems and identify important software issues and needed changes and functions. Microsoft then rewrites the software, testing it internally at the company and then externally through its beta-testing process where customers who volunteer or are selected by Microsoft give the company extensive feedback which is then used to make improvements. After final corrections are made to the software, the company distributes and sells it to customers. They start the process again by giving Microsoft more feedback.

Organizational process is just as important as organizational structure, and you'll learn about both in this chapter.

Departmentalization subdividing work and workers into separate organizational units responsible for completing particular tasks

Designing Organizational Structures

With offices and operations in 58 countries, products in over 200, and more than 150,000 employees worldwide, Sara Lee Corporation owns some of the best-known brands (Sara Lee, Hillshire Farms, Ball Park, and Jimmy Dean) in the world. To improve company performance, Sara Lee changed its organizational structure to focus on three key customer/geographic markets: North American retail (bakery, packaged meats, and Senseo coffee), North American food service (bakery goods, coffee, and meats sold to restaurants), and Sara Lee International (bakery and beverage businesses outside North America and global household products). Companies or divisions that didn't fit the new structure, like the European meats division and the branded apparel businesses (including Champion and Playtex) were sold. As a result, Sara Lee is now focused on its core businesses—food, beverage, and household and body care.[3]

Why would a large company like Sara Lee completely restructure its organizational design? What can be gained from such a change?

 After reading the next three sections, you'll have a better understanding of the importance of organizational structure because you should be able to

1 describe the departmentalization approach to organizational structure.

2 explain organizational authority.

3 discuss the different methods for job design.

1 Departmentalization

Traditionally, organizational structures have been based on some form of departmentalization. **Departmentalization** is a method of subdividing work and workers

Exhibit 9.3

Functional Departmentalization

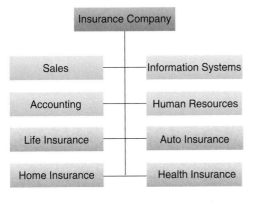

into separate organizational units that take responsibility for completing particular tasks.[4]

Traditionally, organizational structures have been created by departmentalizing work according to five methods: **1.1 functional, 1.2 product, 1.3 customer, 1.4 geographic,** *and* **1.5 matrix.**

1.1 Functional Departmentalization

The most common organizational structure is functional departmentalization. Companies tend to use this structure when they are small or just starting out. **Functional departmentalization** organizes work and workers into separate units responsible for particular business functions or areas of expertise. A common functional structure might have individuals organized into accounting, sales, marketing, production, and human resources departments.

Not all functionally departmentalized companies have the same functions. The insurance company and the advertising agency shown in Exhibit 9.3 both have sales, accounting, human resources, and information systems departments, as indicated by the orange boxes. The purple and green boxes indicate the functions that are different. As would be expected, the insurance com-

pany has separate departments for life, auto, home, and health insurance. The advertising agency has departments for artwork, creative work, print advertising, and radio advertising. So the functional departments in a company that uses functional structure depend in part on the business or industry the company is in.

Functional departmentalization has some advantages. First, it allows work to be done by highly qualified specialists. While the accountants in the accounting department take responsibility for producing accurate revenue and expense figures, the engineers in research and development can focus their efforts on designing a product that is reliable and simple to manufacture. Second, it lowers costs by reducing duplication. When the engineers in research and development come up with that fantastic new product, they don't have to worry about creating an aggressive advertising campaign to sell it. That task belongs to the advertising experts and sales representatives in marketing. Third, with everyone in the same department having similar work experience or training, communication and coordination are less problematic for departmental managers.

At the same time, functional departmentalization has a number of disadvantages. To start, cross-department coordination can be difficult. Managers and employees are often more interested in doing what's right for their function than in doing what's right for the entire organization. As companies grow, functional departmentalization may also lead to slower decision making and produce managers and workers with narrow experience and expertise.

1.2 Product Departmentalization

Product departmentalization organizes work and workers into separate units responsible for producing particular products or services. Exhibit 9.4 on the next page shows the product departmentalization structure used by United Technologies (UTC), which is organized along seven different product lines: Carrier, Chubb, Hamilton Sundstrand, Otis, Pratt & Whitney, Sikorsky, and UTC Power.[5]

One of the advantages of product departmentalization is that, like functional departmentalization, it allows managers and workers to specialize in one area of expertise. Unlike the narrow expertise and experiences in functional departmentalization, however, managers and workers develop a broader set of

Functional departmentalization organizing work and workers into separate units responsible for particular business functions or areas of expertise

Product departmentalization organizing work and workers into separate units responsible for producing particular products or services

Exhibit 9.4

Product Departmentalization: United Technologies

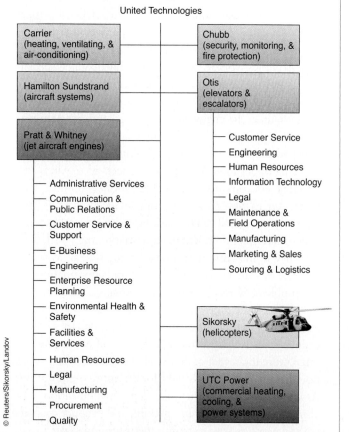

United Technologies

- Carrier (heating, ventilating, & air-conditioning)
- Chubb (security, monitoring, & fire protection)
- Hamilton Sundstrand (aircraft systems)
- Otis (elevators & escalators)
- Pratt & Whitney (jet aircraft engines)
  - Administrative Services
  - Communication & Public Relations
  - Customer Service & Support
  - E-Business
  - Engineering
  - Enterprise Resource Planning
  - Environmental Health & Safety
  - Facilities & Services
  - Human Resources
  - Legal
  - Manufacturing
  - Procurement
  - Quality

Otis:
  - Customer Service
  - Engineering
  - Human Resources
  - Information Technology
  - Legal
  - Maintenance & Field Operations
  - Manufacturing
  - Marketing & Sales
  - Sourcing & Logistics

- Sikorsky (helicopters)
- UTC Power (commercial heating, cooling, & power systems)

Source: *United Technologies Corporation 2005 Annual Report,* United Technologies, available online at http://www.utc.com/annual_reports/2005/html, [accessed 8 August 2008].

experiences and expertise related to an entire product line. Likewise, product departmentalization makes it easier for top managers to assess work-unit performance. For example, because of the clear separation of their seven different product divisions, United Technologies' top managers can easily compare the performance of its Chubb fire and security and its Sikorsky helicopter divisions. The divisions had similar profits—$235 million for Chubb and $250 million for Sikorsky—but Chubb's revenues were much higher at $4.3 billion compared to Sikorsky's $2.8 billion.[6] Finally, decision making should be faster because managers and workers are responsible for the entire product line rather than

for separate functional departments; in other words, there are fewer conflicts compared to functional departmentalization.

The primary disadvantage of product departmentalization is duplication. For example, you can see in Exhibit 9.4 that UTC's Otis elevators and Pratt & Whitney divisions both have customer service, engineering, human resources, legal, manufacturing, and procurement (similar to sourcing and logistics) departments. If United Technologies were instead organized by function, by contrast, one lawyer could handle matters related to both elevators and aircraft engines rather than working only on one or the other. Duplication like this often results in higher costs.

A second disadvantage is the challenge of coordinating across the different product departments. United Technologies would probably have difficulty standardizing its policies and procedures in product departments as different as the Carrier (heating, ventilating, and air-conditioning) and Sikorsky (military and commercial helicopters) divisions.

1.3 Customer Departmentalization

Customer departmentalization organizes work and workers into separate units responsible for particular kinds of customers. For example, as Exhibit 9.5 shows, the telecommunications company Sprint Nextel is organized into departments that cater to businesses, consumers, 4G mobile broadband operations, and product development.

The primary advantage of customer departmentalization is that it focuses the organization on customer needs rather than on products or business functions. Furthermore, creating separate departments to serve specific kinds of customers allows companies to specialize and adapt their products and services to customer needs and problems.

The primary disadvantage of customer departmentalization is that, like product departmentalization, it leads to duplication of resources. It can also be difficult to achieve coordination across different customer departments. Finally, the emphasis on meeting customers' needs may lead workers to make decisions that please customers but hurt the business.

1.4 Geographic Departmentalization

Geographic departmentalization organizes work and workers into separate units responsible for doing business in particular geographic areas. For example, Exhibit 9.6 shows the geographic departmentalization used by Coca-Cola Enterprises (CCE), the largest bottler and dis-

Customer departmentalization organizing work and workers into separate units responsible for particular kinds of customers

Geographic departmentalization organizing work and workers into separate units responsible for doing business in particular geographic areas

tributor of Coca-Cola products in the world. As shown in Exhibit 9.6, CCE has two regional groups: North America and Europe. As the table in the exhibit shows, each of these regions would be a sizable company by itself.

The primary advantage of geographic departmentalization is that it helps companies respond to the demands of different markets. This can be especially important when the company sells in different countries, as cultural preferences can vary widely. For example, CCE's geographic divisions sell products suited to taste preferences in different countries. CCE bottles and distributes the following products in Europe but not in the United States: Aquarius, Bonaqua, Burn, Coca-Cola Light (which is somewhat different from Diet Coke), Cresta flavors, Five Alive, Kia-Ora, Kinley, Lilt, Malvern, and Oasis.[7] Another advantage is that geographic departmentaliza-

Exhibit 9.5

Customer Departmentalization: Sprint Corporation

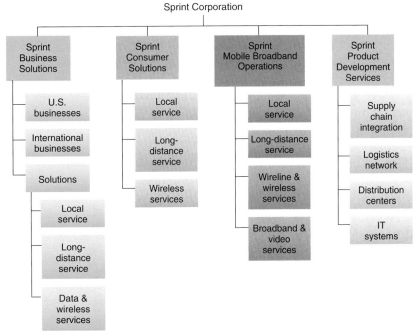

Source: "Overview," Sprint, available online at http://www.sprint.com/sprint/fastfacts/overview/index.html [accessed 1 May 2005].

Exhibit 9.6

Geographic Departmentalization: Coca-Cola Enterprises

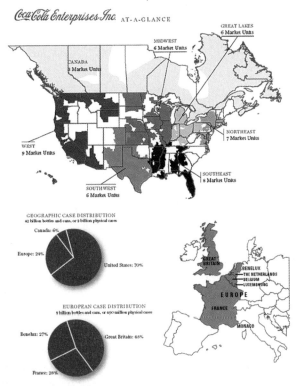

Source: "Territories of Operation, 2007 Annual Report," Coca-Cola Enterprises, available online at http://www.cokecce.com/brochures/cce_2007/index.html#territories [accessed 7 September 2008].

tion can reduce costs by locating unique organizational resources closer to customers. For instance, it is much cheaper for CCE to build bottling plants in Belgium than to bottle Coke in England and then transport it across the English Channel to Belgium.

The primary disadvantage of geographic departmentalization is that it can lead to duplication of resources. For example, while it may be necessary to adapt products and marketing to different geographic locations, it's doubtful that CCE needs significantly different inventory tracking systems from location to location. Also, even more than with the other forms of departmentalization, it can be difficult to coordinate departments that are literally thousands of miles from each other and whose managers have very limited contact with each other.

1.5 Matrix Departmentalization

Matrix departmentalization is a hybrid structure in which two or more forms of departmentalization are used together. The most common matrix combines the product and functional forms of departmentalization, but other forms may also be

> **Matrix departmentalization** a hybrid organizational structure in which two or more forms of departmentalization, most often product and functional, are used together

used. Exhibit 9.7 shows the matrix structure used by Procter & Gamble, which has 98,000 employees working in 80 different countries. Across the top of Exhibit 9.7, you can see that the company uses a product unit structure with managers responsible for the global efforts of their branded products. The left side of the figure, however, shows that the company is also using a geographic structure. Geographic managers are responsible for taking P&G's globally positioned products and adapting them to fit the cultures of the countries where they are sold—more than 140 countries in all. P&G's roster of brands includes Pampers (diapers), Tide (laundry detergent), Always (feminine protection), Pantene (shampoo), Bounty (dryer sheets), Folgers (coffee), Pringles (snack food), Charmin (toilet paper), Downy (fabric softener), Iams (dog and cat food), Crest (toothpaste), Actonel (prescription drug), and Olay (body care). The company also has two groups that cut across the entire matrix; they take care of customer service and administration.

Exhibit 9.7

Matrix Departmentalization: Procter & Gamble

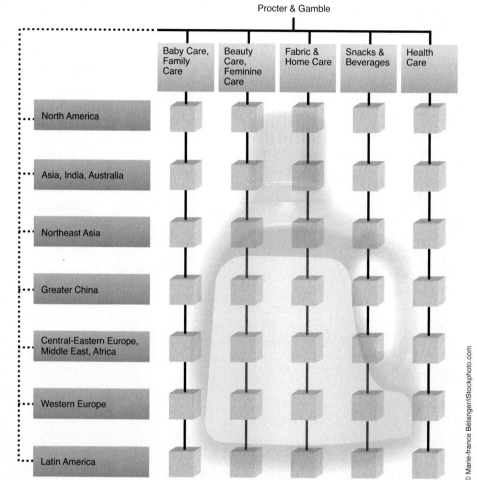

Source: "Corporate Info: Structure," P&G, available online at http://www.pg.com/jobs/corporate_structure/four_pillars.shtml [accessed 8 August 2008].

© Marie-france Bélanger/iStockphoto.com

The boxes in the figure represent the matrix structure, created by combining the geographic and product structures. For example, in the health care business in Central-Eastern Europe, Middle East, and Africa, country managers in Hungary, United Arab Emirates, or Kenya are responsible for developing P&G's business in products such as Metamucil, Pepto-Bismol, Prilosec OTC, and Vicks.

Several things distinguish matrix departmentalization from the other traditional forms of departmentalization.[8] First, most employees report to two bosses, one from each core part of the matrix. For example, in Exhibit 9.7, the manager responsible for Charmin in France would report both to the president for Global Baby Care/Family Care and to the president for Western Europe. Second, by virtue of their hybrid design, matrix structures lead to much more cross-functional interaction than other forms of departmentalization. In fact, while matrix workers are typically members

of only one functional department (based on their work experience and expertise), they are also commonly members of several ongoing project, product, or customer groups. Third, because of the high level of cross-functional interaction, matrix departmentalization requires significant coordination between managers in the different parts of the matrix. In particular, managers have the complex job of tracking and managing the multiple demands (project, product, customer, or functional) on employees' time.

The primary advantage of matrix departmentalization is that it allows companies to efficiently manage large, complex tasks like researching, developing, and marketing pharmaceuticals or carrying out complex global businesses. Efficiency comes from avoiding duplication. For example, rather than having an entire marketing function for each project, the company simply assigns and reassigns workers from the marketing department as they are needed at various stages of product completion. More specifically, an employee from a department may simultaneously be part of five different ongoing projects, but may be actively completing work on only a few projects at a time.

Another advantage is the pool of resources available to carry out large, complex tasks. Because of the ability to quickly pull in expert help from all the functional areas of the company, matrix project managers have a much more diverse set of expertise and experience at their disposal than do managers in the other forms of departmentalization.

The primary disadvantage of matrix departmentalization is the high level of coordination required to manage the complexity involved with running large, ongoing projects at various levels of completion. Matrix structures are notorious for confusion and conflict between project bosses in different parts of the matrix. At P&G, such confusion or conflict might occur between managers in the Global Fabric and Home Care Division and the president of operations in greater China. Disagreements or misunderstandings about schedules, budgets, available resources, and the availability of employees with particular functional expertise are common. Another disadvantage is that matrix structures require much more management skill than the other forms of departmentalization.

Because of these problems, many matrix structures evolve from a **simple matrix,** in which managers in different parts of the matrix negotiate conflicts and resources directly, to a **complex matrix,** in which specialized matrix managers and departments are added to the organizational structure. In a complex matrix, managers from different parts of the matrix might report to the same matrix manager, who helps them sort out conflicts and problems.

> Matrix structures are notorious for confusion and conflict between project bosses in different parts of the matrix.

2 Organizational Authority

The second part of traditional organizational structures is authority. **Authority** is the right to give commands, take action, and make decisions to achieve organizational objectives.[9]

Traditionally, organizational authority has been characterized by the following dimensions: 2.1 chain of command, 2.2 line versus staff authority, 2.3 delegation of authority, and 2.4 degree of centralization.

2.1 Chain of Command

Turn back a few pages to Sony's organizational chart in Exhibit 9.1. If you place your finger on any position in the chart, say, VAIO Business Group (under Electronics Business), you can trace a line upward to the company's CEO, Howard Stringer. This line, which vertically connects every job in the company to higher levels of management, represents the chain of command. The **chain of command** is the vertical line of authority that clarifies who reports to whom throughout the organization. People higher in the chain of command have the right, *if they so choose,* to give commands, take action, and make decisions concerning activities occurring anywhere below them in the chain. In the following discussion about delegation and decentralization, you will learn that managers don't always choose to exercise their authority directly.[10]

One of the key assumptions underlying the chain of command is **unity of command,** which means that workers should report to just one boss.[11] In practical terms, this means that only one

Simple matrix a form of matrix departmentalization in which managers in different parts of the matrix negotiate conflicts and resources

Complex matrix a form of matrix departmentalization in which managers in different parts of the matrix report to matrix managers, who help them sort out conflicts and problems

Authority the right to give commands, take action, and make decisions to achieve organizational objectives

Chain of command the vertical line of authority that clarifies who reports to whom throughout the organization

Unity of command a management principle that workers should report to just one boss

person can be in charge at a time. Matrix organizations, in which employees have two bosses, automatically violate this principle. This is one of the primary reasons that matrix organizations are difficult to manage. Unity of command serves an important purpose: to prevent the confusion that might arise when an employee receives conflicting commands from two different bosses.

2.2 Line versus Staff Authority

A second dimension of authority is the distinction between line and staff authority. **Line authority** is the right to command immediate subordinates in the chain of command. For example, Sony CEO Howard Stringer has line authority over the head of Sony Entertainment Business Group, which contains Sony Pictures. Stringer can issue orders to that division president and expect them to be carried out.

In turn, the head of Sony Entertainment Business Group can issue orders to his subordinates and expect them to be carried out.

Staff authority is the right to *advise* but not command others who are not subordinates in the chain of command. For example, a manager in human resources at Sony might advise the manager in charge of Sony's TV Business Group on a hiring decision but cannot order him or her to hire a certain applicant.

The terms *line* and *staff* are also used to describe different functions within the organization. A **line function** is an activity that contributes directly to creating or selling the company's products. So, for example, activities that take place within the

Exhibit 9.8

Delegation: Responsibility, Authority, and Accountability

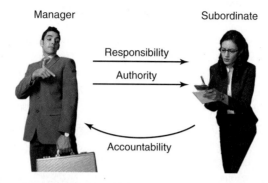

Source: C. D. Pringle, D. F. Jennings, and J. G. Longenecker, *Managing Organizations: Functions and Behaviors* © 1990. Adapted by permission of Pearson Education, Inc., Upper Saddle River, NJ.

manufacturing and marketing departments would be considered line functions. A **staff function,** such as accounting, human resources, or legal services, does not contribute directly to creating or selling the company's products but instead supports line activities. For example, marketing managers might consult with the legal staff to make sure the wording of a particular advertisement is legal.

2.3 Delegation of Authority

Managers can exercise their authority directly by completing the tasks themselves, or they can choose to pass on some of their authority to subordinates. **Delegation of authority** is the assignment of direct authority and responsibility to a subordinate to complete tasks for which the manager is normally responsible.

When a manager delegates work, three transfers occur, as illustrated in Exhibit 9.8. First, the manager transfers full

Line authority the right to command immediate subordinates in the chain of command

Staff authority the right to advise, but not command, others who are not subordinates in the chain of command

Line function an activity that contributes directly to creating or selling the company's products

Staff function an activity that does not contribute directly to creating or selling the company's products, but instead supports line activities

Delegation of authority the assignment of direct authority and responsibility to a subordinate to complete tasks for which the manager is normally responsible

How to Be a More Effective Delegator

1. Trust your staff to do a good job. Recognize that others have the talent and ability to complete projects.

2. Avoid seeking perfection. Establish a standard of quality and provide a time frame for reaching it.

3. Give effective job instructions. Make sure employees have enough information to complete the job successfully.

4. Know your true interests. Delegation is difficult for some people who actually prefer doing the work themselves rather than managing it.

5. Follow up on progress. Build in checkpoints to help identify potential problems.

6. Praise the efforts of your staff.

7. Don't wait until the last minute to delegate. Avoid crisis management by routinely delegating work.

8. Ask questions, expect answers, and assist employees to help them complete the work assignments as expected.

9. Provide the resources you would expect if you were doing an assignment yourself.

10. Delegate to the lowest possible level to make the best possible use of organizational resources, energy, and knowledge.

Source: S. B. Wilson, "Are You an Effective Delegator?" *Female Executive*, 1 November 1994, 19.

percent to 80 percent as well as you can today, you delegate it immediately." Why? Many tasks don't need to be done perfectly; they just need to be *done*. And delegating tasks that someone else can do frees managers to assume other important responsibilities.

Delegating authority can generate a related problem: micromanaging. Sometimes managers delegate only to later interfere with how the employee is performing the task. "Why are you doing it that way? That's not the way I do it." But delegating full responsibility means that the employee—not the manager—is now completely responsible for task completion. Good managers need to trust their subordinates to do the job.

The second transfer that occurs with delegation is that the manager gives the subordinate full authority over the budget, resources, and personnel needed to do the job. To do the job effectively, subordinates must have the same tools and information at their disposal that managers had when they were responsible for the same task. In other words, for delegation to work, delegated authority must be commensurate with delegated responsibility.

The third transfer that occurs with delegation is the transfer of accountability. The subordinate now has the authority and responsibility to do the job and in return is accountable for getting the job done. In other words, managers delegate their authority and responsibility to subordinates in exchange for results.

2.4 Degree of Centralization

If you've ever called a company's toll-free number with a complaint or a special request and been told by the customer service representative, "I'll have to ask my manager," or "I'm not authorized to do that," you know that centralization of authority exists in that company. **Centralization of authority** is the location of most authority at the upper levels of the organization. In a centralized organization, managers make most decisions, even the relatively small ones. That's why the customer service representative you called couldn't make a decision without first asking the manager.

If you are lucky, however, you may have talked to a customer service representative at another company who said, "I can take care of that for you right now." In other words, the person was able to handle your problem without any input from or consultation with

Centralization of authority the location of most authority at the upper levels of the organization

Decentralization the location of a significant amount of authority in the lower levels of the organization

responsibility for the assignment to the subordinate. Many managers find giving up full responsibility somewhat difficult. For example, Steve Ballmer and Bill Gates have been compatriots at Microsoft nearly since its beginning. But when Gates ceded the position of CEO to Ballmer in 2000, taking a number-two position as Chief Software Architect, he had difficulty giving up the reigns of the company. Part of the problem was that Gates is an icon, and it's hard to give up status. As Ballmer tried to take the reins as CEO, Gates would sometimes undermine his authority, creating unproductive tension. Debates between the two had a negative effect on decision-making at Microsoft…and that may be putting it mildly. Their conflict sometimes stopped business-strategy decisions dead in their tracks, leaving fallout that Microsoft continues to clean up today. Fortunately, the two gradually settled their differences. Gates recognized the need to change his behavior and let Ballmer take charge. Gates even came to understand the impact of symbolic actions, as he publicly deferred to Ballmer on a decision in a board meeting. Gates has now fully shifted his energies to philanthropy, leaving Ballmer to run the company.[12]

One reason it is difficult for some managers to delegate is that they often fear the task won't be done as well as if they did it themselves. However, one CEO says, "If you can delegate a task to somebody who can do it 75

company management. **Decentralization** is the location of a significant amount of authority in the lower levels of the organization. An organization is decentralized if it has a high degree of delegation at all levels. In a decentralized organization, workers closest to problems are authorized to make the decisions necessary to solve the problems on their own.

Decentralization has a number of advantages. It develops employee capabilities throughout the company and leads to faster decision making and more satisfied customers and employees. Furthermore, a study of 1,000 large companies found that those with a high degree of decentralization outperformed those with a low degree of decentralization in terms of return on assets (6.9 percent versus 4.7 percent), return on investment (14.6 percent versus 9.0 percent), return on equity (22.8 percent versus 16.6 percent), and return on sales (10.3 percent versus 6.3 percent). Surprisingly, the same study found that few large companies actually are decentralized. Specifically, only 31 percent of employees in these 1,000 companies were responsible for recommending improvements to

3 Job Design

1. "Welcome to McDonald's. May I have your order please?"
2. Listen to the order. Repeat it for accuracy. State the total cost. "Please drive to the second window."
3. Take the money. Make change.
4. Give customers drinks, straws, and napkins.
5. Give customers food.
6. "Thank you for coming to McDonald's."

Could you stand to do the same simple tasks an average of 50 times per hour, 400 times per day, 2,000 times per week, 8,000 times per month? Few can. Fast-food workers rarely stay on the job more than six months. Indeed, McDonald's and other fast-food restaurants have well over 100 percent employee turnover each year.[15]

The shape of a job is closely related to how happy and fulfilled an employee feels doing it. In this next section, you will learn about **job design**—the number,

> The key question is no longer **whether** companies should decentralize, but **where** they should decentralize.

management. Overall, just 10 percent of employees received the training and information needed to support a truly decentralized approach to management.[13]

With results like these, the key question is no longer *whether* companies should decentralize, but *where* they should decentralize. One rule of thumb is to stay centralized where standardization is important and to decentralize where standardization is unimportant. **Standardization** is solving problems by consistently applying the same rules, procedures, and processes. Each year, General Motors purchases roughly $85 billion worth of automotive parts, many of which are only slightly different from each other. For instance, GM makes 26 different types of seat frames, 20 different fuel pumps, and 12 V6 engines. GM, however, has started standardizing the parts it uses across its product lines and today uses only 6 types of fuel pump, and management wants to cut that number to 5.[14]

kind, and variety of tasks that individual workers perform in doing their jobs.

*You will learn **3.1 why companies continue to use specialized jobs like the McDonald's drive-through job** and **3.2 how job rotation, job enlargement, job enrichment, and 3.3 the job characteristics model are being used to overcome the problems associated with job specialization.***

3.1 Job Specialization

Job specialization occurs when a job is composed of a small part of a larger task or process. Specialized jobs are characterized by simple, easy-to-learn steps, low variety, and high repetition, like the McDonald's drive-through window job just described. One of the clear disadvantages of specialized jobs is that, being so easy to learn, they quickly become boring. This, in turn, can lead to low job satisfaction and high absenteeism and employee turnover, all of which are very costly to organizations.

Why, then, do companies continue to create and use specialized jobs? The primary reason is that specialized jobs are very economical. As we learned from Taylor and the Gilbreths in Chapter 2, economy is a key reason why the pioneers of scientific management

Standardization solving problems by consistently applying the same rules, procedures, and processes

Job design the number, kind, and variety of tasks that individual workers perform in doing their jobs

Job specialization a job composed of a small part of a larger task or process

sought to standardize tasks. Once a job has been specialized, it takes little time to learn and master. Consequently, when experienced workers quit or are absent, the company can replace them with new employees and lose little productivity. For example, next time you're at McDonald's, notice the pictures of the food on the cash registers. These pictures make it easy for McDonald's trainees to quickly learn to take orders. Likewise, to simplify and speed operations, the drink dispensers behind the counter are set to automatically fill drink cups. Put a medium cup below the dispenser. Punch the medium drink button. The soft drink machine then fills the cup to within a half-inch of the top while that same worker goes to get your fries. At McDonald's, every task has been simplified in this way. Because the work is designed to be simple, wages can remain low since it isn't necessary to pay high salaries to attract highly experienced, educated, or trained workers.

3.2 Job Rotation, Enlargement, and Enrichment

Because of the efficiency of specialized jobs, companies are often reluctant to eliminate them. Consequently, job redesign efforts have focused on modifying jobs to keep the benefits of specialized jobs while reducing their obvious costs and disadvantages. Three methods—job rotation, job enlargement, and job enrichment—have been used to try to improve specialized jobs.[16]

Job rotation attempts to overcome the disadvantages of job specialization by periodically moving workers from one specialized job to another to give them more variety and the opportunity to use different skills. For example, an office receptionist who does nothing but answer phones could be systematically rotated to a different job, such as typing, filing, or data entry, every day or two. Likewise, a "mirror attacher" in an automobile plant might attach mirrors in the first half of the day's work shift and then install bumpers during the second half. Because employees simply switch from one specialized job to another, job rotation allows companies to retain the economic benefits of specialized work. At the same time, the greater variety of tasks makes the work less boring and more satisfying for workers.

Another way to counter the disadvantages of specialization is to enlarge the job. **Job enlargement** increases

the number of different tasks that a worker performs within one particular job. So, instead of being assigned just one task, workers with enlarged jobs are given several tasks to perform. For example, an enlarged "mirror attacher" job might include attaching the mirror, checking to see that the mirror's power adjustment controls work, and then cleaning the mirror's surface. Though job enlargement increases variety, many workers report feeling more stress when their jobs are enlarged. Consequently, many workers view enlarged jobs as simply more work, especially if they are not given additional time to complete the additional tasks. In

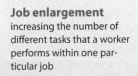

Job rotation periodically moving workers from one specialized job to another to give them more variety and the opportunity to use different skills

Job enlargement increasing the number of different tasks that a worker performs within one particular job

comparison, **job enrichment** attempts to overcome the deficiencies in specialized work by increasing the number of tasks and by giving workers the authority and control to make meaningful decisions about their work.[17]

3.3 Job Characteristics Model

In contrast to job rotation, job enlargement, and job enrichment, which focus on providing variety in job tasks, the **job characteristics model (JCM)** is an approach to job redesign that seeks to formulate jobs in ways that motivate workers and lead to positive work outcomes.[18] As shown in the far right column of Exhibit 9.9, the primary goal of the model is to create jobs that result in positive personal and work outcomes such as internal work motivation, satisfaction with one's job, and work effectiveness. Of these, the central concern of the JCM is internal motivation. **Internal motivation** is motivation that comes from the job itself rather than from outside rewards, such as a raise or praise from the boss. If workers feel that performing the job well is itself rewarding, then the job has internal motivation. Statements such as "I get a nice sense of accomplishment" or "I feel good about myself and what I'm producing" are examples of internal motivation.

Moving to the left in Exhibit 9.9, you can see that the JCM specifies three critical psychological states that must occur for work to be internally motivating. First, workers must *experience the work as meaningful;* that is, they must view their job as being important. Second, they must *experience responsibility for work outcomes*—they must feel personally responsible for the work being done well. Third, workers must have *knowledge of results;* that

Exhibit 9.9

Job Characteristics Model

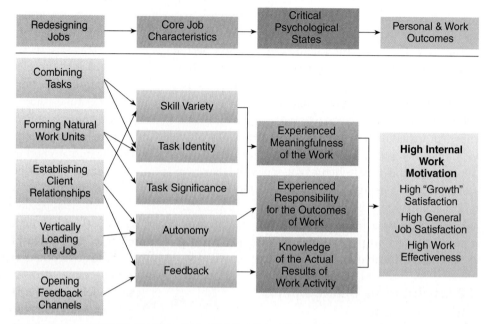

Source: J. R. Hackman and G. R. Oldham, *Work Redesign* (Reading, MA: Addison-Wesley, 1980). Reprinted by permission of Pearson Education.

is, they must know how well they are performing their jobs. All three critical psychological states must occur for work to be internally motivating.

For example, grocery store cashiers usually have knowledge of results. When you're slow, your checkout line grows long. If you make a mistake, customers point it out: "No, I think that's on sale for $2.99, not $3.99." Likewise, cashiers experience responsibility for work outcomes. At the end of the day, the register is totaled and the money is counted. Ideally, the money matches the total sales in the register. If the money in the till is less than what's recorded in the register, most stores make the cashier pay the difference. Consequently, most cashiers are very careful to avoid being caught short at the end of the day. Nonetheless,

Job enrichment increasing the number of tasks in a particular job and giving workers the authority and control to make meaningful decisions about their work

Job characteristics model (JCM) an approach to job redesign that seeks to formulate jobs in ways that motivate workers and lead to positive work outcomes

Internal motivation motivation that comes from the job itself rather than from outside rewards

Bottom-Up Job Design

Most jobs are designed and assigned by management from the top down. But at Linden Labs, a software engineering company that creates the Second Life Grid, a platform where people can create a virtual presence online, employees define their jobs. You go to work, decide what direction the company should move in and how you can help it move, and then execute. Scott Cook, founder of Intuit, says, "This challenges one of the longest-held tenets of business: that the senior executives of a company have responsibility to figure out what needs to be done, to tell people what needs to be done and assign them to do that work." But it makes for happy, productive employees and growth: while subscriptions to the Second Life virtual world were flat in the second quarter of 2007, landmass, for which users pay a fee, grew over 44%.

Source: "A Conversation With Scott Cook," *Inc.*, September 2007, 213-215; The Tao of Linden, available online at http://lindenlab.com/about/tao [accessed 11 August 2008].

satisfying or motivating. To start, skill variety is low. Except for the size of an order or special requests ("no onions"), the process is the same for each customer. At best, task identity is moderate. Although you take the order, handle the money, and deliver the food, others are responsible for a larger part of the process—preparing the food. Task identity will be even lower if the McDonald's has two drive-through windows because each drive-through window worker will have an even more specialized task. The first is limited to taking the order and making change, while the second just delivers the food. Task significance, the impact you have on others, is probably low. Autonomy is also very low: McDonald's has strict rules about dress, cleanliness, and procedures. But the job does provide immediate feedback, such as positive and negative customer comments, car horns honking, the amount of time it takes to process orders, and the number of cars in the drive-through. With the exception of feedback, the

WHY ISN'T THE DRIVE-THROUGH JOB PARTICULARLY SATISFYING OR MOTIVATING?

despite knowing the results and experiencing responsibility for work outcomes, most grocery store cashiers (at least where I shop) aren't internally motivated because they don't experience the work as meaningful. With scanners, it takes little skill to learn or do the job. Anyone can do it. In addition, cashiers have few decisions to make, and the job is highly repetitive.

What kinds of jobs produce the three critical psychological states? Moving another step to the left in Exhibit 9.9, you can see that these psychological states arise from jobs that are strong on five core job characteristics: skill variety, task identity, task significance, autonomy, and feedback. **Skill variety** is the number of different activities performed in a job. **Task identity** is the degree to which a job, from beginning to end, requires completion of a whole and identifiable piece of work. **Task significance** is the degree to which a job is perceived to have a substantial impact on others inside or outside the organization. **Autonomy** is the degree to which a job gives workers the discretion, freedom, and independence to decide how and when to accomplish the work. Finally, **feedback** is the amount of information the job provides to workers about their work performance.

To illustrate how the core job characteristics work together, let's use them to more thoroughly assess why the McDonald's drive-through window job is not particularly

low levels of the core job characteristics show why the drive-through window job is not internally motivating for many workers.

What can managers do when jobs aren't internally motivating? The far left column of Exhibit 9.9 lists five job redesign techniques that managers can use to strengthen a job's core characteristics. *Combining tasks* increases skill variety and task identity by joining separate, specialized tasks into larger work modules. For example, some trucking firms are now requiring truck drivers to load their rigs as well as drive them. The hope is that involving drivers in loading will ensure that trucks are properly loaded, thus reducing damage claims.

Work can be formed into *natural work units* by arranging tasks according to

Skill variety the number of different activities performed in a job

Task identity the degree to which a job, from beginning to end, requires the completion of a whole and identifiable piece of work

Task significance the degree to which a job is perceived to have a substantial impact on others inside or outside the organization

Autonomy the degree to which a job gives workers the discretion, freedom, and independence to decide how and when to accomplish the job

Feedback the amount of information the job provides to workers about their work performance

logical or meaningful groups. Although many trucking companies randomly assign drivers to trucks, some have begun assigning drivers to particular geographic locations (e.g., the Northeast or Southwest) or to truckloads that require special driving skill when being transported (e.g., oversized loads, chemicals, etc.). Forming natural work units increases task identity and task significance.

Establishing client relationships increases skill variety, autonomy, and feedback by giving employees direct contact with clients and customers. In some companies, truck drivers are expected to establish business relationships with their regular customers. When something goes wrong with a shipment, customers are told to call drivers directly.

Vertical loading means pushing some managerial authority down to workers. For truck drivers, this means that they have the same authority as managers to resolve customer problems. In some companies, if a late shipment causes problems for a customer, the driver has the authority to fully refund the cost of that shipment (without first obtaining management's approval).

The last job redesign technique offered by the model, *opening feedback channels,* means finding additional ways to give employees direct, frequent feedback about their job performance.

Designing Organizational Processes

Mechanistic organization an organization characterized by specialized jobs and responsibilities; precisely defined, unchanging roles; and a rigid chain of command based on centralized authority and vertical communication

Organic organization an organization characterized by broadly defined jobs and responsibility; loosely defined, frequently changing roles; and decentralized authority and horizontal communication based on task knowledge

Intraorganizational process the collection of activities that take place within an organization to transform inputs into outputs that customers value

More than 40 years ago, Tom Burns and G. M. Stalker described how two kinds of organizational designs, mechanistic and organic, are appropriate for different kinds of organizational environments.[19] **Mechanistic organizations** are characterized by specialized jobs and responsibilities; precisely defined, unchanging roles; and a rigid chain of command

based on centralized authority and vertical communication. This type of organization works best in stable, unchanging business environments. By contrast, **organic organizations** are characterized by broadly defined jobs and responsibility; loosely defined, frequently changing roles; and decentralized authority and horizontal communication based on task knowledge. This type of organization works best in dynamic, changing business environments.

The organizational design techniques described in the first half of this chapter—departmentalization, authority, and job design—are better suited for mechanistic organizations and the stable business environments that were more prevalent before 1980. In contrast, the organizational design techniques discussed next, in the second part of the chapter, are more appropriate for organic organizations and the increasingly dynamic environments in which today's businesses compete.

The key difference between these approaches is that mechanistic organizational designs focus on organizational structure while organic organizational designs are concerned with organizational process, or the collection of activities that transform inputs into outputs valued by customers.

After reading the next two sections, you should be able to

4 explain the methods that companies are using to redesign internal organizational processes (i.e., intraorganizational processes).

5 describe the methods that companies are using to redesign external organizational processes (i.e., interorganizational processes).

4 Intraorganizational Processes

An **intraorganizational process** is the collection of activities that take place within an organization to transform inputs into outputs that customers value.

*Let's take a look at how companies are using **4.1 reengineering** and **4.2 empowerment** to redesign intraorganizational processes like these.*

4.1 Reengineering

In their best-selling book *Reengineering the Corporation,* Michael Hammer and James Champy define **reengineering** as "the *fundamental* rethinking and *radical* redesign of business *processes* to achieve *dramatic* improvements in critical, contemporary measures of performance, such as cost, quality, service and speed."[20] Hammer and Champy further explained the four key words shown in italics in this definition. The first key word is *fundamental.* When reengineering organizational designs, managers must ask themselves, "Why do we do what we do?" and "Why do we do it the way we do?" The usual answer is, "Because that's the way we've always done it." Fundamental rethinking involves getting behind "that's the way we've always done it" and pursuing answers to these questions down to the foundations so that processes are actually achieving business goals. The second key word is *radical.* Reengineering is about significant change, about starting over by throwing out the old ways of getting work done. The third key word is *processes.* Hammer and Champy noted that "most business people are not process oriented; they are focused on tasks, on jobs, on people, on structures, but not on processes." The fourth key word is *dramatic.* Reengineering is about achieving quantum improvements in company performance.

An example from IBM Credit's operation illustrates how work can be reengineered.[21] IBM Credit lends businesses money to buy IBM computers. Previously, the loan process began when an IBM salesperson called the home office to obtain credit approval for a customer's purchase. The first department involved in the process took the credit information over the phone from the salesperson and recorded it on the credit form. The credit form was sent to the credit checking department, then to the pricing department (where the interest rate was determined), and on through a total of five departments. In all, it took the five departments six days to approve or deny the customer's loan. Of course, this delay cost IBM business. Some customers got their loans elsewhere. Others, frustrated by the wait, simply canceled their orders.

Finally, two IBM managers decided to walk a loan straight through each of the departments involved in the process. At each step, they asked the workers to stop what they were doing and immediately process their loan application. They were shocked by what they found. From start to finish, the entire process took just 90 minutes! The six-day turnaround time was almost entirely due to delays in handing off the work from one department to another. The solution: IBM redesigned the process so that one

© Bogdanov Oleg/Itar-Tass/Landov

In Plain English . . .

The definition of intraorganizational process tells you exactly what it is, but here's a quick example to help you get to "Oh, that's it."

The steps involved in an automobile insurance claim are a good example of an intraorganizational process:

1. Document the loss (i.e., the accident).
2. Assign an appraiser to determine the dollar amount of damage.
3. Make an appointment to inspect the vehicle.
4. Inspect the vehicle.
5. Write an appraisal and get the repair shop to agree to the damage estimate.
6. Pay for the repair work.
7. Return the repaired car to the customer.

person, not five people in five separate departments, now handles the entire loan approval process without any handoffs. Approval time dropped from six days to four hours and allowed IBM Credit to increase the number of loans it handled by a factor of 100!

Reengineering changes an organization's orientation from vertical to horizontal. Instead of taking orders from upper management, lower- and middle-level managers and workers take orders from a customer who is at the beginning and end of each process. Instead of running independent functional departments, managers and workers in different departments take ownership of cross-functional processes. Instead of simplifying work so that it becomes increasingly specialized, reengineering complicates work

Reengineering fundamental rethinking and radical redesign of business processes to achieve dramatic improvements in critical measures of performance, such as cost, quality, service, and speed

Task interdependence the extent to which collective action is required to complete an entire piece of work

Pooled interdependence work completed by having each job or department independently contribute to the whole

Sequential interdependence work completed in succession, with one group's or job's outputs becoming the inputs for the next group or job

Reciprocal interdependence work completed by different jobs or groups working together in a back-and-forth manner

Empowering workers permanently passing decision-making authority and responsibility from managers to workers by giving them the information and resources they need to make and carry out good decisions

Exhibit 9.10

Reengineering and Task Interdependence

Pooled Interdependence

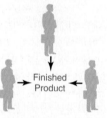

Sequential Interdependence

Reciprocal Interdependence

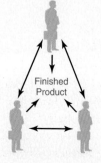

by giving workers increased autonomy and responsibility for complete processes.

In essence, reengineering changes work by changing **task interdependence,** the extent to which collective action is required to complete an entire piece of work. As shown in Exhibit 9.10, there are three kinds of task interdependence.[22] In **pooled interdependence,** each job or department independently contributes to the whole. In **sequential interdependence,** work must be performed in succession, as one group's or job's outputs become the inputs for the next group or job. Finally, in **reciprocal interdependence,** different jobs or groups work together in a back-and-forth manner to complete the process. By reducing the handoffs between different jobs or groups, reengineering decreases sequential interdependence. Likewise, reengineering decreases pooled interdependence by redesigning work so that formerly independent jobs or departments now work together to complete processes. Finally, reengineering increases reciprocal interdependence by making groups or individuals responsible for larger, more complete processes in which several steps may be accomplished at the same time.

As an organizational design tool, reengineering promises big rewards, but it has also come under severe criticism. The most serious complaint is that because it allows a few workers to do the work formerly done by many, reengineering is simply a corporate code word for cost cutting and worker layoffs.[23] Likewise, for that reason, detractors claim that reengineering hurts morale and performance. Today, even reengineering gurus Hammer and Champy admit that roughly 70 percent of all reengineering projects fail because of the effects on people in the workplace. Says Hammer, "I wasn't smart enough about that [the people issues]. I was reflecting my engineering background and was insufficiently appreciative of the human dimension. I've [now] learned that's critical."[24]

4.2 Empowerment

Another way of redesigning intraorganizational processes is through empowerment. **Empowering workers** means permanently passing decision-making authority and responsibility from managers to workers. For workers to be fully empowered, companies must give them the information and resources they need to make and carry out good decisions and then reward them for taking individual initiative.[25] Unfortunately, this doesn't happen often enough. As Michael Schrage, author and MIT researcher, wrote:

© Claudio Arnese/iStockphoto.com

A warehouse employee can see on the intranet that a shipment is late but has no authority to accelerate its delivery. A project manager knows—and can mathematically demonstrate—that a seemingly minor spec change will bust both her budget and her schedule. The spec must be changed anyway. An airline reservations agent tells the Executive Platinum Premier frequent flier that first class appears wide open for an upgrade. However, the airline's yield management software won't permit any upgrades until just four hours before the flight, frequent fliers (and reservations) be damned. In all these cases, the employee has access to valuable information. Each one possesses the "knowledge" to do the job better. But the knowledge and information are irrelevant and useless. Knowledge isn't power; the ability to act on knowledge is power.[26]

When workers are given the proper information and resources and are allowed to make good decisions, they experience strong feelings of empowerment. **Empowerment** is a feeling of intrinsic motivation in which workers perceive their work to have meaning and perceive themselves to be competent, having an impact, and capable of self-determination.[27] Work has meaning when it is consistent with personal standards and beliefs. Workers feel competent when they believe they can perform an activity with skill. The belief that they are having an impact comes from a feeling that they can affect work outcomes. A feeling of self-determination arises from workers' belief that they have the autonomy to choose how best to do their work.

Empowerment can lead to changes in organizational processes because meaning, competence, impact, and self-determination produce empowered employees who take active, rather than passive, roles in their work.

5 Interorganizational Processes

An **interorganizational process** is a collection of activities that occur *among companies* to transform inputs into outputs that customers value. In other words, many companies work together to create a product or service that keeps customers happy. For example, when you purchase a Liz Claiborne outfit, you're not just buying from Liz Claiborne; you're also buying from a network of 250 suppliers in 35 countries and a sourcing team in Hong Kong that produces the right fabrics and the entire line of clothing. Those companies then manufacture the first product prototypes and send them back to the New York designers for final inspection and possibly last-minute changes.[28]

In this section, you'll explore interorganizational processes by learning about **5.1 modular organizations** *and* **5.2 virtual organizations.**[29]

5.1 Modular Organizations

Except for the core business activities that they can perform better, faster, and cheaper than others, **modular organizations** outsource all remaining business activities

Empowerment feelings of intrinsic motivation, in which workers perceive their work to have impact and meaning and perceive themselves to be competent and capable of self-determination

Interorganizational process a collection of activities that take place among companies to transform inputs into outputs that customers value

Modular organization an organization that outsources noncore business activities to outside companies, suppliers, specialists, or consultants

to outside companies, suppliers, specialists, or consultants. The term *modular* is used because the business activities purchased from outside companies can be added and dropped as needed, much like adding pieces to a three-dimensional puzzle. Exhibit 9.11 depicts a modular organization in which the company has chosen to keep training, human resources, sales, product design, manufacturing, customer service, research and development, and information technology as core business activities, but it has outsourced the noncore activities of product distribution, Web page design, advertising, payroll, accounting, and packaging.

Modular organizations have several advantages. First, because modular organizations pay for outsourced labor, expertise, or manufacturing capabilities only when needed, they can cost significantly less to run than traditional organizations. For example, when Apple came up with its iPod digital music player, it outsourced the audio chip design and manufacture to SigmaTel in Austin, Texas, and final assembly to Asutek Computers in Taiwan. Doing so not only reduced costs and sped up production (beating Sony's Network Walkman to market), but also allowed Apple to do what it does best—design innovative products with easy-to-use software.[30] To obtain these advantages, however, modular organizations need reliable partners—vendors and suppliers that they can work closely with and trust.

Exhibit 9.11

Modular Organization

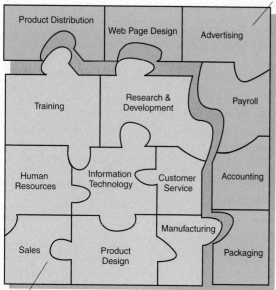

Outsourced Noncore Business Activities

Product Distribution · Web Page Design · Advertising · Training · Research & Development · Payroll · Human Resources · Information Technology · Customer Service · Accounting · Sales · Product Design · Manufacturing · Packaging

Core Business Activities

CROWD**SOURCING**

Companies—and individuals—are tapping into an army of people willing to work for literally pennies. Amazon's Mechanical Turk allows people (called "requesters") to post repetitive tasks that can only be completed by human intelligence. Some examples are identifying the best of a set of photos, writing product descriptions, and color coding clothing sold by online retailers. But requesters can also post tasks that are more involved. One manager paid a consultant $2,000 for a flow chart of his company's repair process. When the company needed additional work, however, it enlisted a "Turker," The second flow chart cost $5. Keep your eyes on the trend of crowdsourcing.

Sources: J. Howe, "The Rise of Crowdsourcing," *Wired,* June 2006, 176.

Trivia: What was the original Mechanical Turk? See the Review card for the answer.

mgmt trend

Modular organizations have disadvantages, too. The primary disadvantage is the loss of control that occurs when key business activities are outsourced to other companies. Also, companies may reduce their competitive advantage in two ways if they mistakenly outsource a core business activity. First, as a result of competitive and technological change, the noncore business activities a company has outsourced may suddenly become the basis for competitive advantage. Second, related to that point, suppliers to whom work is outsourced can sometimes become competitors.

5.2 Virtual Organizations

In contrast to modular organizations in which the interorganizational process revolves around a central company, a **virtual organization** is part of a network in which many companies share skills, costs, capabilities, markets, and customers with each other. Exhibit 9.12 shows a virtual organization in which, for "today," the parts of a virtual company consist of product design, purchasing, manufacturing, advertising, and information technology. Unlike modular organizations, in which the outside organizations are tightly linked to one central company, virtual organizations work with some companies in the network alliance but not with all. So, whereas a puzzle with various pieces is a fitting metaphor for a modular organization, a potluck dinner is an appropriate metaphor for a virtual organization. All participants bring their finest food dish but eat only what they want.

Another difference is that the working relationships between modular organizations and outside companies tend to be more stable and longer lasting than the shorter, often temporary relationships found among the virtual companies in a network alliance. The composition of a virtual organization is always changing. The combination of network partners that a virtual corporation has at any one time depends on the expertise needed to solve a particular problem or provide a specific product or service. This is why the businessperson in the network organization shown in the photo is saying, "Today, I'll have . . . ." Tomorrow, the business could want something completely different. In this sense, the term *virtual organization* means the organization that exists "at the moment." Virtual organizations have a number of advantages. They let companies share costs. And, because members can quickly combine their efforts to meet customers' needs, they are fast and flexible.

As with modular organizations, a disadvantage of virtual organizations is that once work has been outsourced, it can be difficult to control the quality of work done by network partners. The greatest disadvantage, however, is that tremendous managerial skills are required to make a network of independent organizations work well together, especially since their relationships tend to be short and based on a single task or project. Virtual organizations are using two methods to solve this problem. The first is to use a *broker*. In traditional, hierarchical organizations, managers plan, organize, and control. But with the horizontal, interorganizational processes that characterize virtual organizations, the job of a broker is to create and assemble the knowledge, skills, and resources from different companies for outside parties, such as customers.[31] The second way to make networks of virtual organizations more manageable is to use a *virtual organization agreement* that, somewhat like a contract, specifies the schedules, responsibilities, costs, payouts, and liabilities for participating organizations.

Exhibit 9.12

Virtual Organizations

Today, I'll have...

Purchasing

Product Design

Information Technology

Manufacturing

Advertising

> **Virtual organization**
> an organization that is part of a network in which many companies share skills, costs, capabilities, markets, and customers to collectively solve customer problems or provide specific products or services

MANAGING TEAMS

Why Use Work Teams?

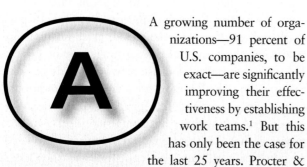

A growing number of organizations—91 percent of U.S. companies, to be exact—are significantly improving their effectiveness by establishing work teams.[1] But this has only been the case for the last 25 years. Procter & Gamble and Cummins Engine began using teams in 1962 and 1973, respectively. But many companies, like Boeing, Caterpillar, Champion International, Ford Motor Company, and General Electric, did not set up their first teams until the 1980s.[2] In other words, teams are a relatively new phenomenon, and there's still much for organizations to learn about managing them.

Work teams consist of a small number of people with complementary skills who hold themselves mutually accountable for pursuing a common purpose, achieving performance goals, and improving interdependent work processes.[3] Though work teams are not the answer for every situation or organization, if the right teams are used properly and in the right settings, teams can dramatically improve company performance and instill a sense of vitality in the workplace that is otherwise difficult to achieve.

Work team a small number of people with complementary skills who hold themselves mutually accountable for pursuing a common purpose, achieving performance goals, and improving interdependent work processes

Learning Outcomes

1 explain the good and bad of using teams.

2 recognize and understand the different kinds of teams.

3 understand the general characteristics of work teams.

4 explain how to enhance work team effectiveness.

After reading the next two sections, you should be able to

1 explain the good and bad of using teams.

2 recognize and understand the different kinds of teams.

1 The Good and Bad of Using Teams

*Let's begin our discussion of teams by learning about **1.1 the advantages of teams, 1.2 the disadvantages of teams, and 1.3 when to use and not use teams.***

1.1 The Advantages of Teams

Companies are making greater use of teams because they have been shown to improve customer satisfaction, product and service quality, employee job satisfaction, and decision making.[4] Teams help businesses increase *customer satisfaction* in several ways. For example, work teams can be trained to meet the needs of specific customers. Hewitt Associates, a consulting firm, manages benefits administration for hundreds of multinational client firms. To ensure customer satisfaction, Hewitt reengineered its customer service center and created specific teams to handle benefits-related questions posed by employees of specific client organizations.[5] Businesses also create problem-solving teams and employee involvement teams to study ways to improve overall customer satisfaction and make recommendations for improvements. Teams like these typically meet on a weekly or monthly basis.

Teams also help firms improve *product and service quality* in several ways.[6] In contrast to traditional organizational structures where management is responsible for organizational outcomes and performance, teams

take direct responsibility for the quality of the products and services they produce. At Whole Foods, a super-market chain that sells groceries and health foods, the ten teams that manage each store are responsible for store quality and performance; they are also directly ac-countable because the size of their team bonus depends on the store's performance. Productive teams get an ex-tra $1.50 to $2.00 per hour in every other paycheck.[7]

Another reason for using teams is that teamwork often leads to increased *job satisfaction*.[8] One reason that teamwork can be more satisfying than traditional work is that it gives workers a chance to improve their skills. This is often accomplished through **cross-training**, in which team members are taught how to do all or most of the jobs performed by the other team members. The advantage for the organization is that cross-train-ing allows a team to function normally when one mem-ber is absent, quits, or is transferred. The advantage for workers is that cross-training broadens their skills and increases their capabilities while also making their work more varied and interesting. A second reason that teamwork is satisfying is that work teams often receive proprietary business information that is available only to managers at most companies. For example, Whole Foods has an "open books, open door, open people" philosophy.[9] Team members are given full access to their store's financial information and everyone's salaries, including those of the store manager and the CEO.[10] Team members also gain job satisfaction from unique leadership responsibilities that are not typically avail-able in traditional organizations. For example, rotat-ing leadership among team members can lead to more participation and cooperation in team decision making and improved team performance.[11]

Finally, teams share many of the advantages of group decision making discussed in Chapter 5. For instance, because team members possess different knowledge, skills, abilities, and experiences, a team is able to view problems from multiple perspectives. This diversity of viewpoints increases the odds that team decisions will solve the un-derlying causes of problems and not just address the symptoms. The increased knowledge and informa-tion available to teams also make it easier for them to generate more alternative solutions, a critical part of improving the quality of decisions. Because team members are involved in decision-making processes, they are also likely to be more committed to making those decisions work. In short, teams can do a much better job than individuals in two important steps of the decision-making process: defining the problem and generating alternative solutions.

1.2 The Disadvantages of Teams

Although teams can significantly improve customer satisfaction, product and service quality, speed and efficiency in product development, employee job sat-isfaction, and decision making, using teams does not guarantee these positive outcomes. In fact, if you've ever participated in team projects in your classes, you're probably already aware of some of the problems inher-ent in work teams. Despite all of their promise, teams and teamwork are also prone to these significant disad-vantages: initially high turnover, social loafing, and the problems associated with group decision making.

The first disadvantage of work teams is *initially high turnover*. Teams aren't for everyone, and some workers balk at the responsibility, effort, and learning required in team settings.

Social loafing is another disadvantage of work teams. **Social loafing** occurs when workers withhold their ef-forts and fail to perform their share of the work.[12] A 19th-century French engineer named Maximilian Ring-lemann first documented social loafing when he found that one person pulling on a rope alone exerted an aver-age of 63 kilograms of force on the rope. In groups of three, the average force dropped to 53 kilograms per

Cross-training training team members to do all or most of the jobs performed by the other team members

Social loafing behavior in which team members withhold their efforts and fail to perform their share of the work

© Image Source Pink/Getty Images

person. In groups of eight, the average dropped to just 31 kilograms per person. Ringlemann concluded that the larger the team, the smaller the individual effort. In fact, social loafing is more likely to occur in larger groups, where identifying and monitoring the efforts of individual team members can be difficult.[13] In other words, social loafers count on being able to blend into the background where their lack of effort isn't easily spotted. From team-based class projects, most students already know about social loafers or "slackers," who contribute poor, little, or no work whatsoever. Not surprisingly, a study of 250 student teams found that the most talented students are typically the least satisfied with teamwork because of having to carry slackers and do a disproportionate share of their team's work. Perceptions of fairness are negatively related to the extent of social loafing within teams.[14]

Finally, teams share many of the *disadvantages of group decision making* discussed in Chapter 5, such as groupthink. In *groupthink,* members of highly cohesive groups feel intense pressure not to disagree with each other so that the group can approve a proposed solution. Because groupthink restricts discussion and leads to consideration of a limited number of alternative solutions, it usually results in poor decisions. Also, team decision making takes considerable time, and team meetings can often be unproductive and inefficient. Another possible pitfall is *minority domination,* where just one or two people dominate team discussions,

> ### FACTORS THAT ENCOURAGE PEOPLE TO WITHHOLD EFFORT IN TEAMS
>
> **1.** **The presence of someone with expertise.** Team members will withhold effort when another team member is highly qualified to make a decision or comment on an issue.
>
> **2.** **The presentation of a compelling argument.** Team members will withhold effort if the arguments for a course of action are very persuasive or similar to their own thinking.
>
> **3.** **Lacking confidence in one's ability to contribute.** Team members will withhold effort if they are unsure about their ability to contribute to discussions, activities, or decisions. This is especially so for high-profile decisions.
>
> **4.** **An unimportant or meaningless decision.** Team members will withhold effort by mentally withdrawing or adopting a "who cares" attitude if decisions don't affect them or their units, or if they don't see a connection between their efforts and their team's successes or failures.
>
> **5.** **A dysfunctional decision-making climate.** Team members will withhold effort if other team members are frustrated or indifferent or if a team is floundering or disorganized.
>
> Source: P. W. Mulvey, J. F. Veiga, and P. M. Elsass, "When Teammates Raise a White Flag," *Academy of Management Executive* 10, no. 1 (1996): 40–49.

restricting consideration of different problem definitions and alternative solutions. Finally, team members may not feel accountable for the decisions and actions taken by the team.

1.3 When to Use Teams

As the two previous subsections made clear, teams have significant advantages *and* disadvantages. Therefore, the question is not *whether* to use teams, but *when* and *where* to use teams for maximum benefit and minimum cost. As Doug Johnson, associate director at the Center for the Study of Work Teams, puts it, "Teams are a means to an end, not an end in themselves."[15] Exhibit 10.1 on the next page provides some additional guidelines on when to use or not use teams.[16]

First, teams should be used when there is a clear, engaging reason or purpose for using them. Too many companies use teams because they're popular or because the companies assume that teams can fix all problems. Teams are much more likely to succeed if they know why they exist and what they are supposed to accomplish and more likely to fail if they don't.

Exhibit 10.1

When to Use and When Not to Use Teams

USE TEAMS WHEN . . .		DON'T USE TEAMS WHEN . . .
✓ there is a clear, engaging reason or purpose.		✗ there isn't a clear, engaging reason or purpose.
✓ the job can't be done unless people work together.		✗ the job can be done by people working independently.
✓ rewards can be provided for teamwork and team performance.		✗ rewards are provided for individual effort and performance.
✓ ample resources are available.		✗ the necessary resources are not available.

Source: R. Wageman, "Critical Success Factors for Creating Superb Self-Managing Teams," *Organizational Dynamics* 26, no. 1 (1997): 49–61.

© James Dawson/Image Farm/Jupiterimages / © Hill Street Studios/Brand X Pictures/Jupiterimages

Second, teams should be used when the job can't be done unless people work together. This typically means that teams are needed when tasks are complex, require multiple perspectives, or require repeated interaction with others to complete. If tasks are simple and don't require multiple perspectives or repeated interaction with others, however, teams should not be used.[17] For instance, production levels dropped by 23 percent when Levi Strauss introduced teams in its factories. Levi Strauss's mistake was assuming that teams were appropriate for garment work, where workers perform single, specialized tasks, like sewing zippers or belt loops. Because this kind of work does not require interaction with others, Levi Strauss unwittingly pitted the faster workers against the slower workers on each team. Arguments, infighting, insults, and threats were common between faster workers and the slower workers who held back team performance. One seamstress even had to physically restrain an angry coworker who was about to throw a chair at a faster worker who constantly nagged her about her slow pace.[18]

Third, teams should be used when rewards can be provided for teamwork and team performance. Rewards that depend on team performance rather than individual performance are the key to rewarding team behaviors and efforts. You'll read more about team rewards later in the chapter, but for now it's enough to know that if the type of reward (individual versus team) is not matched to the type of performance (individual versus team), teams won't work.

Traditional work group a group composed of two or more people who work together to achieve a shared goal

2 Kinds of Teams

Let's continue our discussion of teams by learning about the different kinds of teams that companies use to make themselves more competitive. We look first at *2.1 how teams differ in terms of autonomy, which is the key dimension that makes one team different from another,* and then at *2.2 some special kinds of teams.*

2.1 Autonomy, the Key Dimension

Teams can be classified in a number of ways, such as permanent or temporary, functional or cross-functional. However, studies indicate that the amount of autonomy possessed by a team is the key difference among teams.[19] *Autonomy* is the degree to which workers have the discretion, freedom, and independence to decide how and when to accomplish their jobs.

Exhibit 10.2 shows how five kinds of teams differ in terms of autonomy. Moving left to right across the autonomy continuum at the top of the exhibit, traditional work groups and employee involvement groups have the least autonomy, semi-autonomous work groups have more autonomy, and, finally, self-managing teams and self-designing teams have the most autonomy. Moving from bottom to top along the left side of the exhibit, note that the number of responsibilities given to each kind of team increases directly with its autonomy. Let's review each of these kinds of teams and their autonomy and responsibilities in more detail.

The smallest amount of autonomy is found in **traditional work groups,** where two or more people work together to achieve a shared goal. In these groups, workers are responsible for doing the work or executing the task, but they do not have direct responsibility

Exhibit 10.2
Team Autonomy Continuum

RESPONSIBILITIES	TRADITIONAL WORK GROUPS	EMPLOYEE INVOLVEMENT GROUPS	SEMI-AUTONOMOUS WORK GROUPS	SELF-MANAGING TEAMS	SELF-DESIGNING TEAMS
Control Design of					
Team					✓
Tasks					✓
Membership					✓
Production/Service Tasks					
Make Decisions				✓	✓
Solve Problems				✓	✓
Major Production/Service Tasks					
Make Decisions			✓	✓	✓
Solve Problems			✓	✓	✓
Information			✓	✓	✓
Give Advice/Make Suggestions		✓	✓	✓	✓
Execute Task	✓	✓	✓	✓	✓

Sources: R. D. Banker, J. M. Field, R. G. Schroeder, and K. K. Sinha, "Impact of Work Teams on Manufacturing Performance: A Longitudinal Field Study," *Academy of Management Journal* 39 (1996): 867-890; J. R. Hackman, "The Psychology of Self-Management in Organizations," in *Psychology and Work: Productivity, Change, and Employment*, ed. M. S. Pallak and R. Perlof (Washington, DC: American Psychological Association), 85–136.

or control over their work. Workers report to managers who are responsible for their performance and have the authority to hire and fire them, make job assignments, and control resources.

Employee involvement teams, which have somewhat more autonomy, meet on company time on a weekly or monthly basis to provide advice or make suggestions to management concerning specific issues such as plant safety, customer relations, or product quality.[20] Though they offer advice and suggestions, they do not have the authority to make decisions. Membership on these teams is often voluntary, but members may be selected because of their expertise. The idea behind em-

ployee involvement teams is that the people closest to the problem or situation are best able to recommend solutions.

Semi-autonomous work groups not only provide advice and suggestions to management but also have the authority to make decisions and solve problems related to the major tasks required to produce a

Employee involvement team team that provides advice or makes suggestions to management concerning specific issues

Semi-autonomous work group a group that has the authority to make decisions and solve problems related to the major tasks of producing a product or service

product or service. Semi-autonomous groups regularly receive information about budgets, work quality and performance, and competitors' products. Furthermore, members of semi-autonomous work groups are typically cross-trained in a number of different skills and tasks. In short, semi-autonomous work groups give employees the authority to make decisions that are typically made by supervisors and managers.

That authority is not complete, however. Managers still play a role, though much reduced compared to traditional work groups, in supporting the work of semi-autonomous work groups. In semi-autonomous work groups, managers ask good questions, provide resources, and facilitate performance of group goals.

Self-managing teams differ from semi-autonomous work groups in that team members manage and control *all* of the major tasks *directly related* to production of a product or service without first getting approval from management. This includes managing and controlling the acquisition of materials, making a product or providing a service, and ensuring timely delivery.

Self-designing teams have all the characteristics of self-managing teams, but they can also control and change the design of the teams themselves, the tasks they do and how and when they do them, and the membership of the teams.

2.2 Special Kinds of Teams

Companies are also increasingly using several other kinds of teams that can't easily be categorized in terms of autonomy: cross-functional teams, virtual teams, and project teams. Depending on how these teams are designed, they can be either low- or high-autonomy teams.

Cross-functional teams are intentionally composed of employees from different functional areas of the organization.[21] Because their members have different functional backgrounds, education, and experience,

> **S**elf-designing teams have a high failure rate—as high as 50 percent—but when they work, they really work. A self-directed team at GTE Industries in Dallas-Fort Worth increased the number of phone books produced by 150 percent in a five-year period while reducing errors by half. They also reduced the response time on customer complaints from 18 days to three.

Source: C. Joinson, :"Teams at Work," *HR Magazine*, May 1999, available online at http://www.shrm.org/hrmagazine/articles/0599cov.asp [accessed 12 August 2008].

© Oktay Ortakcioglu/iStockphoto.com

cross-functional teams usually attack problems from multiple perspectives and generate more ideas and alternative solutions, all of which are especially important when trying to innovate or do creative problem solving.[22] Cross-functional teams can be used almost anywhere in an organization and are often used in conjunction with matrix and product organizational structures (see Chapter 9). They can also be used either with part-time or temporary team assignments or with full-time, long-term teams.

Cessna, which manufactures airplanes, created cross-functional teams for purchasing parts. With workers from purchasing, manufacturing engineering, quality engineering, product design engineering, reliability engineering, product support, and finance, each team addressed make-versus-buy decisions (make it themselves or buy from others), sourcing (who to buy from), internal plant and quality improvements, and the external training of suppliers to reduce costs and increase quality.[23]

Virtual teams are groups of geographically and/or organizationally dispersed coworkers who use a combination of telecommunications and information technologies to accomplish an organizational task.[24] Members of virtual teams rarely meet face-to-face; instead, they use email, videoconferencing, and group communication software. For example, MySQL, an open source database software developer, has 320 workers in 25 countries, strewn from Tennessee to the Ukraine. They communicate with each other using a company chat room (or Skype when live voice conversations are necessary) and are accountable for completing tasks on a program called Worklog. Oleksandr Byelkin lives in Lugansk, Ukraine; not only does he have poor phone service, but he also doesn't speak English very well. Even MySQL's holiday party was online.[25] Virtual teams can be employee involvement teams, self-managing teams, or nearly any kind

---

Self-managing team a team that manages and controls all of the major tasks of producing a product or service

Self-designing team a team that has the characteristics of self-managing teams but also controls team design, work tasks, and team membership

Cross-functional team a team composed of employees from different functional areas of the organization

Virtual team a team composed of geographically and/or organizationally dispersed coworkers who use telecommunication and information technologies to accomplish an organizational task

of team discussed in this chapter. Virtual teams are often (but not necessarily) temporary teams that are set up to accomplish a specific task.[26]

The principal advantage of virtual teams is their flexibility. Employees can work with each other regardless of physical location, time zone, or organizational affiliation.[27] Because the team members don't meet in a physical location, virtual teams also find it much easier to include other key stakeholders such as suppliers and customers. Plus, virtual teams have certain efficiency advantages over traditional team structures. Because the teammates do not meet face-to-face, a virtual team typically requires a smaller time commitment than a traditional team does.[28] A drawback of virtual teams is that the team members must learn to express themselves in new contexts.[29] The give-and-take that naturally occurs in face-to-face meetings is more difficult to achieve through video conferencing or other methods of virtual teaming. Indeed, several studies have shown that physical proximity enhances information processing in teams.[30] Therefore, some companies bring virtual team members together in offices or special trips on a regular basis to try to minimize these problems.

Project teams are created to complete specific, one-time projects or tasks within a limited time.[31] Project teams are often used to develop new products, significantly improve existing products, roll out new information systems, or build new factories or offices. The project team is typically led by a project manager who has the overall responsibility for planning, staffing, and managing the team, which usually includes employees from different functional areas. Effective project teams demand both individual and collective responsibility.[32] One advantage of project teams is that drawing employees from different functional areas can reduce or eliminate communication barriers. In turn, as long as team members feel free to express their

ideas, thoughts, and concerns, free-flowing communication encourages cooperation among separate departments and typically speeds up the design process.[33] Another advantage of project teams is their flexibility. When projects are finished, project team members either move on to the next project or return to their functional units. For example, publication of

Tips for Managing Successful Virtual Teams

GOOD TIP!

- Select people who are self-starters and strong communicators.
- Keep the team focused by establishing clear, specific goals and by explaining the consequences and importance of meeting these goals.
- Provide frequent feedback so that team members can measure their progress.
- Keep team interactions upbeat and action-oriented by expressing appreciation for good work and completed tasks.
- Personalize the virtual team by periodically bringing team members together and by encouraging team members to share information with each other about their personal lives. This is especially important when the virtual team first forms.
- Improve communication through increased telephone calls, emails, and Internet messaging and videoconference sessions.
- Periodically ask team members how well the team is working and what can be done to improve performance.
- Empower virtual teams so they have the discretion, freedom, and independence to decide how and when to accomplish their jobs.

Sources: W. F. Cascio, "Managing a Virtual Workplace," *Academy of Management Executive* 14 (2000): 81–90; B. Kirkman, B. Rosen, P. Tesluk, and C. Gibson, "The Impact of Team Empowerment on Virtual Team Performance: The Moderating Role of Face-to-Face Interaction," *Academy of Management Journal* 47 (2004): 175–192; S. Furst, M. Reeves, B. Rosen, and R. Blackburn, "Managing the Life Cycle of Virtual Teams," *Academy of Management Executive* (May 2004): 6–20; C. Solomon, "Managing Virtual Teams," *Workforce* 80 (June 2001): 60.

Project team a team created to complete specific, one-time projects or tasks within a limited time

this book required designers, editors, page compositors, and Web designers, among others. When the task was finished, these people applied their skills to other textbook projects. Because of this flexibility, project teams are often used with the matrix organizational designs discussed in Chapter 9.

Managing Work Teams

"Why did I ever let you talk me into teams? They're nothing but trouble."[34] Lots of managers have this reaction after making the move to teams. Many don't realize that this reaction is normal, both for them and for workers. In fact, such a reaction is characteristic of the *storming* stage of team development (discussed in Section 3.5). Managers who are familiar with these stages and with the other important characteristics of teams will be better prepared to manage the predictable changes that occur when companies make the switch to team-based structures.

 After reading the next two sections, you should be able to

3 understand the general characteristics of work teams.

4 explain how to enhance work team effectiveness.

3 Work Team Characteristics

Norms informally agreed-on standards that regulate team behavior

Understanding the characteristics of work teams is essential for making teams an effective part of an organization. Therefore, in this section you'll learn about *3.1 team norms, 3.2 team cohesiveness, 3.3 team size, 3.4 team conflict,* and *3.5 the stages of team development.*

3.1 Team Norms

Over time, teams develop **norms,** informally agreed-upon standards that regulate team behavior.[35] Norms are valuable because they let team members know what is expected of them. At Nucor Steel, work groups expect their members to get to work on time. To reinforce this norm, anyone who is late to work will not receive the team bonus for that day (assuming the team is productive). A worker who is more than 30 minutes late will not receive the team bonus for the entire week. Losing a bonus matters at Nucor because work group bonuses can easily double the size of a worker's take-home pay.[36]

Studies indicate that norms are one of the most powerful influences on work behavior because they regulate the everyday actions that allow teams to function effectively. Effective work teams develop norms about the quality and timeliness of job performance, absenteeism, safety, and expression of ideas. Team norms are often associated with positive outcomes, such as stronger organizational commitment, more trust in management, and stronger job and organizational satisfaction.[37]

Norms can also influence team behavior in negative ways. For example, most people would agree that damaging organizational property; saying or doing something to hurt someone at work; intentionally doing one's work badly, incorrectly, or slowly; griping about coworkers; deliberately breaking rules; or doing something to harm the company are negative behaviors. A study of workers from 34 teams in twenty different organizations found that teams with negative norms strongly influenced their team members to engage in these negative behaviors. In fact, the longer individuals were members of a team with negative norms and the more frequently they interacted with their teammates, the more likely they were to perform negative behaviors. Since team norms typically develop early in the life of a team, these results indicate how important it is for teams to establish positive norms from the outset.[38]

3.2 Team Cohesiveness

Cohesiveness is another important characteristic of work teams. **Cohesiveness** is the extent to which team members are attracted to a team and motivated to remain in it.[39] The level of cohesiveness in a group is important for several reasons. To start, cohesive groups have a better chance of retaining their members. As a result, cohesive groups typically experience lower turnover.[40] In addition, team cohesiveness promotes cooperative behavior, generosity, and a willingness on the part of team members to assist each other.[41] When team cohesiveness is high, team members are more motivated to contribute to the team because they want to gain the approval of other team members. For these reasons and others, studies have clearly established that cohesive teams consistently perform better.[42] Furthermore, cohesive teams quickly achieve high levels of performance. By contrast, teams low in cohesion take much longer to reach the same levels of performance.[43]

What can be done to promote team cohesiveness? First, make sure that all team members are present at team meetings and activities. Team cohesiveness suffers when members are allowed to withdraw from the team and miss team meetings and events.[44] Second, create additional opportunities for teammates to work together by rearranging work schedules and creating common workspaces. When task interdependence is high and team members have lots of chances to work together, team cohesiveness tends to increase.[45] Third, engaging in nonwork activities as a team can help build cohesion. At a company where teams put in extraordinarily long hours coding computer software, the software teams maintained cohesion by doing "fun stuff" together. Team leader Tammy Urban says, "We went on team outings at least once a week. We'd play darts, shoot pool.

Teams work best when you get to know each other outside of work—what people's interests are, who they are. Personal connections go a long way when you're developing complex applications in our kind of time frames."[46] Finally, companies build team cohesiveness by making employees feel that they are part of a special organization. For example, all the new hires at Disney World in Orlando are required to take a course entitled "Traditions One," where they learn the traditions and history of the Walt Disney Company (including the names of the seven dwarfs!). The purpose of Traditions One is to instill a sense of team pride in working for Disney.

3.3 Team Size

The relationship between team size and performance appears to be curvilinear. Very small or very large teams may not perform as well as moderately sized teams. For most teams, the right size is somewhere between six and nine members.[47] This size is conducive to high team cohesion, which has a positive effect on team performance, as discussed above. A team of this size is small enough for the team members to get to know each other and for each member to have an opportunity to contribute in a meaningful way to the success of the team. At the same time, the team is also large enough to take advantage of team members' diverse skills, knowledge, and perspectives. It is also easier to instill a sense of responsibility and mutual accountability in teams of this size.[48]

By contrast, when teams get too large, team members find it difficult to get to know one another, and the team may splinter into smaller subgroups. When this occurs, subgroups some-

Teams work best when you get to know each other outside of work.

© Rubberball/Jupiter Images

Cohesiveness the extent to which team members are attracted to a team and motivated to remain in it

times argue and disagree, weakening overall team cohesion. As teams grow, there is also a greater chance of *minority domination,* where just a few team members dominate team discussions. Even if minority domination doesn't occur, larger groups may not have time for all team members to share their input. And when team members feel that their contributions are unimportant or not needed, the result is less involvement, effort, and accountability to the team.[49] Large teams also face logistical problems such as finding an appropriate time or place to meet. Finally, the incidence of social loafing, discussed earlier in the chapter, is much higher in large teams.

Team performance can also suffer when a team is too small. Teams with just a few people may lack the diversity of skills and knowledge found in larger teams. Also, teams that are too small are unlikely to gain the advantages of team decision making (i.e., multiple perspectives, generating more ideas and alternative solutions, and stronger commitment) found in larger teams.

What signs indicate that a team's size needs to be changed? If decisions are taking too long, if the team has difficulty making decisions or taking action, if a few members dominate the team, or if the commitment or efforts of team members are weak, chances are the team is too big. In contrast, if a team is having difficulty coming up with ideas or generating solutions, or if the team does not have the expertise to address a specific problem, chances are the team is too small.

3.4 Team Conflict

Conflict and disagreement are inevitable in most teams. But this shouldn't surprise anyone. From time to time, people who work together are going to disagree about what and how things get done. What causes conflict in teams? Although almost anything can lead to conflict—casual remarks that unintentionally offend a team member or fighting over scarce resources—the primary cause of team conflict is disagreement over team goals and priorities.[50] Other common causes of team conflict include disagreements over task-related issues, interpersonal incompatibilities, and simple fatigue.

Though most people view conflict negatively, the key to dealing with team conflict is not avoiding it, but rather making sure that the team experiences the right kind of conflict. In Chapter 5, you learned about *c-type conflict,* or *cognitive conflict,* which focuses on problem-related differences of opinion, and *a-type conflict,* or *affective conflict,* which refers to the emotional reactions that can occur when disagreements become personal rather than professional.[51] Cognitive conflict is strongly associated with improvements in team performance, whereas affective conflict is strongly associated with decreases in team performance.[52] Why does this happen? With cognitive conflict, team members disagree because their different experiences and expertise lead them to different views of the problem and solutions. Indeed, managers who participated on teams that emphasized cognitive conflict described their teammates as "smart," "team players," and "best in the business." They described their teams as "open," "fun," and "productive." One manager summed up the positive attitude that team members had about cognitive conflict by saying, "We scream a lot, then laugh, and then resolve the issue."[53] Thus, cognitive conflict is also characterized by a willingness to examine, compare, and reconcile differences to produce the best possible solution.

By contrast, affective conflict often results in hostility, anger, resentment, distrust, cynicism, and apathy. Managers who participated on teams that emphasized affective conflict described their teammates as "manipulative," "secretive," "burned out," and "political."[54] Not surprisingly, affective conflict can make people uncomfortable and cause them to withdraw and decrease their commitment to a team.[55] Affective conflict also lowers the satisfaction of team members, may lead to personal hostility between coworkers, and can decrease team cohesiveness.[56] Although cognitive conflict is a benefit,

© Inmagine/Inspirestock/Jupiter Images

How to Have a Good Fight

- Work with more information to make discussion productive rather than contentious.
- Generate several alternative solutions. Two solutions will generate debate. More than two will generate productive discussion.
- Establish common goals.
- Use your sense of humor.
- Create and maintain a balance of power.
- Do not force consensus.

Source: K. M. Eisenhard, J. L. Kahwajy, and L. J. Bourgeois III, "How Management Teams Can Have a Good Fight," *Harvard Business Review* 75, no. 4 (July-August 1997): 77-85.

© Walik/iStockphoto.

affective conflict undermines team performance by preventing teams from engaging in the kinds of activities that are critical to team effectiveness.

So, what can managers do to manage team conflict? First, they need to realize that emphasizing cognitive conflict alone won't be enough. Studies show that cognitive and affective conflicts often occur together in a given team activity! Sincere attempts to reach agreement on a difficult issue can quickly deteriorate from cognitive to affective conflict if the discussion turns personal and tempers and emotions flare. While cognitive conflict is clearly the better approach to take, efforts to engage in cognitive conflict should be managed well and checked before they deteriorate and the team becomes unproductive.

Can teams disagree and still get along? Fortunately, they can. In an attempt to study this issue, researchers examined team conflict in twelve high-tech companies. In four of the companies, work teams used cognitive conflict to address problems but did so in a way that minimized the occurrence of affective conflict.

There are several ways teams can have a good fight.[57] First, work with more, rather than less, information. If data are plentiful, objective, and up-to-date, teams will focus on issues, not personalities. Second, develop multiple alternatives to enrich debate. Focusing on multiple solutions diffuses conflict by getting the team to keep searching for a better solution. Positions and opinions are naturally more flexible with five alternatives than with just two. Third, establish common goals. Remember, most team conflict arises from disagreements over team goals and priorities. Therefore, common goals encourage collaboration and minimize conflict over a team's purpose. Fourth, inject humor into the workplace. Humor relieves tension, builds cohesion,

and just makes being in teams fun. Fifth, maintain a balance of power by involving as many people as possible in the decision process. And sixth, resolve issues without forcing a consensus. Consensus means that everyone must agree before decisions are finalized. Effectively, requiring consensus gives everyone on the team veto power. Nothing gets done until everyone agrees, which, of course, is nearly impossible. As a result, insisting on consensus usually promotes affective rather than cognitive conflict. If team members can't agree after constructively discussing their options, it's better to have the team leader make the final choice. Most team members can accept the team leader's choice if they've been thoroughly involved in the decision process.

3.5 Stages of Team Development

As teams develop and grow, they pass through four stages of development. As shown in Exhibit 10.3, those stages are forming, storming, norming, and performing.[58] Although not every team passes through each of these stages, teams that do tend to be better performers.[59] This holds true even for teams composed of seasoned executives. After a period of time, however, if a team is not managed well, its performance may start to deteriorate as the team begins a process of decline and progresses through the stages of de-norming, de-storming, and de-forming.[60]

Exhibit 10.3
Stages of Team Development

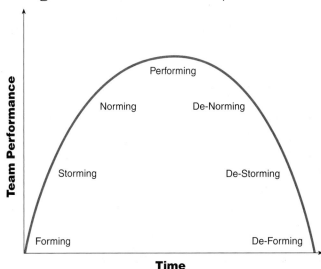

Sources: J. F. McGrew, J. G. Bilotta, and J. M. Deeney, "Software Team Formation and Decay: Extending the Standard Model for Small Groups," *Small Group Research* 30, no. 2 (1999): 209–234; B. W. Tuckman, "Development Sequence in Small Groups," *Psychological Bulletin* 63, no. 6 (1965): 384–399.

Forming is the initial stage of team development. This is the getting-acquainted stage in which team members first meet each other, form initial impressions, and try to get a sense of what it will be like to be part of the team. Some of the first team norms will be established during this stage, as team members begin to find out what behaviors will and won't be accepted by the team. During this stage, team leaders should allow time for team members to get to know each other, set early ground rules, and begin to set up a preliminary team structure.

Conflicts and disagreements often characterize the second stage of team development, **storming.** As team members begin working together, different personalities and work styles may clash. Team members become more assertive at this stage and more willing to state opinions. This is also the stage when team members jockey for position and try to establish a favorable role for themselves on the team. In addition, team members are likely to disagree about what the group should do and how it should do it. Team performance is still relatively low, given that team cohesion is weak and team members are still reluctant to support each other. Since teams that get stuck in the storming stage are almost always ineffective, it is important for team leaders to focus the team on team goals and on improving team performance. Team members need to be particularly patient and tolerant with each other in this stage.

During **norming,** the third stage of team development, team members begin to settle into their roles as team members. Positive team norms will have developed by this stage, and teammates should know what to expect from each other. Petty differences should have been resolved, friendships will have developed, and group cohesion will be relatively strong. At this point, team members will have accepted team goals, be operating as a unit, and, as indicated by the increase in performance, be working together effectively. This stage can be very short and is often characterized by someone on the team saying, "I think things are finally coming together." Note, however, that teams may also cycle back and forth between storming and norming several times before finally settling into norming.

In the last stage of team development, **performing,** performance improves because the team has finally matured into an effective, fully functioning team. At this point, members should be fully committed to the team and think of themselves as members of a team and not just employees. Team members often become intensely loyal to one another at this stage and feel mutual accountability for team successes and failures. Trivial disagreements, which can take time and energy away from the work of the team, should be rare. At this stage, teams get a lot of work done, and it is fun to be a team member. But the team should not become complacent. Without effective management, its performance may begin to decline as it passes through the stages of de-norming, de-storming, and de-forming.[61]

4 Enhancing Work Team Effectiveness

Making teams work is a challenging and difficult process. Nonetheless, companies can increase the likelihood that teams will succeed by carefully managing *4.1 the setting of team goals and priorities* and *4.2 how work team members are selected, 4.3 trained,* and *4.4 compensated.*[62]

4.1 Setting Team Goals and Priorities

In Chapter 5, you learned that having specific, measurable, attainable, realistic, and timely (i.e., S.M.A.R.T.) goals is one of the most effective means for improv-

Forming the first stage of team development, in which team members meet each other, form initial impressions, and begin to establish team norms

Storming the second stage of development, characterized by conflict and disagreement, in which team members disagree over what the team should do and how it should do it

Norming the third stage of team development, in which team members begin to settle into their roles, group cohesion grows, and positive team norms develop

Performing the fourth and final stage of team development, in which performance improves because the team has matured into an effective, fully functioning team

ing individual job performance. Fortunately, team goals also improve team performance, especially when they are *specific* and *challenging*. In fact, team goals lead to much higher team performance 93 percent of the time.[63] For example, Nucor Steel sets specific, challenging hourly goals for each of its production teams, which consist of first-line supervisors and production and maintenance workers. The average in the steel industry is tons of steel per hour. Nucor production teams have a goal of 8 tons per hour, but get a 5 percent bonus for every ton over 8 tons that they produce each hour. With no limit on the bonuses they can receive, Nucor's production teams produce an average of 35 to 40 tons of steel per hour![64]

Why is setting *specific* team goals so critical to team success? One reason is that increasing a team's performance is inherently more complex than just increasing one individual's job performance. For instance, consider that any team is likely to involve at least four different kinds of goals: each member's goal for the team, each member's goal for himself or herself on the team, the team's goal for each member, and the team's goal for itself.[65] In other words, without a specific, challenging goal for the team itself (the last of the four goals listed), team members may head off in all directions at once

pursuing these other goals. Consequently, setting a specific, challenging goal *for the team* clarifies team priorities by providing a clear focus and purpose.

Challenging team goals affect how hard team members work. In particular, they greatly reduce the incidence of social loafing. When faced with reasonably difficult goals, team members necessarily expect everyone to contribute. Consequently, they are much more likely to notice and complain if a teammate isn't doing his or her share. In fact, when teammates know each other well, when team goals are specific, when team communication is good, and when teams are rewarded for team performance (discussed below), there is only a 1 in 16 chance that teammates will be social loafers.[66]

What can companies and teams do to ensure that team goals lead to superior team performance? One increasingly popular approach is to give teams stretch goals. *Stretch goals* are extremely ambitious goals that workers don't know how to reach.[67] The purpose of stretch goals is to achieve extraordinary improvements in performance by forcing managers and workers to throw away old, comfortable solutions and adopt radical, never-before-used solutions.[68]

Four things must occur for stretch goals to effectively motivate teams.[69] First, teams must have a high de-

© Stephanie Sinclair/Corbis

Two Sheets and a Blanket

The organization with arguably some of the highest performing teams in the United States (maybe the world) is the U.S. Marine Corps. One of the many exercises the Marines use to get new arrivals at its Parris Island boot camp to perform as a team is called "two sheets and a blanket." An entire platoon (about 50 recruits) gets three minutes to make all the beds in the barracks—with hospital corners tight enough to bounce a quarter. If the entire platoon doesn't finish, the drill instructor orders the platoon to strip the beds and start over. So it goes—all day if necessary—until the recruits realize that they can finish in time and to specification only if they work together with the faster guys helping the slower guys.

Source: J. Vesterman, "From Wharton to War," *Fortune*, 12 June 2006, 105

mgmt trend

TEAMS:

Ferraris of Work Design

Structural accommodation the ability to change organizational structures, policies, and practices in order to meet stretch goals

Bureaucratic immunity the ability to make changes without first getting approval from managers or other parts of an organization

Individualism-collectivism the degree to which a person believes that people should be self-sufficient and that loyalty to one's self is more important than loyalty to team or company

Team level the average level of ability, experience, personality, or any other factor on a team

gree of autonomy or control over how they achieve their goals. Second, teams must be empowered with control over resources such as budgets, workspaces, computers, or whatever else they need to do their jobs. Steve Kerr, Goldman Sachs' chief learning officer, says, "We have a moral obligation to try to give people the tools to meet tough goals. I think it's totally wrong if you don't give employees the tools to succeed, then punish them when they fail."[70]

Third, teams need structural accommodation. **Structural accommodation** means giving teams the ability to change organizational

structures, policies, and practices if doing so helps them meet their stretch goals. Finally, teams need bureaucratic immunity. **Bureaucratic immunity** means that teams no longer have to go through the frustratingly slow process of multilevel reviews and sign-offs to get management approval before making changes. Once granted bureaucratic immunity, teams are immune from the influence of various organizational groups and are accountable only to top management. Therefore, teams can act quickly and even experiment with little fear of failure.

4.2 Selecting People for Teamwork

University of Southern California professor Edward Lawler says, "People are very naive about how easy it is to create a team. Teams are the Ferraris of work design. They're high performance but high maintenance and expensive."[71] It's almost impossible to have an effective work team without carefully selecting people who are suited for teamwork or for working on a particular team. A focus on teamwork (individualism-collectivism), team level, and team diversity can help companies choose the right team members.[72]

Are you more comfortable working alone or with others? If you strongly prefer to work alone, you may not be well suited for teamwork. Indeed, studies show that job satisfaction is higher in teams when team members prefer working with others.[73] An indirect way to measure someone's *preference for teamwork* is to assess the person's degree of individualism or collectivism. **Individualism-collectivism** is the degree to which a person believes that people should be self-sufficient and that loyalty to oneself is more important than loyalty to one's team or company.[74] *Individualists,* who put their own welfare and interests first, generally prefer independent tasks in which they work alone. In contrast, *collectivists,* who put group or team interests ahead of self-interests, generally prefer interdependent tasks in which they work with others. Collectivists would also rather cooperate than compete and are fearful of disappointing team members or of being ostracized from teams. Given these differences, it makes sense to select team members who are collectivists rather than individualists. Indeed, many companies use individualism-collectivism as an initial screening device for team members. If team diversity is desired, however, individualists may also be appropriate, as discussed below. To determine your preference for teamwork, take the Team Player Inventory shown in Exhibit 10.4.

Team level is the average level of ability, experience, personality, or any other factor on a team. For example, a high level of team experience means that a team has

Exhibit 10.4

The Team Player Inventory

	STRONGLY DISAGREE				STRONGLY AGREE
1. I enjoy working on team/group projects.	1	2	3	4	5
2. Team/group project work easily allows others to not pull their weight.	1	2	3	4	5
3. Work that is done as a team/group is better than work done individually.	1	2	3	4	5
4. I do my best work alone rather than in a team/group.	1	2	3	4	5
5. Team/group work is overrated in terms of the actual results produced.	1	2	3	4	5
6. Working in a team/group gets me to think more creatively.	1	2	3	4	5
7. Teams/groups are used too often when individual work would be more effective.	1	2	3	4	5
8. My own work is enhanced when I am in a team/group situation.	1	2	3	4	5
9. My experiences working in team/group situations have been primarily negative.	1	2	3	4	5
10. More soultions/ideas are generated when working in a team/group situation than when working alone.	1	2	3	4	5

Reverse score items 2, 4, 5, 7, and 9. Then add the scores for items 1 to 10. Higher scores indicate a preference for teamwork, whereas lower total scores indicate a preference for individual work.

particularly experienced team members. This does not mean that every member of the team has considerable experience, but that enough team members do to significantly raise the average level of experience on the team. Team level is used to guide selection of teammates when teams need a particular set of skills or capabilities to do their jobs well. For example, at GE's Aerospace Engines manufacturing plant in Durham, North Carolina, everyone hired had to have an FAA-certified mechanic's license.[75]

Whereas team level represents the average level or capability on a team, **team diversity** represents the variances or differences in ability, experience, personality, or any other factor on a team.[76] From a practical perspective, why is team diversity important? Professor John Hollenbeck explains, "Imagine if you put all the extroverts together. Everyone is talking, but nobody is listening. [By contrast,] with a team of [nothing but] introverts, you can hear the clock ticking on the wall."[77] Not only do strong teams have talented members (i.e., team level), but those talented members are also different in terms of ability, experience, or personality.

For example, teams with strong team diversity on job experience have a mix of team members ranging from seasoned veterans to people with three or four years of experience to rookies with little or no experience. Team diversity is used to guide the selection of team members when teams must complete a wide range of different tasks or when tasks are particularly complex.

Once the right team has been put together in terms of individualism-collectivism, team level, and team diversity, it's important to keep the team together as long as practically possible. Interesting research by the National Transportation Safety Board shows that 73 percent of the serious mistakes made by jet cockpit crews are made the very first day that a crew flies together as a team and, of that 73 percent, 44 percent occur on their very first flight together that day (pilot teams fly two to three flights per day). Moreover, research has shown that fatigued pilot crews who have worked together before make significantly fewer errors than

Team diversity the variances or differences in ability, experience, personality, or any other factor on a team

Top 10 Problems Reported by Team Leaders

1. Confusion about their new roles and about what they should be doing differently.
2. Feeling they've lost control.
3. Not knowing what it means to coach or empower.
4. Having personal doubts about whether the team concept will really work.
5. Uncertainty about how to deal with employees' doubts about the team concept.
6. Confusion about when a team is ready for more responsibility.
7. Confusion about how to share responsibility and accountability with the team.
8. Concern about promotional opportunities, especially about whether the "team leader" title carries any prestige.
9. Uncertainty about the strategic aspects of the leader's role as the team matures.
10. Not knowing where to turn for help with team problems, as few, if any, of their organization's leaders have led teams.

Source: B. Filipczak, M. Hequet, C. Lee, M. Picard, and D. Stamps, "More Trouble with Teams," *Training*, Octobert 1996, 21.

rested crews who have never worked together.[78] Their experience working together helps them overcome their fatigue and outperform new teams that have not worked together before. So, once you've created effective teams, keep them together as long as possible.

4.3 Team Training

After selecting the right people for teamwork, you need to train them. To be successful, teams need significant training, particularly in interpersonal skills, decision-making and problem-solving skills, conflict resolution skills, and technical training. Organizations that create work teams *often underestimate the amount of training* required to make teams effective. This mistake occurs frequently in successful organizations where managers assume that if employees can work effectively on their own, they can work effectively in teams. In reality, companies that successfully use teams provide thousands of hours of training to make sure that teams work. Stacy Myers, a consultant who helps com-

Interpersonal skills
skills, such as listening, communicating, questioning, and providing feedback, that enable people to have effective working relationships with others

panies implement teams, says, "When we help companies move to teams, we also require that employees take basic quality and business knowledge classes as well. Teams must know how their work affects the company, and how their success will be measured."[79]

Most commonly, members of work teams receive training in interpersonal skills. **Interpersonal skills** such as listening, communicating, questioning, and providing feedback enable people to have effective working relationships with others. Because of teams' autonomy and responsibility, many companies also give team members training in *decision-making and problem-solving skills* to help them do a better job of cutting costs and improving quality and customer service. Many organizations also teach teams *conflict resolution skills.* "Teams at Delta Faucet have specific protocols for addressing conflict. For example, if an employee's behavior is creating a problem within a team, the team is expected to work it out without involving the team leader. Two team members will meet with the 'problem' team member and work toward a resolution. If this is unsuccessful, the whole team meets and confronts the issue. If necessary, the team leader can be brought in to make a decision, but . . . it is a rare occurrence for a team to reach that stage."[80] Firms must also provide team members with the *technical training* they need to do their jobs, particularly if they are being cross-trained to perform all of the different jobs on the team. Cross-training is less appropriate for teams of highly skilled workers. For instance, it is unlikely that a group of engineers, computer programmers, and systems analysts would be cross-trained for each other's jobs.

Team leaders need training, too, as they often feel unprepared for their new duties. New team leaders face myriad problems ranging from confusion about their new roles as team leaders (compared to their old jobs as managers or employees) to not knowing where to go for help when their teams have problems. The solution is extensive training.

4.4 Team Compensation and Recognition

Compensating teams correctly is very difficult. For instance, one survey found that only 37 percent of companies were satisfied with their team compensation plans and even fewer, just 10 percent, reported being "very positive."[81] One of the problems, according to Monty Mohrman of the Center for Effective Organizations, is

The more each **team member** knows and can do, the better the **whole team** performs.

that "there is a very strong set of beliefs in most organizations that people should be paid for how well they do. So when people first get put into team-based organizations, they really balk at being paid for how well the team does. It sounds illogical to them. It sounds like their individuality and their sense of self-worth are being threatened."[82] Consequently, companies need to carefully choose a team compensation plan and then fully explain how teams will be rewarded. One basic requirement for team compensation to work is that the type of reward (individual versus team) must match the type of performance (individual versus team).

Employees can be compensated for team participation and accomplishments in three ways: skill-based pay, gainsharing, and nonfinancial rewards. **Skill-based pay** programs pay employees for learning additional skills or knowledge.[83] These programs encourage employees to acquire the additional skills they will need to perform multiple jobs within a team and to share knowledge with others within their work groups.[84]

In **gainsharing** programs, companies share the financial value of performance gains such as productivity increases, cost savings, or quality improvements

with their workers.[85] *Nonfinancial rewards* are another way to reward teams for their performance. These rewards, which can range from vacation trips to T-shirts, plaques, and coffee mugs, are especially effective when coupled with management recognition, such as awards, certificates, and praise.[86] Nonfinancial awards tend to be most effective when teams or team-based interventions, such as total quality management (see Chapter 18), are first introduced.[87]

Which team compensation plan should your company use? In general, skill-based pay is most effective for self-managing and self-directing teams performing complex tasks. In these situations, the more each team member knows and can do, the better the whole team performs. By contrast, gainsharing works best in relatively stable environments where employees can focus on improving productivity, cost savings, or quality.

Skill-based pay compensation system that pays employees for learning additional skills or knowledge

Gainsharing a compensation system in which companies share the financial value of performance gains, such as productivity, cost savings, or quality, with their workers

MANAGING HUMAN RESOURCE SYSTEMS

Human resource management (HRM), or the process of finding, developing, and keeping the right people to form a qualified work force, is one of the most difficult and important of all management tasks. This chapter is organized around the three parts of the human resource management process shown in Exhibit 11.1: attracting, developing, and keeping a qualified work force.

Human resource management (HRM) the process of finding, developing, and keeping the right people to form a qualified work force

Exhibit 11.1

The Human Resource Management Process

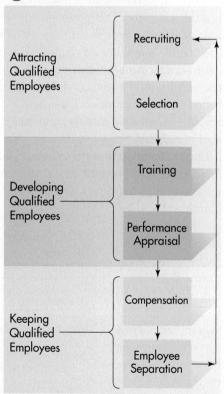

Attracting Qualified Employees
- Recruiting
- Selection

Developing Qualified Employees
- Training
- Performance Appraisal

Keeping Qualified Employees
- Compensation
- Employee Separation

Learning Outcomes

1 explain how different employment laws affect human resource practice.

2 explain how companies use recruiting to find qualified job applicants.

3 describe the selection techniques and procedures that companies use when deciding which applicants should receive job offers.

4 describe how to determine training needs and select the appropriate training methods.

5 discuss how to use performance appraisal to give meaningful performance feedback.

6 describe basic compensation strategies and discuss the four kinds of employee separations.

This chapter will walk you through the steps of the HRM process. We explore how companies use recruiting and selection techniques to attract and hire qualified employees to fulfill those needs. Then we discuss how training and performance appraisal can develop the knowledge, skills, and abilities of the work force. The chapter concludes with a review of compensation and employee separation, that is, how companies can keep their best workers through effective compensation practices and how they can manage the separation process when employees leave the organization.

The Legal Context

B

Before we explore how human resource systems work, you need to better understand the complex legal environment in which they exist. So we'll begin the chapter by reviewing the federal laws that govern human resource management decisions.

1 explain how different employment laws affect human resource practice.

1 Employment Legislation

Since their inception, Hooters restaurants have hired only female servers. Moreover, consistent with the company's marketing theme, the servers wear short nylon shorts and cutoff T-shirts that show their midriffs. The Equal Employment Opportunity Commission (EEOC) began an investigation of Hooters when a Chicago man filed a sex-based discrimination charge. The man alleged that he had applied for a server's job at a Hooters restaurant and was rejected because of his sex. The dispute between Hooters and the EEOC quickly gained national attention. One sarcastic letter to the EEOC printed in *Fortune* magazine read as follows:

> *Dear EEOC:*
>
> *Hi! I just wanted to thank you for investigating those Hooters restaurants, where the waitresses wear those shorty shorts and midriffy T-shirts. I think it's a great idea that you have decided to make Hooters hire men as—how do you say it?—waitpersons. Gee, I never knew so many men wanted to be waitpersons at Hooters. No reason to let them sue on their own either. You're right, the government needs to take the lead on this one.*[1]

This letter characterized public sentiment at the time. Given its backlog of 100,000 job discrimination cases, many wondered if the EEOC didn't have better things to do with its scarce resources.

Three years after the initial complaint, the EEOC ruled that Hooters had violated antidiscrimination laws and offered to settle the case if the company would agree to pay $22 million to the EEOC for distribution to male victims of the "Hooters Girl" hiring policy, establish a scholarship fund to enhance opportunities or education for men, and provide sensitivity training to teach Hooters' employees how to be more sensitive to men's needs. Hooters responded with a $1 million publicity campaign criticizing the EEOC's investigation. Billboards featuring "Vince," a man dressed in a Hooters Girl uniform and blond wig, sprang up all over the country. Hooters customers were given postcards to send complaints to the EEOC. Of course, Hooters paid the postage. As a result of the publicity campaign, restaurant sales increased by 10 percent. Soon thereafter, the EEOC announced that it would not pursue discriminatory hiring charges against Hooters.[2] Nonetheless, the company ended up paying $3.75 million to settle a class-action suit brought by seven men who claimed that their inability to get a job at Hooters violated federal law.[3] Under the settlement, Hooters maintained its women-only policy for server jobs but had to create additional support jobs such as hosts and bartenders that would also be open to men.

As the Hooters example illustrates, the human resource planning process occurs in a very complicated legal environment. Let's explore employment legislation by reviewing **1.1 the major federal employment laws that affect human resource practice, 1.2 how the concept of adverse impact is related to employment discrimination,** and **1.3 the laws regarding sexual harassment in the workplace.**

1.1 Federal Employment Laws

Exhibit 11.2 lists the major federal employment laws and their Web sites, where you can find more detailed information. Except for the Family and Medical Leave Act and the Uniformed Services Employment and Reemployment Rights Act, which are administered by the Department of Labor, all of these laws are administered by the EEOC. The general effect of this body of law, which is still evolving through court decisions, is that employers may not discriminate in employment decisions on the basis of sex, age, religion, color, national origin, race, or disability. The intent is to make these factors irrelevant in employment decisions. Stated another way, employment decisions should be based on factors that are "job related," "reasonably necessary," or a "business necessity" for successful job performance. The only time that sex, age, religion, and the like can be used to make employment decisions is when they are considered a bona fide occupational qualification.[4] Title VII of the 1964 Civil Rights Act says that it is not unlawful to hire and employ someone on the basis of gender, religion, or national origin when there is a **bona fide occupational qualification (BFOQ)** that is "reasonably necessary to the normal operation of that particular business." For example, a Baptist church hiring a new minister can reasonably specify that being

Bona fide occupational qualification (BFOQ) an exception in employment law that permits sex, age, religion, and the like to be used when making employment decisions, but only if they are "reasonably necessary to the normal operation of that particular business." BFOQs are strictly monitored by the Equal Employment Opportunity Commission.

a Baptist rather than a Catholic or Presbyterian is a BFOQ for the position. However, it's unlikely that the church could specify race or national origin as a BFOQ. In general, the courts and the EEOC take a hard look when a business claims that sex, age, religion, color, national origin, race, or disability is a BFOQ.

It is important to understand, however, that these laws apply to the entire HRM process and not just to selection decisions (i.e., hiring and promotion). Thus, these laws also cover all training and development activities, performance appraisals, terminations, and compensation decisions. Employers who use sex, age, race, or religion to make employment-related decisions when those factors are unrelated to an applicant's or employee's ability to perform a job may face charges of discrimination from employee lawsuits or the EEOC. For example, Morgan Stanley, an investment bank, agreed to pay $54 million in damages after the EEOC filed a sex discrimination suit on behalf of 300 of the firm's female employees. The women were paid less and promoted less often than comparable male employees with whom they worked.[5]

In addition to the laws presented in Exhibit 11.2, there are two other important sets of federal laws: labor laws and laws and regulations governing safety standards. Labor laws regulate the interaction between management and labor unions that represent groups of employees. These laws guarantee employees the right to form and join unions of their own choosing. The Occupational Safety and Health Act (OSHA) requires that employers provide employees with a workplace that is "free from recognized hazards that are causing or are likely to cause death or serious physical harm." This law is administered by the Occupational Safety and Health Administration (which, like the act, is referred to as OSHA). OSHA sets safety and health standards for employers and conducts inspections to determine whether those standards are being met. Employers who do not meet OSHA standards may be fined.[6]

1.2 Adverse Impact and Employment Discrimination

The EEOC has investigatory, enforcement, and informational responsibilities. Therefore, it investigates charges of discrimination, enforces the employment discrimination laws in federal court, and publishes guidelines that organizations can use to ensure they are in compliance with the law. One of the most important guidelines jointly is-

Exhibit 11.2

Summary of Major Federal Employment Laws

Law	URL	Description
■ Equal Pay Act of 1963	http://www.eeoc.gov/policy/epa.html	Prohibits unequal pay for males and females doing substantially similar work.
■ Civil Rights Act of 1964	http://www.eeoc.gov/policy/vii.html	Prohibits discrimination on the basis of race, color, religion, gender, or national origin.
■ Age Discrimination in Employment Act of 1967	http://www.eeoc.gov/policy/adea.html	Prohibits discrimination in employment decisions against persons age 40 and over.
■ Pregnancy Discrimination Act of 1978	http://www.eeoc.gov/facts/fs-preg.html	Prohibits discrimination in employment against pregnant women.
■ Americans with Disabilities Act of 1990	http://www.eeoc.gov/policy/ada.html	Prohibits discrimination on the basis of physical or mental disabilities.
■ Civil Rights Act of 1991	http://www.eeoc.gov/policy/cra91.html	Strengthened the provisions of the Civil Rights Act of 1964 by providing for jury trials and punitive damages.
■ Family and Medical Leave Act of 1993	http://www.dol.gov/esa/whd/fmla/index.html	Permits workers to take up to 12 weeks of unpaid leave for pregnancy and/or birth of a new child, adoption or foster care of a new child, illness of an immediate family member, or personal medical leave.
■ Uniformed Services Employment and Reemployment Rights Act of 1994	http://www.osc.gov/userra.htm	Prohibits discrimination against those serving in the Armed Forces Reserve, the National Guard, or other uniformed services; guarantees that civilian employers will hold and then restore civilian jobs and benefits for those who have completed uniformed service.

sued by the EEOC, the Department of Labor, the U.S. Justice Department, and the federal Office of Personnel Management is the *Uniform Guidelines on Employee Selection Procedures.* These guidelines define two important criteria, disparate treatment and adverse impact, that are used in determining whether companies have engaged in discriminatory hiring and promotion practices.

Disparate treatment, which is *intentional* discrimination, occurs when people are *intentionally* not given the same hiring, promotion, or membership opportunities as other employees of their race, color, age, sex, ethnic group, national origin, or religious beliefs despite the fact that they are qualified.[7] Legally, a key element of discrimination lawsuits is establishing motive, meaning that the employer intended to discriminate. If no motive can be established, then a claim of disparate treatment may actually be a case of adverse impact.

Adverse impact, which is *unintentional* discrimination, occurs when members of a particular race, sex, or ethnic group are *unintentionally* harmed or disadvantaged because they are hired, promoted, or trained (or any other employment decision) at substantially lower rates than others. The courts and federal agencies use the **four-fifths (or 80 percent) rule** to determine if adverse impact has occurred. Adverse impact occurs if the decision rate for a protected group of people is less than four-fifths (or 80 percent) of the decision rate for a nonprotected group (usually white males). So, if 100 white applicants and 100 black applicants apply for entry-level jobs, and 60 white applicants are hired (60/100 = 60%), but only 20 black applicants are hired (20/100 = 20%), adverse impact has occurred (0.20/0.60 = 0.33). The criterion for the four-fifths rule in this situation is 0.48 (0.60 × 0.80 = 0.48). Since 0.33 is less than 0.48, the four-fifths rule has been violated.

Violation of the four-fifths rule is not an automatic indication of discrimination, however. If an employer can demonstrate that a selection procedure or test is valid, meaning that the test accurately predicts job performance or that the test is job related because it assesses applicants on specific tasks actually used in the job, then the organization may continue to use the test. If validity cannot be established, however, then a violation of the four-fifths rule may likely result in a lawsuit brought by employees, job applicants, or the EEOC itself.

1.3 Sexual Harassment

According to the EEOC, **sexual harassment** is a form of discrimination in which unwelcome sexual advances, requests for sexual favors, or other verbal or physical conduct of a sexual nature occurs. From a legal perspective, there are two kinds of sexual harassment: quid pro quo and hostile work environment.[8]

Disparate treatment intentional discrimination that occurs when people are purposely not given the same hiring, promotion, or membership opportunities because of their race, color, sex, age, ethnic group, national origin, or religious beliefs

Adverse impact unintentional discrimination that occurs when members of a particular race, sex, or ethnic group are unintentionally harmed or disadvantaged because they are hired, promoted, or trained (or any other employment decision) at substantially lower rates than others

Four-fifths (or 80 percent) rule a rule of thumb used by the courts and the EEOC to determine whether there is evidence of adverse impact. A violation of this rule occurs when the selection rate for a protected group is less than 80 percent or four-fifths of the selection rate for a nonprotected group.

Sexual harassment a form of discrimination in which unwelcome sexual advances, requests for sexual favors, or other verbal or physical conduct of a sexual nature occurs while performing one's job

© Peter Finnie/iStockphoto.com

Quid pro quo sexual harassment occurs when employment outcomes, such as hiring, promotion, or simply keeping one's job, depend on whether an individual submits to being sexually harassed. For example, in a quid pro quo sexual harassment lawsuit against Costco, a female employee alleged that her boss groped her and bumped into her from behind to simulate sex. "He would tell her: 'You work with me and I'll work with you,' motioning to his private area."[9] The supervisor also allegedly told her that he would fire her if she reported his activities to upper management. In quid pro quo cases, requests for sexual acts are linked to economic outcomes (that is, keeping a job). A **hostile work environment** occurs when unwelcome and demeaning sexually related behavior creates an intimidating, hostile, and offensive work environment. There may be no economic injury—that is, requests for sexual acts aren't tied to economic outcomes. However, they can lead to psychological injury from a stressful work environment.

What should companies do to make sure that sexual harassment laws are followed and not violated?[10] First, respond immediately when sexual harassment is reported. A quick response encourages victims of sexual harassment to report problems to management rather than to lawyers or the EEOC. Furthermore, a quick and fair investigation may serve as a deterrent to future harassment. Next, take the time to write a clear, understandable sexual harassment policy that is strongly worded, gives specific examples of what constitutes sexual harassment, spells outs sanctions and punishments, and is widely publicized within the company. This lets potential harassers and victims know what will not be tolerated and how the firm will deal with harassment should it occur.

Next, establish clear reporting procedures that indicate how, where, and to whom incidents of sexual harassment can be reported. The best procedures ensure that a complaint will receive a quick response, that impartial parties will handle the complaint, and that the privacy of the accused and accuser will be protected. At DuPont, Avon, and Texas Industries, employees can call a confidential hotline 24 hours a day, 365 days a year.[11]

Finally, managers should also be aware that most states and many cities or local governments have their own employment-related laws and enforcement agencies. So compliance with federal law is often not enough. In fact, organizations can be in full compliance with federal law and at the same time be in violation of state or local sexual harassment laws.

Finding Qualified Workers

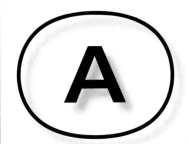

As Gail Hyland-Savage, the CEO of real estate and marketing firm Michaelson, Connor & Boul, says "Staffing is absolutely critical to the success of every company. To be competitive in today's economy, companies need the best people to create ideas and execute them for the organization. Without a competent and talented workforce, organizations will stagnate and eventually perish. The right employees are the most important resources of companies today."[12]

 After reading the next two sections, you should be able to

2 explain how companies use recruiting to find qualified job applicants.

3 describe the selection techniques and procedures that companies use when deciding which applicants should receive job offers.

2 Recruiting

Recruiting is the process of developing a pool of qualified job applicants. Let's examine **2.1 what job analysis is and how it is used in recruiting**, and **2.2 how companies use internal recruiting**, and **2.3 external recruiting to find qualified job applicants.**

2.1 Job Analysis and Recruiting

Job analysis is a "purposeful, systematic process for collecting information on the important work-related aspects of a job."[13] Typically, a job analysis collects four kinds of information:

Quid pro quo sexual harassment a form of sexual harassment in which employment outcomes, such as hiring, promotion, or simply keeping one's job, depend on whether an individual submits to sexual harassment

Hostile work environment a form of sexual harassment in which unwelcome and demeaning sexually related behavior creates an intimidating and offensive work environment

Recruiting the process of developing a pool of qualified job applicants

Job analysis a purposeful, systematic process for collecting information on the important work-related aspects of a job

Exhibit 11.3

Job Description for a Firefighter for the City of Portland, Oregon

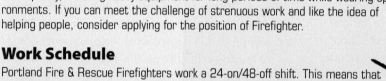

Yes, as a Firefighter you will fight fire and provide emergency medical services to your community. But it doesn't end there: your firefighting career offers you the opportunity to expand your skills to include Hazardous Materials Response, Specialty Response Teams (dive, rope rescue, confined space, etc.), Paramedic Care, Public Education & Information, Fire Investigation, and Fire Code Enforcement.

Teamwork

Professional Firefighters work as a team at emergency scenes. The work day also includes training, fire station and equipment maintenance, fire prevention activities, and public education. As a Firefighter, you must be in excellent physical condition to meet the demands of the job; this means you must work quickly, handling heavy equipment for long periods of time while wearing special protective gear in hot and hazardous environments. If you can meet the challenge of strenuous work and like the idea of helping people, consider applying for the position of Firefighter.

Work Schedule

Portland Fire & Rescue Firefighters work a 24-on/48-off shift. This means that Firefighters report to work at 8:00 a.m. the day of their shift and continue working until 8:00 a.m. the following morning. Our Firefighters then have the following two days (48 hours) off. Firefighters are required to work shifts on holidays and weekends. Portland Fire & Rescue also has 40-hour-a-week firefighters who work in Training, Inspections/Investigations, Public Education, Logistics, and Emergency Management. These positions are usually filled after a Firefighter has met the minimum requirements for these positions.

Source: Portland Fire and Rescue, available online at http://www.portlandonline.com/fire/index.cfm?a=haea&c=cgbil [accessed 13 August 2008].

© Kendall Griffin/iStockphoto.com / © Hemera Technologies/Photos.com/Jupiterimages

---

- work activities, such as what workers do and how, when, and why they do it;
- the tools and equipment used to do the job;
- the context in which the job is performed, such as the actual working conditions or schedule;
- the personnel requirements for performing the job, meaning the knowledge, skills, and abilities needed to do a job well.[14]

Job analysis information can be collected by having job incumbents and/or supervisors complete questionnaires about their jobs, by direct observation, by interviews, or by filming employees as they perform their jobs.

Job description a written description of the basic tasks, duties, and responsibilities required of an employee holding a particular job

Job specifications a written summary of the qualifications needed to successfully perform a particular job

Job descriptions and job specifications are two of the most important results of a job analysis. A **job description** is a written description of the basic tasks, duties, and responsibilities required of an employee holding a particular job. **Job specifications,** which are often included as a separate section of a job description, are a summary of the qualifications needed to successfully perform the job. Exhibit 11.3 shows a job description for a firefighter in the city of Portland, Oregon.

Because a job analysis specifies what a job entails as well as the knowledge, skills, and abilities that are needed to do the job well, companies must complete a job analysis *before* beginning to recruit job applicants. Job analysis, job descriptions, and job specifications are the foundation on which all critical human resource activities are built. They are used during recruiting and selection to match applicant qualifications with the requirements of the job. It is therefore critically important that job descriptions be accurate. Unfortunately, they aren't always so. Apartment Investment & Management Co. (Aimco) discovered that its high turnover rate was due in part to poorly-written job descriptions. The descriptions were more focused on education and experience than actually explaining what an employee would do on the job and what the company culture is like. When they did explain the job, the descriptions were abstract and laden with jargon, making them unclear. Consequently, many new hires found themselves in an incompatible culture or in jobs they did not like or could not do.[15]

Job descriptions are also used throughout the staffing process to ensure that selection devices and the decisions based on these devices are job-related. For example, the questions asked in an interview should be based on the most important work activities identified by a job analysis. Likewise, during performance appraisals, employees should be evaluated in areas that a job analysis has identified as the most important in a job.

Job analyses, job descriptions, and job specifications also help companies meet the legal requirement that their human resource decisions be job-related. To be judged *job-related*, recruitment, selection, training, performance appraisals, and employee separations must be valid and be directly related to the important aspects of the job as identified by a careful job analysis. In fact, in *Griggs v. Duke Power Co.* and *Albemarle Paper Co. v. Moody*, the U.S. Supreme Court stated that companies should use job analyses to help establish the job-relatedness of their human resource procedures.[16] The EEOC's *Uniform Guidelines on Employee Selection Procedures* also recommend that companies base their human resource procedures on job analysis.

2.2 Internal Recruiting

Internal recruiting is the process of developing a pool of qualified job applicants from people who already work in the company. Internal recruiting, sometimes called "promotion from within," improves employee commitment, morale, and motivation. Recruiting current employees also reduces recruitment startup time and costs, and because employees are already familiar with the company's culture and procedures, they are more likely to succeed in new jobs. Job posting and career paths are two methods of internal recruiting.

Job posting is a procedure for advertising job openings within the company to existing employees. A job description and requirements are typically posted on a bulletin board, in a company newsletter, or in an internal computerized job bank that is accessible only to employees.

A *career path* is a planned sequence of jobs through which employees may advance within an organization. For example, a person who starts as a sales representative may move up to sales manager and then to district or regional sales manager. Career paths help employees focus on long-term goals and development while also helping companies increase employee retention.

2.3 External Recruiting

External recruiting is the process of developing a pool of qualified job applicants from outside the company. External recruitment methods include advertising (newspapers, magazines, direct mail, radio, or television), employee referrals (asking current employees to recommend possible job applicants), walk-ins (people who apply on their own), outside organizations (universities, technical/trade schools, professional societies), employment services (state or private employment agencies, temporary help agencies, and professional search firms), special events (career conferences or job fairs), and Internet job sites. Which external recruiting method should you use? Studies show that employee referrals, walk-ins, newspaper advertisements, and state employment agencies tend to be used most frequently for office/clerical and production/service employees. By contrast, newspaper advertisements and college/university recruiting are used most frequently for professional/technical employees. When recruiting managers, organizations tend to rely most heavily on newspaper advertisements, employee referrals, and search firms.[17]

Companies are now hiring non-traditional people in non-traditional ways. Worker shortages have some companies, such as Schneider National, Inc., a transportation and logistics firm in Green Bay, Wisconsin, turning to people of retirement age who want to remain working or come back to work.[18] Baidu, a Beijing-based search engine company, seeks out the best web engineers by hosting an annual programming competition as a recruiting strategy.[19] Recently, the biggest change in external recruiting has been the increased use of the Internet. Some companies now recruit applicants through Internet job sites such as Monster.com, HotJobs.com, Hire.com, and CareerBuilder.com. Companies can post job openings for 30 days on one of these sites for about half of the cost of running an

Internal recruiting
the process of developing a pool of qualified job applicants from people who already work in the company

External recruiting
the process of developing a pool of qualified job applicants from outside the company

Preventing Brain Drain

Recruiting and retaining the most skilled and knowledgeable workers is in every company's best interest. In a global economy that increasingly hinges on information rather than natural resources, it's also in every country's best interest. Some areas of the world are downright dangerous for smart people. 380 of Iraq's academics and doctors were assassinated between 2003 and 2006. But other countries increasingly want to attract the best talent. Saudia Arabia's king, for example, spent $12.5 billion on a new research university to cultivate talent at home. Countries can also attract talent globally by easing "tariffs" on incoming workers and making it easier for them to get work permits. Geoff Colvin, senior editor at *Fortune* magazine, says, "This international fight for talent will get much more serious. With luck it will lead to something new: a free market in brainpower."

Source: G. Colvin, "The Battle for Brainpower," *Fortune* (10 December 2007) 34-35; C. Caulcutt, "Iraq's Deadly Brain Drain," *France* 24 (11 May 2008), available online at http://www.france24.com/en/20080510-iraqs-deadly-brain-drain-iraq [accessed 14 August 2008].

advertisement just once in a Sunday newspaper. Plus, Internet job listings generate nine times as many résumés as one ad in the Sunday newspaper.[20] And because these sites attract so many applicants and offer so many services, companies save by finding qualified applicants without having to use more expensive recruitment and search firms, which typically charge one-third or more of a new hire's salary.[21]

Selection the process of gathering information about job applicants to decide who should be offered a job

Validation the process of determining how well a selection test or procedure predicts future job performance. The better or more accurate the prediction of future job performance, the more valid a test is said to be.

Employment references sources such as previous employers or coworkers who can provide job-related information about job candidates

---

3 Selection

Once the recruitment process has produced a pool of qualified applicants, the selection process is used to determine which applicants have the best chance of performing well on the job. More specifically, **selection** is the process of gathering information about job applicants to decide who should be offered a job. To make sure that selection decisions are accurate and legally defendable, the EEOC's *Uniform Guide-* lines on *Employee Selection Procedures* recommend that all selection procedures be validated. **Validation** is the process of determining how well a selection test or procedure predicts future job performance. The better or more accurate the prediction of future job performance, the more valid a test is said to be.

Let's examine common selection procedures, such as **3.1 application forms and résumés, 3.2 references and background checks, 3.3 selection tests,** and **3.4 interviews.**

3.1 Application Forms and Résumés

The first selection devices that most job applicants encounter when they seek a job are application forms and résumés. Both contain similar information about an applicant, such as name, address, job and educational history, and so forth. Though an organization's application form often asks for information already provided by the applicant's résumé, most organizations prefer to collect this information in their own format for entry into a human resource information system.

Employment laws apply to application forms just as they do to all selection devices. Application forms may ask applicants for only valid, job-related information. Nonetheless, application forms commonly ask applicants for non-job-related information such as marital status, maiden name, age, or date of high school graduation. Indeed, one study found that 73 percent of organizations had application forms that violated at least one federal or state law.[22] There's quite a bit of information that companies may not request in application forms, during job interviews, or in any other part of the selection process. Courts will assume that you consider all of the information you request of applicants, even if you don't. Be sure to ask only those questions that directly relate to the candidate's ability and motivation to perform the job.

Résumés also pose problems for companies but in a different way. Studies show that as many as one-third of job applicants intentionally falsify some information on their résumés and that 80 percent of the information on résumés may be misleading. Therefore, managers should verify the information collected via résumés and application forms by comparing it with additional information collected during interviews and other stages of the selection process, such as references and background checks, which are discussed next.

3.2 References and Background Checks

Nearly all companies ask an applicant to provide **employment references,** such as previous employers or

Don't Ask! (Topics to Avoid in an Interview)

1. *Children.* Don't ask applicants if they have children, plan to have them, or have or need child care. Questions about children can unintentionally single out women.

2. *Age.* Because of the Age Discrimination in Employment Act, employers cannot ask job applicants their age during the hiring process. Since most people graduate high school at the age of 18, even asking for high school graduation dates could violate the law.

3. *Disabilities.* Don't ask if applicants have physical or mental disabilities. According to the Americans with Disabilities Act, disabilities (and reasonable accommodations for them) cannot be discussed until a job offer has been made.

4. *Physical characteristics.* Don't ask for information about height, weight, or other physical characteristics. Questions about weight could be construed as leading to discrimination toward overweight people, and studies show that they are less likely to be hired in general.

5. *Name.* Yes, you can ask an applicant's name, but you cannot ask a female applicant for her maiden name because it indicates marital status. Asking for a maiden name could also lead to charges that the organization was trying to establish a candidate's ethnic background.

6. *Citizenship.* Asking applicants about citizenship could lead to claims of discrimination on the basis of national origin. However, according to the Immigration Reform and Control Act,

companies may ask applicants if they have a legal right to work in the United States.

7. *Lawsuits.* Applicants may not be asked if they have ever filed a lawsuit against an employer. Federal and state laws prevent this to protect whistleblowers from retaliation by future employers.

8. *Arrest records.* Applicants cannot be asked about their arrest records. Arrests don't have legal standing. However, applicants can be asked whether they have been convicted of a crime.

9. *Smoking.* Applicants cannot be asked if they smoke. Smokers might be able to claim that they weren't hired because of fears of higher absenteeism and medical costs. However, they can be asked if they are aware of company policies that restrict smoking at work.

10. *AIDS/HIV.* Applicants can't be asked about AIDS, HIV, or any other medical condition. Questions of this nature would violate the Americans with Disabilities Act, as well as federal and state civil rights laws.

Source: J. S. Pouliot, "Topics to Avoid with Applicants," *Nation's Business* 80, no. 7 (1992): 57.

© iStockphoto.com

> ## 54 percent of employers **will not provide** information about previous employees.

coworkers, that they can contact to learn more about the candidate. **Background checks** are used to verify the truthfulness and accuracy of information that applicants provide about themselves and to uncover negative, job-related background information not provided by applicants. Background checks are conducted by contacting "educational institutions, prior employers, court records, police and governmental agencies, and other informational sources either by telephone, mail, remote computer access, or through in-person investigations."[23]

Unfortunately, previous employers are increasingly reluctant to provide references or background check information for fear of being sued by previous employees for defamation. If former employers provide potential employers with unsubstantiated information that damages applicants' chances of being hired, applicants can (and do) sue for defamation. As a result, 54 percent of employers will not provide information about previous employees.[24] Many provide only dates of employment, positions held, and date of separation.

When previous employers decline to provide meaningful references or background information, they put other employers at risk of *negligent hiring* lawsuits, in which an employer is held liable for the actions of an employee who would not have been hired if the employer had conducted a thorough reference search and background check.[25]

With previous employers generally unwilling to give full, candid references and with negligent hiring lawsuits awaiting companies that don't get such references and background information, what can companies do? They can conduct criminal record checks, especially if the job for which the person is applying involves money, drugs, control over valuable goods, or access to the elderly, children with disabilities, or people's homes.[26]

Background checks
procedures used to verify the truthfulness and accuracy of information that applicants provide about themselves and to uncover negative, job-related background information not provided by applicants

According to the Society for Human Resource Management, 96 percent of companies conduct background checks and 80 percent of companies go further and conduct criminal record checks.[27]

Next, ask applicants to sign a waiver that permits you to check references, run a background check, or contact anyone else with knowledge of their work performance or history. Likewise, ask applicants if there is anything they would like the company to know or if they expect you to hear anything unusual when contacting references.[28] This in itself is often enough to get applicants to share information that they typically withhold. When you've finished checking, keep the findings confidential to minimize the chances of a defamation charge.

Finally, consider hiring private investigators to conduct background checks. They can often uncover surprising information not revealed by traditional background checks.[29]

3.3 Selection Tests

Selection tests give organizational decision makers a chance to know who will likely do well in a job and who won't. The basic idea behind selection testing is to have applicants take a test that measures something directly or indirectly related to doing well on the job. The selection tests discussed here are specific ability tests, cognitive ability tests, biographical data, personality tests, work sample tests, and assessment centers.

Specific ability tests measure the extent to which an applicant possesses the particular kind of ability needed to do a job well. Specific ability tests are also called **aptitude tests** because they measure aptitude for doing a particular task well. For example, if you took the SAT to get into college, then you've taken the aptly named Scholastic Aptitude Test, which is one of the best predictors of how well students will do in college (i.e., scholastic performance). Specific ability tests also exist for mechanical, clerical, sales, and physical work. For example, clerical workers have to be good at accurately reading and scanning numbers as they type or enter data. Exhibit 11.4 shows items similar to

Specific ability tests (aptitude tests) tests that measure the extent to which an applicant possesses the particular kind of ability needed to do a job well

Cognitive ability tests tests that measure the extent to which applicants have abilities in perceptual speed, verbal comprehension, numerical aptitude, general reasoning, and spatial aptitude

Biographical data (biodata) extensive surveys that ask applicants questions about their personal backgrounds and life experiences

Exhibit 11.4

Clerical Test Items Similar to Those Found on the Minnesota Clerical Test

NUMBERS/LETTERS		SAME	
1. 3468251	3467251	Yes O	No O
2. 4681371	4681371	Yes O	No O
3. 7218510	7218520	Yes O	No O
4. ZXYAZAB	ZXYAZAB	Yes O	No O
5. ALZYXMN	ALZYXNM	Yes O	No O
6. PRQZYMN	PRQZYMN	Yes O	No O

Source: N. W. Schmitt and R. J. Klimoski, *Research Methods in Human Resource Management* (Mason, OH: South-Western, 1991). Used with permission.

those found on the Minnesota Clerical Test, in which applicants have only a short time to determine if the two columns of numbers and letters are identical. Applicants who are good at this are likely to do well as clerical or data-entry workers.

Cognitive ability tests measure the extent to which applicants have abilities in perceptual speed, verbal comprehension, numerical aptitude, general reasoning, and spatial aptitude. In other words, these tests indicate how quickly and how well people understand words, numbers, logic, and spatial dimensions. Whereas specific ability tests predict job performance in only particular types of jobs, cognitive ability tests accurately predict job performance in almost all kinds of jobs.[30] Why is this so? The reason is that people with strong cognitive or mental abilities are usually good at learning new things, processing complex information, solving problems, and making decisions, and these abilities are important in almost all jobs.[31] In fact, cognitive ability tests are almost always the best predictors of job performance. Consequently, if you were allowed to use just one selection test, a cognitive ability test would be the one to use.[32] (In practice, though, companies use a battery of different tests because doing so leads to much more accurate selection decisions.)

Biographical data, or **biodata,** are extensive surveys that ask applicants questions about their personal backgrounds and life experiences. The basic idea behind biodata is that past behavior (personal background and life experience) is the best predictor of future behavior. Most biodata questionnaires have over 100 items that gather information about habits and attitudes, health, interpersonal relations, money, what it was like growing up in your family (parents, siblings, childhood years, teen years), personal habits, current home (spouse, children), hobbies, education and training, values, preferences, and work.[33] In general, biodata are very good predictors of future job performance, especially in entry-level jobs.

You may have noticed that some of the information requested in biodata surveys is related to those topics employers should avoid in applications, interviews, or other parts of the selection process. This information can be requested in biodata questionnaires provided that the company can demonstrate that the information is job-related (i.e., valid) and does not result in adverse impact against protected groups of job applicants. Biodata surveys should be validated and tested for adverse impact before they are used to make selection decisions.[34]

Work sample tests, also called *performance tests*, require applicants to perform tasks that are actually done on the job. So, unlike specific ability, cognitive ability, biographical data, and personality tests, which are indirect predictors of job performance, work sample tests directly measure job applicants' capability to do the job. For example, a computer-based work sample test has applicants assume the role of a real estate agent who must decide how to interact with virtual clients in a gamelike scenario. And, as in real life, the clients can be frustrating, confusing, demanding, or indecisive. In one situation, the wife loves the house but the husband hates it. The applicants, just like actual real estate agents, must demonstrate what they would do in these realistic situations.[35] This work sample simulation gives real estate companies direct evidence of whether applicants can do the job if they are hired. Work sample tests are generally very good at predicting future job performance; however, they can be expensive to administer and can be used for only one kind of job. For example, an auto dealership could not use a work sample test for mechanics as a selection test for sales representatives.

Assessment centers use a series of job-specific simulations that are graded by multiple trained observers to determine applicants' ability to perform managerial work. Unlike the previously described selection tests that are commonly used for specific jobs or entry-level jobs, assessment centers are most often used to select applicants who have high potential to be good managers. Assessment centers often last two to five days and require participants to complete a number of tests and exercises that simulate managerial work.

Some of the more common assessment center exercises are in-basket exercises, role-plays, small-group presentations, and leaderless group discussions. An *in-basket exercise* is a paper-and-pencil test in which an applicant is given a manager's in-basket containing memos, phone messages, organizational policies, and other communications normally received by and available to managers. Applicants have a limited time to read through the in-basket, prioritize the items, and decide how to deal with each item. Experienced managers then score the applicants' decisions and recommendations. Exhibit 11.5 shows an item that could be used in an assessment center for evaluating applicants for a job as a store manager.

Exhibit 11.5

In-Basket Item for an Assessment Center for Store Managers

February 28
Sam & Dave's Discount Warehouse
Orange, California

Dear Store Manager,

Last week, my children and I were shopping in your store. After doing our grocery shopping, we stopped in the electronics department and asked the clerk, whose name is Donald Block, to help us find a copy of the latest version of the Madden NFL video game. Mr. Block was rude, unhelpful, and told us to find it for ourselves as he was busy.

I've been a loyal customer for over six years and expect you to immediately do something about Mr. Block's behavior. If you don't, I'll start doing my shopping somewhere else.

Sincerely,
Margaret Quinlan

Source: Adapted from N. W. Schmitt and R. J. Klimoski, *Research Methods in Human Resource Management* (Mason, OH: South-Western 1991).

Work sample tests tests that require applicants to perform tasks that are actually done on the job

Assessment centers a series of managerial simulations, graded by trained observers, that are used to determine applicants' capability for managerial work

© Radius Images/Jupiterimages

In a *leaderless group discussion,* another common assessment center exercise, a group of six applicants is given approximately two hours to solve a problem, but no one is put in charge (hence the name "leaderless" group discussion). Trained observers watch and score each participant on the extent to which he or she facilitates discussion, listens, leads, persuades, and works well with others.

Are tests perfect predictors of job performance? No, they aren't. Some people who do well on selection tests will do poorly in their jobs. Likewise, some people who do poorly on selection tests (and therefore weren't hired) would have been very good performers. Nonetheless, valid tests will minimize these selection errors (hiring people who should not have been hired and not hiring people who should have been hired) while maximizing correct selection decisions (hiring people who should have been hired and not hiring people who should not have been hired). In short, tests increase the chances that you'll hire the right person for the job, that is, someone who turns out to be a good performer. So, although tests aren't perfect, almost nothing predicts future job performance as well as the selection tests discussed here.

3.4 Interviews

In **interviews,** company representatives ask job applicants job-related questions to determine whether they are qualified for the job. Interviews are probably the most frequently used and relied upon selection device. There are several basic kinds of interviews: unstructured, structured, and semistructured.

In **unstructured interviews,** interviewers are free to ask applicants anything they want, and studies show that they do. Because interviewers often disagree about which questions should be asked during interviews, different interviewers tend to ask applicants very different questions.[36] Furthermore, individual interviewers even seem to have a tough time asking the same questions from one interview to the next. This high level of inconsistency lowers the validity of unstructured interviews as a selection device because

comparing applicant responses can be difficult. As a result, unstructured interviews are about half as accurate as structured interviews at predicting which job applicants should be hired.

By contrast, with **structured interviews,** standardized interview questions are prepared ahead of time so that all applicants are asked the same job-related questions.[37] Structuring interviews also ensures that interviewers ask only for important, job-related information. Not only are the accuracy, usefulness, and validity of the interview improved, but the chances that interviewers will ask questions about topics that violate employment laws (the "Don't Ask!" box on page 201 has a list of these topics) are reduced.

The primary advantage of structured interviews is that comparing applicants is much easier because they are all asked the same questions. Structured interviews typically contain four types of questions: situational, behavioral, background, and job-knowledge. Situational questions ask applicants how they would respond in a hypothetical situation (e.g., "What would you do if . . . ?"). These questions are more appropriate for hiring new graduates, as they are unlikely to have encountered real work situations because of their

Interviews a selection tool in which company representatives ask job applicants job-related questions to determine whether they are qualified for the job

Unstructured interviews interviews in which interviewers are free to ask the applicants anything they want

Structured interviews interviews in which all applicants are asked the same set of standardized questions, usually including situational, behavioral, background, and job-knowledge questions

Finding the Perfect Mate

While it may not be healthy to be married to your job, the process of finding one can often feel like dating. Sometimes it even looks like dating. An increasing number of retiring baby boomers and a shortage of skilled workers means that positions need to be filled more quickly, and some companies are turning to speed dating as a new interview strategy. Up to 200 candidates can appear for a daylong interviewing event, where they will spend five minutes each with various recruiters. Ill-fitting candidates can be eliminated early in the process, recruiters can easily remember candidates without searching through notes, and decisions are made more quickly.

Source: S. E. Needleman, "Speed Interviewing Grows as Skills Shortage Looms," *The Wall Street Journal* (6 November 2007) B15.

Exhibit 11.6

Guidelines for Conducting Effective Structured Interviews

Interview Stage	What to Do
 **Planning the Interview**	• Identify and define the knowledge, skills, abilities, and other (KSAO) characteristics needed for successful job performance. • For each essential KSAO, develop key behavioral questions that will elicit examples of past accomplishments, activities, and performance. • For each KSAO, develop a list of things to look for in the applicant's responses to key questions.
 **Conducting the Interview**	• Create a relaxed, nonstressful interview atmosphere. • Review the applicant's application form, résumé, and other information. • Allocate enough time to complete the interview without interruption. • Put the applicant at ease; don't jump right into heavy questioning. • Tell the applicant what to expect. Explain the interview process. • Obtain job-related information from the applicant by asking those questions prepared for each KSAO. • Describe the job and the organization to the applicant. Applicants need adequate information to make a selection decision about the organization.
 **After the Interview**	• Immediately after the interview, review your notes and make sure they are complete. • Evaluate the applicant on each essential KSAO. • Determine each applicant's probability of success and make a hiring decision.

Source: B. M. Farrell, "The Art and Science of Employment Interviews," *Personnel Journal* 65 (1986): 91–94.

limited experience. Behavioral questions ask applicants what they did in previous jobs that is similar to what is required for the job for which they are applying (e.g., "In your previous jobs, tell me about . . . "). These questions are more appropriate for hiring experienced individuals. Background questions ask applicants about their work experience, education, and other qualifications (e.g., "Tell me about the training you received at . . . "). Finally, job-knowledge questions ask applicants to demonstrate their job knowledge (e.g., for nurses, "Give me an example of a time when one of your patients had a severe reaction to a medication. How did you handle it?").[38]

Semistructured interviews are in between structured and unstructured interviews. A major part of the semistructured interview (perhaps as much as 80 percent) is based on structured questions, but some time is set aside for unstructured interviewing to allow the interviewer to probe into ambiguous or missing information uncovered during the structured portion of the interview.

How well do interviews predict future job performance? Contrary to what you've probably heard, recent evidence indicates that even unstructured interviews do a fairly good job.[39] When conducted properly, however, structured interviews can lead to much more accurate hiring decisions than unstructured interviews. In some cases, the validity of structured interviews can rival that of cognitive ability tests. But even more important, because interviews are especially good at assessing applicants' interpersonal skills, they work particularly well with cognitive ability tests. The combination (i.e., smart people who work well in conjunction with others) leads to even better selection decisions than using either alone.[40] Exhibit 11.6 provides a set of guidelines for conducting effective structured employment interviews.

Developing Qualified Workers

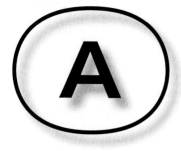

According to the American Society for Training and Development, a typical investment in employee training increases productivity by an average of 17 percent, reduces employee turnover, and makes companies more profitable.[41] Giving employees the knowledge and skills they need to improve their performance is just the first step in developing employees, however. The second step, and not enough companies do this, is giving employees formal feedback about their actual job performance.

After reading the next two sections, you should be able to

4 describe how to determine training needs and select the appropriate training methods.

5 discuss how to use performance appraisal to give meaningful performance feedback.

4 Training

Training means providing opportunities for employees to develop the job-specific skills, experience, and knowledge they need to do their jobs or improve their performance. American companies spend more than $60 billion a year on training. To make sure those training dollars are well spent, companies need to **4.1 determine specific training needs, 4.2 select appropriate training methods, and 4.3 evaluate training.**

4.1 Determining Training Needs

Training developing the skills, experience, and knowledge employees need to perform their jobs or improve their performance

Needs assessment the process of identifying and prioritizing the learning needs of employees

Needs assessment is the process of identifying and prioritizing the learning needs of employees. Needs assessments can be conducted by identifying performance deficiencies, listening to customer complaints, surveying employees and managers, or formally testing employees' skills and knowledge.

Note that training should never be conducted without first performing a needs assessment. Sometimes training isn't needed at all or isn't needed for all employees. Unfortunately, however, many organizations simply require all employees to attend training whether they need to or not. As a result, employees who aren't interested or don't need the training may react negatively during or after training. Likewise, employees who should be sent for training but aren't may also react negatively. Consequently, a needs assessment is an important tool for deciding who should or should not attend training. In fact, employment law restricts employers from discriminating on the basis of age, sex, race, color, religion, national origin, or disability when selecting training participants. Just like hiring decisions, the selection of training participants should be based on job-related information.

4.2 Training Methods

Assume that you're a training director for a major oil company and that you're in charge of making sure all employees know to respond effectively in case of an oil spill.[42] Exhibit 11.7 lists a number of training methods you could use: films and videos, lectures, planned readings, case studies, coaching and mentoring, group discussions, on-the-job training, role-playing, simulations and games, vestibule training, and computer-based learning. Which method would be best?

To choose the best method, you should consider a number of factors such as the number of people to be trained, the cost of training, and the objectives of the training. For instance, if the training objective is to impart information or knowledge to trainees, then you should use films and videos, lectures, and planned readings. In our example, trainees might read a manual or attend a lecture about how to seal a shoreline to keep it from being affected by the spill.

© Natalie Fobes/Stone/Getty Images

Exhibit 11.7

Training Objectives and Methods

TRAINING OBJECTIVE	TRAINING METHODS
Impart Information and Knowledge	• *Films and videos*. Films and videos share information, illustrate problems and solutions, and effectively hold trainees' attention. • *Lectures*. Trainees listen to instructors' oral presentations. • *Planned readings*. Trainees read about concepts or ideas before attending training.
Develop Analytical and Problem-Solving Skills	• *Case studies*. Cases are analyzed and discussed in small groups. The cases present a specific problem or decision, and trainees develop methods for solving the problem or making the decision. • *Coaching and mentoring*. Coaching and mentoring of trainees by managers involves informal advice, suggestions, and guidance. This method is helpful for reinforcing other kinds of training and for trainees who benefit from support and personal encouragement. • *Group discussions*. Small groups of trainees actively discuss specific topics. The instructor may perform the role of discussion leader.
Practice, Learn, or Change Job Behaviors	• *On-the-job training (OJT)*. New employees are assigned to experienced employees. The trainee learns by watching the experienced employee perform the job and eventually by working alongside the experienced employee. Gradually, the trainee is left on his or her own to perform the job. • *Role-playing*. Trainees assume job-related roles and practice new behaviors by acting out what they would do in job-related situations. • *Simulations and games*. Experiential exercises place trainees in realistic job-related situations and give them the opportunity to experience a job-related condition in a relatively low-cost setting. The trainee benefits from hands-on experience before actually performing the job, where mistakes may be more costly. • *Vestibule training*. Procedures and equipment similar to those used in the actual job are set up in a special area called a "vestibule." The trainee is then taught how to perform the job at his or her own pace without disrupting the actual flow of work, making costly mistakes, or exposing the trainee and others to dangerous conditions.
Impart Information and Knowledge; Develop Analytical and Problem-Solving Skills; and Practice, Learn, or Change Job Behaviors	• *Computer-based learning*. Interactive videos, software, CD-ROMs, personal computers, teleconferencing, and the Internet may be combined to present multimedia-based training.

Source: A. Fowler, "How to Decide on Training Methods," *People Management* 25, no. 1 (1995): 36.

If developing analytical and problem-solving skills is the objective, then use case studies, coaching and mentoring, and group discussions. In our example, trainees might view a video documenting how a team handled exposure to hazardous substances, talk with first responders, and discuss what they would do in a similar situation.

If practicing, learning, or changing job behaviors is the objective, then use on-the-job training, role-playing, simulations and games, and vestibule training. In our example, trainees might participate in a mock shoreline cleanup to learn what do in the event oil comes to shore. This simulation could take place on an actual shoreline or on a video-game-like virtual shoreline.

If training is supposed to meet more than one of these objectives, then your best choice may be to combine one of the previous methods with computer-based training.

These days, many companies are adopting Internet training, or "e-learning." E-learning can offer several advantages. Because employees don't need to leave their jobs, travel costs are greatly reduced. Also, because employees can take training modules when it is convenient (in other words, they don't have to fall behind at their jobs to attend week-long training courses), workplace productivity should increase and employee stress should decrease. Finally, if the company's technology infrastructure can support it, e-learning can be much faster than traditional training methods.

There are, however, several disadvantages to e-learning. First, despite its increasing popularity, it's not always the appropriate training method. E-learning can be a good way to impart information, but it isn't always as effective for changing job behaviors or developing problem-solving and analytical skills. Second, e-learning requires a significant investment in computers and high-speed Internet and network connections for all employees. Finally, though e-learning can be faster, many employees find it so boring and unengaging that they may choose to do their jobs rather than complete e-learning courses when sitting alone at their desks. E-learning may become more interesting, however, as more companies incorporate gamelike features such as avatars and competition into their e-learning courses.

Dow Chemical now has the ability to provide electronic learning or training to all 40,000 employees in 70 countries through its Learn@dow.now Web-based training system.[43] Likewise, Cisco Systems offers 4,500 e-learning courses to its managers and employees.[44] And British Telecom used an avatar-based course to train 4,500 salespeople in just over a month. Traditional classroom training would have cost twice as much and taken twice as long to deliver.[45] These companies all determined that the advantages of e-learning far outnumbered the disadvantages.

4.3 Evaluating Training

After selecting a training method and conducting the training, the last step is to evaluate the training. Training can be evaluated in four ways: on *reactions* (how satisfied trainees were with the program), on *learning* (how much employees improved their knowledge or skills), on *behavior* (how much employees actually changed their on-the-job behavior because of training), or on *results* (how much training improved job performance, such as increased sales or quality, or decreased costs).[46] In general,

Performance appraisal
the process of assessing how well employees are doing their jobs

if done well, training provides meaningful benefits for most companies. For example, a study by the American Society for Training and Development shows that a training budget as small as $680 per employee can increase a company's total return on investment by 6 percent.[47]

5 Performance Appraisal

Performance appraisal is the process of assessing how well employees are doing their jobs. Most employees and managers intensely dislike the performance appraisal process. One manager says "I hate annual performance reviews. I hated them when I used to get them, and I hate them now that I give them. If I had to choose between performance reviews and paper cuts, I'd take paper cuts every time. I'd even take razor burns and the sound of fingernails on a blackboard."[48] Unfortunately, attitudes like this are all too common. In fact, 70 percent of employees are dissatisfied with the performance appraisal process in their companies. Likewise, according to the Society for Human Resource Management, 90 percent of human resource managers are dissatisfied with the performance appraisal systems used by their companies.[49]

*Let's explore how companies can avoid some of these problems with performance appraisals by **5.1 accurately measuring job performance** and **5.2 effectively sharing performance feedback with employees**.*

5.1 Accurately Measuring Job Performance

Workers often have strong doubts about the accuracy of their performance appraisals—and they may be right. For example, it's widely known that assessors are prone

Common Rating Errors

Central tendency error occurs when assessors rate all workers as average or in the middle of the scale. Halo error occurs when assessors rate a particular worker as performing at the same level (good, bad, or average) in all parts of his or her job. Leniency error occurs when assessors rate all workers as performing particularly well.

to errors when rating worker performance. One of the reasons that managers make these errors is that they often don't spend enough time gathering or reviewing performance data. What can be done to minimize rating errors and improve the accuracy with which job performance is measured? In general, two approaches have been used: improving performance appraisal measures themselves and training performance raters to be more accurate.

One of the ways companies try to improve performance appraisal measures is to use as many objective performance measures as possible. **Objective performance measures** are measures of performance that are easily and directly counted or quantified. Common objective performance measures include output, scrap, waste, sales, customer complaints, and rejection rates.

But when objective performance measures aren't available, and frequently they aren't, subjective performance measures have to be used instead. Subjective performance measures require that someone judge or assess a worker's performance. The most common kind of subjective performance measure is the Graphic Rating Scale (GRS) shown in Exhibit 11.8. Graphic rating scales are most widely used because they are easy to construct, but they are very susceptible to rating errors.

A popular alternative to graphic rating scales is the **Behavior Observation Scale (BOS)**. BOS requires raters to rate the frequency with which workers perform specific behaviors representative of the job dimensions that are critical to successful job performance. Exhibit 11.8 shows a BOS for two important job dimensions for a retail salesperson: customer service and money handling. Notice that each dimension lists several specific behaviors characteristic of a worker who excels in that dimension of job performance. (Normally, the scale would list seven to twelve items per dimension, not three as in the exhibit.) Notice also that the behaviors are good behaviors, meaning they indicate good performance, and the rater is asked to judge how frequently an employee engaged in those good behaviors. The logic behind the BOS is that better performers engage in good behaviors more often.

Not only do BOSs work well for rating critical dimensions of performance, but studies also show that managers strongly prefer BOSs for giving performance feedback;

Exhibit 11.8

Subjective Performance Appraisal Scales

Graphic Rating Scale

	Very poor	Poor	Average	Good	Very good
Example 1: Quality of work performed is	1	2	3	4	5

	Very poor (20% errors)	Poor (15% errors)	Average (10% errors)	Good (5% errors)	Very good (less than 5% errors)
Example 2: Quality of work performed is	1	2	3	4	5

Behavioral Observation Scale

Dimension: Customer Service

	Almost Never				Almost Always
1. Greets customers with a smile and a "hello."	1	2	3	4	5
2. Calls other stores to help customers find merchandise that is not in stock.	1	2	3	4	5
3. Promptly handles customer concerns and complaints.	1	2	3	4	5

Dimension: Money Handling

	Almost Never				Almost Always
1. Accurately makes change from customer transactions.	1	2	3	4	5
2. Accounts balance at the end of the day, no shortages or surpluses.	1	2	3	4	5
3. Accurately records transactions in computer system.	1	2	3	4	5

accurately differentiating between poor, average, and good workers; identifying training needs; and accurately measuring performance. And in response to the statement, "If I were defending a company, this rating format would be an asset to my case," attorneys strongly preferred BOSs over other kinds of subjective performance appraisal scales.[50]

The second approach to improving the measurement of workers' job performance

Objective performance measures measures of job performance that are easily and directly counted or quantified

Behavioral observation scales (BOSs) rating scales that indicate the frequency with which workers perform specific behaviors that are representative of the job dimensions critical to successful job performance is **rater training**. The most effective is frame-of-reference training in which a group of trainees learns how to do performance appraisals by watching a videotape of an employee at work. Next, they evaluate the performance of the person in the videotape. A trainer (i.e., subject matter expert) then shares his or her evaluations, and trainees' evaluations are compared with the expert's. The expert then explains rationales behind his or her evaluations. This process is repeated until the difference in evaluations given by trainees and evaluations by the expert are minimized. The underlying logic behind the frame-of-reference training is that by adopting the frame of reference used by an expert, trainees will be able to accurately observe, judge, and use the scale to evaluate performance of others.[51]

5.2 Sharing Performance Feedback

After gathering accurate performance data, the next step is to share performance feedback with employees. Unfortunately, even when performance appraisal ratings are accurate, the appraisal process often breaks down at the feedback stage. Employees become defensive and dislike hearing any negative assessments of their work, no matter how small. Managers become defensive, too, and dislike giving appraisal feedback as much as employees dislike receiving it.

What can be done to overcome the inherent difficulties in performance appraisal feedback sessions? Since performance appraisal ratings have traditionally been the judgments of just one person, the boss, one possibility is to use **360-degree feedback.** In this approach, feedback comes from four sources: the boss, subordinates, peers and coworkers, and the employees themselves. The data, which are obtained anonymously (except for the boss'), are compiled into a feedback report comparing the employee's self-ratings with those of the boss, subordinates, and peers and coworkers. Usually, a consultant or human resource specialist discusses the results with the employee. The advantage of 360-degree programs is that negative feedback ("You don't listen") is often more credible when it comes from several people.

Herbert Meyer, who has been studying performance appraisal feedback for more than 30 years, recommends a list of topics for discussion in performance appraisal feedback sessions listed in Exhibit 11.9.[52]

Rater training training performance appraisal raters in how to avoid rating errors and increase rating accuracy

360-degree feedback a performance appraisal process in which feedback is obtained from the boss, subordinates, peers and coworkers, and the employees themselves

Exhibit 11.9

What to Discuss in a Performance Appraisal Feedback Session

- ✔ Overall progress—an analysis of accomplishments and shortcomings.
- ✔ Problems encountered in meeting job requirements.
- ✔ Opportunities to improve performance.
- ✔ Long-range plans and opportunities—for the job and for the individual's career.
- ✔ General discussion of possible plans and goals for the coming year.

Source: H. H. Meyer, "A Solution to the Performance Appraisal Feedback Enigma," *Academy of Management Executive* 5, no. 1 (1991): 68–76.

How these topics are discussed in a review session is important for its success. Managers can do three different things to make performance reviews as comfortable and productive as possible. First, managers should separate developmental feedback, which is designed to improve future performance, from administrative feedback, which is used as a reward for past performance, such as for raises. When managers give developmental feedback, they're acting as coaches, but when they give administrative feedback, they're acting as judges. These roles, coaches and judges, are clearly incompatible. As coaches, managers are encouraging, pointing out opportunities for growth and improvement, and employees are typically open and receptive to feedback. But as judges, managers are evaluative, and employees are typically defensive and closed to feedback.

Second, Meyer suggests that performance appraisal feedback sessions be based on self-appraisals, in which employees carefully assess their own strengths, weaknesses, successes, and failures in writing. Because employees play an active role in the review of their performance, managers can be coaches rather than judges. Also, because the focus is on future goals and development, both employees and managers are likely to be more satisfied with the process and more committed to future plans and changes. And, because the focus is on development and not administrative assessment, studies show that self-appraisals lead to more candid self-assessments than traditional supervisory reviews.[53] See Exhibit 11.9 for a list of topics that Meyer recommends for discussion in performance appraisal feedback sessions.

Finally, what people do with the performance feedback they receive really matters. A study of 1,361 senior managers found that managers who reviewed their 360-degree feedback with an executive coach (hired by the company) were more likely to set specific goals for improvement, ask their bosses for ways to improve, and subsequently improve their performance.[54]

Managers need to receive feedback as well as give it. Not only does HCL Technologies, an outsourcer of technology services, have team members rate their bosses, but the evaluations are made public on the company's intranet to hold top managers accountable. This was the *boss'* idea.[55] A five-year study of 252 managers found that their performance improved dramatically if they met with their subordinates to discuss their 360-degree feedback ("You don't listen") and how they were going to address it ("I'll restate what others have said before stating my opinion"). Performance was dramatically lower for managers who never discussed their 360-degree feedback with subordinates and for managers who did not routinely do so (some managers did not review their 360-degree feedback with subordinates each year of the study). Why is discussing 360-degree feedback with subordinates so effective? These discussions help managers better understand their weaknesses, force them to develop a plan to improve, and demonstrate to the subordinates the managers' public commitment to improving.[56] In short, it helps to have people discuss their performance feedback with others, but it particularly helps to have them discuss their feedback with the people who provided it.

Keeping Qualified Workers

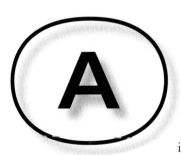

After Motorola's mobile devices division lost $1.2 billion in 2007, the company decided to split in half. In such times of transition and uncertainty, it is easy for a company to lose valuable employees as job security decreases and people seek opportunities elsewhere. In an effort to retain its human resources, Motorola established an incentive program which offered bonuses to employees in key roles who remained on the job and to their supervisors for keeping them there.[57]

After reading the next section, you should be able to

6   describe basic compensation strategies and discuss the four kinds of employee separations.

6 Compensation and Employee Separation

Compensation includes both the financial and the nonfinancial rewards that organizations give employees in exchange for their work. **Employee separation** is a broad term covering the loss of an employee for any reason. *Involuntary separation* occurs when employers decide to terminate or lay off employees. *Voluntary separation* occurs when employees decide to quit or retire. Because employee separations affect recruiting, selection, training, and compensation, organizations should forecast the number of employees they expect to lose through terminations, layoffs, turnover, or retirements when doing human resource planning.

Let's learn more about compensation and employee separation by examining the **6.1 compensation decisions that managers must make** *as well as* **6.2 terminations, 6.3 downsizing, 6.4 retirements,** *and* **6.5 turnover.**

6.1 Compensation Decisions

There are three basic kinds of compensation decisions: pay level, pay variability, and pay structure.[58]

Pay-level decisions are decisions about whether to pay workers at a level that is below, above, or at current market wages. Companies use job evaluation to set their pay structures. **Job evaluation** determines

Compensation the financial and nonfinancial rewards that organizations give employees in exchange for their work

Employee separation the voluntary or involuntary loss of an employee

Job evaluation a process that determines the worth of each job in a company by evaluating the market value of the knowledge, skills, and requirements needed to perform it

the worth of each job by determining the market value of the knowledge, skills, and requirements needed to perform it. After conducting a job evaluation, most companies try to pay the going rate, meaning the current market wage. There are always companies, however, whose financial situation causes them to pay considerably less than current market wages. The child-care industry, for example, has chronic difficulties filling jobs because it pays well below market wages. While a director of a childcare center in Vermont may make up to $25 an hour, teachers make only $9-11 an hour.[59] According to the American Federation of Teachers, the average annual wage for early childcare workers is $18,820, and hourly wages have increased only 39 cents in the last 25 years.[60]

Some companies choose to pay above-average wages to attract and keep employees. *Above-market wages* can attract a larger, more qualified pool of job applicants, increase the rate of job acceptance, decrease the time it takes to fill positions, and increase the time that employees stay.[61]

Pay-variability decisions concern the extent to which employees' pay varies with individual and organizational performance. Linking pay to performance is intended to increase employee motivation, effort, and job performance. Piecework, sales commissions, profit sharing, employee stock ownership plans, and stock options are common pay-variability options. For instance, under **piecework** pay plans, employees are paid a set rate for each item produced up to some standard (e.g., 35 cents per item produced for output up to 100 units per day). Once productivity exceeds the standard, employees are paid a set amount for each unit of output over the standard (e.g., 45 cents for each unit above 100 units). Under a sales **commission** plan, salespeople are paid a percentage of the purchase price of items they sell. The more they sell, the more they earn.

Because pay plans such as piecework and commissions are based on individual performance, they can reduce the incentive that people have to work together. Therefore, companies also use group incentives (dis-

Piecework a compensation system in which employees are paid a set rate for each item they produce

Commission a compensation system in which employees earn a percentage of each sale they make

Profit sharing a compensation system in which a company pays a percentage of its profits to employees in addition to their regular compensation

Employee stock ownership plan (ESOP) a compensation system that awards employees shares of company stock in addition to their regular compensation

How Do Options Work?

Options work like this. Let's say that you are awarded the right (or option) to buy 100 shares of stock from the company for $5 a share. If the company's stock price rises to $15 a share, you can exercise your options and make $1,000. When you exercise your options, you pay the company $500 (100 shares at $5 a share), but because the stock is selling for $15 in the stock market, you can sell your 100 shares for $1,500 and make $1,000. Of course, as the company's profits and share values increase, stock options become even more valuable to employees. Stock options have no value, however, if the company's stock falls below the option "grant price," the price at which the options have been issued to you. For instance, the options you have on 100 shares of stock with a grant price of $5 aren't going to do you a lot of good if the company's stock is worth $2.50. Why exercise your stock options and pay $5 a share for stock that sells for $2.50 a share in the stock market? (Stock options are said to be "underwater" when the grant price is lower than the market price.)

© Stephen Chernin/Getty Images

cussed in Chapter 10) and organizational incentives such as profit sharing, employee stock ownership plans, and stock options to encourage teamwork and cooperation.

With **profit sharing** employees receive a portion of the organization's profits over and above their regular compensation. The more profitable the company, the more profit is shared. Employees of Delta Airlines share profits on 5.5% of eligible earnings. Delta paid out $158 million to its employees in 2007.[62]

Employee stock ownership plans (ESOPs) compensate employees by awarding them shares of the company stock in addition to their regular compensation. By contrast, **stock options** give employees the right to purchase shares of stock at a set price. Proponents of stock options argue that this gives employees and managers a strong incentive to work hard to make the company successful. If they do, the company's profits and stock price increase, and their stock options increase in value. If they don't, profits stagnate or turn into losses, and their stock options decrease in value or become worthless.

The incentive has to be more than just a piece of paper, however. At Van Meter Industrial, based in Cedar Rapids, Iowa, some employees didn't know what stock was, let alone care about their ESOP program, until the company created a committee of employees to educate their peers about how the program works. Workers now take a vested interest in what they can do to save the company money on a daily basis. The company holds an annual "guess the value" contest for employees with a cash prize for the closest guess. Although Van Meter's stock value was barely keeping up with inflation before the program, it went up 78% after the program was implemented.[63]

Pay-structure decisions are concerned with internal pay distributions, meaning the extent to which people in the company receive very different levels of pay.[64] With *hierarchical pay structures,* there are big differences from one pay level to another. The highest pay levels are for people near the top of the pay distribution. The basic idea behind hierarchical pay structures is that large differences in pay between jobs or organizational levels should motivate people to work harder to obtain those higher-paying jobs. Many publicly owned companies have hierarchical pay structures by virtue of the huge amounts they pay their top managers and CEOs. For example, the average CEO now makes 364 times as much as the average worker, down from 525 times the pay of average workers just eight years ago. But with CEO pay packages averaging $18.8 million per year and average workers earning just $36,140, the difference is still incredible and can have a significant detrimental impact on employee morale.[65]

By contrast, *compressed pay structures* typically have fewer pay levels and smaller differences in pay between levels. Pay is less dispersed and more similar across jobs in the company. The basic idea behind compressed pay structures is that similar pay levels should lead to higher levels of cooperation, feelings of fairness and a common purpose, and better group and team performance.

So should companies choose hierarchical or compressed pay structures? The evidence isn't straightforward, but studies seem to indicate that there are significant problems with the hierarchical approach. The most damaging finding is that there appears to be little link between organizational performance and the pay of top managers.[66] Furthermore, studies of professional athletes indicate that hierarchical pay structures (e.g., paying superstars 40 to 50 times more than the lowest-paid athlete on the team) hurt the performance of teams and individual players.[67] Likewise, managers are twice as likely to quit their jobs when their companies have very strong hierarchical pay structures (i.e., when they're paid dramatically less than the people above them).[68] For now, it seems that hierarchical pay structures work best for independent work, where it's easy to determine the contributions of individual performers and little coordination with others is needed to get the job done. In other words, hierarchical pay structures work best when clear links can be drawn between individual performance and individual rewards. By contrast, compressed pay structures, in which everyone receives similar pay, seem to work best for interdependent work, which requires employees to work together. Some companies are pursuing a middle ground: combining hierarchical and compressed pay structures by giving ordinary workers the chance to earn more through ESOPs, stock options, and profit sharing.

6.2 Terminating Employees

Hopefully, the words "You're fired!" have never been directed at you. Lots of people hear them, however, as more than 400,000 people a year get fired from their jobs. Getting fired is a terrible thing, but many managers make it even worse by bungling the firing process, needlessly provoking the person who was fired and unintentionally inviting lawsuits. Though firing is never pleasant (and managers hate firings nearly as much as employees do), managers can do several things to minimize the problems inherent in firing employees.

First, in most situations, firing should not be the first option. Instead, employees should be given a chance to change their behavior. When

Stock options a compensation system that gives employees the right to purchase shares of stock at a set price, even if the value of the stock increases above that price

© Mark Von Holden/FilmMagic/Getty Images

problems arise, employees should have ample warning and must be specifically informed as to the nature and seriousness of the trouble they're in. After being notified, they should be given sufficient time to change. If the problems continue, the employees should again be counseled about their job performance, what could be done to improve it, and the possible consequences if things don't change (e.g., written reprimand, suspension without pay, or firing). Sometimes this is enough to solve the problem. If the problem isn't corrected after several rounds of warnings and discussions, however, the employee may be terminated.[69]

Second, employees should be fired only for a good reason. Employers used to hire and fire employees under the legal principle of employment at will, which allowed them to fire employees for a good reason, a bad reason, or no reason at all. (Employees could also quit for a good reason, a bad reason, or no reason whenever they desired.) As employees began contesting their firings in court, however, the principle of wrongful discharge emerged. **Wrongful discharge** is a legal doctrine that requires employers to have a job-related reason to terminate employees. In other words, like other major human resource decisions, termination decisions should be made on the basis of job-related factors, such as violating company rules or consistently poor performance.

6.3 Downsizing

Downsizing is the planned elimination of jobs in a company. Whether it's because of cost cutting, declining market share, previous overaggressive hiring and growth, or outsourcing, companies typically eliminate 1.5 million jobs a year.[70] Two-thirds of companies that downsize will downsize a second time within a year.

Does downsizing work? In theory, downsizing is supposed to lead to higher productivity and profits, better stock performance, and increased organizational flexibility. However, numerous studies demonstrate that it doesn't. For instance, a fifteen year study of downsizing found that downsizing 10 percent of a company's work force produced only a 1.5 percent decrease in costs; that firms that downsized in-

Wrongful discharge a legal doctrine that requires employers to have a job-related reason to terminate employees

Downsizing the planned elimination of jobs in a company

Outplacement services employment-counseling services offered to employees who are losing their jobs because of downsizing

Early retirement incentive programs (ERIPs) programs that offer financial benefits to employees to encourage them to retire early

creased their stock price by only 4.7 percent over three years, compared with 34.3 percent for firms that didn't; and that profitability and productivity were generally not improved by downsizing.[71] Downsizing can also result in the loss of skilled workers that would be expensive to replace when the company grows again.[72] These results make it clear that the best strategy is to conduct effective human resource planning and avoid downsizing altogether. Indeed, downsizing should always be a last resort.

If companies do find themselves in financial or strategic situations where downsizing is required for survival, however, they should train managers in how to break the news to downsized employees, have senior managers explain in detail why downsizing is necessary, and time the announcement so that employees hear it from the company and not from other sources such as TV or newspaper reports.[73] Finally, companies should do everything they can to help downsized employees find other jobs. One of the best ways to do this is to use **outplacement services** that provide employment-counseling services for employees faced with downsizing. Outplacement services often include advice and training in preparing résumés, getting ready for job interviews, and even identifying job opportunities in other companies.

6.4 Retirement

Early retirement incentive programs (ERIPs) offer financial benefits to employees to encourage them to retire early. Companies use ERIPs to reduce the number of employees in the organization, to lower costs by eliminating positions after employees retire, to lower costs by replacing high-paid retirees with lower-paid, less-experienced employees, or to create openings and job opportunities for people inside the company.

Although ERIPs can save companies money, they can pose a big problem for managers if they fail to accurately predict which employees—the good performers or the poor performers—and how many will retire early. Consultant Ron Nicol says, "The thing that doesn't work is just asking for volunteers. You get the wrong volunteers. Some of your best people will feel they can get a job anywhere. Or you have people who are close to retirement and are a real asset to the company."[74] When Ameritech Corporation (now part of AT&T) offered an ERIP, it carefully identified the number of employees near retirement age and estimated that 5,000 to 6,000 of its 48,000 employees would take advantage of the program. Instead, nearly 22,000 employees accepted the ERIP offer and applied for early retirement![75]

Because of the problems associated with ERIPs, many companies are now offering **phased retirement,** in which employees transition to retirement by working reduced hours over a period of time before completely retiring. The advantage for employees is that they have more free time but continue to earn salaries and benefits without changing companies or careers. The advantage for companies is that it allows them to reduce salaries as well as hiring and training costs and retain experienced, valuable workers.[76]

6.5 Employee Turnover

Employee turnover is the loss of employees who voluntarily choose to leave the company. In general, most companies try to keep the rate of employee turnover low to reduce recruiting, hiring, training, and replacement costs. Not all kinds of employee turnover are bad for organizations, however. In fact, some turnover can actually be good. For instance, **functional turnover** is the loss of poor-performing employees who choose to leave the organization.[77] Functional turnover gives the organization a chance to replace poor performers with better workers. In fact, one study found that simply replacing poor-performing leavers with average workers would increase the revenues produced by retail salespeople in an upscale department store by $112,000 per person per year.[78] By contrast, **dysfunctional turnover,** the loss of high performers who choose to leave, is a costly loss to the organization.

Employee turnover should be carefully analyzed to determine whether good or poor performers are choosing to leave the organization. If the company is losing too many high performers, managers should determine the reasons and find ways to reduce the loss of valuable employees. The company may have to raise salary levels, offer enhanced benefits, or improve working conditions to retain skilled workers. One of the best ways to influence functional and dysfunctional turnover is to link pay directly to performance. A study of four sales forces found that when pay was strongly linked to performance via sales commissions and bonuses, poor performers were much more likely to leave (i.e., functional turnover). By contrast, poor performers were much more likely to stay when paid large, guaranteed monthly salaries and small sales commissions and bonuses.[79]

Phased retirement employees transition to retirement by working reduced hours over a period of time before completely retiring

Employee turnover loss of employees who voluntarily choose to leave the company

Functional turnover loss of poor-performing employees who voluntarily choose to leave a company

Dysfunctional turnover loss of high-performing employees who voluntarily choose to leave a company

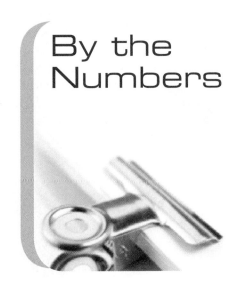

By the Numbers

$3.75 million amount Hooters paid to settle class-action lawsuit brought by 7 men

80% of companies conduct criminal record checks

$680 smallest training budget per employee that can increase company's ROI by 6%

$7.86 average hourly wage for a U.S. child-care worker

2 million number of job openings in Pearl River delta region of China

MANAGING INDIVIDUALS AND A DIVERSE WORK FORCE

Workplace diversity as we know it today is changing. Exhibit 12.1 (on page 216) shows predictions from the U.S. Bureau of the Census of how the U.S. population will change over the next 65 years. The percentage of white, non-Hispanic Americans in the general population is expected to decline from 69.3 percent in 2005 to 46.8 percent by the year 2070. By contrast, the percentage of African Americans will increase (from 12.3 percent to 13.2 percent), as will the percentage of Asian Americans (from 4.3 percent to 10.6 percent). Meanwhile, the proportion of Native Americans will hold steady (at 0.8 percent). The fastest-growing group by far, though, is Hispanics, who are expected to increase from 13.3 percent of the total population in 2005 to 28.6 percent by 2070.

Other significant changes have already occurred. For example, today women hold half the jobs in the United States, up from 38.2 percent in 1970.[1] Furthermore, white males, who composed 63.9 percent of the work force in 1950, hold just 38.2 percent of today's jobs.[2]

These rather dramatic changes have taken place in a relatively short time. And, as these trends clearly show, the work force of the near future will be increasingly Hispanic, Asian American, African American, and female. It will also be older, as the average baby boomer approaches the age of 60 around 2010. Since many boomers are likely to postpone retirement and work well into their 70s to offset predicted reductions in Social Security and Medicare benefits, the work force may become even older than expected.[3]

Learning Outcomes

1 describe diversity and explain why it matters.

2 understand the special challenges that the dimensions of surface-level diversity pose for managers.

3 explain how the dimensions of deep-level diversity affect individual behavior and interactions in the workplace.

4 explain the basic principles and practices that can be used to manage diversity.

Diversity and Why It Matters

Diversity means variety. Therefore, **diversity** exists in an organization when there is a variety of demographic, cultural, and personal differences among the people who work there and the customers who do business there. For example, step into Longo Toyota in El Monte, California, one of Toyota's top-selling dealerships, and you'll find diversity in the form of salespeople who speak Spanish, Korean, Arabic, Vietnamese, Hebrew, and Mandarin Chinese. In fact, the 60 salespeople at Longo Toyota speak 30 different languages. Surprisingly, this level of diversity was achieved without a formal diversity plan in place.[4]

After reading the next section, you should be able to

1 describe diversity and explain why it matters.

Diversity a variety of demographic, cultural, and personal differences among an organization's employees and customers

Exhibit 12.1

Predicted U.S. Population, Distributed by Race, 2005–2070

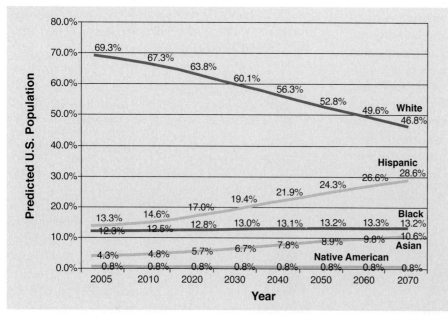

Sources: "Projections of the Resident Population by Race, Hispanic Origin, and Nativity: Middle Series, 2001–2005, 2006–2010, 2011–2015, 2016–2020, 2025–2045, 2050–2070," U.S. Census Bureau, available online at http://www.census.gov/population/projections/nation/summary/np-t5-b.pdf, http://www.census.gov/population/projections/nation/summary/np-t5-c.pdf, http://www.census.gov/population/projections/nation/summary/np-t5-e.pdf, http://www.census.gov/population/projections/nation/summary/np-t5-f.pdf, and http://www.census.gov/population/projections/nation/summary/np-t5-g.pdf.

1 Diversity: Differences That Matter

You'll begin your exploration of diversity by learning **1.1 that diversity is not affirmative action** and **1.2 how to build a business case for diversity.**

1.1 Diversity Is Not Affirmative Action

A common misconception is that workplace diversity and affirmative action are the same, yet these concepts differ in several critical ways, including their purpose, how they are practiced, and the reactions they produce. To start, **affirmative action** refers to purposeful steps taken by an organization to create employment opportunities for minorities and women.[5] By contrast, diversity exists in organizations when there is a variety of demographic, cultural, and personal differences among the people who work there and the customers who do business there. So one key difference is that affirmative action is more narrowly focused on demographics such as sex and race, while diversity has a

Affirmative action purposeful steps taken by an organization to create employment opportunities for minorities and women

broader focus that includes demographic, cultural, and personal differences. A second difference is that affirmative action is a policy for actively creating diversity, but diversity can exist even if organizations don't take purposeful steps to create it. For example, Longo Toyota achieved a high level of diversity without having a formal affirmative action program. Likewise, a local restaurant located near a university in a major city is likely to have a more diverse group of employees than one located in a small town. Affirmative action does not guarantee diversity. An organization can create employment opportunities for women and minorities yet not have a diverse work force.

A third important difference is that affirmative action is required by law (Executive Order 11246, https://www.dol.gov/esa/ofccp/regs/compliance/aa.htm) for private employers with 50 or more employees while diversity is not. Affirmative action originated with Executive Order 11246 but is also related to the 1964 Civil Rights Act, which bans discrimination in voting, public places, federal government programs, federally supported public education, and em-

© Rachel Epstein/PhotoEdit Inc.

> A common misconception is that workplace **diversity** and **affirmative** action are the same.

ployment. Title VII of the Civil Rights Act (http://www.eeoc.gov/policy/vii.html) requires that workers have equal employment opportunities when being hired or promoted. More specifically, Title VII prohibits companies from discriminating on the basis of race, color, religion, sex or national origin. Title VII also created the Equal Employment Opportunity Commission, or EEOC (http://www.eeoc.gov), to administer these laws. By contrast, there is no federal law or agency to oversee diversity. Organizations that pursue diversity goals do so voluntarily.

Fourth, affirmative action programs and diversity programs also have different purposes. The purpose of affirmative action programs is to compensate for past discrimination, which was widespread when legislation was introduced in the 1960s; to prevent ongoing discrimination; and to provide equal opportunities to all regardless of race, color, religion, sex, or national origin. Organizations that fail to uphold these laws may be required to

- hire, promote, or give back pay to those not hired or promoted;
- reinstate those who were wrongly terminated;
- pay attorneys' fees and court costs for those who bring charges against them; or
- take other actions that make individuals whole by returning them to the condition or place

they would have been had it not been for discrimination.[6]

Consequently, affirmative action is basically a punitive approach.[7] By contrast, the general purpose of diversity programs is to create a positive work environment where no one is advantaged or disadvantaged, where "we" is everyone, where everyone can do his or her best work, where differences are respected and not ignored, and where everyone feels comfortable.[8] So, unlike affirmative action, which punishes companies for not achieving specific sex and race ratios in their work forces, diversity programs seek to benefit both organizations and their employees by encouraging organizations to value all kinds of differences.

Despite the overall success of affirmative action in making workplaces much fairer than they used to be, many people argue that some affirmative action programs unconstitutionally offer preferential treatment to females and minorities at the expense of other employees, a view accepted by some courts.[9] The American Civil Rights Institute successfully campaigned to ban race- and sex-based affirmative action in college admissions, government hiring, and government contracting programs in California (1996), Washington (1998) and Michigan (2006). Led by Ward Connerly, the Institute backed similar efforts in Arizona, Colorado, Missouri, Nebraska, and Oklahoma in 2008. Opponents like Connerly feel that affirmative action policies establish only surface-level diversity and, ironically, promote preferential treatment.[10]

Furthermore, research shows that people who have gotten a job or promotion as a result of affirmative action are frequently viewed as unqualified even when clear evidence of their qualifications exists.[11] So, although affirmative action programs have created opportunities for minorities and women, those same minorities and women are frequently presumed to be unqualified when others believe they obtained their jobs as a result of affirmative action.

1.2 Diversity Makes Good Business Sense

Those who support the idea of diversity in organizations often ignore its business aspects altogether, claiming instead that diversity is simply the right thing to do. Yet diversity actually makes good business sense in several

Generational Assets

A mix of older and younger workers may be critical to a company's success in our fast-paced, interconnected global marketplace. Gen-Xers and particularly millennials are flexible; learn new technologies and skills easily; are comfortable with crossing boundaries of space, time, and class; and tend to value collaboration. Baby boomers, while they can be slower to adapt to change, have experience and knowledge that are critical to a company's stability. The challenge? How to overcome generational differences in values, work methods, and communication styles within work groups. Capitalizing on the different strong points of each group and training employees on these differences are essential for success.

Sources: W. Boddie, J. Contardo, and R. Childs, "The Future Workforce: Here They Come," *The Public Manager* 36 (winter 2007) 25-28; E. White, "Age is as Age Does; Making the Generation Gap Work for You," *The Wall Street Journal*, available online at http://online.wsj.com/article/SB121478926535514813.html [accessed 21 August 2008].

ways: cost savings, attracting and retaining talent, and driving business growth.[12] An increase of senior executive positions like "chief diversity officer" (CDO) suggests that more organizations are taking the business end of diversity seriously.[13]

Diversity helps companies with *cost savings* by reducing turnover, decreasing absenteeism, and enabling them to avoid expensive lawsuits.[14] In fact, turnover costs typically amount to more than 90 percent of employees' salaries. So, if an executive who makes $200,000 a year leaves an organization, it would cost approximately $180,000 to find a replacement. Using the 90 percent estimate, losing even the lowest-paid hourly workers can cost companies as much as $10,000 when they quit. Since turnover rates for African Americans average 40 percent higher than for whites, and since women quit their jobs at twice the rate men do, companies that manage diverse work forces well can cut costs by reducing the turnover rates of these employees. And, with women absent from work 60 percent more often than men primarily because of family responsibilities, diversity programs that address the needs of female workers can also reduce the substantial costs of absenteeism.[15]

Diversity programs also save companies money by helping them avoid discrimination lawsuits, which have increased by a factor of 20 since 1970 and quadrupled just since 1995. In one survey conducted by the Society for Human Resource Management, 78 percent of respondents reported that diversity efforts helped them avoid lawsuits and litigation costs.[16] Indeed, because companies lose two-thirds of all discrimination cases that go to trial, the best strategy from a business perspective is not to be sued for discrimination at all.

When companies lose, the average individual settlement amounts to more than $600,000.[17] And settlement costs can be substantially higher in class-action lawsuits, in which individuals join together to sue a company as a group. In fact, the average class-action lawsuit costs companies $58.9 million for racial discrimination and $24.9 million for gender discrimination.[18]

Diversity also makes business sense by helping companies *attract and retain talented workers.*[19] Indeed, diversity-friendly companies tend to attract better and more diverse job applicants. Very simply, diversity begets more diversity. Companies that make *Fortune* magazine's list of the 50 best companies for minorities already attract a diverse and talented pool of job applicants. After being recognized by *Fortune* for their efforts, they experience even bigger increases in both the quality and the diversity of people who apply for jobs. Research shows that companies with acclaimed diversity programs not only attract more talented workers but also have higher stock market performance.[20]

The third way that diversity makes business sense is by *driving business growth.* Diversity helps companies grow by improving their understanding of the marketplace. When companies have diverse work forces, they are better able to understand the needs of their increasingly diverse customer bases. A recent survey conducted by the Society for Human Resource Management found that tapping into "diverse customers and markets" was the number one reason managers gave for implementing diversity programs.[21]

Diversity also helps companies grow through higher-quality problem solving. Though diverse groups initially have more difficulty working together than homogeneous groups, diverse groups eventually establish a rapport and do a better job of identifying problems and generating alternative solutions, the two most important steps in problem solving.[22] In short, "diversity is no longer about counting heads; it's about making heads count," says Amy George, vice president of diversity and inclusion at PepsiCo.[23]

Diversity and Individual Differences

A survey that asked managers, "What is meant by diversity to decision-makers in your organization?" found that they most frequently mentioned race, culture, sex, national origin, age, religion, and regional origin.[24] When managers describe workers this way, they are focusing on surface-level diversity. **Surface-level diversity** consists of differences that are immediately observable, typically unchangeable, and easy to measure.[25] In other words, independent observers can usually agree on dimensions of surface-level diversity, such as another person's age, sex, race/ethnicity, or physical capabilities.

Most people start by using surface-level diversity to categorize or stereotype other people. But those initial categorizations typically give way to deeper impressions formed from knowledge of others' behavior and psychological characteristics such as personality and attitudes.[26] When you think of others this way, you are focusing on deep-level diversity. **Deep-level diversity** consists of differences that are communicated through verbal and nonverbal behaviors and are learned only through extended interaction with others.[27] Examples of deep-level diversity include personality differences, attitudes, beliefs, and values. In other words, as people in diverse workplaces get to know each other, the initial focus on surface-level differences such as age, race/ethnicity, sex, and physical capabilities is replaced by deeper, more complex knowledge of coworkers.

If managed properly, the shift from surface- to deep-level diversity can accomplish two things.[28] First, coming to know and understand each other better can result in reduced prejudice and conflict. Second, it can lead to stronger social integration. **Social integration** is the degree to which group members are psychologically

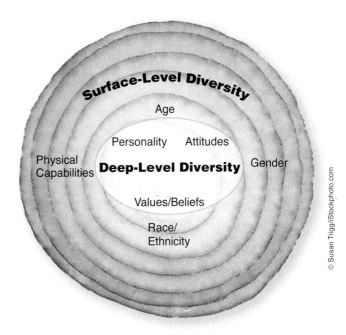

attracted to working with each other to accomplish a common objective, or, as one manager put it, "working together to get the job done."

 After reading the next two sections, you should be able to

2 understand the special challenges that the dimensions of surface-level diversity pose for managers.

3 explain how the dimensions of deep-level diversity affect individual behavior and interactions in the workplace.

2 Surface-Level Diversity

Because age, sex, race/ethnicity, and physical disabilities are usually immediately observable, many managers and workers use these dimensions of surface-level diversity to form initial impressions and categorizations of coworkers, bosses, customers, or job applicants. Whether intentionally or not, sometimes those initial categorizations and impressions lead to decisions or behaviors that discriminate. Consequently, these dimensions of surface-level diversity pose special

Surface-level diversity differences such as age, sex, race/ethnicity, and physical disabilities that are observable, typically unchangeable, and easy to measure

Deep-level diversity differences such as personality and attitudes that are communicated through verbal and nonverbal behaviors and are learned only through extended interaction with others

Social integration the degree to which group members are psychologically attracted to working with each other to accomplish a common objective

challenges for managers who are trying to create positive work environments where everyone feels comfortable and no one is advantaged or disadvantaged.

*Let's learn more about those challenges and the ways that **2.1 age, 2.2 sex, 2.3 race/ethnicity,** and **2.4 mental or physical disabilities** can affect decisions and behaviors in organizations.*

2.1 Age

Age discrimination is treating people differently (e.g., in hiring and firing, promotion, and compensation decisions) because of their age. According to the Society for Human Resource Management, 53 percent of 428 surveyed managers believed that older workers "didn't keep up with technology," and 28 percent said that older workers were "less flexible." When 57-year-old Sam Horgan, a former chief financial officer, was interviewing for a job, he was asked by a 30-something job interviewer, "Would you have trouble working with young bright people?"[29] It is also commonly assumed that older workers cost more, and some companies fear that older workers will require higher salaries and more health-care benefits.[30]

So, what's reality and what's myth? Do older employees actually cost more? In some ways, they do. The older people are and the longer they stay with a company, the more the company pays for salaries, pension plans, and vacation time. But older workers cost companies less, too, because they tend to show better judgment and care more about the quality of their work. They are also less likely to quit, show up late, or be absent, the cost of which can be substantial.[31] A survey by Chicago outplacement firm Challenger, Gray & Christmas found that only 3 percent of employees age 50 and over changed jobs in any given year, compared to 10 percent of the entire work force and 12 percent of workers ages 25 to 34. The study also found that while older workers make up about 14 percent of the work force, they suffer only 10 percent of all workplace injuries and use fewer health-care benefits than younger workers with school-age children.[32] As for the widespread belief that job performance declines with age, the scientific evidence clearly refutes this stereotype. Performance does not decline with age regardless of the type of job.[33]

What can companies do to reduce age discrimina-tion?[34] To start, managers need to recognize that age discrimination is much more pervasive than they probably think. Whereas "old" used to mean mid-50s, in today's workplace, "old" is closer to 40. When 773 CEOs were asked, "At what age does a worker's productivity peak?" the average age they gave was 43. Thus, age discrimination may be affecting more workers because perceptions about age have changed. In addition, age discrimination is more likely to occur with the aging of baby boomers simply because there are millions more older workers than there used to be. And, because studies show that interviewers rate younger job candidates as more qualified (even when they aren't), companies need to train managers and recruiters to make hiring and promotion decisions on the basis of qualifications, not age. Companies also need to monitor the extent to which older workers receive training. The Bureau of Labor Statistics found that the number of training courses and number of hours spent in training drops dramatically after employees reach the age of 44.[35] Finally, companies need to ensure that younger and older workers interact with each other. One study found that younger workers generally hold positive views of older workers and that the more time they spent working with older coworkers, the more positive their attitudes became.[36]

2.2 Sex

Sex discrimination occurs when people are treated differently because of their sex. Sex discrimination and racial/ethnic discrimination (discussed in the next section) are often associated with the so-called **glass ceiling,** the invisible barrier that prevents women and minorities from advancing to the top jobs in organizations.

Exhibit 12.2

Women's Earnings as a Percentage of Men's

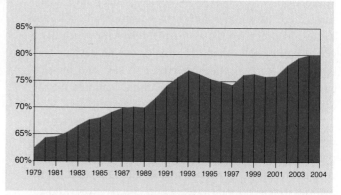

Sources: U. S. Department of Labor. Bureau of Labor Statistics. *Highlights of Women's Earnings in 2006*, available online at http://www.bls.gov/cps/cpswom2006.pdf [accessed 21 August 2008].

Age discrimination treating people differently (e.g., in hiring and firing, promotion, and compensation decisions) because of their age

Sex discrimination treating people differently because of their sex

Glass ceiling the invisible barrier that prevents women and minorities from advancing to the top jobs in organizations

Exhibit 12.3

Women at *Fortune* 500 and 1000 Companies

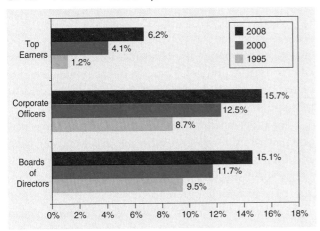

Source: "2008 Catalyst Census of Women Corporate Officers and Top Earners of the Fortune 500," *Catalyst*, available online at http://www.catalyst.org/press-release/141/catalyst-2008-census-of-the-fortune-500-reveals-women-gained-little-ground-advancing-to-business-leadership-positions [accessed 21 August 2008].

To what extent do women face sex discrimination in the workplace? In some ways, there is much less sex discrimination than there used to be. For example, whereas women held only 17 percent of managerial jobs in 1972, they now outnumber men with 50.6 percent of managerial jobs, a percentage that is slightly more than their representation in the work force (46.3 percent). Likewise, women own 40 percent of all U.S. businesses. Whereas women owned 700,000 businesses in 1977 and 4.1 million businesses in 1987, today they own 10 million! Finally, though women still earn less than men on average, the differential is narrowing as shown in Exhibit 12.2 on the previous page. Women earned 80.8 percent of what men did in 2006, up from 63 percent in 1979.[37]

Although progress is being made, sex discrimination continues to operate via the glass ceiling at higher levels in organizations as shown in Exhibit 12.3. For instance, only 16.4 percent of corporate officers (i.e., top management) were women, and the numbers are even lower for women of color. Indra K. Nooyi, CEO of PepsiCo, and Andrea Jung, CEO of Avon, are the only women of color heading *Fortune* 500 companies.[38] Indeed, only 13 of the 500 largest companies in the United States have women CEOs. Angela Braly, CEO of WellPoint, is the only woman to run a *Fortune* 50 company.[39] Similarly, the 2008 Catalyst Census of Women Board of Directors revealed that only 15 percent of the members of corporate boards of directors at top-500 companies in Canada are women.[40]

Is sex discrimination the sole reason for the slow rate at which women have been promoted to middle and up-per levels of management and corporate boards? Some studies indicate that it's not.[41] In some instances, the slow progress appears to be due to career and job choices. Whereas men's career and job choices are often driven by the search for higher pay and advancement, women are more likely to choose jobs or careers that also give them a greater sense of accomplishment, more control over their work schedules, and easier movement in and out of the workplace.[42] Furthermore, women are historically much more likely than men to prioritize family over work at some time in their careers. For example, 96 percent of 600 female Harvard MBAs held jobs while they were in their 20s. That dropped to 71 percent in their late 30s when they had children, but then increased to 82.5 percent in their late 40s as their children became older.[43]

Beyond these reasons, however, it's likely that sex discrimination does play a role in women's slow progress into the higher levels of management. And even if you don't think so, many of the women you work with probably do. Indeed, one study found that more than 90 percent of executive women believed that the glass ceiling had hurt their careers.[44] In another study, 80 percent of women said they left their last organization because the glass ceiling had limited their chances for

The Golf Divide

For decades, golf has been known as the great executive pastime—the white, male executive pastime. Today, however, many executive positions are held by women, who are less likely to be avid golfers, and techies and Silicon Valley executives, who prefer mountain biking, so corporate outings are becoming as diverse as their employees (soccer, cycling, etc.). Still, golf reigns as the activity of choice in many industries and is considered an ideal place to build and sustain business relationships. To get all types of businesspeople prepared to play, the PGA of America has a program called "Golf: For Business and for Life" that sponsors courses at colleges and universities, and the nonprofit Executive Women's Golf Association teaches the game to businesswomen, a growing number of whom are middle managers with executive aspirations.

Source: J.P. Newport and R. Adams, "Business Gold Changes Course," *The Wall Street Journal*, 26-27 May 2007, P1.

The evidence strongly indicates that there is **strong** and **persistent** racial and ethnic discrimination in the hiring processes of many organizations.

advancement.[45] A third study indicated that the glass ceiling is prompting more and more women to leave companies to start their own businesses.[46]

So, what can companies do to make sure that women have the same opportunities for development and advancement as men? One strategy is mentoring, or pairing promising female executives with senior executives from whom they can seek advice and support. A vice president at a utility company says "I think it's the single most critical piece to women advancing career-wise. In my experience you need somebody to help guide you and . . . go to bat for you."[47] In fact, 91 percent of female executives have a mentor at some point and feel their mentor was critical to their advancement.

Another strategy is to make sure that male-dominated social activities don't unintentionally exclude women. Nearly half (47 percent) of women in the work force believe that "exclusion from informal networks" makes it more difficult to advance their careers. By contrast, just 18 percent of CEOs thought this was a problem.[48] One final strategy is to designate a "go-to person" other than their supervisors that women can talk to if they believe that they are being held back or discriminated against because of their sex. Make sure this person has the knowledge and authority to conduct a fair, confidential internal investigation.[49]

2.3 Race/Ethnicity

Racial and ethnic discrimination occurs when people are treated differently because of their race or ethnicity. To what extent is racial and ethnic discrimination a factor in the workplace? Every year, the EEOC receives between 26,000 and 30,000 charges of race discrimination, which is more than any other type of discrimination charge (**http://www.eeoc.gov/stats/race.html**). However, thanks to the 1964 Civil Rights Act and Title VII, there is much less racial and ethnic discrimination than there used to be. For example, only five *Fortune 500* firms had an African American CEO in 2007, whereas none did in 1988.[50] Nonetheless, strong racial and ethnic disparities still exist. For instance, whereas 11 percent of Americans are black, only 8.4 percent of managers and 3.5 percent of top managers are black. Similarly, 14 percent of Americans are Hispanic, but only 7 percent

Racial and ethnic discrimination treating people differently because of their race or ethnicity

are managers and 7.4 percent of CEOs at *Fortune 500* and other companies are Hispanic. By contrast, Asians, who constitute about 4.7 percent of the population, are better represented, holding 6.4 percent of management jobs and 4.3 percent of CEO jobs.[51]

What accounts for the disparities between the percentages of minority groups in the general population and their smaller representation in management positions? Some studies have found that the disparities are due to preexisting differences in training, education, and skills; when African Americans, Hispanics, Asian Americans, and whites have similar skills, training, and education, they are much more likely to have similar jobs and salaries.[52]

Other studies, however, provide increasingly strong direct evidence of racial or ethnic discrimination in the workplace. For example, one study directly tested hiring discrimination by sending pairs of black and white males and pairs of Hispanic and non-Hispanic males to apply for the same jobs. Each pair had résumés with identical qualifications, and all were trained to present themselves in similar ways to minimize differences during interviews. The researchers found that the white males got three times as many job offers as the black males, and that the non-Hispanic males got three times as many offers as the Hispanic males.[53]

Another study, which used similar methods to test hiring procedures at 149 different companies, found that whites received 10 percent more interviews than blacks. Half of the whites interviewed received job offers, but only 11 percent of the blacks. And when job offers were made, blacks were much more likely to be offered lower-level positions, while whites were more likely to be offered jobs at higher levels than the jobs they had applied for.[54]

Critics of these studies point out that it's nearly impossible to train different applicants to give identical responses in job interviews and that differences in interviewing skills may have somehow accounted for the results. However, British researchers found similar kinds of discrimination just by sending letters of inquiry to prospective employers. As in the other studies, the letters were identical except for the applicant's race. Employers frequently responded to letters from Afro-Caribbean, Indian, or Pakistani "applicants" by indicating that the positions had been filled. By contrast, they often responded to white, Anglo-Saxon "applicants" by inviting them to face-to-face interviews. Similar results were found with Vietnamese and Greek "applicants" in Australia.[55] In short, the evidence indicates that there is strong and persistent racial and ethnic discrimination in the hiring processes of many organizations.

What can companies do to make sure that people of all racial and ethnic backgrounds have the same opportunities?[56] Start by looking at the numbers. Compare the hiring rates of whites to the hiring rates for racial and ethnic applicants. Do the same thing for promotions within the company. See if nonwhite workers quit the company at higher rates than white workers. Also, survey employees to compare white and nonwhite employees' satisfaction with jobs, bosses, and the company, as well as their perceptions concerning equal treatment. Next, if the numbers indicate racial or ethnic disparities, consider employing a private firm to test your hiring system by having applicants of different races with identical qualifications apply for jobs in your company.[57] Although disparities aren't proof of discrimination, it's much better to investigate hiring and promotion disparities yourself than to have the EEOC or a plaintiff's lawyer do it for you.

Another step companies can take is to eliminate unclear selection and promotion criteria. Vague criteria allow decision makers to focus on non-job-related characteristics that may unintentionally lead to employment discrimination. Instead, selection and promotion criteria should spell out the specific knowledge, skills, abilities, education, and experience needed to perform a job well.

Finally, creating a culture that is visionary in its approach to diversity is key. It's not surprising that when it came time for PepsiCo to choose a new CEO, the board picked Indian-born Indra Nooyi. PepsiCo has a long history of diversity, stretching back to the end of World War II, when President Walter Mack hired Edward Boyd away from the National Urban League to head a team charged with launching a marketing program for African American consumers. In every area of the country where Boyd's team ran a marketing blitz, Pepsi sales increased, and soon Pepsi-Cola overtook market leader Coca-Cola in cities like Cleveland and Chicago. One of the most successful campaigns was a series of print advertisements titled "Leaders in Their Fields," which profiled the accom-

© Image Source Black/Jupiterimages

plishments of professional and successful African Americans. Pepsi's print campaign was the first to shun the stereotypical images of African Americans used in print and other advertisements. As you can see from PepsiCo's history, it takes a long time and a lot of effort to create a culture of diversity. But good hiring practices contribute to such an organizational culture and make it easier to achieve what PepsiCo has.[58]

2.4 Mental or Physical Disabilities

According to the Americans with Disabilities Act (http://www.usdoj.gov/crt/ada/adahom1.htm), a **disability** is a mental or physical impairment that substantially limits one or more major life activities.[59] One in every five Americans, or more than 54 million people, has a disability.[60] **Disability discrimination** occurs when people are treated differently because of their disabilities.

To what extent is disability discrimination a factor in the workplace? Although 79.7 percent of the overall U.S. population was employed in 2006, only 37.7 percent of people with disabilities were. Individuals with sensory disabilities such as blindness or deafness had the highest employment rates, while those with self-care disabilities, which inhibit their motor skills and their ability to care for their grooming needs, were the least represented in the work force.[61] Furthermore, people with disabilities are disproportionately employed in low-status or part-time jobs, have little chance for advancement, and, on

Disability a mental or physical impairment that substantially limits one or more major life activities

Disability discrimination treating people differently because of their disabilities

Work Force Health on the Decline

According to the Council for Disability Awareness, the general health of the American work force is declining because of age and questionable lifestyle choices (poor diet, lack of exercise, etc.). Rising obesity rates are causing back pain, hip and knee injury (often leading to joint replacement), and diabetes. Claims for depression and other nervous disorders, chronic bronchitis, and asthma are also increasing. Many companies are finding ways to accommodate workers. American Express has made its cafeteria wheelchair accessible and rearranged work schedules to coincide with the paratransit system. Sylvania has created flexible shifts for disabled employees, and General Motors enlists the help of an ergonomic specialist to help assign disabled workers to jobs that won't aggravate their ailments.

© BananaStock/JupiterImages

Source: M. P. McQueen, "Workplace Disabilities Are on the Rise," *The Wall Street Journal*, 1 May 2007, D1.

average, are twice as likely to live in poverty as able people.[62] Numerous studies also indicate that managers and the general public believe that discrimination against people with disabilities is common and widespread.[63]

What accounts for the disparities between the employment and income levels of able people and people with disabilities? Contrary to popular opinion, it has nothing to do with how well people with disabilities can do their jobs. Studies show that as long as companies make reasonable accommodations for disabilities (e.g., changing procedures or equipment), people with disabilities perform their jobs just as well as able people. They also have better safety records and are no more likely to be absent or quit their jobs.[64]

What can companies do to make sure that people with disabilities have the same opportunities as everyone else? Beyond educational efforts to address incorrect stereotypes and expectations, a good place to start is to commit to reasonable workplace accommodations such as changing work schedules, reassigning jobs, acquiring or modifying equipment, or providing assistance when needed. Accommodations for disabilities needn't be expensive. According to the Job Accommodation Network, 71 percent of accommodations cost employers $500 or less, and 20 percent of accommodations don't cost anything at all.[65]

Finally, companies should actively recruit qualified workers with disabilities. Numerous organizations such as Mainstream, Kidder Resources, the American Council of the Blind (http://www.acb.org), the National Federation of the Blind (http://www.nfb.org), the National Association of the Deaf (http://www.nad.org), the Epilepsy Foundation of America (http://www.epilepsyfoundation.org), and the National Amputation Foundation (http://www.nationalamputation.org) actively work with employers to find jobs for qualified people with disabilities. Companies can also place advertisements in publications such as *Careers and the Disabled* that specifically target workers with disabilities.[66]

3 Deep-Level Diversity

As you learned in Section 2, people often use the dimensions of surface-level diversity to form initial impressions about others. Over time, however, as people have a chance to get to know each other, initial impressions based on age, sex, race/ethnicity, and mental or physical disabilities give way to deeper impressions based on behavior and psychological characteristics. When we think of others this way, we are focusing on deep-level diversity. *Deep-level diversity* represents differences that can be learned only through extended interaction with others. Examples of deep-level diversity include differences in personality, attitudes, beliefs, and values. In short, recognizing deep-level diversity requires getting to know and understand one another better. And that matters because it can result in less prejudice, discrimination, and conflict in the workplace. These changes can then lead to better *social integration*, the degree to which organizational or group members are psychologically attracted to working with each other to accomplish a common objective.

Stop for a second and think about your boss (or the boss you had in your last job). What words would you use to describe him or her? Is your boss introverted or extraverted? Emotionally stable or unstable? Agreeable or disagreeable? Organized or disorganized? Open or closed to new experiences? When you describe your boss or others in this way, what you're really doing is describing dispositions and personality.

A **disposition** is the tendency to respond to situations and events in a predetermined manner. **Personality** is the

Disposition the tendency to respond to situations and events in a predetermined manner

Personality the relatively stable set of behaviors, attitudes, and emotions displayed over time that makes people different from each other

relatively stable set of behaviors, attitudes, and emotions displayed over time that makes people different from each other.[67] For example, which of your aunts or uncles is a little offbeat, a little out of the ordinary? What was that aunt or uncle like when you were small? What is she or he like now? Chances are she or he is pretty much the same wacky person. In other words, the person's core personality hasn't changed. For years, personality researchers studied thousands of different ways to describe people's personalities. In the last decade, however, personality research conducted in different cultures, different settings, and different languages has shown that five basic dimensions of personality account for most of the differences in people's behaviors, attitudes, and emotions. The *Big Five Personality Dimensions* are extraversion, emotional stability, agreeableness, conscientiousness, and openness to experience.[68]

Extraversion is the degree to which someone is active, assertive, gregarious, sociable, talkative, and energized by others. In contrast to extraverts, introverts are less active, prefer to be alone, and are shy, quiet, and reserved. For the best results in the workplace, introverts and extraverts should be correctly matched to their jobs.

Emotional stability is the degree to which someone is not angry, depressed, anxious, emotional, insecure, or excitable. People who are emotionally stable respond well to stress. In other words, they can maintain a calm, problem-solving attitude in even the toughest situations (e.g., conflict, hostility, dangerous conditions, or extreme time pressures). By contrast, emotionally unstable people find it difficult to handle the most basic demands of their jobs under only moderately stressful situations and become distraught, tearful, self-doubting, and anxious. Emotional stability is particularly important for high-stress jobs such as police work, fire fighting, emergency medical treatment, piloting planes, or commanding rockets.

Agreeableness is the degree to which someone is cooperative, polite, flexible, forgiving, good-natured, tolerant, and trusting. Basically, agreeable people are easy to work with and be around, whereas disagreeable

> Introverts and extraverts should be correctly matched to their jobs.

people are distrusting and difficult to work with and be around.

Conscientiousness is the degree to which someone is organized, hardworking, responsible, persevering, thorough, and achievement oriented. One management consultant wrote about his experiences with a conscientious employee: "He arrived at our first meeting with a typed copy of his daily schedule, a sheet bearing his home and office phone numbers, addresses, and his email address. At his request, we established a timetable for meetings for the next four months. He showed up on time every time, day planner in hand, and carefully listed tasks and due dates. He questioned me exhaustively if he didn't understand an assignment and returned on schedule with the completed work or with a clear explanation as to why it wasn't done."[69]

Openness to experience is the degree to which someone is curious, broad-minded, and open to new ideas, things, and experiences; is spontaneous; and

Extraversion the degree to which someone is active, assertive, gregarious, sociable, talkative, and energized by others

Emotional stability the degree to which someone is not angry, depressed, anxious, emotional, insecure, and excitable

Agreeableness the degree to which someone is cooperative, polite, flexible, forgiving, good-natured, tolerant, and trusting

Conscientiousness the degree to which someone is organized, hardworking, responsible, persevering, thorough, and achievement oriented

Openness to experience the degree to which someone is curious, broad-minded, and open to new ideas, things, and experiences; is spontaneous; and has a high tolerance for ambiguity

92 studies across five occupational groups (professionals, police, managers, sales, and skilled/semiskilled jobs) with a combined total of 12,893 study participants indicated that, on average, conscientious people are inherently more motivated and are better at their jobs.[70]

has a high tolerance for ambiguity. People in marketing, advertising, research, or other creative jobs need to be curious, open to new ideas, and spontaneous. By contrast, openness to experience is not particularly important to accountants, who need to consistently apply stringent rules and formulas to make sense out of complex financial information.

Which of the Big Five Personality Dimensions has the largest impact on behavior in organizations? The cumulative results indicate that conscientiousness is related to job performance across five different occupational groups (professionals, police, managers, sales, and skilled or semiskilled jobs).[71] In short, people "who are dependable, persistent, goal directed, and organized tend to be higher performers on virtually any job; viewed negatively, those who are careless, irresponsible, low-achievement striving, and impulsive tend to be lower performers on virtually any job."[72] The results also indicate that extraversion is related to performance in jobs, such as sales and management, that involve significant interaction with others. In people-intensive jobs like these, it helps to be sociable, assertive, and talkative and to have energy and be able to energize others. Finally, people who are extraverted and open to experience seem to do much better in training. Being curious and open to new experiences as well as sociable, assertive, talkative, and full of energy helps people perform better in learning situations.[73]

How Can Diversity Be Managed?

How much should companies change their standard business practices to accommodate the diversity of their workers? What do you do when a talented top executive has a drinking problem that only seems to affect his behavior at company business parties (for entertaining clients), where he has made inappropriate advances toward female employees? What do you do when, despite aggressive company policies against racial discrimination, employees continue to tell racial jokes and publicly post cartoons displaying racial humor? And, since many people confuse diversity with affirmative action, what do you do to make sure that your company's diversity practices and policies are viewed as benefiting all workers and not just some workers?

White Males Lead Diversity?

At PricewaterhouseCoopers (PwC), the chief diversity officer, Chris Simmons, who is black, asked Keith Ruth to help lead the company's diversity effort. Ruth was surprised to be asked—because he is white. An emerging trend in managing diversity is to put white males in charge. The rationale is that unless white males are heavily involved and even champion diversity efforts, those efforts will not ever become part of the mainstream. PwC, Coca-Cola, and Georgia Power all have white men running diversity programs. For PwC's Simmons, it's an important step away from thinking that only women and minorities should be leading the diversity movement.

Source: E. White, "Diversity Programs Look to Involve White Males as Leaders," *The Wall Street Journal*, 7 May 2007, B4.

© BananaStock/JupiterImages

No doubt about it, questions like these make managing diversity one of the toughest challenges that managers face.[74] Nonetheless, there are steps companies can take to begin to address these issues.

 After reading the next section, you should be able to

4 explain the basic principles and practices that can be used to manage diversity.

© Robert Bremec/iStockphoto.com

IF YOU DON'T MEASURE SOMETHING, . . .

4 Managing Diversity

As discussed earlier, diversity programs try to create a positive work environment where no one is advantaged or disadvantaged, where "we" is everyone, where everyone can do his or her best work, where differences are respected and not ignored, and where everyone feels comfortable. *Let's begin to address those goals by learning about 4.1 different diversity paradigms, 4.2 diversity principles,* and *4.3 diversity training and practices.*

4.1 Diversity Paradigms

There are several different methods or paradigms for managing diversity: the discrimination and fairness paradigm, the access and legitimacy paradigm, and the learning and effectiveness paradigm.[75] The *discrimination and fairness paradigm,* which is the most common method of approaching diversity, focuses on equal opportunity, fair treatment, recruitment of minorities, and strict compliance with the equal employment opportunity laws. Under this approach, success is usually measured by how well companies achieve recruitment, promotion, and retention goals for women, people of different racial/ethnic backgrounds, or other underrepresented groups. According to a recent workplace diversity practices survey conducted by the Society for Human Resource Management, 77 percent of companies with more than 500 employees systematically collect measurements on diversity-related practices.[76] For example, one manager says "If you don't measure something, it doesn't count. You measure your market share. You measure your profitability. The same should be true for diversity. There has to be some way of measuring whether you did, in fact, cast your net widely, and whether the company is better off today in terms of the experience of people of color than it was a few years ago. I measure my market share and my profitability. Why not this?"[77] The primary benefit of the discrimination and fairness paradigm is that it

generally brings about fairer treatment of employees and increases demographic diversity. The primary limitation is that the focus of diversity remains on the surface-level dimensions of sex, race, and ethnicity.

The *access and legitimacy paradigm* focuses on the acceptance and celebration of differences to ensure that the diversity within the company matches the diversity found among primary stakeholders such as customers, suppliers, and local communities. This is similar to the *business growth* advantage of diversity discussed earlier in the chapter. The basic idea behind this approach is attracting a broader customer base by creating a more diverse workforce. "We are living in an increasingly multicultural country, and new ethnic groups are quickly gaining consumer power. Our company needs a demographically more diverse work force to help us gain access to these differentiated segments."[78] Consistent with this goal, Ed Adams, vice president of human resources for Enterprise Rent-a-Car, says "We want people who speak the same language, literally and figuratively, as our customers. We don't set quotas. We say [to our managers], 'Reflect your local market.'"[79] The primary benefit of this approach is that it establishes a clear business reason for diversity. Like the discrimination and fairness paradigm, however, it focuses only on the surface-level diversity dimensions of sex, race, and ethnicity. Furthermore, employees who are assigned responsibility for customers and stakeholders on the basis of their sex, race, or ethnicity may eventually feel frustrated and exploited.

IT DOESN'T COUNT.

Whereas the discrimination and fairness paradigm focuses on assimilation (having a demographically representative work force), and the access and legitimacy paradigm focuses on differentiation (having demographic differences inside the company match those of key customers and stakeholders), the *learning and effectiveness paradigm* focuses on integrating deep-level diversity differences, such as personality, attitudes, beliefs, and values, into the actual work of the organization. Aetna's 28,000 employees are diverse not only in terms of sex, ethnicity and race, but also by age group, sexual orientation, work styles and levels, perspective, education, skills, and other characteristics. Raymond Arroyo, head of diversity at Aetna, says, "Diversity at Aetna means treating individuals individually, leveraging everyone's best, and maximizing the powerful potential of our workforce." He adds, "Part of a top diversity executive's role in any organization is to integrate diversity into every aspect of a business, including the workforce, customers, suppliers, products, services and even into the community a business serves."[80]

The learning and effectiveness paradigm is consistent with achieving organizational plurality. **Organizational plurality** is a work environment where (1) all members are empowered to contribute in a way that maximizes the benefits to the organization, customers, and themselves, and (2) the individuality of each member is respected by not segmenting or polarizing people on the basis of their membership in a particular group.[81]

The learning and effectiveness diversity paradigm offers four benefits.[82] First, it values common ground. Dave Thomas of the Harvard Business School explains: "Like the fairness paradigm, it promotes equal opportunity for all individuals. And like the access paradigm, it acknowledges cultural differences among people and recognizes the value in those differences. Yet this new model for managing diversity lets the organization internalize differences among employees so that it learns and grows because of them. Indeed, with the model fully in place, members of the organization can say, 'We are all on the same team, with our differences—not despite them.'"[83]

Second, this paradigm makes a distinction between individual and group differences. When diversity focuses only on differences between groups, such as females versus males, large differences within groups are ignored.[84]

Organizational plurality a work environment where (1) all members are empowered to contribute in a way that maximizes the benefits to the organization, customers, and themselves, and (2) the individuality of each member is respected by not segmenting or polarizing people on the basis of their membership in a particular group

For example, think of the women you know at work. Now, think for a second about what they have in common. After that, think about how they're different. If your situation is typical, the list of differences should be just as long as the list of commonalities if not longer. In short, managers can achieve a greater understanding of diversity and their employees by treating them as individuals and by realizing that not all African Americans, Hispanics, women, or white males want the same things at work.[85]

Third, because the focus is on individual differences, the learning and effectiveness paradigm is less likely to encounter the conflict, backlash, and divisiveness sometimes associated with diversity programs that focus only on group differences. Ray Haines, a consultant who has helped companies deal with the aftermath of diversity programs that became divisive, says, "There's a large amount of backlash related to diversity training. It stirs up a lot of hostility, anguish, and resentment but doesn't give people tools to deal with [the backlash]. You have people come in and talk about their specific ax to grind."[86]

© Alexey Gorichenskiy/iStockphoto.com/ © Lit Liu/iStockphoto.com

Not all diversity programs are divisive or lead to conflict. But, by focusing on individual rather than group differences, the learning and effectiveness paradigm helps to minimize these potential problems.

Finally, unlike the other diversity paradigms that simply focus on the value of being different (primarily in terms of surface-level diversity), the learning and effectiveness paradigm focuses on bringing different talents and perspectives *together* (i.e., deep-level diversity) to make the best organizational decisions and to produce innovative, competitive products and services.

4.2 Diversity Principles

Diversity paradigms are general approaches or strategies for managing diversity. Whatever diversity paradigm a manager chooses, diversity principles will help managers do a better job of *managing company diversity programs.*[87]

Begin by *carefully and faithfully following and enforcing federal and state laws regarding equal opportunity employment.* Diversity programs can't and won't succeed if the company is being sued for discriminatory actions and behavior. Faithfully following the law will also reduce the time and expense associated with EEOC investigations or lawsuits. Start by learning more at the EEOC Web site (**http://www.eeoc.gov**). Following the law also means strictly and fairly enforcing company policies.

Treat group differences as important but not special. Surface-level diversity dimensions such as age, sex, and race/ethnicity should be respected but should not be treated as more important than other kinds of differences (i.e., deep-level diversity). Remember, the shift from surface- to deep-level diversity helps people know and understand each other better, reduces prejudice and conflict, and leads to stronger social integration, as people want to work together and get the job done. Also, *find the common ground.* Respecting differences is important. But it's just as important, especially with diverse work forces, to actively find ways for employees to see and share commonalities.

Tailor opportunities to individuals, not groups. Special programs for training, development, mentoring, or promotions should be based on individual strengths and weaknesses, not on group status. Instead of making mentoring available for just one group of workers, create mentoring opportunities for everyone who wants to be mentored. At Pacific Enterprises, all programs, including Career Conversations forums, in which upper-level managers are publicly interviewed about themselves and how they got their jobs, are open to all employees.[88]

Solicit negative as well as positive feedback. Diversity is one of the most difficult management issues. No company or manager gets it right from the start. Consequently, companies should aggressively seek positive and negative feedback about their diversity programs. One way to do that is to use a series of measurements to see if progress is being made. L'Oréal, the cosmetics firm, has goals and measurements to track its progress in diversity with respect to recruitment, retention, and advancement as well as the extent to which the company buys goods and services from minority- and women-owned suppliers.[89]

Set high but realistic goals. Just because diversity is difficult doesn't mean that organizations shouldn't try to accomplish as much as possible. The general purpose of diversity programs is to try to create a positive work environment where no one is advantaged or disadvantaged, where "we" is everyone, where everyone can do his or her best work, where

differences are respected and not ignored, and where everyone feels comfortable. Even if progress is slow, companies should not shrink from these goals.

4.3 Diversity Training and Practices

Organizations use diversity training and several common diversity practices to manage diversity. There are two basic types of diversity training programs. **Awareness training** is designed to raise employees' awareness of diversity issues, such as the five dimensions discussed in this chapter, and to get employees to challenge underlying assumptions or stereotypes they may have about others. As a starting point in awareness training, some companies have begun using the Implicit Association Test (IAT), which measures the extent to which people associate positive or negative thoughts (i.e., underlying assumptions or stererotypes) with blacks or whites, men or women, homosexuals or heterosexuals, young or old, or other groups. For example, test takers are shown black or white faces that they must instantly pair with various words. Response times (shorter responses generally indicate stronger associations) and the pattern of associations indicates the extent to which people are biased. Most people are, and strongly so. For example, 88 percent of whites have a more positive mental as-

sociation toward whites than toward blacks, but, surprisingly, so do blacks, 48 percent of whom show the same bias. Taking the IAT is a good way to increase awareness of diversity issues. To take the IAT and to learn more about the decade of research behind it, go to **http://implicit.harvard.edu**.[90] By contrast, **skills-based diversity training** teaches employees the practical skills they need for managing a diverse work force such as flexibility and adaptability, negotiation, problem solving, and conflict resolution.[91]

Companies also use diversity audits, diversity pairing, and minority experiences for top executives to better manage diversity. **Diversity audits** are formal assessments that measure employee and management attitudes, investigate the extent to which people are advantaged or disadvantaged with respect to hiring and promotions, and review companies' diversity-related policies and procedures. For example, the results of a formal diversity audit prompted BRW, an architecture and engineering firm, to increase job advertising in minority publications, set up a diversity committee to make recommendations to upper management, provide diversity training for all employees, and rewrite the company handbook to make a stronger statement about the company's commitment to a diverse work force.[92]

Awareness training training that is designed to raise employees' awareness of diversity issues and to challenge the underlying assumptions or stereotypes they may have about others

Skills-based diversity training training that teaches employees the practical skills they need for managing a diverse work force, such as flexibility and adaptability, negotiation, problem solving, and conflict resolution

Diversity audits formal assessments that measure employee and management attitudes, investigate the extent to which people are advantaged or disadvantaged with respect to hiring and promotions, and review companies' diversity-related policies and procedures

Earlier in the chapter you learned that *mentoring,* pairing a junior employee with a senior employee, is a common strategy for creating learning and promotional opportunities for women. Diversity pairing is a special kind of mentoring. In **diversity pairing,** people of different cultural backgrounds, sexes, or races/ethnicities are paired for mentoring. The hope is that stereotypical beliefs and attitudes will change as people get to know each other as individuals.[93] Pat Carmichael, an African American female vice president at JPMorgan Chase, who was mentored early in her career by a white male, mentors men and women of all backgrounds. Regarding a current mentee, John Imperiale, a white assistant branch manager, she says, "My hope is that the exposure John has to me will give him insights when he's managing a diverse group of employees."[94]

Finally, because top managers are still overwhelmingly white and male, a number of companies believe that it is worthwhile to *have top executives experience what it is like to be in the minority.* This can be done by having top managers go to places or events where nearly everyone else is of a different sex or racial/ethnic background. At Hoechst Celanese (which has now split into two companies), top managers would join two organizations in which they were a minority. For instance, the CEO, a white male, joined the board of Hampton University, a historically African American college, and Jobs for Progress, a Hispanic organization that helps people prepare for jobs. Commenting on his experiences, he said, "The only way to break out of comfort zones is to be exposed to other people. When we are, it becomes clear that all people are similar." A Hoechst vice president who joined three organizations in which he was in the minority said, "Joining these organizations has been more helpful to me than two weeks of diversity training."[95]

Diversity pairing a mentoring program in which people of different cultural backgrounds, sexes, or races/ethnicities are paired together to get to know each other and change stereotypical beliefs and attitudes

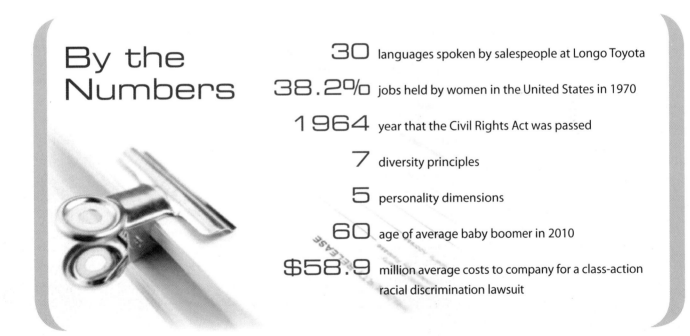

By the Numbers

30 languages spoken by salespeople at Longo Toyota

38.2% jobs held by women in the United States in 1970

1964 year that the Civil Rights Act was passed

7 diversity principles

5 personality dimensions

60 age of average baby boomer in 2010

$58.9 million average costs to company for a class-action racial discrimination lawsuit

Part 4 - Leading

MOTIVATION

What Is Motivation?

What makes people happiest and most productive at work? Is it money, benefits, opportunities for growth, interesting work, or something else altogether? And if people desire different things, how can a company keep everyone motivated? It takes insight and hard work to motivate workers to join the company, perform well, and then stay with the company. Indeed, when asked to name their biggest management challenge, nearly one-third of executives polled by Creative Group, a specialized staffing service in Menlo Park, California, cited "motivating employees."[1]

So what is motivation? **Motivation** is the set of forces that initiates, directs, and makes people persist in their efforts to accomplish a goal.[2] *Initiation of effort* is concerned with the choices that people make about how much effort to put forth in their jobs. ("Do I really knock myself out for these performance appraisals or just do a decent job?") *Direction of effort* is concerned with the choices that people make in deciding where to put forth effort in their jobs. ("I should be spending time with my high-dollar accounts instead of learning this new computer system!") *Persistence of effort* is concerned with the choices that people make about how long they will put forth effort in their jobs before reducing or eliminating those efforts. ("I'm only halfway through the project, and I'm exhausted. Do I plow through to the end, or just

Motivation the set of forces that initiates, directs, and makes people persist in their efforts to accomplish a goal

Learning Outcomes

1 explain the basics of motivation.

2 use equity theory to explain how employees' perceptions of fairness affect motivation.

3 use expectancy theory to describe how workers' expectations about rewards, effort, and the link between rewards and performance influence motivation.

4 explain how reinforcement theory works and how it can be used to motivate.

5 describe the components of goal-setting theory and how managers can use them to motivate workers.

6 discuss how the entire motivation model can be used to motivate workers.

call it quits?") Initiation, direction, and persistence are at the heart of motivation.

After reading the next section, you should be able to

1   explain the basics of motivation.

1 Basics of Motivation

Take your right hand and point the palm toward your face. Keep your thumb and pinky finger straight and bend the three middle fingers so the tips are touching your palm. Now rotate your wrist back and forth. If you were in the Regent Square Tavern in Pittsburgh, Pennsylvania, that hand signal would tell waitress Marjorie Landale that you wanted a Yuengling beer. Marjorie, who isn't deaf, would not have understood that sign a few years ago. But with a state school for the deaf nearby, the tavern always has its share of deaf customers, so she decided on her own to take classes to learn how to sign. At first, deaf customers would signal for a pen and paper to write out their orders. But after Marjorie signaled that she was learning to sign, "their eyes [would] light up, and they [would] finger-spell their order." Word quickly spread as the students started bringing in their friends, classmates, teachers, and hearing friends as well. Says Marjorie, "The deaf customers are patient with my amateur signing. They appreciate the effort."[3]

What would motivate an employee like Marjorie to voluntarily learn a new language like American Sign

Language? (Sign language is every bit as much of a language as French or Spanish.) She wasn't paid to take classes in her free time. She chose to do it on her own. And while she undoubtedly makes more tip money with a full bar than with an empty one, it's highly unlikely that she began her classes with the objective of making more money. Just what is it that motivates employees like Marjorie Landale?

*Let's learn more about motivation by building a basic model of motivation out of **1.1 effort and performance, 1.2 need satisfaction,** and **1.3 extrinsic and intrinsic rewards.** Then we'll discuss **1.4 how to motivate people with this basic model of motivation.***

1.1 Effort and Performance

When most people think of work motivation, they think that working hard (effort) should lead to a good job (performance). Exhibit 13.1 shows a basic model of work motivation and performance, displaying this process. The first thing to notice about Exhibit 13.1 is that this is a basic model of work motivation *and* performance. In practice, it's almost impossible to talk about one without mentioning the other. Not surprisingly, managers often assume motivation to be the only determinant of performance when they say things such as "Your performance was really terrible last quarter. What's the matter? Aren't you as motivated as you used to be?" In fact, motivation is just one of three primary determinants of job performance. In industrial psychology, job performance is frequently represented by this equation:

$$\text{Job Performance} = \text{Motivation} \times \text{Ability} \times \text{Situational Constraints}$$

In this formula, *job performance* is how well someone performs the requirements of the job. *Motivation,* as defined above, is effort, the degree to which someone works hard to do the job well. *Ability* is the degree to which workers possess the knowledge, skills, and talent needed to do a job well. And *situational constraints* are factors beyond the control of individual employees such as tools, policies, and resources that have an effect on job performance.

Since job performance is a multiplicative function of motivation times ability

Needs the physical or psychological requirements that must be met to ensure survival and well-being

times situational constraints, job performance will suffer if any one of these components is weak. Does this mean that motivation doesn't matter? No, not at all. It just means that all the motivation in the world won't translate into high performance when you have little ability and high situational constraints. So, while we will spend this chapter developing a model of work motivation, it is important to remember that ability and situational constraints affect job performance as well.

1.2 Need Satisfaction

In Exhibit 13.1, we started with a very basic model of motivation in which effort leads to job performance. But managers want to know, "What leads to effort?" Determining employee needs is the first step to answering that question.

Needs are the physical or psychological requirements that must be met to ensure survival and well-being.[4] As shown on the left side of Exhibit 13.2, a person's unmet need creates an uncomfortable, internal state of tension that must be resolved. For example, if you normally skip breakfast but then have to work through lunch, chances are you'll be so hungry by late afternoon that the only thing you'll be motivated to do is find something to eat. So, according to needs theories, people are motivated by unmet needs. But a need no longer motivates once it is met. When this occurs, people become satisfied, as shown on the right side of Exhibit 13.2.

Note: Throughout the chapter, as we build on this basic model, the parts of the model that we've already discussed will appear shaded in color. Since we've already discussed the effort $\longrightarrow$ performance part of the model, those components are shown with a colored background. When we add new parts to the model, they will have a white background. Since we're adding need satisfaction to the model at this step, the need-satisfaction components of unsatisfied need, tension, energized

Exhibit 13.1

A Basic Model of Work Motivation and Performance

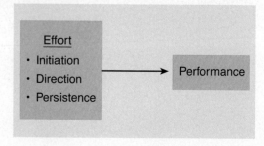

Exhibit 13.2

Adding Need Satisfaction to the Model

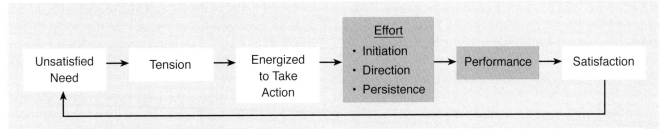

As shown on the left side of this exhibit, a person's unsatisfied need creates an uncomfortable, internal state of tension that must be resolved. So, according to needs theories, people are motivated by unmet needs. But once a need is met, it no longer motivates. When this occurs, people become satisfied, as shown on the right side of the exhibit.

to take action, and satisfaction are shown with a white background. This shading convention should make it easier to understand the work motivation model as we add to it in each section of the chapter.

Since people are motivated by unmet needs, managers must learn what those unmet needs are and address them. This is not always a straightforward task, however, because different needs theories suggest different needs categories. Consider three well-known needs theories. Maslow's Hierarchy of Needs suggests that people are motivated by *physiological* (food and water), *safety* (physical and economic), *belongingness* (friendship, love, social interaction), *esteem* (achievement and recogni-

tion), and *self-actualization* (realizing your full potential) needs.[5] Alderfer's ERG Theory collapses Maslow's five needs into three: *existence* (safety and physiological needs), *relatedness* (belongingness), and *growth* (esteem and self-actualization).[6] McClelland's Learned Needs Theory suggests that people are motivated by the need for *affiliation* (to be liked and accepted), the need for *achievement* (to accomplish challenging goals), or the need for *power* (to influence others).[7]

Things become even more complicated when we consider the different predictions made by these theories. According to Maslow, needs are arranged in a hierarchy from low (physiological) to high (self-actualization), and

> Since people are motivated by **unmet needs**, managers must learn what those unmet needs are and **address them**.

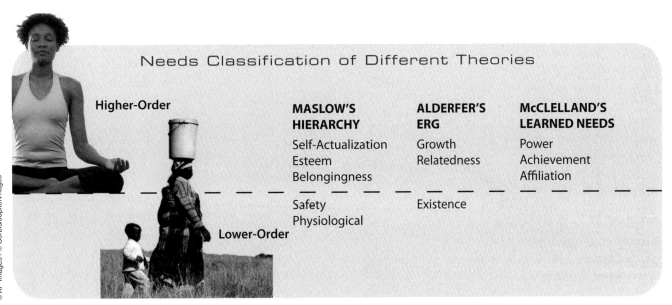

Needs Classification of Different Theories

Higher-Order

MASLOW'S HIERARCHY	ALDERFER'S ERG	McCLELLAND'S LEARNED NEEDS
Self-Actualization	Growth	Power
Esteem	Relatedness	Achievement
Belongingness		Affiliation
Safety	Existence	
Physiological		

Lower-Order

people are motivated by their lowest unsatisfied need. As each need is met, they work their way up the hierarchy from physiological to self-actualization needs. By contrast, Alderfer says that people can be motivated by more than one need at a time. Furthermore, he suggests that people are just as likely to move down the needs hierarchy as up, particularly when they are unable to achieve satisfaction at the next higher need level. McClelland argues that the degree to which particular needs motivate varies tremendously from person to person, with some people being motivated primarily by achievement and others by power or affiliation. Moreover, McClelland says that needs are learned, not innate. For instance, studies show that children whose parents own a small business or hold a managerial position are much more likely to have a high need for achievement.[8]

So, with three different sets of needs and three very different ideas about how needs motivate, how do we provide a practical answer to managers who just want to know "What leads to effort?" Fortunately, the research simplifies things a bit. To start, studies indicate that there are two basic kinds of needs categories.[9] As you would expect, *lower-order needs* are concerned with safety and with physiological and existence requirements, whereas *higher-order needs* are concerned with relationships (belongingness, relatedness, and affiliation); challenges and accomplishments (esteem, self-actualization, growth, and achievement); and in-

> **Extrinsic reward** a reward that is tangible, visible to others, and given to employees contingent on the performance of specific tasks or behaviors

fluence (power). Studies generally show that higher-order needs will not motivate people as long as lower-order needs remain unsatisfied.[10]

For example, imagine that you graduated from college six months ago and are still looking for your first job. With money running short (you're probably living on your credit cards) and the possibility of having to move back in with your parents looming (if this doesn't motivate you, what will?), your basic needs for food, shelter, and security drive your thoughts, behavior, and choices at this point. But once you land that job, find a great place (of your own!) to live, and put some money in the bank, these basic needs should decrease in importance as you begin to think about making new friends and taking on challenging work assignments. In fact, once lower-order needs are satisfied, it's difficult for managers to predict which higher-order needs will motivate behavior.[11] Some people will be motivated by affiliation, while others will be motivated by growth or esteem. Also, the relative importance of the various needs may change over time but not necessarily in any predictable pattern.

1.3 Extrinsic and Intrinsic Rewards

So, what leads to effort? In part, needs do. But rewards are important, too, and no discussion of motivation would be complete without considering them. Let's add two kinds of rewards, extrinsic and intrinsic, to the model in Exhibit 13.3.[12]

Extrinsic rewards are tangible and visible to others and are given to employees contingent on the performance of specific tasks or behaviors.[13] External agents (managers, for example) determine and control the dis-

Exhibit 13.3

Adding Rewards to the Model

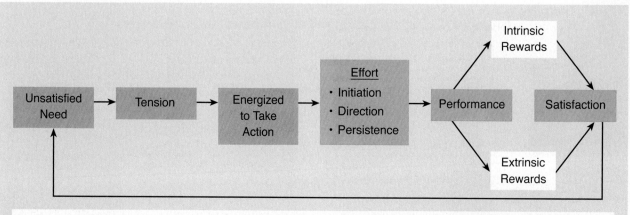

Performing a job well can be rewarding intrinsically (the job itself is fun, challenging, or interesting) or extrinsically (as you receive better pay or promotions, etc.). Intrinsic and extrinsic rewards lead to satisfaction of various needs.

Win-Win Motivation

Shari Adler took six months off from her job at Pfizer and spent it in Tanzania. But she wasn't on safari. She was working for the Tanzanian Ministry of Health. Adler reaped the benefits of Pfizer's paid volunteerism program, a strategy increasingly adopted by companies for a host of reasons. Younger workers want to see companies do more than write a check to help society. Moreover, meaningful volunteer opportunities help attract and retain workers who are motivated to use their job skills to help others in need. Paid volunteerism benefits companies too, since employees return with broader perspectives, more independence and confidence, and new skills that can enhance their motivation and on-the-job performance.

Source: S. E. Needleman, "The Latest Office Perk: Getting Paid to Volunteer," *The Wall Street Journal,* 29 April 2008, D1.

© Charles O. Cecil/Alamy

tribution, frequency, and amount of extrinsic rewards such as pay, company stock, benefits, and promotions. For example, IKEA, the Sweden-based home furniture retailer, awarded its employees $80 million in bonuses to celebrate the company's 54 years of success. IKEA promoted the "Big Thank You" sale as a way to encourage customers to make purchases on its 54th anniversary, and all of the profits earned that day were distributed to its employees.[14]

Why do companies need extrinsic rewards? To get people to do things they wouldn't otherwise do. Companies use extrinsic rewards to motivate people to perform four basic behaviors: join the organization, regularly attend their jobs, perform their jobs well, and stay with the organization.[15] Think about it. Would you show up to work every day to do the best possible job that you could just out of the goodness of your heart? Very few people would. This is why Cognex, maker of industrial vision systems (robots that "see"), rewards its employees for perseverance, or staying with the company—for a long time. To Dr. Robert Shillman, perseverance means not only longevity but the willingess and ability to keep working on difficult issues for an extended period. The longer an employee perseveres, the greater the rewards.[16]

By contrast, **intrinsic rewards** are the natural rewards associated with performing a task or activity for its own sake. For example, aside from the external rewards management offers for doing something well, employees often find the activities or tasks they perform interesting and enjoyable. Examples of intrinsic rewards include a sense of accomplishment or achievement, a feeling of responsi-

bility, the chance to learn something new or interact with others, or simply the fun that comes from performing an interesting, challenging, and engaging task.

Which types of rewards are most important to workers in general? A number of surveys suggest that both extrinsic and intrinsic rewards are important. One survey found that the most important rewards were good benefits and health insurance, job security, a week or more of vacation (all extrinsic rewards), interesting work, the opportunity to learn new skills, and independent work situations (all intrinsic rewards). And employee preferences for intrinsic and extrinsic rewards appear to be relatively stable. Studies conducted over the last three decades have consistently found that employees are twice as likely to indicate that important and meaningful work matters more to them than what they are paid.[17]

1.4 Motivating with the Basics

So, given the basic model of work motivation based on needs and rewards in Exhibit 13.3, what practical steps can managers take to motivate employees to increase their effort?

Well, *start by asking people what their needs are.* If managers don't know what workers' needs are, they won't be able to provide them the opportunities and rewards that can satisfy those needs. Tommy Lee Hayes-Brown, who is in charge of recognition programs at MetLife, illus-

> **Intrinsic reward** a natural reward associated with performing a task or activity for its own sake

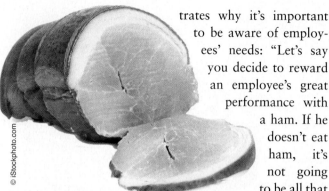

trates why it's important to be aware of employees' needs: "Let's say you decide to reward an employee's great performance with a ham. If he doesn't eat ham, it's not going to be all that meaningful."[18]

Next, *satisfy lower-order needs first.* Since higher-order needs will not motivate people as long as lower-order needs remain unsatisfied, companies should satisfy lower-order needs first. In practice, this means providing the equipment, training, and knowledge to create a safe workplace free of physical risks, paying employees well enough to provide financial security, and offering a benefits package that will protect employees and their families through good medical coverage and health and disability insurance.

Third, managers should *expect people's needs to change.* As some needs are satisfied or situations change, what motivated people before may not motivate them now. Likewise, what motivates people to accept a job (pay and benefits) may not necessarily motivate them once they have the job (the job itself, opportunities for advancement). Managers should also expect needs to change as people mature.[19] For older employees, benefits are as important as pay, which is always ranked as more important by younger employees. Older employees also rank job security as more important than personal and family time, which is more important to younger employees.[20]

Finally, *as needs change and lower-order needs are satisfied, create opportunities for employees to satisfy higher-order needs.* Recall that intrinsic rewards such as accomplishment, achievement, learning something new, and interacting with others are the natural rewards associated with performing a task or activity for its own sake. And, with the exception of influence (power), intrinsic rewards correspond very closely to higher-order needs that are concerned with relationships (belongingness, relatedness, and affiliation) and challenges and accomplishments (esteem, self-actualization, growth, and achievement). Therefore, one way for managers to meet employees' higher-order needs is to create opportunities for employees to experience intrinsic

Equity theory a theory that states that people will be motivated when they perceive that they are being treated fairly

rewards by providing challenging work, encouraging employees to take greater responsibility for their work, and giving employees the freedom to pursue tasks and projects they find naturally interesting.

How Perceptions and Expectations Affect Motivation

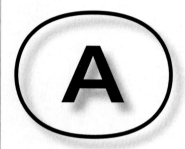

So we've now seen that people are motivated to achieve intrinsic and extrinsic rewards. When employees believe that rewards are not fairly awarded, or if they don't believe they can achieve the performance goals the company has set for them, they won't be very motivated.

 After reading the next two sections, you should be able to

2 use equity theory to explain how employees' perceptions of fairness affect motivation.

3 use expectancy theory to describe how workers' expectations about rewards, effort, and the link between rewards and performance influence motivation.

2 Equity Theory

Fairness, or what people perceive to be fair, is a critical issue in organizations. **Equity theory** says that people will be motivated at work when they *perceive* that they are being treated fairly. In particular, equity theory stresses the importance of perceptions. So, regardless of the actual level of rewards people receive, they must also perceive that they are being treated fairly relative to others. For example, you learned in Chapter 11 that the average CEO now makes 364 times more than the average worker.[21] Many people believe that CEO pay is obscenely high and unfair. In order to keep CEO salaries in check, companies like Aflac, a Georgia insurance company, have adopted "say-on-pay" policies that allow investors a vote on executive compensation packages.[22] Others believe that CEO pay is fair because if it were easier to find good CEOs, then CEOs would be paid much less. Equity theory doesn't focus on objective equity (i.e., that CEOs make 364 times more than blue-collar workers). Instead, it says that equity, like beauty, is in the eye of the beholder.

*Let's learn more about equity theory by examining **2.1 the components of equity theory, 2.2 how people react to perceived inequities,** and **2.3 how to motivate people using equity theory.***

2.1 Components of Equity Theory

The basic components of equity theory are inputs, outcomes, and referents. **Inputs** are the contributions employees make to the organization. Inputs include education and training, intelligence, experience, effort, number of hours worked, and ability. **Outcomes** are what employees receive in exchange for their contributions to the organization. Outcomes include pay, fringe benefits, status symbols, and job titles and assignments. And, since perceptions of equity depend on comparisons, **referents** are others with whom people compare themselves to determine if they have been treated fairly. The referent can be a single person (comparing yourself with a coworker), or a generalized other (comparing yourself with "students in general," for example), or could be with yourself over time ("I was better off last year than I am this year"). Usually, people choose to compare themselves to referents who hold the same or similar jobs or who are otherwise similar in gender, race, age, tenure, or other characteristics.[23]

According to equity theory, employees compare their outcomes (the rewards they receive from the organization) to their inputs (their contributions to the organization). This comparison of outcomes to inputs is called the **outcome/input (O/I) ratio.**

$$\frac{\text{OUTCOMES}_{\text{SELF}}}{\text{INPUTS}_{\text{SELF}}} = \frac{\text{OUTCOMES}_{\text{REFERENT}}}{\text{INPUTS}_{\text{REFERENT}}}$$

After an internal comparison in which they compare their outcomes to their inputs, employees then make an external comparison in which they compare their O/I ratio with the O/I ratio of a referent.[24] When people perceive that their O/I ratio is equal to the referent's O/I ratio, they conclude that they are being treated fairly. But, when people perceive that their O/I ratio is different from their referent's O/I ratio, they conclude that they have been treated inequitably or unfairly.

Inequity can take two forms, underreward and overreward. **Underreward** occurs when your O/I ratio is worse than your referent's O/I ratio. In other words, you are getting fewer outcomes relative to your inputs than your referent is getting. When people perceive that

Change in China

In chapter 5, you learned about Geert Hofstede's studies of cultural differences. Hofstede studied China in the 1980s, when he found Chinese workers to be motivated by money (high masculinity), collectivist, and ill-inclined to offer suggestions to a supervisor (high power distance). Not so for the Chinese worker of today, who is individualist, values leisure time alongside salary, has plenty of ideas about how the company can improve, and shares them in culturally sensitive ways. This is important information for Western companies seeking to hire and motivate workers in China, as they might respond better to a recognition dinner than a bonus or a plaque.

Source: K. King-Metters and R. Metters, "Misunderstanding the Chinese Worker," *The Wall Street Journal*, 7 July 2008, R11.

they have been underrewarded, they tend to experience anger or frustration.

By contrast, **overreward** occurs when your O/I ratio is better than your referent's O/I ratio. In this case, you are getting more outcomes relative to your inputs than your referent is. In theory, when people perceive that they have been overrewarded, they experience guilt. But, not surprisingly, people have a very high tolerance for overreward. It takes a tremendous amount of overpayment before people decide that their pay or benefits are more than they deserve.

2.2 How People React to Perceived Inequity

So what happens when people perceive that they have been treated inequitably at work? Exhibit 13.4 on the next page shows that perceived inequity affects satisfaction. In the case of underreward, this usually translates into frustration or anger; with overreward, the reaction is guilt. These reactions lead to tension and a strong need to take action to restore equity in some way. At first, a slight inequity may not be strong enough to motivate an employee to take immediate action. If the inequity continues or there are multiple inequities, however, tension may build over time until a point of intolerance is reached, and the person is energized to take action.[25]

Inputs in equity theory, the contributions employees make to the organization

Outcomes in equity theory, the rewards employees receive for their contributions to the organization

Referents in equity theory, others with whom people compare themselves to determine if they have been treated fairly

Outcome/input (O/I) ratio in equity theory, an employee's perception of how the rewards received from an organization compare with the employee's contributions to that organization

Underreward a form of inequity in which you are getting fewer outcomes relative to inputs than your referent is getting

Overreward a form of inequity in which you are getting more outcomes relative to inputs than your referent

Exhibit 13.4

Adding Equity Theory to the Model

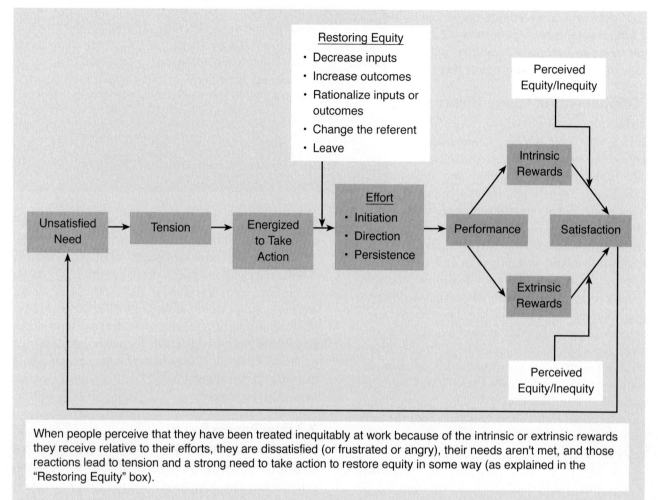

Restoring Equity
- Decrease inputs
- Increase outcomes
- Rationalize inputs or outcomes
- Change the referent
- Leave

Perceived Equity/Inequity

Unsatisfied Need → Tension → Energized to Take Action → **Effort**: Initiation, Direction, Persistence → Performance → Intrinsic Rewards / Extrinsic Rewards → Satisfaction

Perceived Equity/Inequity

When people perceive that they have been treated inequitably at work because of the intrinsic or extrinsic rewards they receive relative to their efforts, they are dissatisfied (or frustrated or angry), their needs aren't met, and those reactions lead to tension and a strong need to take action to restore equity in some way (as explained in the "Restoring Equity" box).

When people perceive that they have been treated unfairly, they may try to restore equity by reducing inputs, increasing outcomes, rationalizing inputs or outcomes, changing the referent, or simply leaving. We will discuss these possible responses in terms of the inequity associated with underreward, which is much more common than the inequity associated with overreward.

People who perceive that they have been underrewarded may try to restore equity by *decreasing or withholding their inputs (i.e., effort)*. Pilots at American Airlines took a 23 percent pay cut after 9/11 to help keep the airline solvent. When American began doing well again, and top managers collectively received a quarter-billion dollars in stock, the pilots requested their old salary back. It is common for airline pilots to protest their employers in such circumstances by calling in sick or going on strike.[26]

Increasing outcomes is another way people try to restore equity. This might include asking for a raise or

pointing out the inequity to the boss and hoping that he or she takes care of it. Sometimes, however, employees may go to external organizations such as labor unions, federal agencies, or the courts for help in increasing outcomes to restore equity.

Another method of restoring equity is to *rationalize or distort inputs or outcomes.* Instead of decreasing inputs or increasing outcomes, employees restore equity by making mental or emotional adjustments to their O/I ratios or the O/I ratios of their referents. For example, suppose that a company downsizes 10 percent of its work force. It's likely that the survivors, the people who still have jobs, will be angry or frustrated with company management because of the layoffs. If alternative jobs are difficult to find, however, these survivors may rationalize or distort their O/I ratios and conclude, "Well, things could be worse. At least I still have my job." Rationalizing or distorting outcomes may be used when other ways to restore equity aren't available.

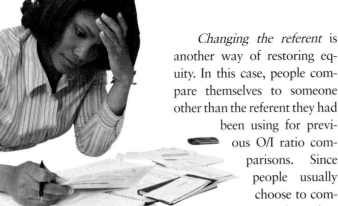

Changing the referent is another way of restoring equity. In this case, people compare themselves to someone other than the referent they had been using for previous O/I ratio comparisons. Since people usually choose to compare themselves to others who hold the same or similar jobs or who are otherwise similar (i.e., friends, family members, neighbors who work at other companies), they may change referents to restore equity when their personal situations change, such as a decrease in job status or pay.[27] Finally, when none of these methods are possible or restore equity, *employees may leave* by quitting their jobs, transferring, or increasing absenteeism.[28]

2.3 Motivating with Equity Theory

What practical steps can managers take to use equity theory to motivate employees? They can *start by looking for and correcting major inequities.* Among other things, equity theory makes us aware that an employee's sense of fairness is based on subjective perceptions. What one employee considers grossly unfair may not affect another employee's perceptions of equity at all. Although these different perceptions make it difficult for managers to create conditions that satisfy all employees, it's critical that they do their best to take care of major inequities that can energize employees to take disruptive, costly, or harmful actions such as decreasing inputs or leaving. So, whenever possible, managers should look for and correct major inequities.

Second, managers can *reduce employees' inputs.* Increasing outcomes is often the first and only strategy that companies use to restore equity, yet reducing employee inputs is just as viable a strategy. In fact, with dual-career couples working 50-hour weeks, more and more employees are looking for ways to reduce stress and restore a balance between work and family. Consequently, it may make sense to ask employees to do less, not more; to have them identify and eliminate the 20 percent of their jobs that doesn't increase productivity or add value for customers; and to eliminate company-imposed requirements that really aren't critical to the performance of managers, employees, or the company (e.g., unnecessary meetings and reports).

Finally, managers should *make sure decision-making processes are fair.* Equity theory focuses on **distributive justice,** the degree to which outcomes and rewards are fairly distributed or allocated. However, **procedural justice,** the fairness of the procedures used to make reward allocation decisions, is just as important.[29] Procedural justice matters because even when employees are unhappy with their outcomes (i.e., low pay), they're much less likely to be unhappy with company management if they believe that the procedures used to allocate outcomes were fair. For example, employees who are laid off tend to be hostile toward their employer when they perceive that the procedures leading to the layoffs were unfair. By contrast, employees who perceive layoff procedures to be fair tend to continue to support and trust their employers.[30] Also, if employees perceive that their outcomes are unfair (i.e., distributive injustice), but that the decisions and procedures leading to those outcomes were fair (i.e., procedural justice), they are much more likely to seek constructive ways of restoring equity such as discussing these matters with their manager. In contrast, if employees perceive both distributive and procedural injustice, they may resort to more destructive tactics such as withholding effort, absenteeism, tardiness, or even sabotage and theft.[31]

3 Expectancy Theory

One of the hardest things about motivating people is that rewards that are attractive to some employees are unattractive to others. **Expectancy theory** says that people will be motivated to the extent to which they believe that their efforts will lead to good performance, that good performance will be rewarded, and that they will be offered attractive rewards.[32]

*Let's learn more about expectancy theory by examining **3.1 the components of expectancy theory** and **3.2 how to use expectancy theory as a motivational tool.***

3.1 Components of Expectancy Theory

Expectancy theory holds that people make conscious choices about their motivation. The three factors that affect those choices are

Distributive justice the perceived degree to which outcomes and rewards are fairly distributed or allocated

Procedural justice the perceived fairness of the process used to make reward allocation decisions

Expectancy theory a theory that states that people will be motivated to the extent to which they believe that their efforts will lead to good performance, that good performance will be rewarded, and that they will be offered attractive rewards

valence, expectancy, and instrumentality.

Valence is simply the attractiveness or desirability of various rewards or outcomes. Expectancy theory recognizes that the same reward or outcome—say, a promotion—will be highly attractive to some people, will be highly disliked by others, and will not make much difference one way or the other to still others. Accordingly, when people are deciding how much effort to put forth, expectancy theory says that they will consider the valence of all possible rewards and outcomes that they can receive from their jobs. The greater the sum of those valences, each of which can be positive, negative, or neutral, the more effort people will choose to put forth on the job.

Expectancy is the perceived relationship between effort and performance. When expectancies are strong, employees believe that their hard work and efforts will result in good performance, so they work harder. By contrast, when expectancies are weak, employees figure that no matter what they do or how hard they work, they won't be able to perform their jobs successfully, so they don't work as hard.

Instrumentality is the perceived relationship between performance and rewards. When instrumentality is strong, employees believe that improved performance will lead to better and more rewards, so they choose to work harder. When instrumentality is weak, employees don't believe that better performance will result in more or better rewards, so they choose not to work as hard.

Expectancy theory holds that for people to be highly motivated, all three variables—valence, expectancy, and instrumentality—must be high. Thus, expectancy theory can be represented by the following simple equation:

Motivation = Valence × Expectancy × Instrumentality

If any one of these variables (valence, expectancy, or instrumentality) declines, overall motivation will decline, too.

Exhibit 13.5 incorporates the expectancy theory variables into our motivation model. Valence and instrumentality combine to affect employees' willingness to put forth effort (i.e., the degree to which they are energized to take action),

Valence the attractiveness or desirability of a reward or outcome

Expectancy the perceived relationship between effort and preformance

Instrumentality the perceived relationship between performance and rewards

while expectancy transforms intended effort ("I'm really going to work hard in this job") into actual effort. If you're offered rewards that you desire and you believe that you will in fact receive these rewards for good performance, you're highly likely to be energized to take action. However, you're not likely to actually exert effort unless you also believe that you can do the job (i.e., that your efforts will lead to successful performance).

3.2 Motivating with Expectancy Theory

What practical steps can managers take to use expectancy theory to motivate employees? First, they can *systematically gather information to find out what employees want from their jobs.* In addition to individual managers directly asking employees what they want from their jobs (see Subsection 1.4 "Motivating with the Basics"), companies need to survey their employees regularly to determine their wants, needs, and dissatisfactions. Since people consider the valence of all the possible rewards and outcomes that they can receive from their jobs, regular identification of wants, needs, and dissatisfactions gives companies the chance to turn negatively valent rewards and outcomes into positively valent rewards and outcomes, thus raising overall motivation and effort. Therefore, employers should routinely survey employees to identify not only the range of rewards that are valued by most employees but also to understand the preferences of specific employees.

Second, managers can *take specific steps to link rewards to individual performance in a way that is clear and understandable to employees.* Unfortunately, most employees are extremely dissatisfied with the link between pay and performance in their organizations. In one study, based on a representative sample, 80 percent of the employees surveyed wanted to be paid according to a different kind of pay system! Moreover, only 32 percent of employees were satisfied with how their annual pay raises were determined, and only 22 percent were happy with the way the starting salaries for their jobs were determined.[33] One way to make sure that employees see the connection between pay and performance (see Chapter 11 for a discussion of compensation strategies) is for managers to publicize the way in which pay decisions are made. This is especially important given that only 41 percent of employees know how their pay increases are determined.[34]

Exhibit 13.5

Adding Expectancy Theory to the Model

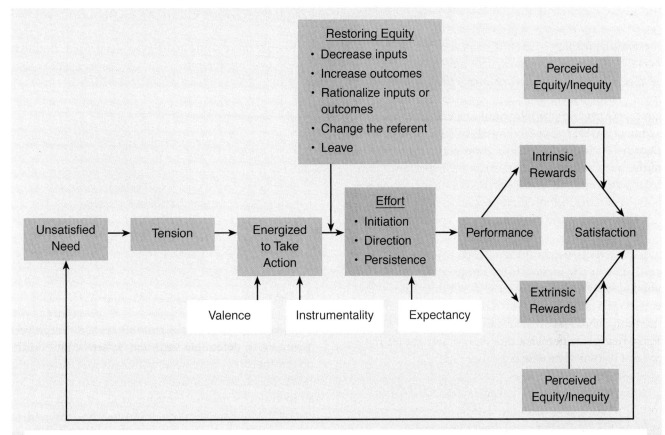

If rewards are attractive (valence) and linked to performance (instrumentality), then people are energized to take action. In other words, good performance gets them rewards that they want. Intended effort (i.e., energized to take action) turns into actual effort when people expect that their hard work and efforts will result in good performance. After all, why work hard if that hard work is wasted?

© Image Source Black/JupiterImages

$50 Windfall?

Employees at Kimley-Horn, a big civil-engineering firm in North Carolina, can at any time, for any reason, award a bonus of $50 to another employee. Bonuses don't have to be approved by anyone, and there are no strings attached. An employee who wants to award a bonus to a coworker downloads a form, fills it out, and often delivers it to the awardee in person. The awardee then redeems the form at the payroll department for a $50 check. Kimley-Horn employees give out over 6,100 bonuses per year for a total corporate expense nearing $340,000.

Source: A. C. Pasquariello, "Grant Makers," *Fast Company*, April 2007, 32.

Finally, managers should *empower employees to make decisions if management really wants them to believe that their hard work and effort will lead to good performance.* If valent rewards are linked to good performance, people should be energized to take action. However, this works only if they also believe that their efforts will lead to good performance. One of the ways that managers destroy the expectancy that hard work and effort will lead to good performance is by restricting what employees can do or by ignoring employees' ideas. In Chapter 9, you learned that *empowerment* is a feeling of intrinsic motivation, in which workers perceive their work to have meaning and perceive themselves to be competent, to have an impact, and to be capable of self-determination.[35] So, if managers want workers to have strong expectancies, they should empower them to make decisions. Doing so will motivate employees to take active rather than passive roles in their work.

Reinforcement theory a theory that states that behavior is a function of its consequences, that behaviors followed by positive consequences will occur more frequently, and that behaviors followed by negative consequences, or not followed by positive consequences, will occur less frequently

Reinforcement the process of changing behavior by changing the consequences that follow behavior

Reinforcement contingencies cause-and-effect relationships between the performance of specific behaviors and specific consequences

Schedule of reinforcement rules that specify which behaviors will be reinforced, which consequences will follow those behaviors, and the schedule by which those consequences will be delivered

How Rewards and Goals Affect Motivation

When used properly, rewards motivate and energize employees. But when used incorrectly, they can demotivate, baffle, and even anger them. Goals are also supposed to motivate employees. But leaders who fo-cus blindly on meeting goals at all costs often find that they destroy motivation.

After reading the next three sections, you should be able to

4 explain how reinforcement theory works and how it can be used to motivate.

5 describe the components of goal-setting theory and how managers can use them to motivate workers.

6 discuss how the entire motivation model can be used to motivate workers.

4 Reinforcement Theory

Reinforcement theory says that behavior is a function of its consequences, that behaviors followed by positive consequences (i.e., reinforced) will occur more frequently, and that behaviors followed by negative consequences, or not followed by positive consequences, will occur less frequently.[36] More specifically, **reinforcement** is the process of changing behavior by changing the consequences that follow behavior.[37]

Reinforcement has two parts: reinforcement contingencies and schedules of reinforcement. **Reinforcement contingencies** are the cause-and-effect relationships between the performance of specific behaviors and specific consequences. For example, if you get docked an hour's pay for being late to work, then a reinforcement contingency exists between a behavior (being late to work) and a consequence (losing an hour's pay). A **schedule of reinforcement** is the set of rules regarding reinforcement contingencies such as which behaviors will be reinforced, which consequences will follow those behaviors, and the schedule by which those consequences will be delivered.[38]

Exhibit 13.6 incorporates reinforcement contingencies and reinforcement schedules into our motivation model. First, notice that extrinsic rewards and the schedules of reinforcement used to deliver them are the primary method for creating reinforcement contingencies in organizations. In turn, those reinforcement contingencies directly affect valences (the attractiveness of rewards), instrumentality (the perceived link between rewards and performance), and effort (how hard employees will work).

*Let's learn more about reinforcement theory by examining **4.1 the components of reinforcement theory, 4.2 the different schedules for delivering reinforcement,** and **4.3 how to motivate with reinforcement theory.***

4.1 Components of Reinforcement Theory

As just described, *reinforcement contingencies* are the cause-and-effect relationships between the performance of specific behaviors and specific consequences. There are four kinds of reinforcement contingencies: positive reinforcement, negative reinforcement, punishment, and extinction.

Positive reinforcement strengthens behavior (i.e., increases its frequency) by following behaviors with desirable consequences. By contrast, **negative reinforcement** strengthens behavior by withholding an unpleasant con-

sequence when employees perform a specific behavior. Negative reinforcement is also called *avoidance learning* because workers perform a behavior to *avoid* a negative consequence. For example, at the Florist Network, a small business in Buffalo, New York, company management instituted a policy of requiring good attendance for employees to receive their annual bonuses. Employee attendance improved significantly when excessive absenteeism threatened to result in the loss of $1,500 or more.[39]

> **Positive reinforcement** reinforcement that strengthens behavior by following behaviors with desirable consequences
>
> **Negative reinforcement** reinforcement that strengthens behavior by withholding an unpleasant consequence when employees perform a specific behavior

Exhibit 13.6

Adding Reinforcement Theory to the Model

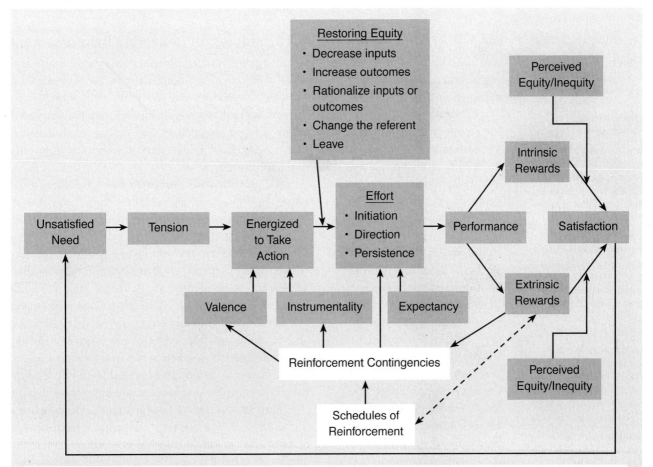

Extrinsic rewards and the schedules of reinforcement used to deliver them are the primary method for creating reinforcement contingencies in organizations. In turn, those reinforcement contingencies directly affect valences (the attractiveness of rewards), instrumentality (the perceived link between rewards and performance), and effort (how hard employees will work).

By contrast, **punishment** weakens behavior (i.e., decreases its frequency) by following behaviors with undesirable consequences. For example, the standard disciplinary or punishment process in most companies is an oral warning ("Don't ever do that again"), followed by a written warning ("This letter is to discuss the serious problem you're having with . . . "), followed by three days off without pay ("While you're at home not being paid, we want you to think hard about . . . "), followed by being fired ("That was your last chance"). Though punishment can weaken behavior, managers have to be careful to avoid the backlash that sometimes occurs when employees are punished at work. For example, Frito-Lay began getting complaints from customers that they were finding potato chips with obscene messages written on them. Frito-Lay eventually traced the problem to a potato chip plant where supervisors had fired 58 out of the 210 workers for disciplinary reasons over a nine-month period. The remaining employees were so angry over what they saw as unfair treatment from management that they began writing the phrases on potato chips with felt-tipped pens.[40]

Extinction is a reinforcement strategy in which a positive consequence is no longer allowed to follow a previously reinforced behavior. By removing the positive consequence, extinction weakens the behavior, making it less likely to occur. Based on the idea of positive reinforcement, most companies give company leaders and managers substantial financial rewards when the company performs well. Based on the idea of extinction, you would then expect that leaders and managers would not be rewarded (i.e., removing the positive consequence) when companies perform poorly. If companies really want pay to reinforce the right kinds of behaviors, then rewards have to be removed when company management doesn't produce successful performance.

4.2 Schedules for Delivering Reinforcement

As mentioned earlier, a *schedule of reinforcement* is the set of rules regarding reinforcement contingencies such as which behaviors will be reinforced, which consequences will follow those behaviors, and the schedule by which those consequences will be delivered. There are two categories of reinforcement schedules: continuous and intermittent.

With **continuous reinforcement schedules,** a consequence follows every instance of a behavior. For example, employees working on a piece-rate pay system earn money (consequence) for every part they manufacture (behavior). The more they produce, the more they earn. By contrast, with **intermittent reinforcement schedules,** consequences are delivered after a specified or average time has elapsed or after a specified or average number of behaviors has occurred. As Exhibit 13.7 shows, there are four types of intermittent reinforcement schedules. Two of these are based on time and are called *interval reinforcement schedules,* while the other two, known as *ratio schedules,* are based on behaviors.

With **fixed interval reinforcement schedules,** consequences follow a behavior only after a fixed time has elapsed. For example, most people receive their paychecks on a fixed interval schedule (e.g., once or twice per month). As long as they work (behavior) during a specified pay period (interval), they get a paycheck (consequence). With **variable interval reinforcement schedules,** consequences follow a behavior after dif-

---

Punishment reinforcement that weakens behavior by following behaviors with undesirable consequences

Extinction reinforcement in which a positive consequence is no longer allowed to follow a previously reinforced behavior, thus weakening the behavior

Continuous reinforcement schedule a schedule that requires a consequence to be administered following every instance of a behavior

Intermittent reinforcement schedule a schedule in which consequences are delivered after a specified or average time has elapsed or after a specified or average number of behaviors has occurred

Fixed interval reinforcement schedule an intermittent schedule in which consequences follow a behavior only after a fixed time has elapsed

Variable interval reinforcement schedule an intermittent schedule in which the time between a behavior and the following consequences varies around a specified average

Exhibit 13.7

Intermittent Reinforcement Schedules

INTERMITTENT REINFORCEMENT SCHEDULES		
	FIXED	**VARIABLE**
INTERVAL (TIME)	Consequences follow behavior after a fixed time has elapsed.	Consequences follow behavior after different times, some shorter and some longer, that vary around a specific average time.
RATIO (BEHAVIOR)	Consequences follow a specific number of behaviors.	Consequences follow a different number of behaviors, sometimes more and sometimes less, that vary around a specified average number of behaviors.

ferent times, some shorter and some longer, that vary around a specified average time. On a 90-day variable interval reinforcement schedule, you might receive a bonus after 80 days or perhaps after 100 days, but the average interval between performing your job well (behavior) and receiving your bonus (consequence) would be 90 days.

With **fixed ratio reinforcement schedules,** consequences are delivered following a specific number of behaviors. For example, a car salesperson might receive a $1,000 bonus after every 10 sales. Therefore, a salesperson with only 9 sales would not receive the bonus until he or she finally sold a 10th car.

With **variable ratio reinforcement schedules,** consequences are delivered following a different number of behaviors, sometimes more and sometimes less, that vary around a specified average number of behaviors. With a 10-car variable ratio reinforcement schedule, a salesperson might receive the bonus after 7 car sales, or after 12, 11, or 9 sales, but the average number of cars sold before receiving the bonus would be 10 cars.

Which reinforcement schedules work best? In the past, the standard advice was to use continuous reinforcement when employees were learning new behaviors because reinforcement after each success leads to faster learning. Likewise, the standard advice was to use intermittent reinforcement schedules to maintain behavior after it is learned because intermittent rewards are supposed to make behavior much less subject to extinction.[41] Research shows, however, that except for interval-based systems, which usually produce weak results, the effectiveness of continuous reinforcement, fixed ratio, and variable ratio schedules differs very little.[42] In organizational settings, all three produce consistently large increases over noncontingent reward schedules. So managers should choose whichever of these three is easiest to use in their companies.

4.3 Motivating with Reinforcement Theory

What practical steps can managers take to use reinforcement theory to motivate employees? University of Nebraska business professor Fred Luthans, who has been studying the effects of reinforcement theory in organizations for more than a quarter of a century, says that there are five steps to motivating workers with reinforcement theory: *identify, measure, analyze, intervene,* and *evaluate* critical performance-related behaviors.[43]

Identify means identifying critical, observable, performance-related behaviors. These are the behaviors that are most important to successful job performance. In addition, they must also be easily observed so that they can be accurately measured. *Measure* means measuring the baseline frequencies of these behaviors. In other words, find out how often workers perform them. *Analyze* means analyzing the causes and consequences of these behaviors. Analyzing the causes helps managers create the conditions that produce these critical behaviors, and analyzing the consequences helps them determine if these behaviors produce the results that they want. *Intervene* means changing the organization by using positive and negative reinforcement to increase the frequency of these critical behaviors. *Evaluate* means evaluating the extent to which the intervention actually changed workers' behavior. This is done by comparing behavior after the intervention to the original baseline of behavior before the intervention.

In addition to these five steps, managers should remember three other key things when motivating

Fixed ratio reinforcement schedule an intermittent schedule in which consequences are delivered following a specific number of behaviors

Variable ratio reinforcement schedule an intermittent schedule in which consequences are delivered following a different number of behaviors, sometimes more and sometimes less, that vary around a specified average number of behaviors

Trashing the Workweek

Giving employees freedom to go to a baseball game on Wednesday afternoon might seem like a risky way to motivate them. But the Results-Only Work Environment (ROWE) approach, pioneered at Best Buy by Cali Ressler and Jodi Thompson, taps into employees' need for independence in order to get them to perform at their best. Employees at J. A. Counter, an insurance and investment advisory company in New Richmond, Wisconsin, determine for themselves when and how they work. Want to go hunting mid-week? Go for it. Instead of being responsible to the clock, employees are responsible to outcomes, making them "mini-entrepreneurs" for the company. ROWE has boosted morale and productivity in many companies.

Source: S. Westcott, "Beyond Flextime: Trashing the Workweek," *Inc.*, August 2008, 30-31.

with reinforcement theory. *Don't reinforce the wrong behaviors.* Although reinforcement theory sounds simple, it's actually very difficult to put into practice. One of the most common mistakes is accidentally reinforcing the wrong behaviors. Sometimes managers reinforce behaviors that they don't want!

Managers should also *correctly administer punishment at the appropriate time.* Many managers believe that punishment can change workers' behavior and help them improve their job performance. Furthermore, managers believe that fairly punishing workers also lets other workers know what is or isn't acceptable.[44] A danger of using punishment is that it can produce a backlash against managers and companies. But, if administered properly, punishment can weaken the frequency of undesirable behaviors without creating a backlash.[45] To be effective, the punishment must be strong enough to stop the undesired behavior and must be administered objectively (same rules applied to everyone), impersonally (without emotion or anger), consistently and contingently (each time improper behavior occurs), and quickly (as soon as possible following the undesirable behavior). In addition, managers should clearly explain what the appropriate

Goal a target, objective, or result that someone tries to accomplish

Goal-setting theory a theory that states that people will be motivated to the extent to which they accept specific, challenging goals and receive feedback that indicates their progress toward goal achievement

behavior is and why the employee is being punished. Employees typically respond well when punishment is administered this way.[46]

Finally, managers should *choose the simplest and most effective schedule of reinforcement.* When choosing a schedule of reinforcement, managers need to balance effectiveness against simplicity. In fact, the more complex the schedule of reinforcement, the more likely it is to be misunderstood and resisted by managers and employees. Since continuous reinforcement, fixed ratio, and variable ratio schedules are about equally effective, continuous reinforcement schedules may be the best choice in many instances by virtue of their simplicity.

5 Goal-Setting Theory

The basic model of motivation with which we began this chapter showed that individuals feel tension after becoming aware of an unfulfilled need. Once they experience tension, they search for and select courses of action that they believe will eliminate this tension. In other words, they direct their behavior toward something. This something is a goal. A **goal** is a target, objective, or result that someone tries to accomplish. **Goal-setting theory** says that people will be motivated to the extent they ac-

ONE OF THE SIMPLEST, MOST EFFECTIVE WAYS TO MOTIVATE WORKERS...

cept specific, challenging goals and receive feedback that indicates their progress toward goal achievement.

*Let's learn more about goal setting by examining **5.1 the components of goal-setting theory** and **5.2 how to motivate with goal-setting theory**.*

5.1 Components of Goal-Setting Theory

The basic components of goal-setting theory are goal specificity, goal difficulty, goal acceptance, and performance feedback.[47] **Goal specificity** is the extent to which goals are detailed, exact, and unambiguous. Specific goals, such as "I'm going to have a 3.0 average this semester," are more motivating than general goals, such as "I'm going to get better grades this semester."

Goal difficulty is the extent to which a goal is hard or challenging to accomplish. Difficult goals, such as "I'm going to have a 3.5 average and make the Dean's List this semester," are more motivating than easy goals, such as "I'm going to have a 2.0 average this semester."

Goal acceptance, which is similar to the idea of goal commitment discussed in Chapter 5, is the extent to which people consciously understand and agree to goals. Accepted goals, such as "I really want to get a 3.5 average this semester to show my parents how much I've improved," are more motivating than unaccepted goals, such as "My parents really want me to get a 3.5 average this semester, but there's so much more I'd rather do on campus than study!"

Performance feedback is information about the quality or quantity of past performance and indicates whether progress is being made toward the accomplishment of a goal. Performance feedback, such as "My prof said I need a 92 on the final to get an 'A' in that class," is more motivating than no feedback, "I have no idea what my grade is in that class." In short, goal-setting theory says that people will be motivated to the extent to which they accept specific, challenging goals and receive feedback that indicates their progress toward goal achievement.

How does goal setting work? To start, challenging goals focus employees' attention (i.e., direction of effort) on the critical aspects of their jobs and away from unimportant areas. Goals also energize behavior. When faced with unaccomplished goals, employees typically develop plans and strategies to reach those goals. Goals also create tension between the goal, which is the desired future state of affairs, and where the employee or company is now, meaning the current state of affairs. This tension can be satisfied only by achieving or abandoning the goal. Finally, goals influence persistence. Since goals only go away when they are accomplished, employees are more likely to persist in their efforts in the presence of goals. Exhibit 13.8 on the next page incorporates goals into the motivation model by showing how they directly affect tension, effort, and the extent to which employees are energized to take action.

5.2 Motivating with Goal-Setting Theory

What practical steps can managers take to use goal-setting theory to motivate employees? One of the simplest, most effective ways to motivate workers is to *assign them specific, challenging goals.*

Second, managers should *make sure workers truly accept organizational goals.* Specific, challenging goals won't motivate workers unless they really accept, understand, and agree to the organization's goals. For this to occur, people must see the goals as fair and reasonable. Plus, they must trust management and believe that managers are using goals to clarify what is expected from them rather than to exploit or threaten them ("If you don't achieve these goals . . ."). Participative goal setting, in which managers and employees generate goals together, can help increase trust and understanding and thus acceptance of goals. Furthermore, providing workers with training can help increase goal acceptance, particularly when workers don't believe they are capable of reaching the organization's goals.[48]

Finally, managers should *provide frequent, specific, performance-related feedback.*

Goal specificity the extent to which goals are detailed, exact, and unambiguous

Goal difficulty the extent to which a goal is hard or challenging to accomplish

Goal acceptance the extent to which people consciously understand and agree to goals

Performance feedback information about the quality or quantity of past performance that indicates whether progress is being made toward the accomplishment of a goal

...IS TO ASSIGN THEM SPECIFIC, CHALLENGING GOALS.

Exhibit 13.8
Adding Goal-Setting Theory to the Model

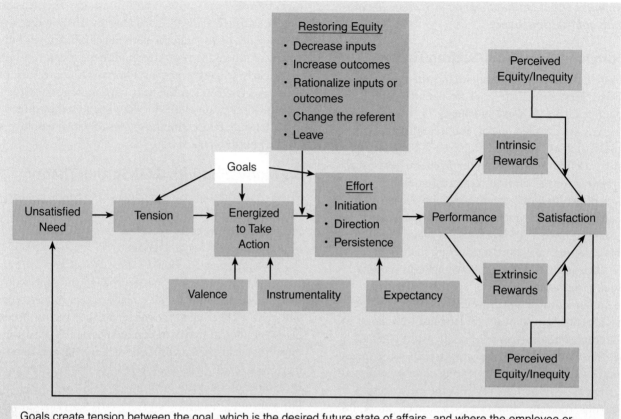

Goals create tension between the goal, which is the desired future state of affairs, and where the employee or company is now, meaning the current state of affairs. This tension can be satisfied only by achieving or abandoning the goal. Goals also energize behavior. When faced with unaccomplished goals, employees typically develop plans and strategies to reach those goals. Finally, goals influence persistence.

Once employees have accepted specific, challenging goals, they should receive frequent performance-related feedback so that they can track their progress toward goal completion. Feedback leads to stronger motivation and effort in three ways.[49] Receiving specific feedback that indicates how well they're performing can encourage employees who don't have specific, challenging goals to set goals to improve their performance. Once people meet goals, performance feedback often encourages them to set higher, more difficult goals. And, feedback lets people know whether they need to increase their efforts or change strategies in order to accomplish their goals. So, to motivate employees with goal-setting theory, make sure they receive frequent performance-related feedback so that they can track their progress toward goal completion.

6 Motivating with the Integrated Model

We began this chapter by defining motivation as the set of forces that initiates, directs, and makes people persist in their efforts to accomplish a goal. We also asked the basic question that managers ask when they try to figure out how to motivate their workers: "What leads to effort?" Though the answer to that question is likely to be somewhat different for each employee, the diagram on your Review Card for this chapter helps you begin to answer it by consolidating the practical advice from the theories reviewed in this chapter in one convenient location. So, if you're having difficulty figuring out why people aren't motivated where you work, check your Review Card for a useful, theory-based starting point.

"They are written in **concise, down-to-earth language**. There are tons of pictures and interesting blurbs of information. It's very relevant to my life. It's nice to have a book/website that seems to **reach out to students and actually care** about how we learn and try to tailor to our needs as much as possible. Thank you for this."

– Alice Brent, Student at Arizona State University

SPEAK UP!

SHE DID

MGMT2 was built on a simple principle: to create a new teaching and learning solution that reflects the way today's faculty teach and the way you learn.

Through conversations, focus groups, surveys, and interviews, we collected data that drove the creation of the current version of MGMT2 that you are using today. But it doesn't stop there – in order to make MGMT2 an even better learning experience, we'd like you to SPEAK UP and tell us how MGMT2 worked for you.

What did you like about it?
What would you change?
Are there additional ideas you have that would help us build a better product for next semester's principles of management students?

At **4ltrpress.cengage.com/mgmt** you'll find all of the resources you need to succeed in principles of management – **video podcasts, audio downloads, flash cards, interactive quizzes** and more!

Speak Up! Go to
4ltrpress.cengage.com/mgmt.

LEADERSHIP

What Is Leadership?

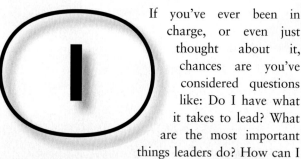

If you've ever been in charge, or even just thought about it, chances are you've considered questions like: Do I have what it takes to lead? What are the most important things leaders do? How can I transform a poorly performing department, division, or company? Do I need to adjust my leadership depending on the situation and the employee? Why doesn't my leadership inspire people? If you feel overwhelmed at the prospect of being a leader, you're not alone—millions of leaders in organizations across the world struggle with fundamental leadership issues on a daily basis.

How does an ensemble of 100 or more musicians, all playing different parts at different times on different instruments, manage to produce something as beautiful as Beethoven's Fifth Symphony? (Or, if Gustav Mahler's "Symphony of a Thousand," is on the program, a lot more people might be involved!) The conductor, like a CEO, is responsible for managing all of this complexity and ensuring great output. But his or her job is about much more than just keeping the beat with a baton. According to Ramona Wis, author of *The Conductor as Leader: Principles of Leadership Applied to Life on the Podium*, conductors must also build connections between people, inspire them with vision, command their trust, and persuade them to participate in the ensemble at their very best.

Whether the end result is a stirring musical performance, innovation of new products, or increased profits, **leadership** is the process of influencing others to achieve group or orga-

Learning Outcomes

1 explain what leadership is.

2 describe who leaders are and what effective leaders do.

3 explain Fiedler's contingency theory.

4 describe how path-goal theory works.

5 explain the normative decision theory.

6 explain how visionary leadership (i.e., charismatic and transformational leadership) helps leaders achieve strategic leadership.

Leadership the process of influencing others to achieve group or organizational goals

nizational goals. The knowledge and skills you'll learn in this chapter won't make the task of leadership less daunting, but they will help you navigate it.

After reading the next two sections, you should be able to

1   explain what leadership is.

2   describe who leaders are and what effective leaders do.

1 Leaders versus Managers

According to University of Southern California business professor Warren Bennis, the primary difference between leaders and managers is that leaders are concerned with do-

ing the right thing, whereas managers are concerned with doing things right.[1] In other words, leaders begin with the question, "What should we be doing?" while managers start with "How can we do what we're already doing better?" Leaders focus on vision, mission, goals, and objectives, while managers focus on productivity and efficiency. Managers see themselves as preservers of the status quo, while leaders see themselves as promoters of change and challengers of the status quo. Leaders, consequently, encourage creativity and risk taking. At Maddock Douglas, an Elmhurst, Illinois firm that helps companies develop new products, President Louis Viton leads by encouraging creativity and risk-taking with an annual "Fail Forward" award for ambitious ideas that end in disaster—even if they end up costing the company huge amounts of money. Viton says the

latest "Fail Forward" winner produced a new product design that was a total embarrassment. . . . But she was trying to do something new and different and better. She went for it, and she won an award for it."[2]

Another difference is that managers have a relatively short-term perspective, while leaders take a long-term view. Managers are also more concerned with *means,* how to get things done, while leaders are more concerned with *ends,* what gets done. Managers are concerned with control and limiting the choices of others, while leaders are more concerned with expanding people's choices and options.[3] Finally, managers solve problems so that others can do their work, while leaders inspire and motivate others to find their own solutions.

Though leaders are different from managers, organizations need them both. Managers are critical to getting out the day-to-day work, and leaders are critical to inspiring employees and setting the organization's long-term direction. The key issue for any organization is the extent to which it is properly led and properly managed. As Warren Bennis said in summing up the difference between leaders and managers, "American organizations (and probably those in much of the rest of the industrialized world) are underled and overmanaged. They do not pay enough attention to doing the right thing, while they pay too much attention to doing things right."[4]

2 Who Leaders Are and What Leaders Do

Trait theory a leadership theory that holds that effective leaders possess a similar set of traits or characteristics

Traits relatively stable characteristics, such as abilities, psychological motives, or consistent patterns of behavior

Indra Nooyi, PepsiCo's CEO, talks straight, has a sharp sense of humor, and sings in the hallways wherever she is. Nooyi is an extrovert. By contrast, J.C. Penney's CEO, Mike Ullman, who is soft-spoken and easy to approach, is an introvert.[5] Which one is likely to be more successful

as a CEO? According to a survey of 1,542 senior managers, it's the extrovert. Forty-seven percent of those 1,542 senior managers felt that extroverts make better CEOs, while 65 percent said that being an introvert hurts a CEO's chances of success.[6] So clearly senior managers believe that extroverted CEOs are better leaders. But are they? Not necessarily. In fact, a relatively high percentage of CEOs, 40 percent, are introverts. Sara Lee CEO Brenda Barnes says, "I've always been shy. . . . People wouldn't call me that [an introvert], but I am."[7] Indeed, Barnes turns down all speaking requests and rarely gives interviews.

*So, what makes a good leader? Does leadership success depend on who leaders are, such as introverts or extroverts, or on what leaders do and how they behave? Let's learn more about who leaders are by investigating **2.1 leadership traits** and **2.2 leadership behaviors.***

2.1 Leadership Traits

Trait theory is one way to describe who leaders are. **Trait theory** says that effective leaders possess a similar set of traits or characteristics. **Traits** are relatively stable characteristics, such as abilities, psychological motives, or consistent patterns of behavior. For example, according to trait theory, leaders are taller and more confident and have greater physical stamina (i.e., higher energy levels) than nonleaders. Indeed, while just 14.5 percent of men are six feet tall, 58 *percent* of *Fortune* 500 CEOs are six feet or taller.[8] Trait theory is also known as the "great person" theory because early versions of the theory stated that leaders are born, not made. In other words, you either have the right stuff to be a leader or you don't. And if you don't, there is no way to get it.

For some time, it was thought that trait theory was wrong and that there are no consistent trait differences between leaders and nonleaders or between effective and ineffective leaders. However, more recent evidence shows that "successful leaders are not like other people," that successful leaders are indeed different from the rest of us.[9] More specifically, leaders are different from nonleaders in the following traits: drive, the desire to lead, honesty/integrity, self-confidence, emotional stability, cognitive ability, and knowledge of the business.[10]

Drive refers to a high level of effort and is characterized by achievement, motivation, initiative, energy, and tenacity. In terms of achievement and ambition, leaders always try to make improvements or achieve success in what they're doing. Because of their initiative, they have a strong desire to promote change or solve problems. Leaders typically have more energy—they have to, given the long hours they put in and followers' expectations that they be positive and upbeat. Leaders are also more tenacious than nonleaders and are better at overcoming obstacles and problems that would deter most of us.

Successful leaders also have a stronger *desire to lead.* They want to be in charge and think about ways to influence or convince others about what should or shouldn't be done. *Honesty/integrity* is also important to leaders. *Honesty,* being truthful with others, is a cornerstone of leadership. Leaders won't be trusted if they are dishonest. When they are honest, subordinates are willing to overlook other flaws. *Integrity* is the extent to which leaders do what they say they will do. Leaders may be honest and have good intentions, but they also won't be trusted if they don't consistently deliver on what they promise.

Self-confidence, believing in one's abilities, also distinguishes leaders from nonleaders. Self-confident leaders are more decisive and assertive and are more likely to gain others' confidence. Moreover, self-confident leaders will admit mistakes because they view them as learning opportunities rather than as refutation of their leadership capabilities. This also means that leaders have *emotional stability.* Even when things go wrong, they remain even-tempered and consistent in their outlook and in the way they treat others. Leaders who can't control their emotions, who anger quickly or attack and blame others for mistakes, are unlikely to be trusted.

Leaders are also smart. Leaders typically have strong *cognitive abilities.* This doesn't mean that leaders are necessarily geniuses—far from it. But it does mean that leaders have the capacity to analyze large amounts of seemingly unrelated, complex information and see patterns, opportunities, or threats where others might not see them. Finally, leaders also know their stuff, which means they have superior technical knowledge about the businesses they run. Leaders who have a good *knowledge of the business* understand the key technological decisions and concerns facing their companies. More often than not, studies indicate that effective leaders have long, extensive experience in their industries. Ann Livermore, in charge of storage and servers at Hewlett-Packard, has her thumb on the business of data networks. She has regular conversations with customers to assess their needs and market trends, and new products—as well as business growth—emerge from her research.[11]

2.2 Leadership Behaviors

Thus far, you've read about who leaders *are.* It's hard to imagine a truly successful leader who lacks all of these qualities. But traits alone are not enough to make a successful leader. Leaders who have all these traits (or many of them) must then take actions that encourage people to achieve group or organizational goals.[12] So we will now examine what leaders *do,* meaning the behaviors they perform or the actions they take to influence others to achieve group or organizational goals. When she interviewed the CEO of Procter & Gamble on

Don't Judge a Leader by Her Chanel

How much do physical traits affect our perception of a person's ability to lead? One study showed that female candidates tend to fare worse in elections than their male opponents because of their gender…and worse yet if they are perceived as unattractive. Although it is just as easy to judge a leader by the clothes he or she is wearing as it is to judge a book by its cover, it is best to focus on whether a person has strong personal—rather than physical—traits, such as persistence, attention to detail, efficiency, analytical skills, and high standards.

Sources: J. N. Schubert and M. A. Curran, "Stereotyping Effects in Candidate Evaluation: The Interaction of Gender and Attractiveness Bias," available online at http://www3.niu.edu/~ti0jns1/mpsa2001_paper.htm, [accessed 27 August 2008]; G. Anders, "Tough CEOs Often Most Successful, a Study Finds," *The Wall Street Journal*, 19 November 2007, B3.

Followers as Leaders

© Marcel Pelletier/iStockphoto.com

As more organizations become flatter, or adopt less hierarchical organizational structures, it is becoming increasingly clear that leaders and followers are dependent on one another. One thing good leaders need is good followers. Barbara Kellerman, James MacGregor Burns Lecturer in Public Leadership at Harvard's John F. Kennedy School of Government, outlines five different types of followers and urges leaders to understand what kind of followers they have. Isolates and bystanders are not invested. They just do their jobs and tend to impede change. They can be useful for leaders who want to maintain the status quo but are otherwise dead weight. Good followers, by contrast, support a leader they've invested in. Consequently, they are good assets. Participants are self-motivated and driven to make a difference, activists are eager and will go the extra mile, while diehards will support their leader even if it means going down with the ship. But leaders beware: These types of followers can be a liability if you have not inspired their loyalty. So followers are leaders, too. As Kellerman notes, "[W]hile they may lack authority, at least in comparison with their superiors, followers do not lack power and influence."

Source: B. Kellerman, "What Every Leader Needs to Know About Followers," *Harvard Business Review* (December 2007): 84–91.

the subject of leadership, Associated Press reporter Elise Amendola asked, "Are leaders born or made?" Debunking the "great person" theory, A.G. Lafley answered, "Clearly made. You choose to lead. You choose to want to make a difference, to make the world better in some meaningful way. Until that choice is made, you don't have a leader. You have a lump of clay."[13]

Researchers at the University of Michigan, Ohio State University, and the University of Texas examined the specific behaviors that leaders use to improve the satisfaction and performance of their subordinates. Hundreds of studies were conducted and hundreds of leader behaviors were examined. At all three universities, two basic leader behaviors emerged as central to successful leadership: initiating structure (called *job-centered leadership* at the University of Michigan and *concern for production* at the University of Texas) and considerate leader behavior (called *employee-centered leadership* at the University of Michigan and *concern for people* at the University of Texas).[14] These two leader behaviors form the basis for many of the leadership theories discussed in this chapter.

Initiating structure is the degree to which a leader

structures the roles of followers by setting goals, giving directions, setting deadlines, and assigning tasks. A leader's ability to initiate structure primarily affects subordinates' job performance. When Jamie Dimon became CEO of JPMorgan Chase, the financial services company had four different computer systems from previously acquired companies. Branch bankers couldn't access checking histories or determine whether customers qualified for credit cards or mortgages. Dimon initiated structure by telling his executives to put one system in place, and, "If you don't do it in six weeks, I'll make all the choices myself."[15] The deadline was met.

Consideration is the extent to which a leader is friendly, approachable, and supportive and shows concern for employees. Consideration primarily affects subordinates' job sat-

Initiating structure
the degree to which a leader structures the roles of followers by setting goals, giving directions, setting deadlines, and assigning tasks

Consideration the extent to which a leader is friendly, approachable, and supportive and shows concern for employees

© Shalom Ormsby/Digital Vision/Getty Images

Leaders are shaped by the choices they make.

isfaction. Specific leader consideration behaviors include listening to employees' problems and concerns, consulting with employees before making decisions, and treating employees as equals. Twenty-five years ago Wal-Mart's CEO, Lee Scott, received a lesson in the importance of consideration from founder Sam Walton. Scott, who was then in charge of a transportation unit, was known for his tough management style and for sending blistering memos. When "Mr. Sam" called him into his office, Scott found nine of his truck drivers there waiting for him. The drivers, who were taking advantage of Wal-Mart's open-door policy, had complained to Walton about the way Scott treated them and asked that he be fired. According to Scott, "They just wanted to do their work and be appreciated for it. So Mr. Walton asked me, with them there, if I could do it differently."[16] After agreeing that he could, Scott said that Walton "had me stand at the door as they were leaving and thank each one for having the courage to use the open door, which is one of the very basic principles of Wal-Mart."[17] That office is now Scott's, and Wal-Mart has the same open door through which any Wal-Mart employee can walk to talk with the CEO.

Although researchers at all three universities generally agreed that initiating structure and consideration were basic leader behaviors, their interpretation differed on how these two behaviors are related to one another and which are necessary for effective leadership. The University of Michigan studies indicated that initiating structure and consideration were mutually exclusive behaviors on opposite ends of the same continuum. In other words, leaders who wanted to be more considerate would have to do less initiating of structure (and vice versa). The University of Michigan studies also indicated that only considerate leader behaviors (i.e., employee-centered behaviors) were associated with successful leadership. By contrast, researchers at Ohio State University and the University of Texas found that initiating structure and consideration were independent behaviors, meaning that leaders can be considerate and initiate structure at the same time. Additional evidence confirms this finding.[18] The same researchers also concluded that the most effective leaders excelled at both initiating structure and considerate leader behaviors.

This "high-high" approach can be seen in the upper right corner of the Blake/Mouton leadership grid, shown in Exhibit 14.1. Blake and Mouton used two leadership behaviors—concern for people (i.e., consideration) and concern for production (i.e., initiat-

Exhibit 14.1

Blake/Mouton Leadership Grid

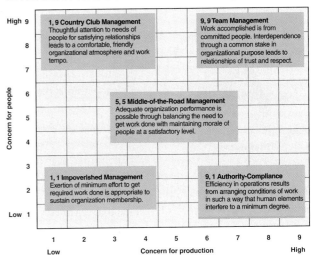

Source: R. R. Blake and A. A. McCanse, "The Leadership Grid®," *Leadership Dilemmas—Grid Solutions* (Houston: Gulf Publishing Company), 21. Copyright © 1991, by Scientific Methods, Inc. Reproduced by permission of the owners.

ing structure)—to categorize five different leadership styles. Both behaviors are rated on a 9-point scale, with 1 representing "low" and 9 representing "high." Blake and Mouton suggest that a "high-high" or 9,9 leadership style is the best. They call this style *team management* because leaders who use it display a high concern for people (9) and a high concern for production (9).

By contrast, leaders use a 9,1 *authority-compliance* leadership style when they have a high concern for production and a low concern for people. A 1,9 *country club* style occurs when leaders care about having a friendly enjoyable work environment but don't really pay much attention to production or performance. The worst leadership style, according to the grid, is the 1,1 *impoverished* leader, who shows little concern for people or production and does the bare minimum needed to keep his or her job. Finally, the 5,5 *middle-of-the-road* style occurs when leaders show a moderate amount of concern for both people and production.

Is the team management style, with a high concern for production and a high concern for people, really the best leadership style? Logically, it would seem so. Why wouldn't you want to show high concern for both people and production? Nonetheless, nearly 50 years of research indicates that there isn't one best leadership style. The best leadership style depends on the situation. In other words, no one leadership behavior by itself and no one combination of leadership behaviors works well across all situations and employees.

Situational Approaches to Leadership

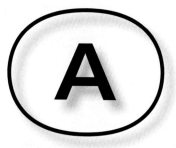

After leader traits and behaviors, the situational approach to leadership is the third major method used in the study of leadership. We'll review three major situational approaches to leadership—Fiedler's contingency theory, path-goal theory, and Vroom and Yetton's normative decision model. All assume that the effectiveness of any **leadership style,** the way a leader generally behaves toward followers, depends on the situation.[19]

According to situational leadership theories, there is no one best leadership style. But, one of these situational theories differs from the other three in one significant way. Fiedler's contingency theory assumes that leadership styles are consistent and difficult to change. Therefore, leaders must be placed in or "matched" to a situation that fits their leadership style. In contrast, the other situational theories assume that leaders are capable of adapting and adjusting their leadership styles to fit the demands of different situations.

After reading the next three sections, you should be able to

3 explain Fiedler's contingency theory.

4 describe how path-goal theory works.

5 explain the normative decision theory.

3 Putting Leaders in the Right Situation: Fiedler's Contingency Theory

Leadership style the way a leader generally behaves toward followers

Contingency theory a leadership theory that states that in order to maximize work group performance, leaders must be matched to the situation that best fits their leadership style

Fiedler's **contingency theory** states that in order to maximize work group performance, leaders must be matched to the right leadership situation.[20] More specifically, the first basic assumption of Fiedler's theory is that leaders are effective when the work groups they

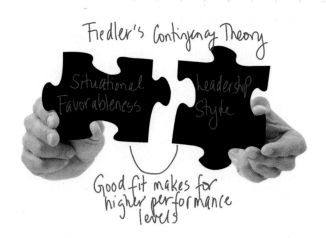

Fiedler's Contingency Theory
Situational Favorableness — Leadership Style
Good fit makes for higher performance levels

© rubberball/Getty Images

lead perform well. So, instead of judging leaders' effectiveness by what the leaders do (i.e., initiating structure and consideration) or who they are (i.e., trait theory), Fiedler assesses leaders by the conduct and performance of the people they supervise. Second, Fiedler assumes that leaders are generally unable to change their leadership styles and that they will be more effective when their styles are matched to the proper situation. Third, Fiedler assumes that the favorableness of a situation for a leader depends on the degree to which the situation permits the leader to influence the behavior of group members. Fiedler's third assumption is consistent with our definition of leadership as the process of influencing others to achieve group or organizational goals. In other words, in addition to traits, behaviors, and a favorable situation to match, leaders have to be allowed to lead.

Let's learn more about Fiedler's contingency theory by examining **3.1 the least preferred coworker** *and* **leadership styles, 3.2 situational favorableness,** *and* **3.3 how to match leadership styles to situations.**

3.1 Leadership Style: Least Preferred Coworker

When Fiedler refers to *leadership style,* he means the way that leaders generally behave toward their followers. Do the leaders yell and scream and blame others when things go wrong? Or do they correct mistakes by listening and then quietly but directly making their point? Do they let others make their own decisions and hold them accountable for the results? Or do they micromanage, insisting that all decisions be approved first by them? Fiedler also assumes that leadership styles are tied to leaders' underlying needs and personalities. Since personality and needs are relatively stable, he assumes that leaders are generally incapable of changing their leadership styles. In other words, the way that leaders treat people now is probably the way they've always treated others.

Exhibit 14.2

Situational Favorableness

Leader-Member Relations	Good	Good	Good	Good	Poor	Poor	Poor	Poor
Task Structure	High	High	Low	Low	High	High	Low	Low
Position Power	Strong	Weak	Strong	Weak	Strong	Weak	Strong	Weak
Situation	I	II	III	IV	V	VI	VII	VIII
		Favorable		Moderately Favorable		Unfavorable		

Fiedler uses a questionnaire called the Least Preferred Coworker (LPC) scale to measure leadership style. When completing the LPC scale, people are instructed to consider all of the people with whom they have ever worked and then to choose the one person with whom they have worked *least* well. Fiedler explains, "This does not have to be the person you liked least well, but should be the one person with whom you have the most trouble getting the job done."[21] How you describe this person is a clue to your own preferred leadership style.

Would you describe your LPC as pleasant, friendly, supportive, interesting, cheerful, and sincere? Or would you describe the person as unpleasant, unfriendly, hostile, boring, gloomy, and insincere? People who describe their LPC in a positive way (scoring 64 and above on the full inventory of 18 oppositional pairs) have *relationship-oriented* leadership styles. After all, if they can still be positive about their least preferred coworker, they must be people-oriented. By contrast, people who describe their LPC in a negative way (scoring 57 or below) have *task-oriented* leadership styles. Given a choice, they'll focus first on getting the job done and second on making sure everyone gets along. Finally, those with moderate scores (from 58 to 63) have a more flexible leadership style and can be somewhat relationship-oriented or somewhat task-oriented.

3.2 Situational Favorableness

Fiedler assumes that leaders will be more effective when their leadership styles are matched to the proper situation. More specifically, Fiedler defines **situational favorableness** as the degree to which a particular situation either permits or denies a leader the chance to influence the behavior of group members.[22] In highly favorable situations, leaders find that their actions influence followers. But in highly unfavorable situations, leaders have little or no success influencing the people they are trying to lead.

Three situational factors determine the favorability of a situation: leader-member relations, task structure, and position power. The most important situational factor is **leader-member relations,** which refers to how well followers respect, trust, and like their leaders. When leader-member relations are good, followers trust the leader and there is a friendly work atmosphere. **Task structure** is the degree to which the requirements of a subordinate's tasks are clearly specified. With highly structured tasks, employees have clear job responsibilities, goals, and procedures. **Position power** is the degree to which leaders are able to hire, fire, reward, and punish workers. The more influence leaders have over hiring, firing, rewards, and punishments, the greater their power.

Exhibit 14.2 shows how leader-member relations, task structure, and position power can be combined into eight situations that differ in their favorability to leaders. In general, Situation I, on the left side of Exhibit 14.2, is the most favorable leader situation. Followers like and trust their leaders and know what to do because their tasks are highly structured. Also, the leaders have the formal power to influence workers through hiring, firing, rewarding, and punishing them. Therefore, in Situation I, it's relatively easy for a leader to influence followers. By contrast, Situation VIII, on the right side of Exhibit 14.2, is the least favorable situation for leaders. Followers don't like or trust their leaders. Plus, followers are not sure what they're supposed to be doing because their tasks or jobs are highly unstructured. Finally, leaders find it difficult to influence followers without the ability

Situational favorableness the degree to which a particular situation either permits or denies a leader the chance to influence the behavior of group members

Leader-member relations the degree to which followers respect, trust, and like their leaders

Task structure the degree to which the requirements of a subordinate's tasks are clearly specified

Position power the degree to which leaders are able to hire, fire, reward, and punish workers

Exhibit 14.3

Matching Leadership Styles to Situations

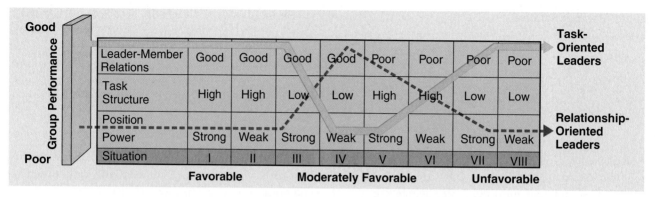

Leader-Member Relations	Good	Good	Good	Good	Poor	Poor	Poor	Poor	Task-Oriented Leaders
Task Structure	High	High	Low	Low	High	High	Low	Low	
Position Power	Strong	Weak	Strong	Weak	Strong	Weak	Strong	Weak	Relationship-Oriented Leaders
Situation	I	II	III	IV	V	VI	VII	VIII	

Favorable · Moderately Favorable · Unfavorable

to hire, fire, reward, or punish the people who work for them. In short, it's very difficult to influence followers given the conditions found in Situation VIII.

3.3 Matching Leadership Styles to Situations

After studying thousands of leaders and followers in hundreds of different situations, Fiedler found that the performance of relationship- and task-oriented leaders followed the pattern displayed in Exhibit 14.3.

Relationship-oriented leaders, with high LPC scores, were better leaders (i.e., their groups performed more effectively) under moderately favorable situations. In moderately favorable situations, the leader may be liked somewhat, tasks may be somewhat structured, and the leader may have some position power. In this situation, a relationship-oriented leader improves leader-member relations, which is the most important of the three situational factors. In turn, morale and performance improve.

By contrast, as Exhibit 14.3 shows, task-oriented leaders, with low LPC scores, are better leaders in highly favorable and unfavorable situations. Task-oriented leaders do well in favorable situations where leaders are liked, tasks are structured, and the leader has the power to hire, fire, reward, and punish. In these favorable situations, task-oriented leaders effectively step on the gas of a well-tuned car. Their focus on performance sets the goal for the group, which then charges forward to meet it. But task-oriented leaders also do well in unfavorable situations where leaders are disliked, tasks are unstructured, and the leader doesn't have the power to hire, fire, reward, and punish. In these unfavorable situations, the task-oriented leader sets goals which focus attention on performance and clarify what needs to be done, thus overcoming low task structure. This is enough to jump-start performance even if workers don't like or trust the leader.

Finally, though not shown in Exhibit 14.3, people with moderate LPC scores (who can be somewhat relationship-oriented or somewhat task-oriented) tend to do fairly well in all situations because they can adapt their behavior. Typically, though, they don't perform quite as well as relationship-oriented or task-oriented leaders whose leadership styles are well matched to the situation.

Recall, however, that Fiedler assumes leaders to be incapable of changing their leadership styles. Accordingly, the key to applying Fiedler's contingency theory

How would you rank your least-preferred coworker? He or she is:

Pleasant	⑧ ⑦ ⑥ ⑤ ④ ③ ② ①	Unpleasant
Friendly	⑧ ⑦ ⑥ ⑤ ④ ③ ② ①	Unfriendly
Supportive	⑧ ⑦ ⑥ ⑤ ④ ③ ② ①	Hostile
Boring	① ② ③ ④ ⑤ ⑥ ⑦ ⑧	Interesting
Gloomy	① ② ③ ④ ⑤ ⑥ ⑦ ⑧	Cheerful
Insincere	① ② ③ ④ ⑤ ⑥ ⑦ ⑧	Sincere

Source: F. E. Fiedler and M. M. Chemers, *Improving Leadership Effectiveness: The Leader Match Concept*, 2nd ed. (New York: John Wiley & Sons, 1984). Reprinted by permission of the authors.

Dark Days in Detroit

At the time this text was written, the chief executives of the big three Detroit automakers, Chrysler, Ford, and General Motors, were meeting with Congress to ask for a $25 billion loan package to keep their companies from going into bankruptcy (a scenario for which GM admitted having no contingency plan). Ford burned through nearly $7.7 billion in cash during the third quarter of 2008, and losses at GM and Chrysler could put both companies into bankruptcy within the year. So who's to blame? Is it the slumping auto sales resulting from the economic downturn, or is it leadership that has been slow to restructure and adopt more fuel-efficient vehicles? All three CEOs flew their companies' private jets to the hearing, and while Chrysler's CEO Robert Nardelli offered to take $1 in annual compensation, Ford and GM CEOs Alan Mulally and Richard Wagoner (who received $15.7 million and $21.7 million respectively in 2007) made no such offers.

Sources: N. Boudette, J. Mitchell, and S. Hughes, "Ford, GM: Bankruptcy is Not an Option," *The Wall Street Journal*, 19 November 2008, available online at http://online.wsj.com/article/SB122710695099540967.html [Accessed 19 November 2008]; J. Murphy, "Ford Cuts Mazda Stake," *The Wall Street Journal*, 18 November 2008, available online at http://online.wjs.com/article/SB122699454190736773.html [Accessed 19 November 2008]; D. Milbank, "Auto Execs Fly Corporate Jets to D.C., Tin Cups in Hand," *The Washington Post*, 20 November 2008, available online at http://www.washingtonpost.com/wp-dyn/content/article/2008/11/19/AR2008111903669.html?nav=hcmodule [accessed 20 November 2008].

© Chip Somodevilla/Getty Images

in the workplace is to accurately measure and match leaders to situations *or* to teach leaders how to change situational favorableness by changing leader-member relations, task structure, or position power. Though matching or placing leaders in appropriate situations works particularly well, practicing managers have had little luck reengineering situations to fit their leadership styles. The primary problem, as you've no doubt realized, is the complexity of the theory. In a study designed to teach leaders how to reengineer their situations to fit

their leadership styles, Fiedler found that most of the leaders simply did not understand what they were supposed to do to change their situations. Furthermore, if they didn't like their LPC profile (perhaps they felt they were more relationship-oriented than their scores indicated), they arbitrarily changed it to better suit their view of themselves. Of course, the theory won't work as well if leaders are attempting to change situational factors to fit their perceived leadership style rather than their real leadership style.[23]

4 Adapting Leader Behavior: Path-Goal Theory

Just as its name suggests, **path-goal theory** states that leaders can increase subordinate satisfaction and performance by clarifying and clearing the paths to goals and by increasing the number and kinds of rewards available for goal attainment. Said another way, leaders need to clarify how followers can achieve organizational goals, take care of problems that prevent followers from achieving goals, and then find more and varied rewards to motivate followers to achieve those goals.[24]

Leaders must meet two conditions if path clarification, path clearing, and rewards are to increase followers' motivation. First, leader behavior must be a source of immediate or future satisfaction for followers. The things you do as a leader must please your followers today or lead to activities or rewards that will satisfy them in the future.

Second, while providing the coaching, guidance, support, and rewards necessary for effective work performance, leader behaviors must complement and not duplicate the characteristics of followers' work environments. Thus, leader behaviors must offer something unique and valuable to followers beyond what they're already experiencing as they do their jobs or what they can already do for themselves.

In contrast to Fiedler's contingency theory, path-goal theory assumes that leaders *can* change and adapt their leadership styles.

> **Path-goal theory** a leadership theory that states that leaders can increase subordinate satisfaction and performance by clarifying and clearing the paths to goals and by increasing the number and kinds of rewards available for goal attainment

(The things you do as a leader must please your followers today or satisfy them in the future.)

setting standards of performance, and making sure that people follow standard rules and regulations.

Supportive leadership involves being approachable and friendly to employees, showing concern for them and their welfare, treating them as equals, and creating a friendly climate. Supportive leadership is very similar to considerate leader behavior. Supportive leadership often results in employee satisfaction with the job and with leaders. This leadership style may also result in improved performance when it increases employee confidence, lowers employee job stress, or improves relations and trust between employees and leaders.[26]

Participative leadership involves consulting employees for their suggestions and input before making decisions. Participation in decision making should help followers understand which goals are most important and clarify the paths to accomplishing them. Furthermore, when people participate in decisions, they become more committed to making them work.

Achievement-oriented leadership means setting challenging goals, having high expectations of employees, and displaying confidence that employees will assume responsibility and put forth extraordinary effort. Simon Cooper, president and COO of the Ritz-Carlton luxury hotel chain, uses the phrase "He who says it, does" to describe achievement-oriented leadership. Cooper explains, "I use this phrase whenever someone convinces me that they can achieve something I consider to be unachievable. In the past I've been known to add focus to a goal by making a bet to see if they can make it—sometimes with amusing consequences. I remember being at a mountain resort in Canada and proposing an incredible goal for the season. The team convinced me that they could achieve it, and I offered

Exhibit 14.4 illustrates this process, showing that leaders change and adapt their leadership styles contingent on their subordinates or the environment in which those subordinates work.

*Let's learn more about path-goal theory by examining **4.1 the four kinds of leadership styles that leaders use, 4.2 the subordinate and environmental contingency factors that determine when different leader styles are effective**, and **4.3 the outcomes of path-goal theory in improving employee satisfaction and performance.***

4.1 Leadership Styles

As illustrated in Exhibit 14.4, the four leadership styles in path-goal theory are directive, supportive, participative, and achievement oriented.[25] **Directive leadership** involves letting employees know precisely what is expected of them, giving them specific guidelines for the performance of their tasks, scheduling work,

Directive leadership a leadership style in which the leader lets employees know precisely what is expected of them, gives them specific guidelines for performing tasks, schedules work, sets standards of performance, and makes sure that people follow standard rules and regulations

Supportive leadership a leadership style in which the leader is friendly and approachable, shows concern for employees and their welfare and treats them as equals, and creates a friendly climate

Participative leadership a leadership style in which the leader consults employees for their suggestions and input before making decisions

Achievement-oriented leadership a leadership style in which the leader sets challenging goals, has high expectations of employees, and displays confidence that employees will assume responsibility and put forth extraordinary effort

Exhibit 14.4
Path-Goal Theory

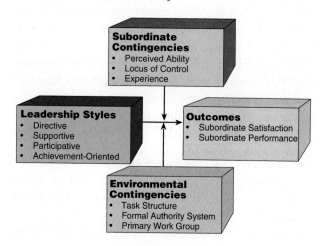

© Ryan McVay/Digital Vision/Getty Images

to jump into the lake if they did. It's a long story, but they made it. There's a great scene of a hole being cut in the ice and an ambulance on standby while I gave a whole new meaning to the term 'dunking'. The cognac [afterwards] was very welcome."[27]

Whatever leadership style you adopt, the ability to persuade and influence others is key to your success. As business becomes more global, and as the way people work changes, organizational structures are becoming flatter, or less hierarchical. This means that leaders must cross traditional boundaries and work with peers and subordinates alike in other divisions or even in other companies. Motivation is thus becoming far more important than direction. Whether you're a directive, supportive, participative, or achievement-oriented leader, your ability to bring others on board with your vision and plan is vital to good leadership.[28]

4.2 Subordinate and Environmental Contingencies

As shown in Exhibit 14.4, path-goal theory specifies that leader behaviors should be fitted to subordinate characteristics. The theory identifies three kinds of subordinate contingencies: perceived ability, experience, and locus of control. *Perceived ability* is simply how much ability

subordinates believe they have for doing their jobs well. Subordinates who perceive that they have a great deal of ability will be dissatisfied with directive leader behaviors. Experienced employees are likely to react in a similar way. Since they already know how to do their jobs (or perceive that they do), they don't need or want close supervision. By contrast, subordinates with little experience or little perceived ability will welcome directive leadership.

Locus of control is a personality measure that indicates the extent to which people believe that they have control over what happens to them in life. *Internals* believe that what happens to them, good or bad, is largely a result of their choices and actions. *Externals,* on the other hand, believe that what happens to them is caused by external forces beyond their control. Accordingly, externals are much more comfortable with a directive leadership style, while internals greatly prefer a participative leadership style because they like to have a say in what goes on at work.

Path-goal theory specifies that leader behaviors should complement rather than duplicate the characteristics of followers' work environments. In other words, a leader should use a leadership style that best responds to the characteristics of the environment as well as the characteristics of the people involved. There are three kinds of environmental contingencies: task structure, the formal authority system, and the primary work group. As in Fiedler's contingency theory, *task structure* is the degree to which the requirements of a subordinate's tasks are clearly specified. When task structure is low and tasks are unclear, directive leadership should be used because it complements the work environment. When task structure is high and tasks are clear, however, directive leadership is not needed because it duplicates what task structure provides. Alternatively, when tasks are stressful, frustrating, or dissatisfying, leaders should respond with supportive leadership.

The *formal authority system* is an organization's set of procedures, rules, and policies. When the formal authority system is unclear, directive leadership complements the situation by reducing uncertainty and increasing clarity. But when the formal authority system is clear, directive leadership is redundant and should not be used.

Primary work group refers to the amount of work-oriented participation or emotional support that is provided by an employee's immediate work group. Participative leadership should be used when tasks are complex and there is little existing work-oriented participation in the primary work group. When tasks are stressful, frustrating, or repetitive, supportive leadership is called for.

Exhibit 14.5

Path-Goal Theory: When to Use Directive, Supportive, Participative, or Achievement-Oriented Leadership

DIRECTIVE LEADERSHIP	SUPPORTIVE LEADERSHIP	PARTICIPATIVE LEADERSHIP	ACHIEVEMENT-ORIENTED LEADERSHIP
Unstructured tasks	Structured, simple, repetitive tasks; Stressful, frustrating tasks	Complex tasks	Unchallenging tasks
Workers with external locus of control	Workers lack confidence	Workers with internal locus of control	
Unclear formal authority system	Clear formal authority system	Workers not satisfied with rewards	
Inexperienced workers		Experienced workers	
Workers with low perceived ability		Workers with high perceived ability	

Finally, since keeping track of all of these subordinate and environmental contingencies can get a bit confusing, Exhibit 14.5 provides a summary of when directive, supportive, participative, and achievement-oriented leadership styles should be used. Above all, using path-goal theory means that a leader must be attuned and responsive to the sometimes changing complexities of his or her environment.

4.3 Outcomes

Does following path-goal theory improve subordinate satisfaction and performance? Preliminary evidence suggests that it does.[29] In particular, people who work for supportive leaders are much more satisfied with their jobs and their bosses. Likewise, people who work for directive leaders are more satisfied with their jobs and bosses (but not quite as much as when their bosses are supportive) and perform their jobs better, too. Does adapting one's leadership style to subordinate and environmental characteristics improve subordinate satisfaction and performance? At this point, because it is difficult to completely test this complex theory, it's too early to tell.[30] However, since the data clearly show that it makes sense for leaders to be both supportive *and* directive, it also makes sense that leaders could improve subordinate satisfaction and performance by adding participative and achievement-oriented leadership styles to their capabilities as leaders.

Normative decision theory a theory that suggests how leaders can determine an appropriate amount of employee participation when making decisions

5 Adapting Leader Behavior: Normative Decision Theory

Many people believe that making tough decisions is at the heart of leadership. Yet experienced leaders will tell you that deciding *how* to make decisions is just as important. The **normative decision theory** (also known as the *Vroom-Yetton-Jago model*) helps leaders decide how much employee participation (from none to letting employees make the entire decision) should be used when making decisions.[31]

*Let's learn more about normative decision theory by investigating **5.1 decision styles** and **5.2 decision quality and acceptance**.*

5.1 Decision Styles

Unlike nearly all of the other leadership theories discussed in this chapter, which have specified *leadership* styles, the normative decision theory specifies five different *decision* styles, or ways of making decisions. (Refer back to Chapter 5 for a more complete review of decision making in organizations.) As shown in Exhibit 14.6, those styles vary from *autocratic decisions* (AI or AII) on the left, in which leaders make the decisions by themselves, to *consultative decisions* (CI or CII), in which leaders share problems with subordinates but still make the decisions themselves, to *group decisions* (GII) on the right, in which leaders share the problems with subordinates and then have the group make the decisions. GE Aircraft Engines in Durham, North Carolina,

Exhibit 14.6

Normative Theory, Decision Styles, and Levels of Employee Participation

Leader solves the problem or makes the decision				Leader is willing to accept any decision supported by the entire group
AI Using information available at the time, the leader solves the problem or makes the decision.	**AII** The leader obtains necessary information from employees and then selects a solution to the problem. When asked to share information, employees may or may not be told what the problem is.	**CI** The leader shares the problem and gets ideas and suggestions from relevant employees on an individual basis. Individuals are not brought together as a group. Then the leader makes the decision, which may or may not reflect their input.	**CII** The leader shares the problem with employees as a group, obtains their ideas and suggestions, and then makes the decision, which may or may not reflect their input.	**GII** The leader shares the problem with employees as a group. Together, the leader and employees generate and evaluate alternatives and try to reach an agreement on a solution. The leader acts as a facilitator and does not try to influence the group. The leader is willing to accept and implement any solution that has the support of the entire group.

Source: Adapted from V. H. Vroom & P. W. Yetton, *Leadership and Decision Making* (Pittsburgh: University of Pittsburgh Press, 1973), 13.

uses this approach when making decisions. According to *Fast Company* magazine, "At GE/Durham, every decision is either an 'A' decision, a 'B' decision, or a 'C' decision. An 'A' decision is one that the plant manager makes herself, without consulting anyone."[32] Plant manager Paula Sims says, "I don't make very many of those, and when I do make one, everyone at the plant knows it. I make maybe 10 or 12 a year."[33] "B" decisions are also made by the plant manager, but with input from the people affected. "C" decisions, the most common type, are made by consensus, by the people directly involved, with plenty of discussion. With "C" decisions, the view of the plant manager doesn't necessarily carry more weight than the views of those affected."[34]

5.2 Decision Quality and Acceptance

According to the normative decision theory, using the right degree of employee participation improves the quality of decisions and the extent to which employees accept and are committed to decisions. Exhibit 14.7 lists the decision rules that normative decision theory uses to increase the quality of a decision and the degree to which employees accept and commit to a decision. The quality, leader information, subordinate information, goal congruence, and problem structure rules are used to increase decision quality. For example, the leader information rule states that if a leader doesn't have enough information to make a decision on his or her own, then the leader should not use an autocratic decision style.

The commitment probability, subordinate conflict, and commitment requirement rules shown in Exhibit 14.7 on the next page are used to increase employee acceptance and commitment to decisions. For example, the commitment requirement rule says that if decision acceptance and commitment are important and the subordinates share the organization's goals, then you shouldn't use an autocratic or consultative style. In other words, if followers want to do what's best for the company and you need their acceptance and commitment to make a decision work, then use a group decision style and let them make the decision. As you can see, these decision rules help leaders improve decision quality and follower acceptance and commitment by eliminating decision styles that don't fit the particular decision or situation they're facing. Normative decision theory, like path-goal theory, is situational in nature.

The abstract decision rules in Exhibit 14.7 are then framed as yes/no questions, which makes the process of applying these rules more concrete. These questions are

Exhibit 14.7

Normative Theory Decision Rules

DECISION RULES TO INCREASE DECISION QUALITY

Quality Rule. If the quality of the decision is important, then don't use an autocratic decision style.

Leader Information Rule. If the quality of the decision is important, and if the leader doesn't have enough information to make the decision on his or her own, then don't use an autocratic decision style.

Subordinate Information Rule. If the quality of the decision is important, and if the subordinates don't have enough information to make the decision themselves, then don't use a group decision style.

Goal Congruence Rule. If the quality of the decision is important, and subordinates' goals are different from the organization's goals, then don't use a group decision style.

Problem Structure Rule. If the quality of the decision is important, the leader doesn't have enough information to make the decision on his or her own, and the problem is unstructured, then don't use an autocratic decision style.

DECISION RULES TO INCREASE DECISION ACCEPTANCE

Commitment Probability Rule. If having subordinates accept and commit to the decision is important, then don't use an autocratic decision style.

Subordinate Conflict Rule. If having subordinates accept the decision is important and critical to successful implementation and subordinates are likely to disagree or end up in conflict over the decision, then don't use an autocratic or consultative decision style.

Commitment Requirement Rule. If having subordinates accept the decision is absolutely required for successful implementation and subordinates share the organization's goals, then don't use an autocratic or consultative style.

Sources: Adapted from V. H. Vroom, "Leadership," in *Handbook of Industrial and Organizational Psychology*, ed. M. D. Dunnette (Chicago: Rand McNally, 1976); V. H. Vroom & A. G. Jago, *The New Leadership: Managing Participation in Organizations* (Englewood Cliffs, NJ: Prentice Hall, 1988).

shown in the decision tree displayed in Exhibit 14.8. You start at the left side of the model and answer the first question, "How important is the technical quality of this decision?" by choosing "high" or "low." Then you continue by answering each question as you proceed along the decision tree until you get to a recommended decision style.

Let's use the model to make the decision of whether to change from a formal business attire policy to a casual wear policy. The problem sounds simple, but it is actually more complex than you might think. Follow the yellow line in Exhibit 14.8 as we work through the decision in the discussion below.

Problem: Change to Casual Wear?

1. *Quality requirement: How important is the technical quality of this decision?* High. This question has to do with whether there are quality differences in the alternatives and whether those quality differences matter. In other words: Is there a lot at stake in this decision? Although most people would assume that quality isn't an issue here, it really is, given the overall positive changes that generally accompany changes to casual wear.

2. *Commitment requirement: How important is subordinate commitment to the decision?* High.

Changes in culture, like dress codes, require subordinate commitment or they fail.

3. *Leader's information: Do you have sufficient information to make a high-quality decision?* Yes. Let's assume that you've done your homework. Much has been written about casual wear, from how to make the change to the effects it has in companies (almost all positive).

4. *Commitment probability: If you were to make the decision by yourself, is it reasonably certain that your subordinate(s) would be committed to the decision?* No. Studies of casual wear find that employees' reactions are almost uniformly positive. Nonetheless, employees are likely to be angry if you change something as personal as clothing policies without consulting them.

5. *Goal congruence: Do subordinates share the organizational goals to be attained in solving this problem?* Yes. The goals that usually accompany a change to casual dress policies are a more informal culture, better communication, and less money spent on business attire.

6. *Subordinate information: Do subordinates have sufficient information to make a high-quality decision?* No. Most employees know little about casual wear policies or even what constitutes casual wear in most companies. Consequently, most companies have to

Exhibit 14.8

Normative Decision Theory Tree for
Determining the Level of Participation in Decision Making

Leadership Style

Problem Attributes

QR	Quality requirement:	How important is the technical quality of this decision?
CR	Commitment requirement:	How important is subordinate commitment to the decision?
LI	Leader's information:	Do you have sufficient information to make a high-quality decision?
PS	Problem structure:	Is the problem well structured?
CP	Commitment probability:	If you were to make the decision by yourself, is it reasonably certain that your subordinate(s) would be committed to the decision?
GC	Goal congruence:	Do subordinates share the organizational goals to be attained in solving this problem?
CO	Subordinate conflict:	Is conflict among subordinates over preferred solutions likely?
SI	Subordinate information:	Do subordinates have sufficient information to make a high-quality decision?

Source: V. H. Vroom & P. W. Yetton, *Leadership and Decision Making* (Pittsburgh, University of Pittsburgh Press, 1973). Adapted and reprinted by permission of University of Pittsburgh Press.

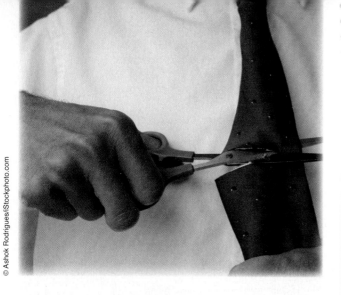
© Ashok Rodrigues/iStockphoto.com

educate employees about casual wear practices and policies before making a decision.

7. *CII is the answer:* With a CII, or consultative decision process, the leader shares the problem with employees as a group, obtains their ideas and suggestions, and then makes the decision, which may or may not reflect their input. So, given the answers to these questions (remember, different managers won't necessarily answer these questions the same way), the normative decision theory recommends that leaders consult with their subordinates before deciding whether to change to a casual wear policy.

How well does the normative decision theory work? A prominent leadership scholar has described it as the best supported of all leadership theories.[35] In general, the more managers violate the decision rules in Exhibit 14.7, the less effective their decisions are, especially with respect to subordinate acceptance and commitment.[36]

Strategic Leadership

Strategic leadership
the ability to anticipate, envision, maintain flexibility, think strategically, and work with others to initiate changes that will create a positive future for an organization

Visionary leadership
leadership that creates a positive image of the future that motivates organizational members and provides direction for future planning and goal setting

Strategic leadership is the ability to anticipate, envision, maintain flexibility, think strategically, and work with others to initiate changes that will create a positive fu-

ture for an organization.[37] Thus, strategic leadership captures how leaders inspire their companies to change and their followers to give extraordinary effort to accomplish organizational goals.

After reading the next section, you should be able to

6 explain how visionary leadership (i.e., charismatic and transformational leadership) helps leaders achieve strategic leadership.

6 Visionary Leadership

In Chapter 5, we defined vision as a statement of a company's purpose or reason for existing. Similarly, **visionary leadership** creates a positive image of the future that motivates organizational members and provides direction for future planning and goal setting.[38]

*Two kinds of visionary leadership are **6.1 charismatic leadership** and **6.2 transformational leadership.***

6.1 Charismatic Leadership

Charisma is a Greek word meaning "divine gift." The ancient Greeks saw people with charisma as inspired by the gods and capable of incredible accomplishments. German sociologist Max Weber viewed charisma as a special bond between leaders and followers.[39] Weber wrote that the special qualities of charismatic leaders enable them to strongly influence followers. For example, Richard Scrushy, a founder and the former CEO of HealthSouth, a worldwide provider of health care (outpatient surgery, diagnostic imaging, and rehabilitation), was undoubtedly a charismatic leader. Says one employee, "When he was talking, you could be hypnotized by him."[40] Weber also noted that charismatic leaders tend to emerge in times of crisis and that the radical solutions they propose enhance the admiration that followers feel for them. Indeed, charismatic leaders tend to have incredible influence over followers who may be inspired by their leaders and become fanatically devoted to them. From this perspective, charismatic leaders are often seen as larger-than-life or more special than other employees of the company.

Charismatic leaders have strong, confident, dynamic personalities that attract followers and enable the leaders to create strong bonds with their followers. Followers trust charismatic leaders, are loyal to them, and are inspired to work toward the accomplishment of the leader's vision. Followers who become devoted to charismatic leaders may go to extraordinary lengths to please them. Therefore, we can define **charismatic leadership** as the behavioral tendencies and personal characteristics of leaders that create an exceptionally strong relationship between them and their followers. Charismatic leaders also

- articulate a clear vision for the future that is based on strongly held values or morals;
- model those values by acting in a way consistent with the vision;
- communicate high performance expectations to followers;
- display confidence in followers' abilities to achieve the vision.[41]

Does charismatic leadership work? Studies indicate that it often does. In general, the followers of charismatic leaders are more committed and satisfied, are better performers, are more likely to trust their leaders, and simply work harder.[42] Nonetheless, charismatic leadership also has risks that are at least as large as its benefits. The problems are likely to occur with ego-driven charismatic leaders who take advantage of fanatical followers.

In general, there are two kinds of charismatic leaders, ethical charismatics and unethical charismatics.[43] **Ethical charismatics** provide developmental opportunities for followers, are open to positive and negative feedback, recognize others' contributions, share information, and have moral standards that emphasize the larger interests of the group, organization, or society.

By contrast, **unethical charismatics** control and manipulate followers, do what is best for themselves instead of their organizations, want to hear only positive feedback, share only information that is beneficial to themselves, and have moral standards that put their interests before everyone else's. Because followers can become just as committed to unethical as to ethical charismatics, unethical charismatics pose a tremendous risk for companies.

Exhibit 14.9 on the next page shows the stark differences between ethical and unethical charismatics on several leader behaviors: exercising power, creating the vision, communicating with followers, accepting feedback, stimulating followers intellectually, developing followers, and living by moral standards. For example, ethical charismatics include followers' concerns and wishes when creating a vision by having them participate in the development of the company vision. By contrast, unethical charismatics develop a vision by themselves solely to meet their personal agendas. One unethical charismatic said, "The key thing is that it is my idea; and I am going to win with it at all costs."[44]

Why do we fall for charismatics? According to **Fast Company,** "We're worshipful of top executives who seem charismatic, visionary, and tough. So long as they're lifting profits and stock prices, we're willing to overlook that they can also be callous, cunning, manipulative, deceitful, verbally and psychologically abusive, remorseless, exploitative, self-delusional, irresponsible, and megalomaniacal."[45]

6.2 Transformational Leadership

While charismatic leadership involves articulating a clear vision, modeling values consistent with that vision, communicating high performance expectations, and establishing very strong relationships with their followers, **transformational leadership** goes further by generating awareness and acceptance of a group's purpose and mission and by getting employees to see beyond their own needs and self-interest for the good of the group.[46] Like charismatic leaders, transformational leaders are visionary, but they transform their organizations by getting their followers to accomplish more than they intended and even more than they thought possible.

Transformational leaders make their followers feel that they are a vital part of the organization and help them see how their jobs fit with the organization's vision. By linking individual

Charismatic leadership the behavioral tendencies and personal characteristics of leaders that create an exceptionally strong relationship between them and their followers

Ethical charismatics charismatic leaders who provide developmental opportunities for followers, are open to positive and negative feedback, recognize others' contributions, share information, and have moral standards that emphasize the larger interests of the group, organization, or society

Unethical charismatics charismatic leaders who control and manipulate followers, do what is best for themselves instead of their organizations, want to hear only positive feedback, share only information that is beneficial to themselves, and have moral standards that put their interests before everyone else's

Transformational leadership leadership that generates awareness and acceptance of a group's purpose and mission and gets employees to see beyond their own needs and self-interests for the good of the group

Exhibit 14.9

Ethical and Unethical Charismatics

CHARISMATIC LEADER BEHAVIORS	ETHICAL Charismatics...	UNETHICAL Charismatics...
Exercising power	...use power to serve others.	...use power to dominate or manipulate others for personal gain.
Creating the vision	...allow followers to help develop the vision.	...are the sole source of vision, which they use to serve their personal agendas.
Communicating with followers	...engage in two-way communication and seek out viewpoints on critical issues. input	...engage in one-way communication and are not and suggestions from others.
Accepting feedback	...are open to feedback and willing to learn from criticism.	...have an inflated ego, thrive on attention and admiration of sycophants, and avoid candid feedback.
Stimulating followers	...want followers to think and question status quo as well as leader's views.	...don't want followers to think but instead want uncritical acceptance of leader's ideas.
Developing followers	...focus on developing people with whom they interact, express confidence in them, and share recognition with others.	...are insensitive and unresponsive to followers' needs and aspirations.
Living by moral standards	...follow self-guided principles that may go against popular opinion and have three virtues: courage, a sense of fairness or justice, and integrity.	...follow standards only if they satisfy immediate self-interests, manipulate impressions so that others think they are doing the right thing, and use communication skills to manipulate others to support their personal agenda.

Source: J. M. Howell and B. J. Avolio, "The Ethics of Charismatic Leadership: Submission or Liberation?" *Academy of Management Executive* 6, no. 2 (1992): 43–54.

and organizational interests, transformational leaders encourage followers to make sacrifices for the organization because they know that they will prosper when the organization prospers. Transformational leadership has four components: charismatic leadership or idealized influence, inspirational motivation, intellectual stimulation, and individualized consideration.[47]

Charismatic leadership or idealized influence means that transformational leaders act as role models for their followers. Because transformational leaders put others' needs ahead of their own and share risks with their followers, they are admired, respected, and trusted, and followers want to emulate them. Thus, in contrast to purely charismatic leaders (especially unethical charismatics), transformational leaders can be counted on to do the right thing and maintain high standards for ethical and personal conduct.

Inspirational motivation means that transformational leaders motivate and inspire followers by providing meaning and challenge to their work. By clearly communicating expectations and demonstrating commitment to goals, transformational leaders help followers envision the future, as one must to do from the organizational vision or mission. In turn, this leads to greater enthusiasm and optimism about the future. *Intellectual stimulation* means that transformational leaders encourage followers to be creative and innovative, to question assumptions, and to look at problems and situations in new ways even if their ideas are different from the leader's.

Individualized consideration means that transformational leaders pay special attention to followers' individual needs by creating learning opportunities, accepting and tolerating individual differences, encouraging two-way communication, and being good listen-

ily on discipline or threats to bring performance up to standards. This may work in the short run, but it's much less effective in the long run. Also, as discussed in Chapters 11 and 13, many leaders and organizations have difficulty successfully linking pay practices to individual performance. As a result, studies consistently show that transformational leadership is much more effective on average than transactional leadership. In the United States, Canada, Japan, and India and at all organizational levels, from first-level supervisors to upper-level executives, followers view transformational leaders as much better leaders and are much more satisfied when working for them. Furthermore, companies with transformational leaders have significantly better financial performance.[49]

ers. Roy Pelaez, who supervises 426 Aramark employees who clean airplanes, believes in attending to employees' needs. He says, "Managers are not supposed to get involved with the personal problems of their employees, but I take the opposite view."[48] With morale low and turnover high, he hired a tutor to improve his employees' English skills. To keep absences low, he found government programs that provided certified babysitters for his low-paid employees. And he set up three computers so that employees could teach each other to use word processors and spreadsheets. Says Pelaez, "All of these things are important, because we want employees who really feel connected to the company." Clearly, they do. Turnover, once almost 100 percent per year, dropped to 12 percent after Pelaez began paying attention to his employees' needs.

Finally, a distinction needs to be drawn between transformational leadership and transactional leadership. While transformational leaders use visionary and inspirational appeals to influence followers, **transactional leadership** is based on an exchange process in which followers are rewarded for good performance and punished for poor performance. When leaders administer rewards fairly and offer followers the rewards that they want, followers will often reciprocate with effort. A problem, however, is that transactional leaders often rely too heav-

© iStockphoto.com

Transactional leadership leadership based on an exchange process, in which followers are rewarded for good performance and punished for poor performance

MANAGING COMMUNICATION

What Is Communication?

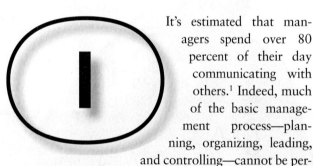

It's estimated that managers spend over 80 percent of their day communicating with others.[1] Indeed, much of the basic management process—planning, organizing, leading, and controlling—cannot be performed without effective communication. If this weren't reason enough to study communication, consider that effective oral communication, such as listening, following instructions, conversing, and giving feedback, is the most important skill for college graduates who are entering the work force.[2] Furthermore, across all industries, poor communication skills rank as the single most important reason that people do not advance in their careers.[3]

Communication is the process of transmitting information from one person or place to another. While some bosses sugarcoat bad news, smart managers understand that in the end effective, straightforward communication between managers and employees is essential for success.

After reading the next two sections, you should be able to

1   explain the role that perception plays in communication and communication problems.

Communication the process of transmitting information from one person or place to another

2   describe the communication process and the various kinds of communication in organizations.

Learning Outcomes

1 explain the role that perception plays in communication and communication problems.

2 describe the communication process and the various kinds of communication in organizations.

3 explain how managers can manage effective one-on-one communication.

4 describe how managers can manage effective organization-wide communication.

1 Perception and Communication Problems

One study found that when *employees* were asked whether their supervisor gave recognition for good work, only 13 percent said their supervisor gave a pat on the back, and a mere 14 percent said their supervisor gave sincere and thorough praise. But when the *supervisors* of these employees were asked if they gave recognition for good work, 82 percent said they gave pats on the back, while 80 percent said that they gave sincere and thorough praise.[4] How could managers and employees have had such different perceptions of something as simple as praise?

*Let's learn more about perception and communication problems by examining **1.1 the basic perception process, 1.2 perception problems, 1.3 how we perceive others**, and **1.4 how we perceive ourselves.** We'll also consider how all of these factors make it difficult for managers to achieve effective communication.*

1.1 Basic Perception Process

As shown in Exhibit 15.1 on the next page, **perception** is the process by which individuals attend to, organize, interpret, and retain informa-

Perception the process by which individuals attend to, organize, interpret, and retain information from their environments

Exhibit 15.1

Basic Perception Process

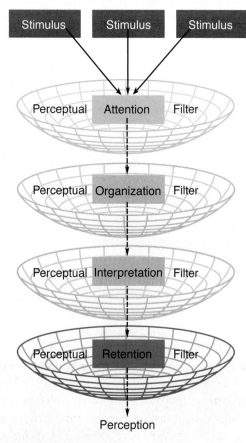

what they saw or heard. As shown in Exhibit 15.1, perceptual filters affect each part of the *perception process:* attention, organization, interpretation, and retention.

Attention is the process of noticing or becoming aware of particular stimuli. Because of perceptual filters, we attend to some stimuli and not others. *Organization* is the process of incorporating new information (from the stimuli that you notice) into your existing knowledge. Because of perceptual filters, we are more likely to incorporate new knowledge that is consistent with what we already know or believe. *Interpretation* is the process of attaching meaning to new knowledge. Because of perceptual filters, our preferences and beliefs strongly influence the meaning we attach to new information (e.g., "This must mean that top management supports our project."). Finally, *retention* is the process of remembering interpreted information. In other words, retention is what we recall and commit to memory after we have perceived something. Of course, perceptual filters also affect retention, that is, what we're likely to remember in the end.

For instance, imagine that you miss the first 10 minutes of a TV show and turn on your TV to see two people talking to each other in a living room. As they talk, they walk around the room, picking up and putting down various items. Some items, such as a ring, watch, and credit card, appear to be valuable, and others appear to be drug-related, such as a water pipe for smoking marijuana. In fact, this situation was depicted on videotape in a well-known study that manipulated people's perceptual filters.[5] Before watching the video, one-third of the study participants were told that the people were there to rob the apartment. Another third of the participants were told that police were on their way to conduct a drug raid and that the people in the apartment were getting rid of incriminating evidence. The remaining third of the participants were told that the people were simply waiting for a friend.

After watching the video, participants were asked to list all of the objects from the video that they could remember. Not surprisingly, the different perceptual filters (theft, drug raid, and waiting for a friend) affected what the participants attended to, how they organized the information, how they interpreted it, and ultimately which objects they remembered. Participants who thought a theft was in progress were more likely to remember the valuable objects in the video. Those who thought a drug raid was imminent were more likely to remember the drug-related objects. There was no discernible pattern to the items remembered by those who thought that the people in the video were simply waiting for a friend.

In short, because of perception and perceptual filters, people are likely to pay attention to different

tion from their environments. And since communication is the process of transmitting information from one person or place to another, perception is obviously a key part of communication. Yet, perception can also be a key obstacle to communication.

As people perform their jobs, they are exposed to a wide variety of informational stimuli such as emails, direct conversations with the boss or coworkers, rumors heard over lunch, stories about the company in the press, or a video broadcast of a speech from the CEO to all employees. Just being exposed to an informational stimulus, however, is no guarantee that an individual will pay attention to that stimulus. People experience stimuli through their own **perceptual filters**—the personality-, psychology-, or experience-based differences that influence them to ignore or pay attention to particular stimuli. Because of filtering, people exposed to the same information will often disagree about

Perceptual filters the personality-, psychology-, or experience-based differences that influence people to ignore or pay attention to particular stimuli things, organize and interpret what they pay attention to differently, and, finally, remember things differently. Consequently, even when people are exposed to the same communications (e.g., organizational memos, discussions with managers or customers), they can end up with very different perceptions and understandings. This is why communication can be so difficult and frustrating for managers. Let's review some of the communication problems created by perception and perceptual filters.

1.2 Perception Problems

Perception creates communication problems for organizations because people exposed to the same communication and information can end up with completely different ideas and understandings. Two of the most common perception problems in organizations are selective perception and closure.

At work, we are constantly bombarded with sensory stimuli—phones ringing, people talking in the background, computers dinging as new email arrives, people calling our names, and so forth. As limited processors of information, we cannot possibly notice, receive, and interpret all of this information. As a result, we attend to and accept some stimuli but screen out and reject others. This isn't a random process. **Selective perception** is the tendency to notice and accept objects and information consistent with our values, beliefs, and expectations while ignoring or screening out inconsistent information. For example, when Jack Smith, the former CEO of General Motors, was a junior-level executive, he traveled to Japan to learn why Toyota's cars were so reliable and why Toyota was so productive. When he learned that Toyota could build a car with half as many people as GM, he wrote a report and shared his findings with GM's all-powerful executive committee. But no one on the committee believed what he told them. The executives just couldn't accept that a Japanese company was so much more effective than GM. Says Smith, "Never in my life have I been so quickly and unceremoniously blown out of the water."[6]

Once we have initial information about a person, event, or process, **closure** is the tendency to fill in the gaps where information is missing, that is, to assume that what we don't know is consistent with what we already know. If employees are told that budgets must be cut by 10 percent, they may automatically assume that 10 percent of employees will lose their jobs, too, even if that isn't the case. Not surprisingly, when closure occurs, people sometimes fill in the gaps with inaccurate information. This, needless to say, can create problems for organizations.

1.3 Perceptions of Others

Attribution theory says that we all have a basic need to understand and explain the causes of other people's behavior.[7] In other words, we need to know why people do what they do. According to attribution theory, we use two general reasons or attributions to explain people's behavior: an *internal attribution,* in which behavior is thought to be voluntary or under the control of the individual, and an *external attribution,* in which behavior is thought to be involuntary and outside of the control of the individual.

For example, have you ever seen someone changing a flat tire on the side of the road and thought to yourself, "What rotten luck—somebody's having a bad day"? If you did, you perceived the

Selective perception the tendency to notice and accept objects and information consistent with our values, beliefs, and expectations while ignoring or screening out or not accepting inconsistent information

Closure the tendency to fill in gaps of missing information by assuming that what we don't know is consistent with what we already know

Attribution theory a theory that states that we all have a basic need to understand and explain the causes of other people's behavior

person through an external attribution known as the defensive bias. The **defensive bias** is the tendency for people to perceive themselves as personally and situationally similar to someone who is having difficulty or trouble.[8] And, when we identify with the person in a situation, we tend to use external attributions (i.e., the situation) to explain the person's behavior. For instance, since flat tires are common, it's easy to perceive ourselves in that same situation and put the blame on external causes such as running over a nail.

Now, let's assume a different situation, this time in the workplace:

A utility company worker puts a ladder on a utility pole and then climbs up to do his work. As he's doing his work, he falls from the ladder and seriously injures himself.[9]

Answer this question: Who or what caused the accident? If you thought, "It's not the worker's fault. Anybody could fall from a tall ladder," then you're still operating from a defensive bias in which you see yourself as personally and situationally similar to someone who is having difficulty or trouble. In other words, you made an external attribution by attributing the accident to an external cause, meaning the situation.

Most accident investigations, however, initially blame the worker (i.e., an internal attribution) and not the situation (i.e., an external attribution). Typically, 60 to 80 percent of workplace accidents each year are blamed on "operator error," that is, the employees themselves. In reality, more complete investigations usually show that workers are responsible for only 30 to 40 percent of all workplace accidents.[10] Why are accident investigators so quick to blame workers? The reason is that they are committing the **fundamental attribution error**,

which is the tendency to ignore external causes of behavior and to attribute other people's actions to internal causes.[11] In other words, when investigators examine the possible causes of an accident, they're much more likely to assume that the accident is a function of the person and not the situation.

Which attribution—the defensive bias or the fundamental attribution error—are workers likely to make when something goes wrong? In general, as shown in Exhibit 15.2, employees and coworkers are more likely to perceive events and explain behavior from a defensive bias. Because they do the work themselves and see themselves as similar to others who make mistakes, have accidents, or are otherwise held responsible for things that go wrong at work, employees and coworkers are likely to attribute problems to external causes such as failed machinery, poor support, or inadequate training. By contrast, because they are typically observers (who don't do the work themselves) and see themselves as situationally and personally different from workers, managers (i.e., the boss) tend to commit the fundamental attribution error and blame mistakes, accidents, and other things that go wrong on workers (i.e., an internal attribution).

Consequently, in most workplaces, when things go wrong, workers and managers can be expected to take opposite views. Therefore, together, the defensive bias, which is typically used by workers, and the fundamental attribution error, which is typically made by managers, present a significant challenge to effective communication and understanding in organizations.

Defensive bias the tendency for people to perceive themselves as personally and situationally similar to someone who is having difficulty or trouble

Fundamental attribution error the tendency to ignore external causes of behavior and to attribute other people's actions to internal causes

Exhibit 15.2

Defensive Bias and Fundamental Attribution Error

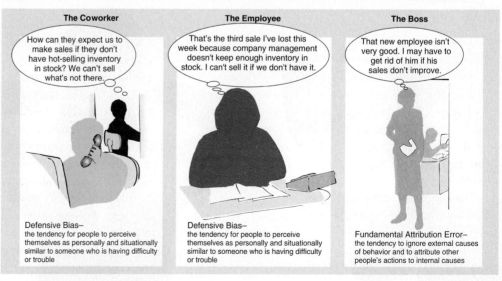

1.4 Self-Perception

The **self-serving bias** is the tendency to overestimate our value by attributing successes to ourselves (internal causes) and attributing failures to others or the environment (external causes).[12] The self-serving bias can make it especially difficult for managers to talk to employees about performance problems. In general, people have a need to maintain a positive self-image. This need is so strong that when people seek feedback at work, they typically want verification of their worth (rather than information about performance deficiencies) or assurance that mistakes or problems weren't their fault.[13] And, when managerial communication threatens people's positive self-image, they can become defensive and emotional. They quit listening, and communication becomes ineffective. In the second half of the chapter, which focuses on improving communication, we'll explain ways in which managers can minimize this self-serving bias and improve effective one-on-one communication with employees.

2 Kinds of Communication

There are many kinds of communication—formal, informal, coaching/counseling, and nonverbal—but they all follow the same fundamental process.

*Let's learn more about the different kinds of communication by examining **2.1 the communication process, 2.2 formal communication channels, 2.3 informal communication channels, 2.4 coaching and counseling, or one-on-one communication,** and **2.5 nonverbal communication.***

2.1 The Communication Process

Earlier in the chapter, we defined *communication* as the process of transmitting information from one person or place to another. Exhibit 15.3 displays a model of the communication process and its major components: the sender (message to be conveyed, encoding the message, transmitting the message); the receiver (receiving message, decoding the message, and the message that was understood); and noise, which interferes with the communication process.

The communication process begins when a *sender* thinks of a message he or she wants to convey to another person. The next step is to encode the message. **Encoding** means putting a message into a verbal (written or spoken) or symbolic form that can be recognized

Exhibit 15.3

The Interpersonal Communication Process

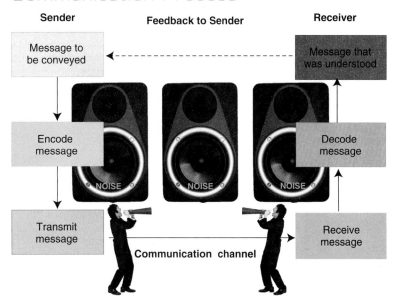

and understood by the receiver. The sender then *transmits the message* via *communication channels.* With some communication channels such as the telephone and face-to-face communication, the sender receives immediate feedback, whereas others such as email (or text messages and file attachments), fax, beepers, voice mail, memos, and letters, make the sender wait for the receiver to respond.

Unfortunately, because of technical difficulties (e.g., fax down, dead battery on the mobile phone, inability to read email attachments) or people-based transmission problems (e.g., forgetting to pass on the message), messages aren't always transmitted. If the message is transmitted and received, however, the next step is for the receiver to decode it. **Decoding** is the process by which the receiver translates the verbal or symbolic form of the message into an understood message. However, the message as understood by the receiver isn't always the same message that was intended by the sender. Because of different experiences or perceptual filters,

Self-serving bias the tendency to overestimate our value by attributing successes to ourselves (internal causes) and attributing failures to others or the environment (external causes)

Encoding putting a message into a written, verbal, or symbolic form that can be recognized and understood by the receiver

Decoding the process by which the receiver translates the written, verbal, or symbolic form of a message into an understood message

Cool or Clear?

Jargon makes you sound smart, but some jargon is very faddish. Take a page from current jargon: *Crowdsource* (v.), to use the skills or tools of a wide variety of freelancers, professional or amateur, paid or unpaid, to work on a single problem. Words like this come and go quickly. They make you sound cool when they're in vogue, but they can also be (and make you) the butt of jokes. More to the point, jargon gets in the way of clear communication. Know what this means?: "Server virtualization is the masking of server resources, including the number and identity of individual physical servers, processors, and operating systems, from server users." Unless you're an IT person, you probably don't. When in doubt, go for simple and clear to get your message across. As Albert Einstein once said, "Any intelligent fool can make things bigger and more complex. It takes a touch of genius and a lot of courage to move in the opposite direction."

Sources: C. Gallo, "Stop Speaking in Jargon," *Business Week Online*, 25 February 2008, available online at http://www.businessweek.com/smallbiz/content/feb2008/sb20080222_627595.htm [accessed 3 September 2008]; G. Barrett, "All We Are Saying," *The New York Times*, 23 December 2007.

---

receivers may attach a completely different meaning to a message than was intended.

The last step of the communication process occurs when the receiver gives the sender feedback. **Feedback to sender** is a return message to the sender that indicates the receiver's understanding of the message (of what the receiver was supposed to know, to do, or not to do). Feedback makes senders aware of possible miscommunications and enables them to continue communicating until the receiver understands the intended message.

Unfortunately, feedback doesn't always occur in the communication process. Complacency and overconfidence about the ease and simplicity of communication can lead senders and receivers to simply assume that they share a common understanding of the message and, consequently, not to use feedback to improve the effectiveness of their communication. This is a serious mistake, especially since messages and feedback are always transmitted with and against a background of noise. **Noise** is anything that interferes with the transmission of the intended message, much like static on a TV or radio station. Noise can occur in any of the following situations:

- The sender isn't sure what message to communicate.
- The message is not clearly encoded.
- The wrong communication channel is chosen.

- The message is not received or decoded properly.
- The receiver doesn't have the experience or time to understand the message.

Jargon, which is vocabulary particular to a profession or group, is another form of noise that interferes with communication in the workplace. Any idea what "rightsizing," "delayering," "unsiloing," and "knowledge acquisition" mean? Rightsizing means laying off workers. Delayering means firing managers, or getting rid of layers of management. Unsiloing means getting workers in different parts of the company (i.e., different vertical silos) to work with others outside their own areas. Knowledge acquisition means teaching workers new knowledge or skills. Unfortunately, the business world is rife with jargon. According to Carol Hymowitz of *The Wall Street Journal*, "A new crop of buzzwords usually sprouts every three to five years, or about the same length of time many top executives have to prove themselves. Some can be useful in swiftly communicating, and spreading, new business concepts. Others are less useful, even devious."[14]

2.2 Formal Communication Channels

An organization's **formal communication channel** is the system of official channels that carry organizationally approved messages and information. Organizational objectives, rules, policies, procedures, instructions, commands, and requests for information are all transmitted via the formal communication system or "channel." There are three formal communication channels: downward communication, upward communication, and horizontal communication.[15]

Feedback to sender in the communication process, a return message to the sender that indicates the receiver's understanding of the message

Noise anything that interferes with the transmission of the intended message

Jargon vocabulary particular to a profession or group

Formal communication channel the system of official channels that carry organizationally approved messages and information

Common Problems with Downward, Upward, and Horizontal Communication

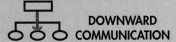

DOWNWARD COMMUNICATION

- Overusing downward communication by sending too many messages

- Issuing contradictory messages

- Hurriedly communicating vague, unclear messages

- Issuing messages that indicate management's low regard for lower-level workers

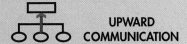

UPWARD COMMUNICATION

- The risk involved with telling upper management about problems (i.e., fear of retribution)

- Managers reacting angrily and defensively when workers report problems

- Not enough opportunities or channels for lower-level workers to contact upper levels of management

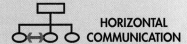

HORIZONTAL COMMUNICATION

- Management discouraging or punishing horizontal communication, viewing it as small talk

- Not giving managers and workers the time or opportunity for horizontal communication

- Not enough opportunities or channels for lower-level workers to engage in horizontal communication

Source: G. L. Kreps, *Organizational Communication: Theory and Practice* (New York: Longman, 1990).

Downward communication flows from higher to lower levels in an organization. Downward communication is used to issue orders down the organizational hierarchy, to give organizational members job-related information, to give managers and workers performance reviews from upper managers, and to clarify organizational objectives and goals.[16]

Upward communication flows from lower levels to higher levels in an organization. Upward communication is used to give higher-level managers feedback about operations, issues, and problems; to help higher-level managers assess organizational performance and effectiveness; to encourage lower-level managers and employees to participate in organizational decision making; and to give those at lower levels the chance to share their concerns with higher-level authorities. At Cisco Systems, the manufacturer of the switches, routers, and computer equipment that form the backbone of the Internet and company computer networks, CEO John Chambers uses monthly birthday breakfasts to create upward communication. Says Chambers, "As for how I hear from employees, I host a monthly birthday breakfast. Anybody who has a birthday in that month gets to come and quiz me for an hour and fifteen minutes. No directors or VPs in the room. It's how I keep my finger on the pulse of what's working and what's not. It's brutal, but it's my most enjoyable session."[17]

Horizontal communication flows among managers and workers who are at the same organizational level, such as when a day shift nurse comes in at 7:30 A.M. for a half-hour discussion with the midnight nurse supervisor who leaves at 8:00 A.M. Horizontal communication helps facilitate coordination and cooperation between different parts of a company and allows coworkers to share relevant information. It also helps people at the same level resolve conflicts and solve problems without involving high levels of management. Studies show that communication breakdowns, which occur most often during horizontal communication, such as when patients are handed over from one nurse or doctor to another, are the largest source of medical errors in hospitals.[18]

In general, what can managers do to improve formal communication? First, decrease reliance on downward communication. Second, increase chances for upward communication by increasing personal contact with lower-level managers and workers. Third, encourage much better use of horizontal communication.

2.3 Informal Communication Channels

An organization's **informal communication channel,** sometimes called the **grapevine,** is the transmission of messages from employee to employee outside of formal

Downward communication communication that flows from higher to lower levels in an organization

Upward communication communication that flows from lower to higher levels in an organization

Horizontal communication communication that flows among managers and workers who are at the same organizational level

Informal communication channel ("grapevine") the transmission of messages from employee to employee outside of formal communication channels

Exhibit 15.4

Grapevine Communication Networks

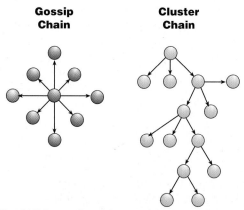

Gossip Chain Cluster Chain

Source: K. Davis & J. W. Newstrom, *Human Behavior at Work: Organizational Behavior*, 8th ed. (New York: McGraw-Hill, 1989).

communication channels. The grapevine arises out of curiosity, that is, the need to know what is going on in an organization and how it might affect you or others. To satisfy this curiosity, employees need a consistent supply of relevant, accurate, in-depth information about "who is doing what and what changes are occurring within the organization."[19] Employee Paul Haze agrees, saying, "If employees don't have a definite explanation from management, they tend to interpret for themselves."[20]

Grapevines arise out of informal communication networks such as the gossip or cluster chains shown in Exhibit 15.4. In a *gossip chain*, one highly connected individual shares information with many other managers and workers. By contrast, in a *cluster chain*, numerous people simply tell a few of their friends. The result in both cases is that information flows freely and quickly through the organization. Some believe that grapevines are a waste of employees' time, that they promote gossip and rumors that fuel political speculation, and that they are sources of highly unreliable, inaccurate information. Yet studies clearly show that grapevines are highly accurate sources of information for a number of reasons.[21] First, because grapevines typically carry "juicy" information that is interesting and timely, information spreads rapidly. At Meghan De Goyler Hauser's former company, the word on the grapevine was that her boss drank on the job, the company accountant was robbing the company blind, and one of her coworkers was a nude model. She says, "The rumors all turned out to be true."[22] Second, since information is typically spread by face-to-face conversation, receivers can send feedback

to make sure they understand the message that is being communicated. This reduces misunderstandings and increases accuracy. Third, since most of the information in a company moves along the grapevine rather than formal communication channels, people can usually verify the accuracy of information by checking it out with others.

What can managers do to manage organizational grapevines? The very worst thing they can do is withhold information or try to punish those who share information with others. The grapevine abhors a vacuum, and rumors and anxiety will flourish in the absence of information from company management. Why does this occur? According to workplace psychologist Nicholas DiFonzo, "The main focus of rumor is to figure out the truth. It's the group trying to make sense of something that's important to them."[23] A better strategy is to embrace the grapevine and keep employees informed about possible changes and strategies. Failure to do so will just make things worse. And, in addition to using the grapevine to communicate with others, managers should not overlook the grapevine as a tremendous source of valuable information and feedback. In fact, information flowing through organizational grapevines is estimated to be 75 to 95 percent accurate.[23]

How to Deal with Internet Gripe Sites

GOOD TIP!

1. Correct misinformation. Put an end to false rumors and set the record straight. Don't be defensive.
2. Don't take angry comments personally.
3. Give your name and contact number to show employees that you're concerned and that they can contact you directly.
4. Hold a town meeting to discuss the issues raised on the gripe site.
5. Set up anonymous internal discussion forums on the company server. Then encourage employees to gripe anonymously on the company intranet, rather than on the Web.

Sources: J. Simons, "Stop Moaning about Gripe Sites and Log On," *Fortune*, 2 April 2001, 181; K. Voight, "Office Intelligence," *Asian Wall Street Journal*, 21 January 2005, P1.

© iStockphoto.com

2.4 Coaching and Counseling: One-on-One Communication

When the Wyatt Company surveyed 531 U.S. companies undergoing major changes and restructuring, it asked their CEOs, "If you could go back and change one thing, what would it be?" The answer? "The way we communicated with our employees." The CEOs said that instead of flashy videos, printed materials, or formal meetings, they would make greater use of one-on-one communication, especially with employees' immediate supervisors rather than higher-level executives that employees didn't know.[24]

Coaching and counseling are two kinds of one-on-one communication. **Coaching** is communicating with someone for the direct purpose of improving the person's on-the-job performance or behavior.[25] Managers tend to make several mistakes when coaching employees, however. First, they wait for a problem before coaching. Jim Concelman, manager for leadership development at Development Dimensions International, says, "Of course, a boss has to coach an employee if a mistake has been made, but they shouldn't be waiting for the error. While it is a lot easier to see a mistake and correct it, people learn more through success than through failure, so bosses should ensure that employees are experiencing as many successes as possible. Successful employees lead to a more successful organization."[26] Second, when mistakes *are* made, managers wait much too long before talking to the employee about the problem. Management professor Ray Hilgert says, "A manager must respond as soon as possible after an incident of poor performance. Don't bury your head. . . . When employees are told nothing, they assume everything is okay."[27]

By contrast, **counseling** is communicating with someone about non-job-related issues such as stress, child care, health issues, retirement planning, or legal issues that may be affecting or interfering with the person's performance. But counseling does not mean that managers should try to be clinicians, even though an estimated 20 percent of employees are dealing with personal problems at any one time. Instead, managers should discuss specific performance problems, listen if the employee chooses to share personal issues, and then recommend that the employee call the company's *Employee Assistance Program (EAP)*. EAPs are typically free when provided as part of a company's benefit package. In emergencies or times of crisis, EAPs can offer immediate counseling and support and provide referrals to organizations and professionals that can help employees and their family members address personal issues.

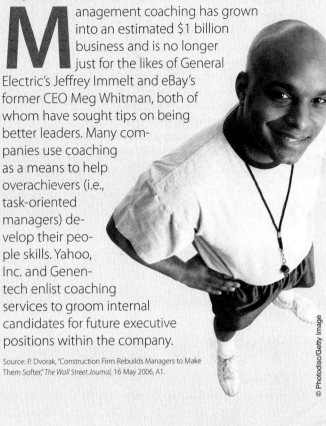
2.5 Nonverbal Communication

Nonverbal communication is any communication that doesn't involve words. Nonverbal communication almost always accompanies verbal communication and may either support and reinforce the verbal message or contradict it. The importance of nonverbal communication is well established. Researchers have estimated that as much as 93 percent of any message is transmitted nonverbally, with 55 percent coming from body language and facial expressions and 38 percent coming from the tone and pitch of the voice.[20] Since many nonverbal cues are unintentional, receivers often consider nonverbal communication to be a more accurate representation of

Coaching communicating with someone for the direct purpose of improving the person's on-the-job performance or behavior

Counseling communicating with someone about non-job-related issues that may be affecting or interfering with the person's performance

Nonverbal communication any communication that doesn't involve words

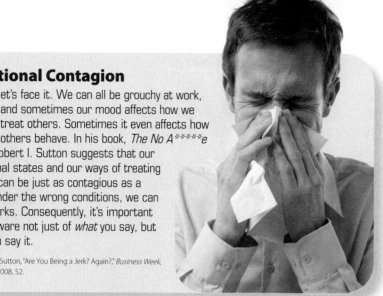

Emotional Contagion

Let's face it. We can all be grouchy at work, and sometimes our mood affects how we treat others. Sometimes it even affects how others behave. In his book, *The No A*****e Rule*, Robert I. Sutton suggests that our emotional states and our ways of treating others can be just as contagious as a cold. Under the wrong conditions, we can all be jerks. Consequently, it's important to be aware not just of *what* you say, but *how* you say it.

Source: R. I. Sutton, "Are You Being a Jerk? Again?," *Business Week,* 25 August 2008, 52.

tend to decrease their communication effectiveness by speaking softly. When people are nervous, they tend to talk faster and louder. These characteristics have a tremendous influence on whether listeners are receptive to what speakers are saying.

In short, because nonverbal communication is so informative, especially when it contradicts verbal communication, managers need to learn how to monitor and control their nonverbal behavior.

what senders are thinking and feeling than the words they use.

Kinesics and paralanguage are two kinds of nonverbal communication.[29] **Kinesics** (from the Greek word *kinesis,* meaning "movement") are movements of the body and face.[30] These movements include arm and hand gestures, facial expressions, eye contact, folding arms, crossing legs, and leaning toward or away from another person.

It turns out that kinesics play an incredibly important role in communication. Studies of married couples' kinesic interactions can predict whether they will stay married with 93 percent accuracy.[31] The key is the ratio of positive to negative kinesic interactions that husbands and wives make as they communicate. Negative kinesic expressions such as eye rolling suggest contempt, whereas positive kinetic expressions such as maintaining eye contact and nodding suggest listening and caring. When the ratio of positive to negative interactions drops below 5 to 1, the chances for divorce quickly increase. Kinesics operate similarly in the workplace, providing clues about people's true feelings, over and above what they say (or don't say). For instance, Louis Giuliano, former CEO of ITT, which makes heavy use of teams, says, "When you get a team together and say to them we're going to change a process, you always have people who say, 'No, we're not.'" They usually don't say it out loud, but "the body language is there," making it clear that their real answer is "no."[32]

Paralanguage includes the pitch, rate, tone, volume, and speaking pattern (i.e., use of silences, pauses, or hesitations) of one's voice. For example, when people are unsure what to say, they

Kinesics movements of the body and face

Paralanguage the pitch, rate, tone, volume, and speaking pattern (i.e., use of silences, pauses, or hesitations) of one's voice

How to Improve Communication

When it comes to improving communication, managers face two primary tasks, managing one-on-one communication and managing organization-wide communication.

After reading the next two sections, you should be able to

3 explain how managers can manage effective one-on-one communication.

4 describe how managers can manage effective organization-wide communication.

3 Managing One-on-One Communication

You learned in Chapter 1 that, on average, first-line managers spend 57 percent of their time with people, middle managers spend 63 percent of their time directly with people, and top managers spend as much as 78 percent of their time dealing with people.[33] These numbers make it clear that managers spend a great deal of time in one-on-one communication with others.

Learn more about managing one-on-one communication by reading how to 3.1 choose the right communication medium, 3.2 be a good listener, and 3.3 give effective feedback.

3.1 Choosing the Right Communication Medium

Sometimes messages are poorly communicated simply because they are delivered using the wrong **communication medium,** which is the method used to deliver a message. For example, the wrong communication medium is being used when an employee returns from lunch, picks up the note left on her office chair, and learns she has been fired.

There are two general kinds of communication media: oral and written communication. *Oral communication* includes face-to-face and group meetings through telephone calls, videoconferencing, or any other means of sending and receiving spoken messages. Studies show that managers generally prefer oral communication over written because it provides the opportunity to ask questions about parts of the message that they don't understand. Oral communication is also a rich communication medium because it allows managers to receive and assess the nonverbal communication that accompanies spoken messages (i.e., body language, facial expressions, and the voice characteristics associated with paralanguage). Furthermore, you don't need a personal computer and an Internet connection to conduct oral communication. Oral communication should not be used for all communication, however. In general, when the message is simple, such as a quick request or a presentation of straightforward information, a memo or email is often the better communication medium.

Written communication includes letters, email, and memos. Although most managers still like and use oral communication, email in particular is changing how they communicate with workers, customers, and each other. Email is the fastest-growing form of communication in organizations primarily because of its convenience and speed. For instance, because people read six times faster than they can listen, they usually can read 30 email messages in 10 to 15 minutes.[34] By contrast, dealing with voice messages can take a considerable amount of time.

Written communication such as email is well suited for delivering straightforward messages and information. Furthermore, with email accessible at the office, at home, and on the road (by laptop computer, cell phone, or Web-based email), managers can use email to stay in touch from anywhere at almost any time. And, since email and other written communications don't have to be sent and received simultaneously, messages can be sent and stored for reading at any time. Consequently, managers can send and receive many more messages using email than using oral communication, which requires people to get together in person or by phone or videoconference.

Email has its own drawbacks, however. One reason is that it lacks the formality of paper memos and letters. It is easy to fire off an email that is not well-written or fully thought through. This is a particular problem in instances when we might be tempted to send a knee-jerk, emotional response to a message that has angered or confused us. Another drawback to email is that it lacks nonverbal cues, making emails very easy to misinterpret. Kristin Byron, assistant professor of management at Syracuse University, says, "People perceive emails as more negative than they are intended to be, and even emails that are intended to be positive can be misinterpreted as more neutral." So take a minute to reflect before you hit reply.[35]

Although written communication is well suited for delivering straightforward messages and information, it is not well suited to complex, ambiguous, or emotionally laden messages, which are better delivered through oral communication.

> Most people, including managers, are **terrible listeners**, retaining only about **25 percent** of what they hear.

3.2 Listening

Are you a good listener? You probably think so. But, in fact, most people, including managers, are terrible listeners, retaining only about 25 percent of what they hear.[36] You qualify as a poor listener if you frequently interrupt others, jump to conclusions about what people will say before they've said it, hurry the speaker to finish his or her point, are a passive listener (not actively working at your listening), or simply don't pay attention to what people are saying.[37] On this last point—attentiveness—college students were periodically asked to record their thoughts during a psychology course. On average, 20 percent of the students were paying atten-

Communication medium the method used to deliver an oral or written message

I'M LISTENING

Radio callers were encouraged to share their troubles when psychiatrist Dr. Frasier Crane (Kelsey Grammer) greeted them with a calm, "I'm listening."

So, what can you do to improve your listening ability? First, understand the difference between hearing and listening. According to *Webster's New World Dictionary,* **hearing** is the act or process of perceiving sounds, whereas **listening** is making a conscious effort to hear. In other words, we react to sounds, such as bottles breaking or music being played too loud, because hearing is an involuntary physiological process. By contrast, listening is a voluntary behavior. So, if you want to be a good listener, you have to choose to be a good listener. Typically, that means choosing to be an active, empathetic listener.[41]

Active listening means assuming half the responsibility for successful communication by actively giving the speaker nonjudgmental feedback that shows you've accurately heard what he or she said. Active listeners make it clear from their behavior that they are listening carefully to what the speaker has to say. Active listeners put the speaker at ease, maintain eye contact, and show the speaker that they are attentively listening by nodding and making short statements.

Several specific strategies can help you be a better active listener. First, *clarify responses* by asking the speaker to explain confusing or ambiguous statements. Second, when there are natural breaks in the speaker's delivery, use this time to paraphrase or summarize what has been said. *Paraphrasing* is restating what has been said in your own words. *Summarizing* is reviewing the speaker's main points or emotions. Paraphrasing and

tion (only 12 percent were actively working at being good listeners), 20 percent were thinking about sex, 20 percent were thinking about things they had done before class, and the remaining 40 percent were thinking about other things unrelated to the class (e.g., worries, religion, lunch, daydreaming).[38]

How important is it to be a good listener? In general, about 45 percent of the total time you spend communicating with others is spent listening. Furthermore, listening is important for managerial and business success, even for those at the top of an organization. Listening is a more important skill for managers than ever, since Generation X employees tend to expect a high level of interaction with their supervisors. They want feedback on their performance, but they also want to offer feedback and know that it is heard.[39] In fact, managers with good listening skills are rated as better managers by their employees and are much more likely to be promoted.[40]

Hearing the act or process of perceiving sounds

Listening making a conscious effort to hear

Active listening assuming half the responsibility for successful communication by actively giving the speaker nonjudgmental feedback that shows you've accurately heard what he or she said

GOOD TIP!

Listen Up!

Communications coach Carmine Gallo offers four tips on how to become a better listener:

1. Fix your gaze. If you're listening to someone, look them in the eyes.

2. Respond to a question with a question. When someone asks you a question, don't just answer and move on. Ask them a meaningful question in return.

3. When people ask for feedback, give it. It shows you were listening and that you take them seriously.

4. Be available for the tough questions. Be attentive, ask questions, and show that you understand (and want to know) the complexities.

Source: C. Gallo, "Why Leadership Means Listening," *Business Week,* 31 January 2008, available online at http://www.businessweek.com/smallbiz/content/jan2007/sb20070131_192848.htm [accessed 3 September 2008].

Exhibit 15.5

Clarifying, Paraphrasing, and Summarizing Responses for Active Listeners

CLARIFYING RESPONSES	PARAPHRASING RESPONSES	SUMMARIZING RESPONSES
Could you explain that again?	What you're really saying is	Let me summarize . . . .
I don't understand what you mean.	If I understand you correctly	Okay, your main concerns are . . . .
I'm not sure how	In other words	To recap what you've said . . . .
I'm confused. Would you run through that again?	So your perspective is that	Thus far, you've discussed . . . .
	Tell me if I'm wrong, but what you seem to be saying is	

Source: E. Atwater, *I Hear You,* rev. ed. (New York: Walker, 1992).

summarizing give the speaker the chance to correct the message if the active listener has attached the wrong meaning to it. Paraphrasing and summarizing also show the speaker that the active listener is interested in the speaker's message. Exhibit 15.5 lists specific statements that listeners can use to clarify responses, paraphrase, or summarize what has been said.

Active listeners also avoid evaluating the message or being critical until the message is complete. They recognize that their only responsibility during the transmission of a message is to receive it accurately and derive the intended meaning from it. Evaluation and criticism can take place after the message is accurately received. To be a good listener, you should avoid thinking about your response while someone is talking and turn all of your attention to listening. Finally, active listeners also recognize that a large portion of any message is transmitted nonverbally and thus pay very careful attention to the nonverbal cues transmitted by the speaker.

Empathetic listening means understanding the speaker's perspective and personal frame of reference and giving feedback that conveys that understanding to the speaker. Empathetic listening goes beyond active listening because it depends on our ability to set aside our own attitudes or relationships to be able to see and understand things through someone else's eyes. Empathetic listening is just as important as active listening, especially for managers, because it helps build rapport and trust with others.

The key to being a more empathetic listener is to show your desire to understand and to reflect people's feelings. You can *show your desire to understand* by listening, that is, asking people to talk about what's most important to them and then giving them sufficient time to talk before responding or interrupting.

Reflecting feelings is also an important part of empathetic listening because it demonstrates that you understand the speaker's emotions. Unlike active listening, in which you restate or summarize the informational content of what has been said, the focus is on the affective part of the message. As an empathetic listener, you can use the following statements to *reflect the speaker's emotions:*

- So, right now it sounds like you're feeling . . . .
- You seem as if you're . . . .
- Do you feel a bit . . . ?
- I could be wrong, but I'm sensing that you're feeling . . . .

In the end, says management consultant Terry Pearce, empathetic listening can be boiled down to these three steps. First, wait 10 seconds before you answer or respond. It will seem an eternity, but waiting prevents you from interrupting others and rushing your response. Second, to be sure you understand what the speaker wants, ask questions to clarify the speaker's intent. Third, only then should you respond first with feelings and then facts (notice that facts *follow* feelings).[42]

This section provides you with important tools to help you become a better listener. Applying them insincerely—or indiscriminately—may make you seem patronizing and derail your attempt to build better working relationships. Not everyone appreciates having what they said repeated back to them—even if you've repeated it in your own words. The key is to respond, rather than repeat or react, in a manner appropriate for the situation and the

Empathetic listening
understanding the speaker's perspective and personal frame of reference and giving feedback that conveys that understanding to the speaker

> *Giving feedback **does not** give managers the right to personally attack workers.*

person with whom you're speaking.[43] The suggestions in Exhibit 15.5 are simply ways to learn the responses that typify active listening. You have to find your own voice to seem genuine.

3.3 Giving Feedback

In Chapter 11, you learned that performance appraisal feedback (i.e., judging) should be separated from developmental feedback (i.e., coaching).[44] We can now focus on the steps needed to communicate feedback one-on-one to employees.

To start, managers need to recognize that feedback can be constructive or destructive. **Destructive feedback** is disapproving without any intention of being helpful and almost always causes a negative or defensive reaction in the recipient. Kent Thiry, CEO of DaVita, a corporation which runs dialysis treatment centers, admits that he regularly gets dinged by his senior executives for giving too much negative feedback. Says Thiry, "They say I'm not harder on them than I am on myself, but my negativity isn't constructive." Thiry now gives himself "a daily score about feedback, to remind myself—and change." Avoiding destructive feedback is important. One study found that 98 percent of employees responded to destructive feedback

from their bosses with either verbal aggression (two-thirds) or physical aggression (one-third).[45]

By contrast, **constructive feedback** is intended to be helpful, corrective, and/or encouraging. It is aimed at correcting performance deficiencies and motivating employees. For feedback to be constructive rather than destructive, it must be immediate, focused on specific behaviors, and problem-oriented. *Immediate feedback* is much more effective than delayed feedback because manager and worker can recall the mistake or incident more accurately and discuss it in detail. For example, if a worker is rude to a customer and the customer immediately reports the incident to management, and if the manager, in turn, immediately discusses the incident with the employee, there should be little disagreement over what was said or done. By contrast, it's unlikely that either the manager or the worker will be able to accurately remember the specifics of what occurred if the manager waits several weeks to discuss the incident. When that happens, it's usually too late to have a meaningful conversation.

Specific feedback focuses on particular acts or incidents that are clearly under the control of the employee. For instance, instead of telling an employee that he or she is "always late for work," it's much more constructive to say, "In the last three weeks, you have been 30 minutes late on four occasions and more than an hour late on two others." Furthermore, specific feedback isn't very helpful unless employees have control over the problems that the feedback addresses. Giving negative feedback about behaviors beyond someone's control is likely to be seen as unfair. Similarly, giving positive feedback about behaviors beyond someone's control may be viewed as insincere.

Last, *problem-oriented feedback* focuses on the problems or incidents associated with the poor performance rather than on the

98 percent of employees responded to destructive feedback from their bosses with either verbal aggression or physical aggression.

© Asia Images/Jupiter Images

Destructive feedback feedback that disapproves without any intention of being helpful and almost always causes a negative or defensive reaction in the recipient

Constructive feedback feedback intended to be helpful, corrective, and/or encouraging

worker or the worker's personality. Giving feedback does not give managers the right to personally attack workers. Though managers may be frustrated by a worker's poor performance, the point of problem-oriented feedback is to draw attention to the problem in a nonjudgmental way so that the employee has enough information to correct it.

4 Managing Organization-Wide Communication

Although managing one-on-one communication is important, managers must also know how to communicate effectively with a larger number of people throughout an organization.

*Learn more about organization-wide communication by reading the following sections about **4.1 improving transmission by getting the message out** and **4.2 improving reception by finding ways to hear what others feel and think.***

4.1 Improving Transmission: Getting the Message Out

Several methods of electronic communication—email, online discussion forums, televised/videotaped speeches and conferences, and broadcast voice mail—now make it easier for managers to communicate with people throughout the organization and get the message out.

New Ways to Get the Word Out

Social media outlets such as Facebook, Twitter, and Jaiku provide a golden opportunity for businesses to get the word out to the public about their products and services. They offer a quick and easy way to get client referrals and to keep in touch with colleagues wherever they are. Because social media users share a lot of information about their activities and personal tastes, companies can also target a ready market by keying advertisements to users' interests.

Source: R. Scoble, "The Next Email: Why Twitter Will Change the Way Business Communicates (Again)," *Fast Company,* September 2007, 72.

© Image Source/Getty Images

Exhibit 15.6

Establishing Online Discussion Forums

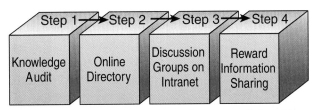

Step 1 → Step 2 → Step 3 → Step 4

| Knowledge Audit | Online Directory | Discussion Groups on Intranet | Reward Information Sharing |

Source: Based on G. McWilliams and M. Stepanek, "Knowledge Management: Taming the Info Monster," *Business Week,* 22 June 1998, 170.

Although we normally think of *email,* or the transmission of messages via computers, as a means of one-on-one communication, it also plays an important role in organization-wide communication. With the click of a button, managers can send email to everyone in the company via email distribution lists. Many CEOs now use this capability regularly to keep employees up to date on changes and developments. On his first day as CEO of Diebold, which makes ATM machines, Thomas Swidarski emailed Diebold's 14,500 employees a message about improving customer loyalty, increasing the speed with which products were manufactured and delivered, and "providing quality products and outstanding service." Swidarski concluded his email by writing that leading Diebold, "does not rest with one person—it rests with each and every one of us."[46] Many CEOs and top executives also make their email addresses public and encourage employees to contact them directly.

Discussion forums are another means of electronically promoting organization-wide communication. **Online discussion forums** are the in-house equivalent of Internet newsgroups; by using Web- or software-based discussion tools that are available across the company, employees can easily ask questions and share knowledge with each other. The point is to share expertise and not duplicate solutions already discovered by others in the company. Furthermore, because online discussion forums remain online, they provide a historical database for people who are dealing with particular problems for the first time.

Exhibit 15.6 lists the steps companies need to take to establish successful online discussion forums. First, pinpoint your company's top intellectual assets through a knowledge audit; then spread that knowledge throughout the organization. Second, create an online directory detailing the expertise of individual workers and make it available to all employees. Third, set up discussion groups on the intranet so that managers and workers can collaborate on problem solving. Finally,

Online discussion forums the in-house equivalent of Internet newsgroups. By using Web- or software-based discussion tools that are available across the company, employees can easily ask questions and share knowledge with each other.

reward information sharing by making the online sharing of knowledge a key part of performance ratings.

Televised/videotaped speeches and meetings are a third electronic method of organization-wide communication. **Televised/videotaped speeches and meetings** are simply speeches and meetings originally made to a smaller audience that are either simultaneously broadcast to other locations in the company or videotaped for subsequent distribution and viewing. Cisco's CEO, John Chambers, tapes ten to fifteen videos a quarter to communicate with his employees and customers.[47]

Voice messaging, or voice mail, is a telephone answering system that records audio messages. In one survey, 89 percent of respondents said that voice messaging is critical to business communication, 78 percent said that it improves productivity, and 58 percent said they would rather leave a message on a voice messaging system than with a receptionist.[48] Nonetheless, most people are unfamiliar with the ability to *broadcast voice mail* by sending a recorded message to everyone in the company. Broadcast voice mail gives top managers a quick, convenient way to address their work forces via oral communication.

4.2 Improving Reception: Hearing What Others Feel and Think

When people think of "organization-wide" communication, they think of the CEO and top managers getting their message out to people in the company. But organization-wide communication also means finding ways to hear what people throughout the organization are feeling and thinking. This is important because most employees and managers are reluctant to share their thoughts and feelings with top managers. Surveys indicate that only 29 percent of first-level managers feel that their companies encourage employees to express their opinions openly. Another study of 22 companies found that 70 percent of the people surveyed were afraid to speak up about problems they knew existed at work.

Withholding information about organizational problems or issues is called **organizational silence.** Organizational silence occurs when employees believe that telling management about problems won't make a difference or that they'll be punished or hurt in some way for sharing such information.[49] Company hotlines, survey feedback, frequent informal meetings, surprise visits, and blogs are ways of overcoming organizational silence.

Company hotlines are phone numbers that anyone in the company can call anonymously to leave information for upper management. For example, Deloitte Touche Tohmatsu has a toll-free hotline for employees to call to report any kind of problem or issue within the company. Hotlines are particularly important because 44 percent of employees will not report misconduct. Why not? The reason is twofold: They don't believe anything will be done, and they "fear that the report will not be kept confidential."[50]

Survey feedback is information that is collected by survey from organization members and then compiled, disseminated, and used to develop action plans for improvement. Many organizations make use of survey feedback by surveying their managers and employees several times a year. FedEx, for example, runs its own Survey Feedback Action program. The online survey, which is completely anonymous, includes sections for employees to evaluate their managers and the overall environment at FedEx including benefits, incentives, and working conditions. The results are compiled and then given back to each FedEx work group to decide where changes and improvements need to be made and to develop specific action plans to address those problems. The final step is to look for improvements in subsequent employee surveys to see if those plans worked.[51]

Frequent *informal meetings* between top managers and lower-level employees are one of the best ways for top managers to hear what others feel and think. Many people assume that top managers are at the center of everything that goes on in organizations, but top managers commonly feel isolated from most of their lower-level managers and employees. Consequently, more and more top managers are scheduling frequent informal meetings with people throughout their companies.

Have you ever been around when a supervisor learns that upper management will be paying a visit? First there's panic, as everyone is told to drop what he or she is doing to polish, shine, and spruce up the workplace so that it looks perfect for the visit. Then, of course, top managers don't get a realistic look at what's going on in the company. Consequently, one of the ways to get an accurate picture is to pay *surprise visits* to various parts of the organization. These visits should not just be surprise inspections but should also be used as an opportunity to encourage meaningful upward communication from those who normally don't get a chance to communicate with upper management. Such surprise visits are now part of the culture at the Royal Mail, the United Kingdom's postal service. Chairman Allan Leighton frequently shows up unannounced at Royal Mail delivery offices. Leighton says the initial reaction is always the same, "Oh s***, it's the chairman." However, Leighton isn't there to catch his employees doing something wrong. He's there to find out, right or wrong, what's really going on. Says Leighton, "Those visits at half past five in the morning [with employees] are the most important part" of turning around the Royal Mail, which was once losing 1.5 million pounds a day.[52] Today, thanks in part to his communication with employees, the Royal Mail delivers 95 percent of first class mail in one day, better than any other postal service in the world and now *earns*, not loses, a profit of 1.5 million pounds per day.

Blogs are another way to hear what people are thinking and saying both inside and outside the organization.

A **blog** is a personal Web site that provides personal opinions or recommendations, news summaries, and reader comments. At Google, which owns the blog-hosting service Blogger, hundreds of employees are writing *internal blogs.* One employee even wrote a blog for posting all the notes from the brainstorming sessions used to redesign the search page used by millions each day.[53] *External blogs*, written by people outside the company, can be a good way to find out what others are saying or thinking about your organization or its products or actions. Situations like this one make it increasingly important for companies to keep tabs on what others are saying about them. Some companies have created the new position of chief blogging officer to manage internal company blogs and to monitor what is said about the company and its products on external blogs.[54]

When a blog entry that was highly critical of the customer service at Home Depot drew more than 7,000 postings, new CEO Frank Blake posted a comment of his own indicating that he was establishing a "dedicated taskforce—working directly with me—that is ready and willing to address each and every issue raised on this [discussion] board.[55]

Blog a personal Web site that provides personal opinions or recommendations, news summaries, and reader comments

By the Numbers

75-95% estimated accuracy of information passing through organizational grapevines

$1 billion estimated value of the management coaching business

30 emails most people can read in 10-15 minutes

25% the amount that most people retain of what they hear

95% first class mail that Royal Mail delivers in one day

CONTROL

For all companies, past success is no guarantee of future success. Even successful companies fall short, face challenges, and have to make changes. **Control** is a regulatory process of establishing standards to achieve organizational goals, comparing actual performance to the standards, and taking corrective action when necessary to restore performance to those standards. Control is achieved when behavior and work procedures conform to standards and company goals are accomplished.[1] Control is not just an after-the-fact process, however. Preventive measures are also a form of control.

Basics of Control

Control is important because there is so much at stake when a company fails to meet standards. After 600 people became ill and four children died from hamburgers consumed at Jack in the Box in 1993, Hallmark/Westland Meat Packing Co. was among a number of companies facing $58.5 million in legal claims. Hallmark/Westland later spent millions to update the inside of its plant. But its neglect to monitor and meet quality standards like proper employee training for the cattle pens outside the plant brought more trouble when a member of the Humane Society of the United States working undercover

Control a regulatory process of establishing standards to achieve organizational goals, comparing actual performance to the standards, and taking corrective action when necessary

Learning Outcomes

1 describe the basic control process.

2 discuss the various methods that managers can use to maintain control.

3 describe the behaviors, processes, and outcomes that today's managers are choosing to control in their organizations.

© iStockphoto.com

at the plant filmed injured cows, or "downer cows," being forced up in the pens. Downer cows are typically removed from the line because they tend to have a higher rate of diseases that can contaminate the food supply. Consequently, Hallmark/Westland had to recall over 143 million pounds of beef, the biggest beef recall in U.S. history. Although it is highly unlikely that the meat would make anyone ill, the recall was necessary due to safety concerns, and the costs are huge. Disposal of the meat alone cost over $1.1 million and CEO Steve Mendell admitted to a congressional committee that "Obviously, my system broke down. Our company is ruined."[2]

After reading the next section, you should be able to

1 describe the basic control process.

1 The Control Process

*The basic control process **1.1 begins with the establishment of clear standards of performance; 1.2 involves a comparison of performance to those standards; 1.3 takes corrective action, if needed, to repair performance deficiencies; 1.4 is a dynamic, cybernetic process;** and **1.5 consists of three basic methods: feedback***

*control, concurrent control, and feedforward control. However, as much as managers would like, **1.6 control isn't always worthwhile or possible.***

1.1 Standards

The control process begins when managers set goals, such as satisfying 90 percent of customers or increasing sales by 5 percent. Companies then specify the performance standards that must be met to accomplish those goals. **Standards** are a basis of comparison for measuring the extent to which organizational performance is satisfactory or unsatisfactory. For example, many pizzerias use 30–40 minutes as the standard for delivery times. Since anything longer is viewed as unsatisfactory, they'll typically reduce the price if they can't deliver a hot pizza to you within that time period.

So how do managers set standards? How do they decide which levels of performance are satisfactory and which are unsatisfactory? The first criterion for a good standard is that it must enable goal achievement. If you're meeting the standard but still not achieving company goals, then the standard may have to be changed. For example, hospitals aim to collect payment for patient services, but the amount of unreimbursed medical care totals $22.3 billion nationwide, significantly short of the goal. So hospitals are changing payment standards by asking that insurance copayments be paid *before* the patient leaves the hospital rather than after. Anyone who can't afford the entire copayment at once is asked to at least make a down payment (those who do are much more likely to pay their entire bill).[3]

Companies also determine standards by listening to customers' comments, complaints, and suggestions, or by observing competitors' products and services. Stan-

Standards a basis of comparison for measuring the extent to which various kinds of organizational performance are satisfactory or unsatisfactory

Benchmarking the process of identifying outstanding practices, processes, and standards in other companies and adapting them to your company

dards are also sometimes set by government authorities. Although the U.S. Food and Drug Administration typically establishes food standards, some companies are not satisfied by the government's slow response to food safety concerns. In order to monitor and enforce quality standards, they have turned to private regulators such as GlobalGap. The private regulator trend started in Europe in 1997 and has since caught on in the United States as companies like WalMart and McDonald's have begun to buy only meat that has been certified by such regulators. Companies can also move more quickly to prompt growers to comply with the standards, improving food quality through the entire system.[4]

Standards can also be determined by benchmarking other companies. **Benchmarking** is the process of determining how well other companies (though not just competitors) perform business functions or tasks. In other words, benchmarking is the process of determining other companies' standards. When setting standards by benchmarking, the first step is to determine what to benchmark. Companies can benchmark anything from cycle time (how fast) to quality (how well) to price (how much). The next step is to identify the companies against which to benchmark your standards. The last step is to collect data to determine other companies' performance standards.

1.2 Comparison to Standards

The next step in the control process is to compare actual performance to performance standards. Although this sounds straightforward, the quality of the comparison largely depends on the measurement and information systems a company uses to keep track of performance. The better the system, the easier it is for companies to track their progress and identify problems that need to be fixed. One way for retailers to verify that performance standards are being met is to use secret shoppers, individuals who visit stores pretending to be customers but are really there to determine whether employees provide helpful customer service. Secret shopper Cliff Fill recalls the fast-food restaurant where the workers discussed their dating plans as he stood in front of them ready to order. After ignoring him for 90 seconds (secret shoppers often carry timers with them), they turned to him and said, "We'll be done with our conversation in a minute and be with you."[5]

1.3 Corrective Action

The next step in the control process is to identify performance deviations, analyze those deviations, and then develop and implement programs to correct them.

Beta versions of software programs are a classic tool that developers use to monitor deviations from the standard and take corrective action *before* the product is released on the market. Microsoft has an internal program called Software Quality Metrics (SQM) that company software developers use when creating new software releases. SQM helps the developers determine how each change in the software code will affect the functionality of the program and uses a system of comparison charts to show how the changes will affect users of new software.[6]

1.4 Dynamic, Cybernetic Process

As shown in Exhibit 16.1, control is a continuous, dynamic, cybernetic process. Control begins by setting standards, measuring performance, and then comparing performance to the standards. If the performance deviates from the standards, then managers and employees analyze the deviations and develop and implement corrective programs that (hopefully) achieve the desired performance by meeting the standards. Managers must repeat the entire process again and again in an endless feedback loop (a continuous process). Thus, control is not a onetime achievement or result. It continues over time (i.e., it is dynamic) and requires daily, weekly, and monthly attention from managers to maintain performance levels at the standard. This constant attention is what makes control a cybernetic process. **Cybernetic** derives from the Greek word *kubernetes,* meaning "steers-

man," that is, one who steers or keeps on course.[7] The control process shown in Exhibit 16.1 is cybernetic because constant attention to the feedback loop is necessary to keep the company's activities on course.

1.5 Feedback, Concurrent, and Feedforward Control

The three basic control methods are feedback control, concurrent control, and feedforward control. **Feedback control** is a mechanism for gathering information about performance deficiencies *after* they occur. This information is then used to correct performance deficiencies or prevent future deficiencies. Study after study has clearly shown that feedback improves both individual and organizational performance. In most instances, any feedback is better than no feedback. If feedback has a downside, it's that it always occurs after the fact, after performance deficiencies have already occurred. Control can minimize the effects, but the damage is already done. For example, American Airlines failed to complete required wiring inspections on its aircraft. Feedback from the Federal Aviation Administration about the failure to meet standards resulted in nearly 2500 delayed flights.[8]

Concurrent control addresses the problems inherent in feedback control by gathering information about performance deficiencies as they occur. Apple and Nike teamed up to create a real-time exercise feedback system called Nike + iPod. After a runner installs a sensor in her shoes, it transmits concurrent information to her iPod. The

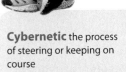

© Brand X Pictures/Jupiterimages

Exhibit 16.1

Cybernetic Control Process

Set Standards

↓

Measure Performance

↓

Compare with Standards

↓

Identify Deviations

→ Analyze Deviations

→ Develop & Implement Program for Corrective Action

→ (back to Measure Performance)

Source: H. Koontz & R. W. Bradspies, "Managing through Feedforward Control: A Future-Directed View," *Business Horizons* 15 (June 1972) 25–36. Reprinted from *Business Horizons*, with permission from Elsevier.

Cybernetic the process of steering or keeping on course

Feedback control a mechanism for gathering information about performance deficiencies after they occur

Concurrent control a mechanism for gathering information about performance deficiencies as they occur, thereby eliminating or shortening the delay between performance and feedback

Guidelines for Using Feedforward Control

1. Plan and analyze thoroughly.
2. Be discriminating as you select input variables.
3. Keep the feedforward system dynamic. Don't let it become a matter of habit.
4. Develop a model of the control system.
5. Collect data on input variables regularly.
6. Assess data on input variables regularly.
7. Take action on what you learn.

Source: H. Koontz and R. W. Bradspies, "Managing through Feedforward Control: A Future Directed View," *Business Horizons* 15 (June 1972): 25–36. Reprinted from *Business Horizons*, with permission from Elsevier.

system measures time, distance, calories burned, and pace. Runners can actually track their efforts every moment of their run and make changes on the fly.[9] Concurrent control is an improvement over feedback because it attempts to eliminate or shorten the delay between performance and feedback about the performance.

Feedforward control is a mechanism for gathering information about performance deficiencies *before* they occur. In contrast to feedback and concurrent control, which provide feedback on the basis of outcomes and results, feedforward control provides information about performance deficiencies by monitoring inputs, not outputs. Thus, feedforward control seeks to prevent or minimize performance deficiencies before they happen. Microsoft uses feedforward controls to try to prevent software problems before they occur. For example, when developing the latest version of its Windows Server software (for network and Internet computer servers), Microsoft taught 8,500 experienced programmers new methods for writing more reliable software code *before* asking them to develop new features for Windows Server software. Microsoft has also developed new software testing tools that let the programmers thoroughly test the code they've written (i.e., input) before passing the code on to others to be used in beta testing and then in final products.[10]

Feedforward control a mechanism for monitoring performance inputs rather than outputs to prevent or minimize performance deficiencies before they occur

Control loss the situation in which behavior and work procedures do not conform to standards

Regulation costs the costs associated with implementing or maintaining control

1.6 Control Isn't Always Worthwhile or Possible

Control is achieved when behavior and work procedures conform to standards and goals are accomplished. By contrast, **control loss** occurs when behavior and work procedures do not conform to standards.[11] Maintaining control is important because loss of control prevents organizations from achieving their goals. When control loss occurs, managers need to find out what, if anything, they could have done to prevent it. Usually, as discussed above, that means identifying deviations from standard performance, analyzing the causes of those deviations, and taking corrective action. Even so, implementing controls isn't always worthwhile or possible. Let's look at regulation costs and cybernetic feasibility to see why.

To determine whether control is worthwhile, managers need to carefully assess **regulation costs,** or costs associated with implementing or maintaining control. If a control process costs more than an an organization gains from its benefits, it may not be worthwhile. Thanks to technology, however, companies are finding it easier (i.e., more feasible) to control many more processes. For example, handwritten prescriptions can be difficult for pharmacists to read, but digital technology can be used to control the accuracy of prescriptions. Doctors can send prescriptions to the pharmacy electronically, and software can alert them to interactions with other drugs that might be harmful to a patient.

Automatic "Green"

Now you don't have to remember to turn down the thermostat when you leave the office in order to control energy costs. Software startup companies are creating "green software" programs that keep tabs on your energy use, turn off lights automatically, and figure out when it is cheapest to use energy for flexible tasks like cooling office space. The convenience doesn't come cheap: one California company paid $350,000 after rebates for its system. But the payoff is big. The system is expected to save the company $110,000 per year and will pay for itself in only three years, generating two kinds of green—energy savings and money.

Source: J. Carlton, "To Cut Fuel Bills, Try High-Tech Help," *The Wall Street Journal*, 11 March 2008, B3.

© Christine Balderas/iStockphoto.com

Still, only about 10 percent of doctors in the United States use this technology despite financial incentives from insurers. While the technology may pay off for large hospitals and practices, the cost is more than the benefit for about 60 percent of doctors who work in smaller practices or on their own.[12]

Another factor to consider is **cybernetic feasibility**, the extent to which it is possible to implement each of the three steps in the control process. If one or more steps cannot be implemented, then maintaining effective control may be difficult or impossible.

How and What to Control

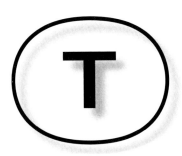

The doors are locked on midnight-shift employees at 10 percent of Sam's Club and Wal-Mart stores to keep out burglars and, some say, also to prevent employee theft. According to Mona Williams, Wal-Mart's vice president for communications, "Wal-Mart secures these stores just as any other business does that has employees working overnight. Doors are locked to protect associates and the store from intruders."[13] But many employees dislike the policy. When Michael Rodriguez injured his ankle at 3 A.M., he had to wait an hour for a store manager to show up to unlock the doors. Says Rodriguez, "Being locked in in an emergency like that, that's not right."[14] Wal-Mart's Mona Williams responds, "Fire doors are always accessible [and unlocked from the inside] for safety, and there will always be at least one manager in the store with a set of keys to unlock the doors."[15]

Does locking in midnight employees jeopardize or improve their safety? Is this policy a reasonable response to employee theft, which can often exceed a store's profits? If you were a Wal-Mart or Sam's Club store manager, what would you do?

After reading the next two sections, you should be able to

2 discuss the various methods that managers can use to maintain control.

3 describe the behaviors, processes, and outcomes that today's managers are choosing to control in their organizations.

2 Control Methods

*Managers can use five different methods to achieve control in their organizations: **2.1 bureaucratic, 2.2 objective, 2.3 normative, 2.4 concertive,** and **2.5 self-control.***

2.1 Bureaucratic Control

When most people think of managerial control, what they have in mind is bureaucratic control. **Bureaucratic control** is top-down control, in which managers try to influence employee behavior by rewarding or punishing employees for compliance or noncompliance with organizational policies, rules, and procedures. Most employees, however, would argue that bureaucratic managers emphasize punishment for noncompliance much more than rewards for compliance. For instance, when visiting the company's regional offices and managers, the president of a training company, who was known for his temper and for micromanaging others, would get some toilet paper from the restrooms and aggressively ask, "What's this?" When the managers answered, "Toilet paper," the president would scream that it was two-ply toilet paper that the company couldn't afford. When told of a cracked toilet seat in one of the women's restrooms, he said, "If you don't like sitting on that seat, you can stand up like I do!"[16]

As you learned in Chapter 2, bureaucratic management and control were created to prevent just this type of managerial behavior. By encouraging managers to apply well-thought-out rules, policies, and procedures in an impartial, consistent manner to everyone in the organization, bureaucratic control is supposed to make companies more efficient, effective, and fair. Ironically, it frequently has just the opposite effect. Managers who use bureaucratic control often emphasize following the rules above all else.

Another characteristic of bureaucratically controlled companies is that due to their rule- and policy-driven decision making, they are highly resistant to change and slow to respond to customers and competitors. Recall from Chapter 2 that even Max Weber, the German philosopher who is largely credited with popularizing bureaucratic ideals in the late 19th century,

Cybernetic feasibility
the extent to which it is possible to implement each step in the control process

Bureaucratic control
the use of hierarchical authority to influence employee behavior by rewarding or punishing employees for compliance or noncompliance with organizational policies, rules, and procedures

referred to bureaucracy as the "iron cage." He said, "Once fully established, bureaucracy is among those social structures which are the hardest to destroy."[17]

2.2 Objective Control

In many companies, bureaucratic control has evolved into **objective control,** which is the use of observable measures of employee behavior or output to assess performance and influence behavior. Whereas bureaucratic control focuses on whether policies and rules are followed, objective control focuses on observing and measuring worker behavior or output. There are two kinds of objective control: behavior control and output control.

Behavior control is regulating behaviors and actions that workers perform on the job. The basic assumption of behavior control is that if you do the right things (i.e., the right behaviors) every day, then

Objective control the use of observable measures of worker behavior or outputs to assess performance and influence behavior

Behavior control the regulation of the behaviors and actions that workers perform on the job

Output control the regulation of workers' results or outputs through rewards and incentives

those things should lead to goal achievement. Behavior control is still management-based, however, which means that managers are responsible for monitoring and rewarding or punishing workers for exhibiting desired or undesired behaviors. Companies that use global positioning satellite (GPS) technology to track where workers are and what they're doing are using behavior control. For example, after getting complaints that his police officers weren't always on the job, Sergeant John Kuczynsky quietly put GPS tracking devices in his Clinton Township, New Jersey, officers' cars. Contrary to the officers' reports indicating that they were patrolling streets or using radar to catch speeding drivers, the GPS tracking software soon showed that five officers were sitting for long periods in parking lots or taking long breaks for meals. All five are now barred from law enforcement jobs.[18]

Instead of measuring what managers and workers do, **output control** measures the results of their efforts. Whereas behavior control regulates, guides, and measures how workers behave on the job, output control gives managers and workers the freedom to behave as they see fit as long as they accomplish prespecified, measurable results. Output control is often coupled with rewards and incentives.

Three things must occur for output control and rewards to lead to improved business results. First, output control measures must be reliable, fair, and accurate. Second, employees and managers must believe that they can produce the desired results. If they don't, then the output controls won't affect their behavior. Third, the rewards or incentives tied to outcome control measures must truly be dependent on achieving established standards of performance. For example, Smithfield Foods CEO Joseph Luter doesn't earn a bonus unless pretax profits exceed $100 million. Ray Goldberg, chairman of the company's compensation committee, says that, "We were trying to make sure [Luter's] rewards are based on the ups and downs of the company."[19] So, with pretax profits of $227.1 million, Luter's bonus, based on 2 percent of earnings between $100 million and $300 million, and 3 percent of profits over $300 million, would total just over $2.5 million. For output control to work with rewards, the rewards must truly be at risk if performance doesn't measure up.

2.3 Normative Control

Rather than monitoring rules, behavior, or output, another way to control what goes on in organizations is to use normative control to shape the beliefs and values of the people who work there. With

normative controls, a company's widely shared values and beliefs guide workers' behavior and decisions. For example, at Nordstrom, a Seattle-based department store chain, one value permeates the entire work force from top to bottom: extraordinary customer service. On the first day of work at Nordstrom, trainees begin their transformation to the "Nordstrom way" by reading the employee handbook. Sounds boring, doesn't it? But Nordstrom's handbook is printed on *one side* of a 3-by-5-inch note card, shown in its entirety in Exhibit 16.2. That's it. No lengthy rules. No specifics about what behavior is or is not appropriate. Just use your judgment.[20]

Normative controls are created in two ways. First, companies that use normative controls are very careful about whom they hire. While many companies screen potential applicants on the basis of their abilities, nor-

stories they tell about the company. At Nordstrom, many of these stories, which employees call "heroics," have been inspired by the company motto, "Respond to Unreasonable Customer Requests!"[22] "Nordies," as Nordstrom employees call themselves, like to tell the story about a customer who just had to have a pair of burgundy Donna Karan slacks that had gone on sale, but she could not find her size. The sales associate who was helping her contacted five nearby Nordstrom stores, but none had the customer's size. So rather than leave the customer dissatisfied with her shopping experience, the sales associate went to her manager for petty cash and then went across the street and paid full price for the slacks at a competitor's store. She then resold them to the customer at Nordstrom's lower sale price.[23] Obviously, Nordstrom would quickly go out of business if this were the norm. Nevertheless, this story makes clear the attitude that drives

Concertive control is **not** established **overnight.**

matively controlled companies are just as likely to screen potential applicants based on their attitudes and values. For example, before building stores in a new city, Nordstrom sends its human resource team into town to interview prospective applicants. In a few cities, the company canceled its expansion plans when it could not find enough qualified applicants who embodied the service attitudes and values for which Nordstrom is known.[21]

Second, with normative controls, managers and employees learn what they should and should not do by observing experienced employees and by listening to the

employee performance at Nordstrom in ways that rules, behavioral guidelines, or output controls could not.

2.4 Concertive Control

Whereas normative controls are based on beliefs that are strongly held and widely shared throughout a company, **concertive controls** are based on beliefs that are shaped and negotiated by work groups.[24] Whereas normative controls are driven by strong organizational cultures, concertive controls usually arise when companies give autonomous work groups complete autonomy and responsibility for task completion. The most autonomous groups operate without managers and are completely responsible for controlling work group processes, outputs, and behavior. Such groups do their own hiring, firing, worker discipline, work schedules, materials ordering, budget making and meeting, and decision making.

Concertive control is not established overnight. Highly autonomous work groups evolve through two phases as they develop concertive control. In phase one, group members learn to work with each other, supervise each other's work, and develop the values and beliefs that will guide and control their behavior. And because they

Exhibit 16.2

Nordstrom's Employee Handbook

Welcome to Nordstrom's. We're glad to have you with our company. Our Number One goal is to provide outstanding customer service. Set both your personal and professional goals high. We have great confidence in your ability to achieve them.

Nordstrom Rules:

Rule #1: Use your good judgment in all situations.

There will be no additional rules. Please feel free to ask your department manager, store manager, or division general manager any question at any time.

Source: S. Williford, "Nordstrom Sets the Standard for Customer Service," *Memphis Business Journal,* 1 July 1996, 21.

Normative control
the regulation of workers' behavior and decisions through widely shared organizational values and beliefs

Concertive control
the regulation of workers' behavior and decisions through work group values and beliefs

develop these values and beliefs themselves, work group members feel strongly about following them.

In the steel industry, Nucor was long considered an upstart compared to the "biggies," U.S. Steel and Bethlehem Steel. Today, however, not only has Nucor managed to outlast many other mills, but the company has also bought out thirteen other mills in the past five years. Nucor has a unique culture that gives real power to employees on the line and fosters teamwork throughout the organization. This type of teamwork can be a difficult thing for a newly acquired group of employees to get used to. For example, at Nucor's first big acquisition in Auburn, New York, David Hutchins is a frontline supervisor or "lead man" in the rolling mill, where steel from the furnace is spread thin enough to be cut into sheets. When the plant was under the previous ownership, if the guys doing the cutting got backed up, the guys doing the rolling—including Hutchins—would just take a break. He says, "We'd sit back, have a cup of coffee, and complain: 'Those guys stink.'" It took six months to convince the employees at the Auburn plant that the Nucor teamwork way was better than the old way. Now, Hutchins says, "At Nucor, we're not 'you guys' and 'us guys.' It's all of us guys. Wherever the bottleneck is, we go there, and everyone works on it."[25]

The second phase in the development of concertive control is the emergence and formalization of objective rules to guide and control behavior. The beliefs and values developed in phase one usually develop into more objective rules as new members join teams. The clearer those rules, the easier it becomes for new members to figure out how and how not to behave.

Ironically, concertive control may lead to even more stress for workers to conform to expectations than bureaucratic control. Under bureaucratic control, most workers only have to worry about pleasing the boss. But with concertive control, their behavior has to satisfy the rest of their team members. For example, one team member says, "I don't have to sit there and look for the boss to be around; and if the boss is not around, I can sit there and talk to my neighbor or do what I want. Now the whole team is around me and the whole team is observing what I'm doing."[26] Plus, with concertive control, team members have a second, much more stressful role to perform—that of making sure that their team members adhere to team values and rules.

Self-control (self-management) a control system in which managers and workers control their own behavior by setting their own goals, monitoring their own progress, and rewarding themselves for goal achievement

2.5 Self-Control

Self-control, also known as **self-management**, is a control system in which managers and workers control their own behavior.[27] Self-control does not result in anarchy, or a state in which everyone gets to do whatever he or she wants. In self-control or self-management, leaders and managers provide workers with clear boundaries within which they may guide and control their own goals and behaviors.[28] Leaders and managers also contribute to self-control by teaching others the skills they need to maximize and monitor their own work effectiveness. In turn, individuals who manage and lead themselves establish self-control by setting their own goals, monitoring their own progress, rewarding or punishing themselves for achieving or for not achieving their self-set goals, and constructing positive thought patterns that remind them of the importance of their goals and their ability to accomplish them.[29]

For example, let's assume you need to do a better job of praising and recognizing the good work that your staff does for you. You can use goal setting, self-observation, and self-reward to self-manage this behavior. For self-observation, write "praise/recognition" on a 3-by-5-inch card. Put the card in your pocket. Put a check on the card each time you praise or recognize someone (wait until the person has left before you do this). Keep track for a week. This serves as your baseline or starting point. Simply keeping track will probably increase how often you do this. After a week, assess your baseline or starting point, and then set a specific goal. For instance, if your baseline was twice a day, you might set a specific goal to praise or recognize others' work five times a day. Continue monitoring your performance with your cards. Once you've achieved your goal every day for a week, give yourself a reward (perhaps a CD, a movie, lunch with a friend at a new restaurant) for achieving your goal.[30]

As you can see, the components of self-management, self-set goals, self-observation, and self-reward have their roots in the motivation theories you read about in Chapter 13. The key difference, though, is that the goals, feedback, and rewards originate from employees themselves and not from their managers or organizations.

3 What to Control?

In the first section of this chapter, we discussed the basics of the control process and that control isn't always worthwhile or possible. In the second section, we looked at the various ways in which control can be obtained. In this third and final section, we address an equally important issue, "What should managers control?" The way managers answer this question has critical implications for most businesses.

If you control for just one thing, such as costs, then other dimensions, like marketing, customer service, and quality, are likely to suffer. If you try to control for too many things, then managers and employees become confused about what's really important. In the end, successful companies find a balance that comes from doing three or four things right, like managing costs, providing value, and keeping customers and employees satisfied.

After reading this section, you should be able to explain
3.1 the balanced scorecard approach to control and how companies can achieve balanced control of company performance by choosing to control 3.2 budgets, cash flows, and economic value added; 3.3 customer defections; 3.4 quality; *and* **3.5 waste and pollution.**

3.1 The Balanced Scorecard

Most companies measure performance using standard financial and accounting measures such as return on cap-

ital, return on assets, return on investments, cash flow, net income, and net margins. The **balanced scorecard** encourages managers to look beyond traditional financial measures to four different perspectives on company performance. How do customers see us (the customer perspective)? At what must we excel (the internal perspective)? Can we continue to improve and create value (the innovation and learning perspective)? How do we look to shareholders (the financial perspective)?[31]

The balanced scorecard has several advantages over traditional control processes that rely solely on financial measures. First, it forces managers at each level of the company to set specific goals and measure performance in each of the four areas. For example, Exhibit 16.3 shows that Southwest Airlines uses nine different measures in its balanced scorecard in order to determine whether it is meeting the standards it has set for itself in the control process. Of those, only three, market value, seat revenue, and plane lease costs (at various compounded annual growth rates, or CAGR), are standard financial measures of performance. In addition, Southwest measures its Federal Aviation Administration (FAA) on-time arrival rating and the cost of its airfares compared to competitors' (customer perspective); how much time each plane spends on the ground after landing and the percentage of planes that depart on time (internal business perspective); and the percentage of its ground crew workers, such as

Exhibit 16.3

Southwest Airlines' Balanced Scorecard

	GOALS	STANDARDS	MEASURES	INITIATIVES
FINANCIAL	Profitability	30% CAGR	Market Value	
	Increased Revenue	20% CAGR	Seat Revenue	
	Lower Costs	5% CAGR	Plane Lease Cost	
CUSTOMER	On-Time Flights	#1	FAA On-Time Arrival Rating	Quality Management, Customer Loyalty Program
	Lowest Prices	#1	Customer Ranking (Market Survey)	
INTERNAL	Fast Ground Turnaround	30 Minutes	Time on Ground	Cycle Time Optimization Program
		90%	On-Time Departure	
LEARNING	Ground Crew Alignment with Company Goals	Year 1: 70% Year 3: 90% Year 5: 100%	% Ground Crew Shareholders	Employee Stock Option Plan Ground Crew Training
			% Ground Crew Trained	

balanced scorecard measurement of organizational performance in four equally important areas: finances, customers, internal operations, and innovation and learning

© image100/Jupiterimages

Sources: G. Anthes, "ROI Guide: Balanced Scorecard," *Computer World,* 17 February 2003, available online at http://www.computerworld.com/action/article.do?command=viewArticleBasic&articleId=78512&intsrc=article_pots_bot [accessed 5 September 2008].

mechanics and luggage handlers, who own company stock and have received job training (learning perspective).

The second major advantage of the balanced scorecard approach to control is that it minimizes the chances of **suboptimization,** which occurs when performance improves in one area at the expense of decreased performance in others. Jon Meliones, chief medical director at Duke Children's Hospital, says, ". . . we could increase productivity . . . by assigning more patients to a nurse, but doing so would raise the likelihood of errors—an unacceptable trade-off."[32]

Let's examine some of the ways in which companies are controlling the four basic parts of the balanced scorecard: the financial perspective (budgets, cash flows, and economic value added), the customer perspective (customer defections), the internal perspective (total quality management), and the innovation and learning perspective (waste and pollution).

3.2 The Financial Perspective: Controlling Budgets, Cash Flows, and Economic Value Added

The traditional approach to controlling financial performance focuses on accounting tools such as cash flow analysis, balance sheets, income statements, financial ratios, and budgets. **Cash flow analysis** predicts how changes in a business will affect its ability to take in more cash than it pays out. **Balance sheets** provide a snapshot of a company's financial position at a particular time (but not the future). **Income statements,** also called profit and loss statements, show what has happened to an organization's income, expenses, and net profit (income less expenses) over a period of time. **Financial ratios** are typically used to track a business' liquidity (cash), efficiency, and profitability over time compared to other businesses in its industry. Finally, **budgets** are used to project costs and revenues, prioritize and control spending, and ensure that expenses don't exceed available funds and revenues. The Financial Review Card bound in the the back of this book contains tables that (a) show the basic steps or parts for cash flow analyses, balance sheets, and income statements; (b) list a few of the most common financial ratios and explain how they are calculated, what they mean, and when to use them; and (c) review the different kinds of budgets managers can use to track and control company finances.

By themselves, none of these tools—cash flow analyses, balance sheets, income statements, financial ratios, or budgets—tell the whole financial story of a business. They must be used together when assessing a company's

---

Suboptimization performance improvement in one part of an organization at the expense of decreased performance in another part

Cash flow analysis a type of analysis that predicts how changes in a business will affect its ability to take in more cash than it pays out

Balance sheets accounting statements that provide a snapshot of a company's financial position at a particular time

Income statements accounting statements, also called "profit and loss statements," that show what has happened to an organization's income, expenses, and net profit over a period of time

Financial ratios calculations typically used to track a business's liquidity (cash), efficiency, and profitability over time compared to other businesses in its industry

Budgets quantitative plans through which managers decide how to allocate available money to best accomplish company goals

---

ACCOUNTING 101

If you struggle to understand how financial ratios can be used where you work, you might find help in the following books:

Accounting the Easy Way, by Peter J. Eisen

Accounting for Dummies and *How to Read a Financial Report: Wringing Vital Signs Out of the Numbers,* both by John A. Tracy

Schaum's Quick Guide to Business Formulas: 201 Decision-Making Tools for Business, Finance, and Accounting Students, by Joel G. Siegel, Jae K. Shim, and Stephen W. Hartman

The Vest-Pocket Guide to Business Ratios, by Michael R. Tyran

Essential Managers: Managing Budgets, by Stephen Brookson

Forecasting Budgets: 25 Keys to Successful Planning (The New York Times Pocket MBA Series), by Norman Moore and Grover Gardner

And don't forget to check out the special Financial Review Card bound in with your Chapter Review cards.

financial performance. Since these tools are reviewed in detail in your accounting and finance classes, only a brief overview is provided here. Still, these are necessary tools for controlling organizational finances and expenses, and they should be part of your business toolbox.

Though no one would dispute the importance of these four accounting tools, accounting research also indicates that the complexity and sheer amount of information contained in them can shut down the brain and glaze over the eyes of even the most experienced manager.[33] Sometimes there's simply too much information to make sense of. The balanced scorecard simplifies things by focusing on one simple question when it comes to finances: How do we look to shareholders? One way to answer that question is through something called economic value added.

Conceptually, **economic value added (EVA)** is not the same thing as profits. It is the amount by which profits exceed the cost of capital in a given year. It is based on the simple idea that capital is necessary to run a business and that capital comes at a cost. Although most people think of capital as cash, once it is invested (i.e., spent), capital is more likely to be found in a business in the form of computers, manufacturing plants, employees, raw materials, and so forth. And just like the interest that a homeowner pays on a mortgage or that a college student pays on a student loan, there is a cost to that capital.

The most common costs of capital are the interest paid on long-term bank loans used to buy all those resources, the interest paid to bondholders (who lend organizations their money), and the dividends (cash payments) and growth in stock value that accrue to shareholders. EVA is positive when company profits (revenues minus expenses minus taxes) exceed the cost of capital in a given year. In other words, if a business is to truly grow, its revenues must be large enough to cover both short-term costs (annual expenses and taxes) and long-term costs (the cost of borrowing capital from bondholders and shareholders). If you're a bit confused, the late Roberto Goizueta, the former CEO of Coca-Cola, explained it this way: "You borrow money at a certain rate and invest it at a higher rate and pocket the difference. It is simple. It is the essence of banking."[34]

Exhibit 16.4 shows how to calculate EVA. First, starting with a company's income statement, you calculate the net operating profit after taxes (NOPAT) by subtracting taxes owed from income from operations. (Remember, a quick review of an income statement is on the Financial Review Card bound at the back of your book). The NOPAT shown in Exhibit 16.4 is $3,500,000. Second, identify how much capital the company has invested (i.e., spent). Total liabilities (what the company owes) less accounts payable and less accrued expenses, neither of which you pay interest on, provides a rough approximation of this amount. In Exhibit 16.4, total capital invested is $16,800,000. Third, calculate the cost (i.e., rate) paid for capital by determining the interest paid to bondholders

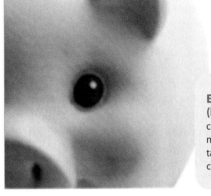

Economic value added (EVA) the amount by which company profits (revenues, minus expenses, minus taxes) exceed the cost of capital in a given year

Exhibit 16.4

Calculating Economic Value Added (EVA)

1. Calculate net operating profit after taxes (NOPAT).	$3,500,000
2. Identify how much capital the company has invested (i.e., spent).	$16,800,000
3. Determine the cost (i.e., rate) paid for capital (usually between 5 percent and 13 percent).	10%
4. Multiply capital used (Step 2) times cost of capital (Step 3).	(10% × $16,800,000) = $1,680,000
5. Subtract the total dollar cost of capital from net profit after taxes.	$3,500,000 NOPAT −$1,680,000 Total cost of capital $1,820,000 Economic value added

(who lend organizations their money), which is usually somewhere between 5 and 8 percent, and the return that stockholders want in terms of dividends and stock price appreciation, which is historically about 13 percent. Take a weighted average of the two to determine the overall cost of capital. In Exhibit 16.4, the cost of capital is 10 percent. Fourth, multiply the total capital ($16,800,000) from Step 2 by the cost of capital (10 percent) from Step 3. In Exhibit 16.4, this amount is $1,680,000. Fifth, subtract the total dollar cost of capital in Step 4 from the NOPAT in Step 1. In Exhibit 16.4, this value is $1,820,000, which means that our example company has created economic value or wealth this year. If our EVA number had been negative, meaning that the company didn't make enough profit to cover the cost of capital from bondholders and shareholders, then the company would have destroyed economic value or wealth by taking in more money than it returned.[35]

Why is EVA so important? First and most importantly, because it includes the cost of capital, it shows whether a business, division, department, profit center, or product is really paying for itself. The key is to make sure that managers and employees can see how their choices and behavior affect the company's EVA.

Second, because EVA can easily be determined for subsets of a company such as divisions, regional offices, manufacturing plants, and sometimes even departments, it makes managers and workers at all levels pay much closer attention to their segment of the business. When company offices were being refurbished at Genesco, a shoe company, a worker who had

Exhibit 16.5

Top Ten U.S. Companies by Market Value Added and Economic Value Added

MVA RANKING	COMPANY	MARKET VALUE ADDED ($ MILLIONS)	ECONOMIC VALUE ADDED ($ MILLIONS)
1	General Electric	$299,810	$5,288
2	ExxonMobil	197,782	14,456
3	Microsoft	178,032	6,426
4	Wal-Mart	161,693	4,972
5	Johnson & Johnson	138,199	5,655
6	United Health Group	112,755	1,897
7	Procter & Gamble	105,858	3,951
8	CitiGroup	99,485	4,536
9	Intel	97,468	1,720
10	Dell	88,086	1,891

Source: R. Grizzetti, "U.S. Performance 1000," *Stern Stewart & Co,* available by request, http://www.sternstewart.com [accessed 20 June 2005].

EVA training handed CEO Ben Harris $4,000 in cash. The worker explained that he now understood the effect his job had on the company's ability to survive and prosper. Since the company was struggling, he had sold the old doors that had been removed during remodeling so that the company could have the cash.[36] In other words, EVA motivates managers and workers to think like small-business owners who must scramble to contain costs and generate enough business to meet their bills each month. And, unlike many kinds of financial controls, EVA doesn't specify what should or should not be done to improve performance. Thus, it encourages managers and workers to be creative in looking for ways to improve EVA performance.

Remember that EVA is the amount by which profits exceed the cost of capital in a given year. So the more that EVA exceeds the total dollar cost of capital, the better a company has used investors' money that year. Market value added (MVA) is simply the cumulative EVA created by a company over time. Thus, MVA indicates how much value or wealth a company has created or destroyed in total during its existence. The

top ten U.S. companies by MVA and EVA are listed in Exhibit 16.5.

3.3 The Customer Perspective: Controlling Customer Defections

The second aspect of organizational performance that the balanced scorecard helps managers monitor is customers. It does so by forcing managers to address the question, "How do customers see us?" Unfortunately, most companies try to answer this question through customer satisfaction surveys, but these are often misleadingly positive. Most customers are reluctant to talk about their problems because they don't know who to complain to or think that complaining will not do any good. Indeed, a study by the Office of Consumer Affairs for South Australia found that 96 percent of unhappy customers never complain to anyone in the company.[37]

One reason that customer satisfaction surveys can be misleading is that sometimes even very satisfied customers will leave to do business with competitors. Rather than poring over customer satisfaction surveys from current customers, studies indicate that companies may do a better job of answering the question "How do customers see us?" by closely monitoring **customer defections,** that is, by identifying which customers are leaving the company and measuring the rate at which they are leaving. Unlike the results of customer satisfaction surveys, customer defections and retention do have a great effect on profits.

For example, very few managers realize that obtaining a new customer costs ten times as much as keeping a current one. In fact, the cost of replacing old customers with new ones is so great that most companies could double their profits by increasing the rate of customer retention by just 5 to 10 percent per year.[38] And, if a company can keep a customer for life, the benefits are even larger. According to Stew Leonard, owner of the Connecticut-based Stew Leonard's grocery store chain, "The lifetime value of a customer in a supermarket is about $246,000. Every time a customer comes through our front door I see, stamped on their forehead in big red numbers, '$246,000.' I'm never going to make that person unhappy with me. Or lose her to the competition."[39]

Beyond the clear benefits to the bottom line, the second reason to study customer defections is that customers who have left are much more likely than current customers to tell you what you were doing wrong. Finally, companies that understand why customers leave can not only take steps to fix ongoing problems, but can also identify which customers are likely to leave and make changes to prevent them from leaving.

3.4 The Internal Perspective: Controlling Quality

The third part of the balanced scorecard, the internal perspective, consists of the processes, decisions, and actions that managers and workers make within the organization. In contrast to the financial perspective of EVA and the outward-looking customer perspective, the internal perspective asks the question "At what must we excel?" Consequently, the internal perspective of the balanced scorecard usually leads managers to a focus on quality.

Quality is typically defined and measured in three ways: excellence, value, and conformance to expectations.[40] When the company defines its quality goal as *excellence,* managers must try to produce a product or service of unsurpassed performance and features. For example, Singapore Airlines is the best airline in the world by almost any standard. It has also received various "best airline" awards from the *Pacific Asia Travel Association, Travel+Leisure, Business Traveller, Conde Nast Traveller,* and *Fortune.*[41] Whereas many airlines try to cram passengers into every available inch on a plane, Singapore Airlines delivers creature comforts to

Customer defections
a performance assessment in which companies identify which customers are leaving and measure the rate at which they are leaving

mgmt trends

An Old Standby Is a Hot Trend

Vertical integration is making a comeback. In an effort to better control resources—namely, raw materials—some companies are buying suppliers who furnish critical components for important product lines. In 2006, Armor Holdings bought the North Carolina textile manufacturer that supplied the super-strong fibers used in its armored cars. Toyota took control of a key battery supplier for hybrid gasoline-electric engines. And Bridgestone Tire bought a rubber plantation in Indonesia. Watch the business press for articles on companies expanding vertically rather than horizontally.

Source: Timothy Aeppel, "A Hot Commodities Market Spurs Buying Spree by Manufacturers," *The Wall Street Journal,* 14 August 2006, A1, A7.

© Steve Corrigan/iStockphoto.com

Aldi, a grocery store company with 7,500 stores worldwide, operates on the single principle of bringing maximum value to customers. Aldi stocks only 3 percent of the products that a typical grocery store carries, and most of its products are store brands. Customers bring their own bags and pick products off pallets rather than store shelves. Yet Aldi's store brands have consistently beaten the name brand rivals in taste and quality, and Aldi was voted the most trusted name in the grocery business in Germany.[43]

When a company defines its quality goal as conformance to specifications, employees must base decisions and actions on whether services and products measure up to the standard. In contrast to excellence and value-based definitions of quality that can be somewhat ambiguous, measuring whether products and services are "in spec" is relatively easy. Although conformance to specifications (i.e., precise tolerances for a part's weight or thickness) is usually associated with manufacturing, it can be used equally well to control quality in nonmanufacturing jobs. Exhibit 16.6 shows

encourage repeat business and customers willing to pay premium prices. On its newer planes, the first-class cabin is divided into eight private mini-rooms, each with an unusually wide leather seat that folds down flat for sleeping, a 23-inch LCD TV that doubles as a computer monitor, and an adjustable table. These amenities and services are common for private jets but truly unique in the com-

> ❝ The **internal perspective** asks the question "At what must we excel?" ❞

mercial airline industry.[42] Singapore Airlines was the first airline, in the 1970s, to introduce a choice of meals, complimentary drinks, and earphones in coach class. It was the first to introduce worldwide video, news, telephone, and fax services and the first to feature personal video monitors for movies, news, documentaries, and games. Singapore Airlines has had AC power for laptop computers for some time, and recently it became the first airline to introduce on-board high-speed Internet access.

Value is the customer perception that the product quality is excellent for the price offered. At a higher price, for example, customers may perceive the product to be less of a value. When a company emphasizes value as its quality goal, managers must simultaneously control excellence, price, durability, or other features of a product or service that customers strongly associate with value.

> **Value** customer perception that the product quality is excellent for the price offered

a checklist that a cook or restaurant owner would use to ensure quality when buying fresh fish.

The way in which a company defines quality affects the methods and measures that workers use to control quality. Accordingly, Exhibit 16.7 shows the advantages and disadvantages associated with the excellence, value, and conformance to specification definitions of quality.

3.5 The Innovation and Learning Perspective: Controlling Waste and Pollution

The last part of the balanced scorecard, the innovation and learning perspective, addresses the question "Can we continue to improve and create value?" Thus, the innovation and learning perspective involves continuous improvement in ongoing products and services (discussed in Chapter 18); relearning and redesigning the processes by which products and services are created (discussed in Chapter 7); and even things like waste and pollution minimization, an increasingly important area of innovation.

Exhibit 16.6

Conformance to Specifications Checklist for Buying Fresh Fish

QUALITY CHECKLIST FOR BUYING FRESH FISH		
FRESH WHOLE FISH	**ACCEPTABLE**	**NOT ACCEPTABLE**
Gills	✓ bright red, free of slime, clear mucus	✗ brown to grayish, thick, yellow mucus
Eyes	✓ clear, bright, bulging, black pupils	✗ dull, sunken, cloudy, gray pupils
Smell	✓ inoffensive, slight ocean smell	✗ ammonia, putrid smell
Skin	✓ opalescent sheen, scales adhere tightly to skin	✗ dull or faded color, scales missing or easily removed
Flesh	✓ firm and elastic to touch, tight to the bone	✗ soft and flabby, separating from the bone
Belly cavity	✓ no viscera or blood visible, lining intact, no bone protruding	✗ incomplete evisceration, cuts or protruding bones, off-odor

Sources: "A Closer Look: Buy It Fresh, Keep It Fresh," *Consumer Reports Online*, available online at http://www.seagrant.sunysb.edu/SeafoodTechnology/SeafoodMedia/CR02-2001/CR-SeafoodII020101.htm [accessed 20 June 2005]; "How to Purchase: Buying Fish," AboutSeaFood, available online at http://www.aboutseafood.com/faqs/purchase1.html [20 June 2005].

© Oxford Scientific/Jupiterimages

Exhibit 16.7

Advantages and Disadvantages of Different Measures of Quality

QUALITY MEASURE	ADVANTAGES	DISADVANTAGES
Excellence	Promotes clear organizational vision.	Provides little practical guidance for managers.
	Being/providing the "best" motivates and inspires managers and employees.	Excellence is ambiguous. What is it? Who defines it?
Value	Appeals to customers, who "know excellence when they see it."	Difficult to measure and control.
	Customers recognize differences in value.	Can be difficult to determine what factors influence whether a product/service is seen as having value.
	Easier to measure and compare whether products/services differ in value.	Controlling the balance between excellence and cost (i.e., affordable excellence) can be difficult.
Conformance to Specifications	If specifications can be written, conformance to specifications is usually measurable.	Many products/services cannot be easily evaluated in terms of conformance to specifications.
	Should lead to increased efficiency.	Promotes standardization, so may hurt performance when adapting to changes is more important.
	Promotes consistency in quality.	May be less appropriate for services, which are dependent on a high degree of human contact.

Source: C. A. Reeves and D. A. Bednar, "Defining Quality: Alternatives and Implications," *Academy of Management Review* 19 (1994): 419–445. Reproduced by permission of *Academy of Management*, PO Box 3020, Briar Cliff Manor, NY, 10510-8020 via Copyright Clearance Center, Inc.

Exhibit 16.8

Four Levels of Waste Minimization

Waste Prevention & Reduction

Recycle & Reuse

Waste Treatment

Waste Disposal

Source: D. R. May and B. L. Flannery, "Cutting Waste with Employee Involvement Teams," *Business Horizons* 38 (September -October 1995): 28–38. Reprinted from *Business Horizons,* with permission from Elsevier.

© Imageshop/Jupiterimages

1. *Good housekeeping*—performing regularly scheduled preventive maintenance for offices, plants, and equipment and quickly fixing leaky valves and making sure machines are running properly so that they don't use more fuel than necessary are examples of good housekeeping.

2. *Material/product substitution*—replacing toxic or hazardous materials with less harmful materials. As part of its Pollution Prevention Pays program over the last 30 years, 3M eliminated 2.2 billion pounds of pollutants and saved $1 billion by using benign substitutes for toxic solvents in its manufacturing processes.[46]

3. *Process modification*—changing steps or procedures to eliminate or reduce waste. Terracycle is a manufacturer of plant food made from the castings (that is, the droppings) of red worms that have feasted on various types of organic waste. But rather than package the plant food in new bottles, Terracycle packages its product in used beverage containers and ships the bottles in recycled boxes to the retailers. The company's entire process operation is 100 percent geared toward reducing or eliminating waste.[47]

At the second level of waste minimization, *recycle and reuse,* wastes are reduced by reusing materials as long as possible or by collecting materials for on- or off-site recycling. A growing trend in recycling is *design for disassembly,* where products are designed from the start for easy disassembly, recycling, and reuse once they are no longer usable. For example, the European Union (EU) is moving toward prohibiting companies from selling products unless most of the product and its packaging can be recycled.[48] Since companies, not consumers, will be held responsible for recycling the products they manufacture, they must design their products from the start with recycling in mind.[49] At reclamation centers throughout Europe, companies will have to be able to recover and recycle 80 percent of the parts that go into their original products.[50] Under the EU's end-of-life vehicle program, all cars built in Europe since June 2002 are already subject to the 80 percent requirement, which rose to 85 percent in 2006 and will be 95 percent by 2015 for autos. Moreover, effective in 2007, the EU requires auto manufacturers to

Exhibit 16.8 shows the four levels of waste minimization ranging from waste disposal, which produces the smallest minimization of waste, to waste prevention and reduction, which produces the greatest minimization.[44] The goals of the top level, *waste prevention and reduction,* are to prevent waste and pollution before they occur or to reduce them when they do occur. For example, United Parcel Service (UPS) uses a software program that helps drivers plan routes with only right turns to save driving time. The strategy also prevents environmental waste, since UPS saves three million gallons of fuel each year and reduces CO2 emissions by 31,000 metric tons.[45] There are three strategies for waste prevention and reduction:

pay to recycle all the cars they made between 1989 and 2002.[51] Today, roughly 160 million cars in Europe are covered by these strict end-of-life regulations.[52]

At the third level of waste minimization, *waste treatment,* companies use biological, chemical, or other processes to turn potentially harmful waste into harmless compounds or useful by-products. For example, during "pickling," a process in the manufacture of steel sheets, the steel is bathed in an acid solution to clean impurities and oxides (which would rust) from its surface. Fortunately, Magnetics International found a safe, profitable way to treat the pickle juice, which it sprays into a 100-foot-high chamber at 1,200 degrees Fahrenheit to form pure iron oxide that can be transformed into a useful magnetic powder which is reused in electric motors, stereo speakers, and refrigerator gaskets.[53]

The fourth and lowest level of waste minimization is waste disposal. Wastes that cannot be prevented, reduced, recycled, reused,

or treated should be safely disposed of in processing plants or in environmentally secure landfills that prevent leakage and contamination of soil and underground water supplies. For example, with the average computer lasting just three years, approximately 60 million computers come out of service each year. But with lead-containing cathode ray tubes in the monitors, toxic metals in the circuit boards, paint-coated plastic, and metal coatings that can contaminate ground water, old computers can't just be thrown away.[54] Hewlett-Packard has started a unique computer disposal program that allows companies or individual computer users to recycle PCs and electronic equipment. Since 1987, HP has collected and recycled over 600 million pounds of used computer equipment. Between 1992 and 2005, they also collected over 91 million printer cartridges. The materials found in these old components can be used to make new HP products as well as new airplane parts, shoe soles, wagons, and fence posts.[55] The service is available at **http://www.hp.com/hpinfo/globalcitizenship/environment/recycle/index.html?jumpid=hpr_R1002_USEN**. With three clicks and a credit card number (prices range from $13 to $34 per item), the old PC equipment will be picked up and properly disposed of. HP makes no profit from this service.

MANAGING SERVICE AND MANUFACTURING OPERATIONS

Managing for Productivity and Quality

Learning Outcomes

1 discuss the kinds of productivity and their importance in managing operations.

2 explain the role that quality plays in managing operations.

3 explain the essentials of managing a service business.

4 describe the different kinds of manufacturing operations.

5 explain why and how companies should manage inventory levels.

Furniture manufacturers, hospitals, restaurants, automakers, airlines, and many other kinds of businesses struggle to find ways to produce quality products and services efficiently and then deliver them in a timely manner. Managing the daily production of goods and services, or operations management, is a key part of a manager's job. But an organization's success depends on the quality of its products and services as well as its productivity. Modeled after U.S.-based Southwest Airlines, European airline Ryanair achieves dramatically lower prices through aggressive price cutting, much higher productivity, and quality customer service. Want a frequent-flier plan? You won't find one at Ryanair. It's too expensive. Want a meal on your flight? Pack a lunch. Ryanair doesn't even serve peanuts because it takes too much time (i.e., expense) to get them out of the seat cushions. Passengers enter and exit the planes using old-fashioned, rolling stairs because they're quicker and cheaper than extendable boarding gates. As a result of such cost-cutting moves, Ryanair does more with less and thus has higher productivity. For example, most airlines break even on their flights when they're 75 percent full, but Ryanair's productivity allows it to break even when its planes are only half full even with its incredibly low prices. With this low break-even point, Ryanair attracts plenty of customers who enable it to fill most of its seats (84 percent) and earn 20 percent net profit margins. Finally, because of its extremely low prices (and its

© Adrian Assalve/iStockphoto.com

competitors' extremely high prices), Ryanair has increased passenger traffic and profits for seventeen straight years.[1]

After reading the next two sections, you should be able to

1   discuss the kinds of productivity and their importance in managing operations.

2   explain the role that quality plays in managing operations.

1 Productivity

At their core, organizations are production systems. Companies combine inputs such as labor, raw materi-als, capital, and knowledge to produce outputs in the form of finished products or services. **Productivity** is a measure of performance that indicates how many in-puts it takes to produce or create an output.

$$\text{Productivity} = \frac{\text{Outputs}}{\text{Inputs}}$$

The fewer inputs it takes to create an output (or the greater the output from one input), the higher the pro-ductivity. For example, a car's gas mileage is a com-mon measure of productiv-ity. A car that gets 35 miles (output) per gallon (input) is more productive and fuel

Productivity a measure of performance that indicates how many inputs it takes to produce or create an output

efficient than a car that gets 18 miles per gallon.

Let's examine **1.1 why productivity matters** and **1.2 the different kinds of productivity**.

1.1 Why Productivity Matters

Why does productivity matter? For companies, higher productivity—that is, doing more with less—results in lower costs for the company, lower prices, faster service, higher market share, and higher profits. For example, every second saved in the drive-through lane at fast-food restaurants increases sales by 1 percent. And with up to 75 percent of all fast-food restaurant sales coming from the drive-through window, it's no wonder that Wendy's (average drive-through time of 138.5 seconds), McDonald's (average time of 167.1 seconds), and Burger King (average time of 179.9 seconds) continue to look for ways to shorten the time it takes to process a drive-through order.[2] Productivity matters so much at the drive-through that McDonald's is experimenting with outsourcing. At roughly 50 McDonald's franchises around the country, drive-through orders are taken by someone at a California call center. An operator can take orders from customers at restaurants in Honolulu one minute and from Gulfport, Mississippi the next. During the 10 seconds it takes for a car to pull away from the microphone at the drive-through, a call center operator can take the order of a different customer who has pulled up to the microphone at another restaurant, even if it's thousands of miles away. According to Jon Anton, co-founder of Bronco Communications, which operates the call center for McDonald's, the goal is "saving seconds to make millions" because more efficient service can lead to more sales and lower labor costs.[3]

The productivity of businesses within a country matters to that country because it results in a higher standard of living. One way productivity leads to a higher standard of living is through increased wages. When companies can do more with less, they can raise employee wages without increasing prices or sacrific-

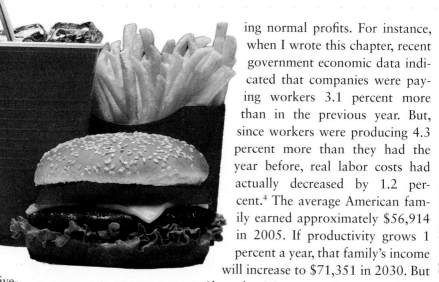

© Comstock/Jupiterimages

ing normal profits. For instance, when I wrote this chapter, recent government economic data indicated that companies were paying workers 3.1 percent more than in the previous year. But, since workers were producing 4.3 percent more than they had the year before, real labor costs had actually decreased by 1.2 percent.[4] The average American family earned approximately $56,914 in 2005. If productivity grows 1 percent a year, that family's income will increase to $71,351 in 2030. But if productivity grows 2 percent a year, their annual income in 2030 will be $90,384, more than $18,000 higher, and that's without working longer hours.[5] Thanks to long-term increases in business productivity, the average American family today earns 33 percent more than the average family in 1980 and 223 percent more than the average family in 1953—and that's after accounting for inflation.[6]

Rising income stemming from increased productivity creates numerous other benefits as well. Productivity increased an average of 3 percent between 1999 and

Multitasking to Higher Productivity?

Think multitasking—or doing multiple tasks *at the same time*—is the answer to increasing productivity? Think again. How effective can you be answering email, reviewing a report, and being attentive at a meeting—all at the same time? James C. Johnston, a research scientist at NASA, says, "Multitasking doesn't look to be one of the great strengths of human cognition. It's almost inevitable that each individual task will be slower and of lower quality." Anyone who's tried to hold a meaningful conversation and text message another person at the same time probably understands this painfully well. (Ever said "yes" when you meant "no," or clicked "send" at the wrong time?) The keys to productivity: focus and concentration, which lead to doing things right the first time. Could "multitasking" be code for not paying attention?

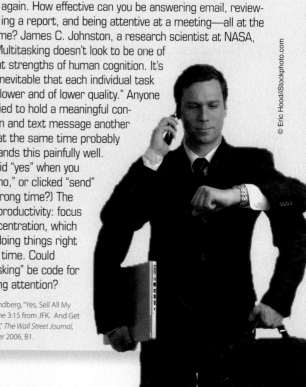

© Eric Hood/iStockphoto.com

Source: J. Sandberg, "Yes, Sell All My Stocks. No, the 3:15 from JFK. And Get Me Mr. Sister," *The Wall Street Journal*, 12 September 2006, B1.

> (**Productivity** matters because it results in a **higher** standard of living.)

2008, and in 2005 alone, the economy added two million jobs.[7] And when more people have jobs that pay more, they give more to charity. For example, in 2005 Americans donated over $260 billion to charities, 6.1 percent more than they gave in 2004.[8]

Another benefit of productivity is that it makes products more affordable or better. For example, while inflation has pushed the average cost of a car to about $29,400 (after incentives and discounts), increases in productivity have actually made cars cheaper.[9] In 1960, the average family needed 26 weeks of income to pay for the average car. Today, the average family needs only 23.9 weeks of income—and today's car is loaded with accessories that weren't even available in 1960, including air bags, power steering and brakes, power windows, cruise control, stereo/CD/DVD players, seat warmers, air-conditioning, and satellite navigation.[10] So productivity gains have actually made today's $29,400 car cheaper than that $2,000 car in 1960 in terms of real purchasing power.[11]

1.2 Kinds of Productivity

Two common measures of productivity are partial productivity and multifactor productivity. **Partial productivity** indicates how much of a particular kind of input it takes to produce an output.

$$\text{Partial Productivity} = \frac{\text{Outputs}}{\text{Single Kind of Input}}$$

Labor is one kind of input that is frequently used when determining partial productivity. *Labor productivity* typically indicates the cost or number of hours of labor it takes to produce an output. In other words, the lower the cost of the labor to produce a unit of output, or the less time it takes to produce a unit of output, the higher the labor productivity. For example, the automobile industry often measures labor productivity by determining the average number of hours of labor needed to completely assemble a car. The three most productive auto manufacturers can assemble a car with 32 or fewer hours of labor. Toyota assembles a car in only 27.9 hours of labor,

Exhibit 18.1

Multifactor Productivity Growth across Industries

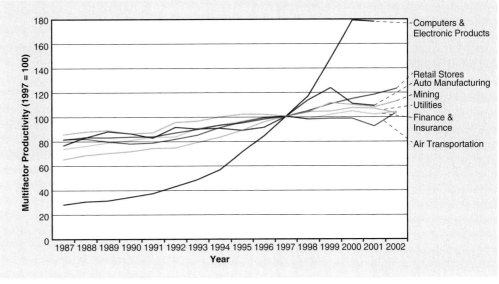

Source: "Productivity and Costs," Bureau of Labor Statistics, available online at http://data.bls.gov/cgi-bin/surveymost?ip [accessed 1 July 2005].

Nissan does it in 29.4 hours, and Honda in 32 hours. These manufacturers have higher labor productivity than General Motors, which needs 34.3 hours of labor to assemble a car, DaimlerChrysler, which needs 35.8 hours, and Ford, which needs 36.9 hours.[12] These lower labor costs give Nissan, Honda, and Toyota an average cost advantage of $350 to $500 per car.[13]

Partial productivity assesses how efficiently companies use only one input, such as labor, when creating outputs. Multifactor productivity is an overall measure of productivity that assesses how efficiently companies use all the inputs it takes to make outputs. More specifically, **multifactor productivity** indicates how much labor, capital, materials, and energy it takes to produce an output.[14]

$$\frac{\text{Multifactor}}{\text{Productivity}} = \frac{\text{Outputs}}{(\text{Labor} + \text{Capital} + \text{Materials} + \text{Energy})}$$

Exhibit 18.1 shows the trends in multifactor productivity across a number of U.S. industries since 1987. With a 78 percent increase between 1997 (scaled at 100) and 2001 (when it reached a level of 178) and nearly a sixfold increase since 1987, the growth in multifactor productivity in the computers and electronic products industry far exceeded the

Partial productivity a measure of performance that indicates how much of a particular kind of input it takes to produce an output

Multifactor productivity an overall measure of performance that indicates how much labor, capital, materials, and energy it takes to produce an output

productivity growth in retail stores, auto manufacturing, mining, utilities, finance and insurance, and air transporation as well as most other industries tracked by the U.S. government.

Should managers use multiple or partial productivity measures? In general, they should use both. Multifactor productivity indicates a company's overall level of productivity relative to its competitors. In the end, that's what counts most. However, multifactor productivity measures don't indicate the specific contributions that labor, capital, materials, or energy make to overall productivity. To analyze the contributions of these individual components, managers need to use partial productivity measures. Doing so can help them determine what factors need to be adjusted or in what areas adjustment can make the most difference in overall productivity.

2 Quality

With the average car costing more than $29,000, car buyers want to make sure that they're getting good quality for their money. Fortunately, as indicated by the number of problems per 100 cars (PP100), today's cars are of much higher quality than earlier models. In 1981, Japanese cars averaged 240 PP100. General Motors' cars averaged 670, Ford's averaged 740, and Chrysler's averaged 870 PP100! In other words, as measured by PP100, the quality of American cars was two to three times worse than that of Japanese cars. In 2007, even the worst cars on the J.D. Power and Associates Survey of Initial Car quality beat the scores of the Japanese cars of decades ago. And high-quality cars like the Mercedes S-Class and Audi A8 even came in with scores under 100 (72 to be exact). That means there's less than one problem per car![15]

The American Society for Quality gives two meanings for **quality**. It can mean a product or service free of deficiencies, such as the number of problems per 100 cars, or it can mean the characteristics of a product or service that satisfy customer needs.[16] Today's cars are of higher quality than those produced twenty years ago in both senses. Not only do they have fewer problems per 100 cars, they also have a number of additional standard features (power brakes and steering, stereo/CD player, power windows and locks, air bags, cruise control, etc.).

In this part of the chapter, you will learn about **2.1 quality-related characteristics for products and servic-**

> **Quality** a product or service free of deficiencies, or the characteristics of a product or service that satisfy customer needs

es, 2.2 ISO 9000 and 14000, 2.3 the Baldrige National Quality Award, and 2.4 total quality management.

2.1 Quality-Related Characteristics for Products and Services

Quality products usually possess three characteristics: reliability, serviceability, and durability.[17] A breakdown occurs when a product quits working or doesn't do what it was designed to do. The longer it takes for a product to break down, or the longer the time between breakdowns, the more reliable the product. Consequently, many companies define product *reliability* in terms of the average time between breakdowns.

Serviceability refers to how easy or difficult it is to fix a product. The easier it is to maintain a working product or fix a broken product, the more serviceable that product is. The Reva is an electric two-seater car, built in India for city use. It goes 50 miles on a single battery charge (a recharge takes just five hours), and its operating costs per mile are one-third that of a typical gasoline-powered car. The Reva has high serviceability by virtue of a computerized diagnostic system that plugs into a portable electronic tool (PET) about the size of a personal digital assistant that assesses how well the car is running. Because the PET can be linked to a phone, customers can easily transmit their Reva's operational history to instantly find out if their car needs work and, if so, what kind.[18]

A product breakdown assumes that a product can be repaired. However, some products don't break down—they fail. *Product failure* means products can't be repaired, only replaced. *Durability* is defined as the mean time to failure. Thus, durability is a quality characteristic that applies to products that can't be repaired.

A high-tech electric Reva cruising the streets of Bangalore on World Environment Day.

© Dibyangshu Sarkar/AFP/Getty Images

Durability is crucial for products such as the defibrillation equipment used by emergency medical technicians, doctors, and nurses to restart patients' hearts. Imagine the lost lives (and lawsuits) that would occur if this equipment were prone to frequent failure!

While high-quality products are characterized by reliability, serviceability, and durability, services are different. There's no point in assessing the durability of a service because services don't last but are consumed the minute they're performed. For example, once a lawn service has mowed your lawn, the job is done until the mowers come back next week to do it again. Services also don't have serviceability. You can't maintain or fix a service. If a service wasn't performed correctly, all you can do is perform it again. Rather than serviceability and durability, the quality of service interactions often depends on how the service provider interacts with the customer. Was the service provider friendly, rude, or helpful? Five characteristics typically distinguish a quality service: reliability, tangibles, responsiveness, assurance, and empathy.[19]

Service reliability is the ability to consistently perform a service well. Studies clearly show that reliability matters more to customers than anything else when buying services. When you take your clothes to the dry cleaner, you don't want them returned with cracked buttons or wrinkles down the front. If your dry cleaner gives you back perfectly clean and pressed clothes every time, it's providing a reliable service.

Also, although services themselves are not tangible (you can't see or touch them), they are provided in tangible places. Thus, *tangibles* refer to the appearance of the offices, equipment, and personnel involved with the delivery of a service. One of the best examples of the effect of tangibles on the perception of quality is the restroom. When you eat at a fancy restaurant, you expect clean, if not upscale, restrooms. How different is your perception of a business, say a gas station, if it has clean restrooms rather than filthy ones?

Responsiveness is the promptness and willingness with which service providers give good service (your dry cleaner returning your laundry perfectly clean and pressed in a day or an hour). *Assurance* is the confidence that service providers are knowledgeable, courteous, and trustworthy. *Empathy* is the extent to which service providers give individual attention and care to customers' concerns and problems.

2.2 ISO 9000 and 14000

ISO, pronounced *eye-so,* comes from the Greek word *isos,* meaning "equal, similar, alike, or identical" and is also an acronym for the International Organization for Standardization, an international organization that helps set standards for 151 countries. The purpose of this agency is to develop and publish standards that facilitate the international exchange of goods and services.[20] **ISO 9000** is a series of five international standards, from ISO 9000 to ISO 9004, for achieving consistency in quality management and quality assurance in companies throughout the world. **ISO 14000** is a series of international standards for managing, monitoring, and minimizing an organization's harmful effects on the environment.[21] (For more on environmental quality and issues, see Section 3.5 of Chapter 16 on controlling waste and pollution.

The ISO 9000 and 14000 standards publications, which are available from the American National Standards Institute, are general and can be used for manufacturing any kind of product or delivering any kind of service. Importantly, the ISO 9000 standards don't describe how to make a better-quality car, computer, or widget. Instead, they describe how companies can extensively document (and thus standardize) the steps they take to create and improve the quality of their products. ISO 9000 certification is increasingly becoming a requirement for doing business with many *Fortune* 500 companies.[22]

To become ISO certified, a process that can take months, a company must show that it is following its own procedures for improving production, updating design plans and specifications, keeping machinery in top condition, educating and training workers, and satisfactorily dealing with customer complaints.[23] Once a company has been certified as ISO 9000 compliant, an accredited third party will issue an ISO 9000 certificate that the company can use in its advertising and publications. This is the quality equivalent of the *Good Housekeeping* Seal of Approval. Continued ISO 9000 certification is not guaranteed, however. Accredited third parties typically conduct periodic audits to make sure the company is still following quality procedures. If it is not, its certification is suspended or canceled.

To get additional information on ISO 9000 guidelines and procedures, see the American National Standards Institute (**http://www.webstore.ansi.org**; the ISO 9000 and ISO 14000 standards publications are avail-

ISO 9000 a series of five international standards, from ISO 9000 to ISO 9004, for achieving consistency in quality management and quality assurance in companies throughout the world

ISO 14000 a series of international standards for managing, monitoring, and minimizing an organization's harmful effects on the environment

able at this site for about $400 and $300, respectively), the American Society for Quality (http://www.asq.org), and the International Organization for Standardization (http://www.iso.org).

2.3 Baldrige National Quality Award

The Baldrige National Quality Award, which is administered by the U.S. government's National Institute for Standards and Technology, is given "to recognize U.S. companies for their achievements in quality and business performance and to raise awareness about the importance of quality and performance excellence as a competitive edge."[24] Each year, up to three awards may be given in these categories: manufacturing, service, small business, education, and health care.

The cost of applying for the Baldrige Award is $6,000 for manufacturing and service companies and $3,000 for small businesses.[25] Why does it cost so much just to apply? Because you get a great deal of information about your business in the process that will be useful even if you don't win. At a minimum, each company that applies receives an extensive report based on 300 hours of assessment from at least eight business and quality experts. At $10 an hour for small businesses and about $20 an hour for manufacturing and service businesses, the *Journal for Quality and Participation* called the Baldrige feedback report "the best bargain in consulting in America."[26]

Businesses that apply for the Baldrige Award are judged on a 1,000-point scale based on the seven criteria in Exhibit 18.2.[27] Results is clearly the most important category, as it takes up 450 out of 1,000 points. In other words, in addition to the six other criteria, companies must show that they have achieved superior quality when it comes to products and services, customers, financial performance and market share, treatment of employees, organizational effectiveness, and leadership and social responsibility. This emphasis on results is what differentiates the Baldrige Award from the ISO 9000 standards. The Baldrige Award indicates the extent to which companies have actually achieved world-class quality. The ISO 9000 standards simply indicate whether a company is following the management system it put in place to improve quality. In fact, ISO 9000 certification covers less than 10 percent of the requirements for the Baldrige Award.[28] Most companies that apply for the Baldrige Award do it to grow, prosper, and stay com-

Total quality management (TQM) an integrated, principle-based, organization-wide strategy for improving product and service quality

Exhibit 18.2

Criteria for the Baldrige National Quality Award

2007 CATEGORIES/ITEMS	POINT VALUES
1 LEADERSHIP	**120**
1.1 Senior Leadership	70
1.2 Governance and Social Responsibilities	50
2 STRATEGIC PLANNING	**85**
2.1 Strategy Development	40
2.2 Strategy Deployment	45
3 CUSTOMER AND MARKET FOCUS	**85**
3.1 Customer and Market Knowledge	40
3.2 Customer Relationships and Satisfaction	45
4 MEASUREMENT, ANALYSIS, AND KNOWLEDGE MANAGEMENT	**90**
4.1 Measurement, Analysis, and Improvement of Organizational Performance	45
4.2 Management of Information, Information Technology, and Knowledge	45
5 WORKFORCE FOCUS	**85**
5.1 Workforce Engagement	45
5.2 Workforce Environment	40
6 PROCESS MANAGEMENT	**85**
6.1 Work Systems Design	35
6.2 Work Process Management and Improvement	50
7 RESULTS	**450**
7.1 Product and Service Outcomes	100
7.2 Customer-Focused Outcomes	70
7.3 Financial and Market Outcomes	70
7.4 Workforce-Focused Outcomes	70
7.5 Process Effectiveness Outcomes	70
7.6 Leadership Outcomes	70
TOTAL POINTS 1,000	

Source: "Criteria for Performance Excellence," *Baldrige National Quality Program 2007*, available online at http://www.quality.nist.gov/PDF_files/2008_Business_Nonprofit_Criteria.pdf [accessed 15 September 2008].

petitive.[29] Furthermore, the companies that have won the Baldrige Award have achieved superior financial returns. Since 1988, an investment in Baldrige Award winners would have outperformed the Standard & Poor's 500 stock index 80 percent of the time.[30]

2.4 Total Quality Management

Total quality management (TQM) is an integrated organization-wide strategy for improving product and service quality.[31] TQM is not a specific tool or technique but a philosophy or overall approach to management that is characterized by three principles: customer focus and satisfaction, continuous improvement, and teamwork.[32]

Although most economists, accountants, and financiers argue that companies exist to earn profits for shareholders, TQM suggests that customer focus and customer satisfaction should be a company's primary goals. **Customer focus** means that the entire organization, from top to bottom, should be focused on meeting customers' needs. The result of that customer focus should be **customer satisfaction,** which occurs when the company's products or services meet or exceed customers' expectations. At companies where TQM is taken seriously, such as Enterprise Rent-a-Car, paychecks and promotions depend on keeping customers satisfied.[33] Enterprise measures customer satisfaction with a detailed survey called the Enterprise Service Quality index. Enterprise not only ranks each branch office by operating profits and customer satisfaction but also makes promotions to higher-paying jobs contingent on above-average customer satisfaction scores.

Continuous improvement is an ongoing commitment to increase product and service quality by constantly assessing and improving the processes and procedures used to create those products and services. How do companies know whether they're achieving continuous improvement? Besides higher customer satisfaction, continuous improvement is usually associated with reduced variation. **Variation** is a deviation in the form, condition, or appearance of a product from the quality standard for that product. The less a product varies from the quality standard, or the more consistently a company's products meet a quality standard, the higher the quality. At Freudenberg-NOK, a manufacturer of seals and gaskets for the automotive industry, continuous improvement means shooting for a goal of Six Sigma quality, meaning just 3.4 defective or nonstandard parts per million (PPM). Achieving this goal would eliminate almost all product variation. In a recent year, Freudenberg-NOK made over 200 million seals and gaskets with a defect rate of 9 PPM, a rate that puts the company almost at its goal.[34] Furthermore, this represents a significant improvement from seven years ago when Freudenberg-NOK was averaging 650 defective PPM. [35]

The third principle of TQM is teamwork. **Teamwork** means collaboration between managers and nonmanagers, across business functions, and between the company and its customers and suppliers. In short, quality improves when everyone in the company is given the incentive to work together and the responsibility and authority to make improvements and solve problems. At Valassis, a printing company long famous for its use of teams, management turned to employees for additional suggestions when business fell during a recession. Teams offered so many ideas to cut costs and raise quality that the company was able to avoid layoffs.[36]

Customer focus and satisfaction, continuous improvement, and teamwork

Robotic Risk Management

Quality control is critical at a pharmacy. The wrong pill or the wrong dosage doesn't happen often, but when it does, it can be lethal to an unsuspecting patient and a costly mistake for the medical facility. Robots significantly reduce such errors. At $1 million each, they're an expensive fix. But Scott Beckman, VP of risk management and insurance for Advocate Health Care Network, says, "I'm going to find every savings I can to try to justify this expense. To me it's a no-brainer. It's a stellar piece of technology that can enhance patient safety and absolutely reduce errors, which means claims go down."

Source: R. Ceniceros, "Robots Reduce Errors in Dispensing Prescriptions," *Business Insurance* (28 April 2008): 30.

Customer focus an organizational goal to concentrate on meeting customers' needs at all levels of the organization

Customer satisfaction an organizational goal to provide products or services that meet or exceed customers' expectations

Continuous improvement an organization's ongoing commitment to constantly assess and improve the processes and procedures used to create products and services

Variation a deviation in the form, condition, or appearance of a product from the quality standard for that product

Teamwork collaboration between managers and nonmanagers, across business functions, and between companies, customers, and suppliers mutually reinforce each other to improve quality throughout a company. Customer-focused continuous improvement is necessary to increase customer satisfaction. At the same time, continuous improvement depends on teamwork from different functional and hierarchical parts of the company.

Managing Operations

At the start of this chapter, you learned that operations management means managing the daily production of goods and services. Then you learned that to manage production, you must oversee the factors that affect productivity and quality. In this half of the chapter, you will learn about managing operations in service and manufacturing businesses. The chapter ends with a discussion of inventory management, a key factor in a company's profitability.

After reading the next three sections, you should be able to

3   explain the essentials of managing a service business.

4   describe the different kinds of manufacturing operations.

5   explain why and how companies should manage inventory levels.

3 Service Operations

Imagine that your trusty VCR breaks down as you try to record your favorite TV show. (You're still saving your money for a TiVo.) You've got two choices. You can run to Wal-Mart and spend $45 to $75 to purchase a new VCR, or you can spend about the same amount (you hope) to have it fixed at a repair shop. Either way you end up with the same thing, a working VCR. However, the first choice, getting a new VCR, involves buying a physical product (a good), while the second, dealing with a repair shop, involves buying a service.

Services differ from goods in several ways. First, goods are produced or made, but services are performed. In other words, services are almost always labor-intensive: someone typically has to perform the service for you. A repair shop could give you the parts needed to repair your old VCR, but you're still going to have a broken VCR without the technician to perform the repairs. Second, goods are tangible, but services are intangible. You can touch and see that new VCR, but you can't touch or see the service provided by the technician who fixed your old VCR. All you can "see" is that the VCR works. Third, services are perishable and unstorable. If you don't use them when they're available, they're wasted. For example, if your VCR repair shop is backlogged on repair jobs, then you'll just have to wait until next week to get your VCR repaired. You can't store an unused service and use it when you like. By contrast, you can purchase a good, such as motor oil, and store it until you're ready to use it. Finally, services account for 59.1 percent of gross national product whereas manufacturing accounts for only 30.9 percent.[37]

*Because services are different from goods, managing a service operation is different from managing a manufacturing or production operation. Let's look at **3.1 the service-profit chain** and **3.2 service recovery and empowerment.***

3.1 The Service-Profit Chain

One of the key assumptions in the service business is that success depends on how well employees—that is, service providers—deliver their services to customers. But success actually begins with how well management treats service employees, as the service-profit chain, depicted in Exhibit 18.3, demonstrates.[38]

The key concept behind the service-profit chain is *internal service quality,* meaning the quality of treatment that employees receive from a company's internal service

SUCCESS BEGINS WITH HOW WELL MANAGEMENT TREATS SERVICE EMPLOYEES.

Exhibit 18.3

Service-Profit Chain

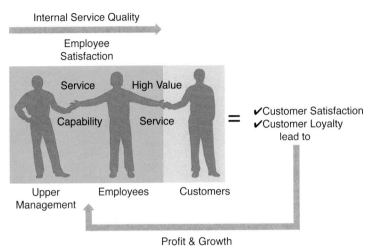

Internal Service Quality

Employee Satisfaction

Service — Capability

High Value Service

= ✔Customer Satisfaction ✔Customer Loyalty lead to

Upper Management — Employees — Customers

Profit & Growth

Sources: R. Hallowell, L. A. Schlesinger, and J. Zornitsky, "Internal Service Quality, Customer and Job Satisfaction: Linkages and Implications for Management," *Human Resource Planning* 19 (1996): 20–31; J. L. Heskett, T. O. Jones, G. W. Loveman, W. E. Sasser, Jr., and L. A. Schlesinger, "Putting the Service-Profit Chain to Work," *Harvard Business Review* (March–April 1994): 164–174.

providers such as management, payroll and benefits, human resources, and so forth. For example, Southwest Airlines is legendary for its positive culture and, to the surprise of many, its excellent customer service. According to Southwest's chairman Herb Kelleher, that's because "employees come first. If you treat them well, then they treat the customers well, and that means your customers come back and your shareholders are happy."[39]

As depicted in Exhibit 18.3, good internal service leads to employee satisfaction and service capability. *Employee satisfaction* occurs when companies treat employees in a way that meets or exceeds their expectations. In other words, the better employees are treated, the more satisfied they are, and the more likely they are to give high-value service that satisfies customers.

How employers treat employees is important because it affects service capability. *Service capability* is an employee's perception of his or her ability to serve customers well. When an organization serves its employees in ways that help them to do their jobs well, employees, in turn, are more likely to believe that they can and ought to provide high-value service to customers.

Finally, according to the service-profit chain shown in Exhibit 18.3, *high-value service* leads to *customer satisfaction* and *customer loyalty*, which, in turn, lead to *long-term profits and growth*. What's the link between customer satisfaction and loyalty, on the one hand, and profits, on the other? To start, the average business keeps only 70 to 90 percent of its existing customers each year. No big deal, you say? Just replace leaving customers with new customers. Well, there's one significant problem with that solution. It costs ten times as much to find a new customer as it does to keep an existing customer. Also, new customers typically buy only 20 percent as much as established customers. In fact, keeping existing customers is so cost-effective that most businesses could double their profits by simply keeping 5 percent more customers per year![40]

3.2 Service Recovery and Empowerment

When mistakes are made, when problems occur, and when customers become dissatisfied with the service they've received, service businesses must switch from the process of service delivery to the process of **service recovery,** or restoring customer satisfaction to strongly dissatisfied customers.[41] Service recovery sometimes requires service employees not only to fix whatever mistake was made but also to perform heroic service acts that delight highly dissatisfied customers by far surpassing their expectations of fair treatment. When accountant Tom Taylor checked into a Hampton Inn in South Carolina, he wasn't happy. The company Web site had given him incorrect directions. The lights in his room weren't plugged in. The shower controls were backwards—"hot" was cold and "cold" was hot. And the air-conditioning was malfunctioning, so his room was freezing cold. When he complained, the employee at the front desk immediately offered him two free nights of lodging.[42]

Unfortunately, when mistakes occur, service employees often don't have the discretion to resolve customer complaints. Customers who want service employees to correct or make up for poor service are frequently told, "I'm not allowed to do that," "I'm just following company rules," or "I'm sorry, only managers are allowed to make changes of any kind." In other words, company rules prevent them from engaging in acts of service recovery meant to turn dissatisfied customers back into satisfied customers. The result is frustration for customers and service employees and lost customers for the company.

Now, however, many companies are empowering their service employees.[43] In Chapter 9, you learned that *empowering workers* means permanently passing decision-making authority and responsibility from managers to workers. With respect to service recovery,

Service recovery restoring customer satisfaction to strongly dissatisfied customers

empowering workers means giving service employees the authority and responsibility to make decisions that immediately solve customer problems.[44] At Hampton Inn, all employees are empowered to solve customer problems. Senior vice president Phil Cordell says, "You don't have to call an 800 number. Just mention it at the front desk or to any employee—a housekeeper, maintenance person or breakfast hostess—and, on the spot, your stay is free."[45] Empowering service workers does entail some costs, although they are usually less than the company's savings from retaining customers.

4 Manufacturing Operations

DaimlerChrysler makes cars, and Dell does computers. Shell produces gasoline, whereas Sherwin-Williams makes paint. Boeing makes jet planes, but Budweiser makes beer. Maxtor makes hard drives, and Maytag makes appliances. The *manufacturing operations* of these companies all produce physical goods. But not all manufacturing operations, especially these, are the same. *Let's learn how various manufacturing operations differ in terms of* **4.1 the amount of processing that is done to produce and assemble a product** *and* **4.2 the flexibility to change the number, kind, and characteristics of products that are produced.**

4.1 Amount of Processing in Manufacturing Operations

Manufacturing operations can be classified according to the amount of processing or assembly that occurs after a customer order is received. The highest degree of processing occurs in **make-to-order operations**. A make-to-order operation does not start processing or assembling products until it receives a customer order. In fact, some make-to-order operations may not even order parts until a customer order is received. Not surprisingly, make-to-order operations produce or assemble highly specialized or customized products for customers.

For example, Dell has one of the most advanced make-to-order operations in the computer business.

Make-to-order operation a manufacturing operation that does not start processing or assembling products until a customer order is received

Assemble-to-order operation a manufacturing operation that divides manufacturing processes into separate parts or modules that are combined to create semicustomized products

Make-to-stock operation a manufacturing operation that orders parts and assembles standardized products before receiving customer orders

Because Dell has no finished goods inventory and no component parts inventory, its computers always have the latest, most advanced components, and Dell can pass on price cuts to customers. Plus, Dell can customize all of its orders, big and small. So whether you're ordering 5,000 personal computers for your company or just one personal computer for your home, Dell doesn't make the computers until you order them.

A moderate degree of processing occurs in **assemble-to-order operations**. A company using an assemble-to-order operation divides its manufacturing or assembly process into separate parts or modules. The company orders parts and assembles modules ahead of customer orders. Then, based on actual customer orders or on research forecasting what customers will want, those modules are combined to create semicustomized products. For example, when a customer orders a new car, General Motors may have already ordered the basic parts or modules it needs from suppliers. Based on sales forecasts, GM may already have ordered enough tires, air-conditioning compressors, brake systems, and seats from suppliers to accommodate nearly all customer orders on a particular day. Special orders from customers and car dealers are then used to determine the final assembly checklist for particular cars as they move down the assembly line.

The lowest degree of processing occurs in **make-to-stock operations** (also called build-to-stock). Because

Is Anything Still Made in the USA?

Conventional wisdom is that all manufacturing will ultimately go to the country where labor is cheapest, which doesn't bode well for, say, the United States. In fact, however, much is still made here. High-end products, bulky products, and delicate products often continue to be produced in the United States and illustrate a key point for consideration in any discussion of globalization: physical and strategic limits do exist. Some business will always be better accomplished close to the customer.

Source: M. Whitehouse, "For Some Manufacturers, There Are Benefits to Keeping Production at Home," *The Wall Street Journal*, 22 January 2007, A2. T. Aeppel, "Still Built on the Homefront," *The Wall Street Journal*, 24 October 2006, B1.

New Balance makes athletic shoes in Orrville, Ohio

Harley-Davidson makes motorcycles in Kansas City, Missouri

Bobcat makes, well, Bobcats in Fargo, North Dakota

© Lester Lefkowitz/Stone/Getty Images

the products are standardized, meaning each product is exactly the same as the next, a company using a make-to-stock operation starts ordering parts and assembling finished products before receiving customer orders. Customers then purchase these standardized products—such as Rubbermaid storage containers, microwave ovens, and vacuum cleaners—at retail stores or directly from the manufacturer. Because parts are ordered and products are assembled before customers order the products, make-to-stock operations are highly dependent on the accuracy of sales forecasts. If sales forecasts are incorrect, make-to-stock operations may end up building too many or too few products, or they may make products with the wrong features or without the features that customers want. These disadvantages are leading many companies to move from make-to-stock to assemble-to-order systems.

4.2 Flexibility of Manufacturing Operations

A second way to categorize manufacturing operations is by **manufacturing flexibility,** meaning the degree to which manufacturing operations can easily and quickly change the number, kind, and characteristics of products they produce. Flexibility allows companies to respond quickly to changes in the marketplace (i.e., competitors and customers) and to reduce the lead time between ordering and final delivery of products. There is often a tradeoff between flexibility and cost, however, with the most flexible manufacturing operations frequently having higher costs per unit and the least flexible operations having lower costs per unit.[46] Some common manufacturing operations, arranged in order from the least flexible to the most flexible, are continuous-flow production, line-flow production, batch production, and job shops.

Most production processes generate finished products at a discrete rate. A product is completed, and then—perhaps a few seconds, minutes, or hours later—another

is completed, and so on. By contrast, in **continuous-flow production,** products are produced continuously rather than at a discrete rate. Like a water hose that is never turned off and just keeps on flowing, production of the final product never stops. Liquid chemicals and petroleum products are examples of continuous-flow production. Because of their complexity, continuous-flow production processes are the most standardized and least flexible manufacturing operations.

Line-flow production processes are preestablished, occur in a serial or linear manner, and are dedicated to making one type of product. Line-flow production processes are inflexible because they are typically dedicated to manufacturing one kind of product. For example, nearly every city has a local bottling plant for soft drinks or beer. The processes or steps in bottling plants are serial, meaning they must occur in a particular order: sterilize; fill with soft drinks or beer; crown or cap bottles; check for underfilling and missing caps; apply label; inspect a final time; and then place bottles in cases, cases on pallets, and pallets on delivery trucks.[47]

Batch production involves the manufacture of large batches of different products in standard lot sizes. This production method is finding increasing use among restaurant chains. To ensure consistency in the taste and quality of their products, many restaurants have central kitchens, or commissaries, that produce batches of food such as mashed potatoes, stuffing, macaroni and cheese, rice, quiche filling, and chili, in volumes ranging from 10 to 200 gallons. These batches are then delivered to restaurants, which serve the food to customers.

Finally, **job shops** are typically small manufacturing operations that handle special manufacturing processes or jobs. In contrast to batch production, which handles large batches of different products, job shops typically handle very small batches, some as small as one product or process per batch. Basically, each job in a job shop is different, and once a

Manufacturing flexibility the degree to which manufacturing operations can easily and quickly change the number, kind, and characteristics of products they produce

Continuous-flow production a manufacturing operation that produces goods at a continuous, rather than a discrete, rate

Line-flow production manufacturing processes that are preestablished, occur in a serial or linear manner, and are dedicated to making one type of product

Batch production a manufacturing operation that produces goods in large batches in standard lot sizes

Job shops manufacturing operations that handle custom orders or small batch jobs

job is done, the job shop moves on to a completely different job or manufacturing process for, most likely, a different customer. For example, Leggett & Platt Machine Products in Carthage, Missouri, is a job shop that makes coil springs, innerspring units, welded metal grids, and various other parts for mattress manufacturers around the world. Since its inception, its 225 employees have made over 25,000 *different* parts; in other words, they have completed 25,000 different jobs for customers.[48]

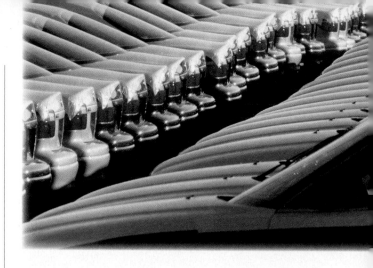

5 Inventory

With SUVs and pickup trucks accounting for nearly 80 percent of its sales, Chrysler was reluctant to stop making them—even when consumer demand dried up. Despite a lack of orders for SUVs and pickups, Chrysler kept building cars—cars that people didn't want—and ended up with nearly a four-month supply of inventory. In addition to what was already on dealer lots, the automaker had 50,000 vehicles sitting on random storage lots around the midwestern United States.[49]

Inventory is the amount and number of raw materials, parts, and finished products a company has in its possession. Like Chrysler, General Motors made the mistake of having too much inventory on hand; GM had to reduce production by over 10 percent at its plants to let existing sales draw down inventory levels to an acceptable and affordable level. Industry experts estimate Chrysler has somewhere between 80 and 126 days of inventory on hand, and it has more SUV inventory (82 days) than GM (77) and Ford (74) and almost three times as much as Toyota (28).[50] *In this section, you will learn about* **5.1 the different types of inventory, 5.2 how to measure inventory levels, 5.3 the costs of maintaining an inventory,** *and* **5.4 the different systems for managing inventory.**

5.1 Types of Inventory

Exhibit 18.4 shows the four kinds of inventory a manufacturer stores: raw materials, component parts, work-in-process, and finished goods. The flow of inventory through a manufacturing plant begins when the purchasing department buys raw materials from vendors. **Raw material inventories** are the basic inputs in the manufacturing process. For example, to begin making a car, automobile manufacturers purchase raw materials like steel, iron, aluminum, copper, rubber, and unprocessed plastic.

Next, raw materials are fabricated or processed into **component parts inventories,** meaning the basic parts used in manufacturing a product. For example, in an automobile plant, steel is fabricated or processed into a car's body panels, and steel and iron are melted and shaped into engine parts like pistons or engine blocks. Some component parts are purchased from vendors rather than fabricated in-house.

The component parts are then assembled to make unfinished **work-in-process inventories,** which are also known as partially finished goods. This process is also called *initial assembly.* For example, steel body panels are welded to each other and to the frame of the car to make a "unibody," which comprises the unpainted interior frame and exterior structure of the car. Likewise, pistons, camshafts, and other engine parts are inserted into the engine block to create a working engine.

Next, all the work-in-process inventories are assembled to create **finished goods inventories,** which are the final outputs of the manufacturing process. This process is also called *final assembly.* For a car, the engine, wheels, brake system, suspension, interior, and electrical system are assembled into a car's painted unibody to make the working automobile, which is the factory's finished product. In the last step in the process, the finished goods are sent to field warehouses, distribution centers, or wholesalers, and then to retailers for final sale to customers.

5.2 Measuring Inventory

As you'll learn below, uncontrolled inventory can lead to huge costs for a manufacturing operation. Consequently, managers need good measures of inventory to prevent inventory costs from becoming too large. Three

Inventory the amount and number of raw materials, parts, and finished products that a company has in its possession

Raw material inventories the basic inputs in a manufacturing process

Component parts inventories the basic parts used in manufacturing that are fabricated from raw materials

Work-in-process inventories partially finished goods consisting of assembled component parts

Finished goods inventories the final outputs of manufacturing operations

Exhibit 18.4

Types of Inventory

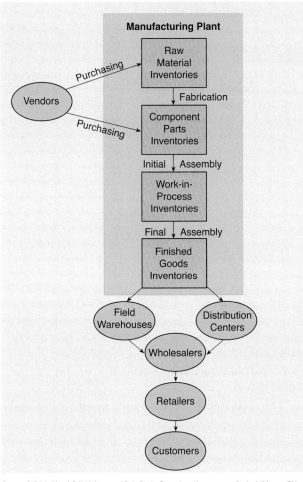

Manufacturing Plant

Vendors → *Purchasing* → Raw Material Inventories

Raw Material Inventories → *Fabrication* → Component Parts Inventories

Vendors → *Purchasing* → Component Parts Inventories

Component Parts Inventories → *Initial Assembly* → Work-in-Process Inventories

Work-in-Process Inventories → *Final Assembly* → Finished Goods Inventories

Finished Goods Inventories → Field Warehouses / Distribution Centers → Wholesalers → Retailers → Customers

Source: R. E. Markland, S. K. Vickery, and R. A. Davis, *Operations Management*, 2nd ed. (Mason, OH: South-Western, 1998). Reprinted with permission.

basic measures of inventory are average aggregate inventory, weeks of supply, and inventory turnover.

If you've ever worked in a retail store and had to take inventory, you probably weren't too excited about the process of counting every item in the store and storeroom. It's an extensive task that's a bit easier today because of bar codes that mark items and computers that can count and track them. Nonetheless, inventories still differ from day to day depending on when in the month or week they're taken. Because of such differences, companies often measure **average aggregate inventory,** which is the average overall inventory during a particular time period. Average aggregate inventory for a month can be determined by simply averaging the inventory counts at the end of each business day for that month. One way companies know whether they're carrying too much or too little inventory is to compare their average aggregate inventory to the industry average for aggregate inventory. For example, 72 days of inventory is the average for the automobile industry. Thus Ford's inventory is about average, whereas Toyota's is quite low and Chrysler's quite high.

Inventory is also measured in terms of *weeks of supply,* meaning the number of weeks it would take for a company to run out of its current supply of inventory. In general, there is an acceptable number of weeks of inventory for a particular kind of business. Too few weeks of inventory on hand, and a company risks a **stockout**—running out of inventory. During a recent holiday season, the busiest shopping time of the year, retail and online stores ran out of Apple Computer's fast-selling iPods.[51] Apple issued a

Average aggregate inventory average overall inventory during a particular time period

Stockout the situation when a company runs out of finished product

> *Uncontrolled inventory can lead to huge costs for a manufacturing operation.*

statement saying, "To try to meet the high demand, we're making and shipping iPods as fast as we can. So, if one store has run out, you may find iPods in another authorized iPod reseller."[52] Nevertheless, iPods were in such short supply that the iPod mini was selling for $380 on eBay, $130 over the suggested retail price. On the other hand, a business that has too many weeks of inventory on hand incurs high costs (discussed below). Excess inventory can be reduced only by cutting prices or temporarily stopping production.

Another common inventory measure, **inventory turnover,** is the number of times per year that a company sells or "turns over" its average inventory. For example, if a company keeps an average of 100 finished widgets in inventory each month, and it sold 1,000 widgets this year, then it turned its inventory 10 times this year.

In general, the higher the number of inventory turns, the better. In practice, a high turnover means that a company can continue its daily operations with just a small amount of inventory on hand. For example, let's take two companies, A and B, which have identical inventory levels (520,000 widget parts and raw materials) over the course of a year. If company A turns its inventories 26 times a year, it will completely replenish its inventory every two weeks and have an average inventory of 20,000 widget parts and raw materials. By contrast, if company B turns its inventories only two times a year, it will completely replenish its inventory every 26 weeks and have an average inventory of 260,000 widget parts and raw materials. So, by turning its inventory more often, company A has 92 percent less inventory on hand at any one time than company B.

The average number of inventory turns across all kinds of manufacturing plants is approximately 8 per year, although the average can be higher or lower for different industries.[53] For example, whereas the average auto company turns its entire inventory 13 times per year, some of the best auto companies more than double that rate, turning their inventory 27.8 times per year, or once every two weeks.[54] Turning inventory more frequently than the industry average can cut an auto company's costs by several hundred million dollars per year. Finally, it should be pointed out that even make-to-order companies like Dell turn their inventory. In theory, make-to-order companies have no inventory. In fact, they've got inventory, but you have to measure it in hours. For example, Dell turns its inventory 500 times a year in its factories, which means that on average it has 17 hours—that's hours and not days—of inventory on hand in its factories.[55]

5.3 Costs of Maintaining an Inventory

Maintaining an inventory results in four kinds of costs: ordering, setup, holding, and stockout. **Ordering cost** is not the cost of the inventory itself but the costs associated with ordering the inventory. It includes the costs of completing paperwork, manually entering data into a computer, making phone calls, getting competing bids, correcting mistakes, and simply determining when and how much new inventory should be reordered. For example, ordering costs are relatively high in the restaurant business because 80 percent of food service orders (in which restaurants reorder food supplies) are processed manually. It's estimated that the food industry could save $6.6 billion if all restaurants converted to electronic data interchange (see Chapter 17).[56]

Setup cost is the cost of changing or adjusting a machine so that it can produce a different kind of inventory.[57] For example, 3M uses the same production machinery to

Sharp Turns

I f it takes an automaker 13 to 28 weeks to turn its inventory, what does that mean for the dealer? How long do cars stay on the dealers' lots?

Surprisingly, the car that sells the fastest is the Mercedes-Benz G-Class (sticker $94,917), sitting on the lot only eight days before being driven off by a happy owner—with a much lighter checkbook. The car that sells the second fastest is almost at the other end of the spectrum: The Honda Fit spends an average of ten days on the lot and sells for only $16,372. The Honda CR-V, BMW X5, Saturn Sky, Lexus LS and ES series, Toyota Tundra, Nissan Versa, and BMW X3 and 5 Series all turn in less than three weeks. Anything else is just old.

Source: "Hot off the Lot," *The Wall Street Journal,* 8 March 2007, D6. Data in article from Power Information Network, a division of J.D. Power & Associates.

© Stockbyte/Getty Images

Inventory turnover the number of times per year that a company sells or "turns over" its average inventory

Ordering cost the costs associated with ordering inventory, including the cost of data entry, phone calls, obtaining bids, correcting mistakes, and determining when and how much inventory to order

Setup cost the costs of downtime and lost efficiency that occur when a machine is changed or adjusted to produce a different kind of inventory

make several kinds of industrial tape, but it must adjust the machines whenever it switches from one kind of tape to another. There are two kinds of setup costs: downtime and lost efficiency. *Downtime* occurs whenever a machine is not being used to process inventory. If it takes five hours to switch a machine from processing one kind of inventory to another, then five hours of downtime have occurred. Downtime is costly because companies earn an economic return only when machines are actively turning raw materials into parts or parts into finished products. The second setup cost is *lost efficiency*. Recalibrating a machine to its optimal settings after a switchover typically takes some time. It may take several days of fine-tuning before a machine finally produces the number of high-quality parts that it is supposed to. So, each time a machine has to be changed to handle a different kind of inventory, setup costs (downtime and lost efficiency) rise.

Holding cost, also known as *carrying* or *storage cost*, is the cost of keeping inventory until it is used or sold. Holding cost includes the cost of storage facilities, insurance to protect inventory from damage or theft, inventory taxes, the cost of obsolescence (holding inventory that is no longer useful to the company), and the opportunity cost of spending money on inventory that could have been spent elsewhere in the company. For example, it's estimated that U.S. airlines have a total of $60 billion worth of airplane parts in stock for maintenance, repair, and overhauling their planes at any one time. The holding cost for managing, storing, and purchasing these parts is nearly $12.5 billion—or roughly one-fifth of the cost of the parts themselves.[58]

Stockout costs are the costs incurred when a company runs out of a product, as happened to Apple when it failed to have enough iPods during the holiday shopping season. There are two basic kinds of stockout costs. First, the company incurs the transaction costs of overtime work, shipping, and the like in trying to quickly replace out-of-stock inventories with new inventories. The second and perhaps more damaging cost is the loss of customers' goodwill when a company cannot deliver the products that it promised.

5.4 Managing Inventory

Inventory management has two basic goals. The first is to avoid running out of stock and thus angering and dissatisfying customers. Consequently, this goal seeks to increase inventory to a safe level that won't risk stockouts. The second goal is to have a minimum level of inventory. This goal is achieved by efficiently reducing inventory levels and costs as much as possible without impairing daily operations. The following inventory management techniques—

economic order quantity (EOQ), just-in-time inventory (JIT), and materials requirement planning (MRP)—are different ways of balancing these competing goals.

Economic order quantity (EOQ) is a system of formulas that helps determine how much and how often inventory should be ordered. EOQ takes into account the overall demand (D) for a product while trying to minimize ordering costs (O) and holding costs (H). The formula for EOQ is

$$EOQ = \sqrt{\frac{2DO}{H}}$$

For example, if a factory uses 40,000 gallons of paint a year (D), ordering costs (O) are $75 per order, and holding costs (H) are $4 per gallon, then the optimal quantity to order is 1,225 gallons:

$$EOQ = \sqrt{\frac{2(40,000)\,(75)}{4}} = 1,225$$

And, with 40,000 gallons of paint being used per year, the factory uses approximately 110 gallons per day:

$$\frac{40,000\ gallons}{365\ days} = 110$$

Consequently, the factory would order 1,225 new gallons of paint approximately every 11 days:

$$\frac{1,225\ gallons}{110\ gallons\ per\ day} = 11.1\ days$$

While EOQ formulas try to minimize holding and ordering costs, the just-in-time (JIT) approach to inventory management attempts to eliminate holding costs by reducing inventory levels to near zero. With a **just-in-time (JIT) inventory system,** component parts arrive from suppliers just as they are needed at each stage of production. By having parts arrive just in time, the manufacturer has little inventory on hand and thus avoids the costs associated with holding inventory.

To have just the right amount of inventory arrive at just the right time requires a tremendous amount of coordination between manufacturing operations and suppliers. One way to promote tight

Holding cost the cost of keeping inventory until it is used or sold, including storage, insurance, taxes, obsolescence, and opportunity costs

Stockout costs the costs incurred when a company runs out of a product, including transaction costs to replace inventory and the loss of customers' goodwill

Economic order quantity (EOQ) a system of formulas that minimizes ordering and holding costs and helps determine how much and how often inventory should be ordered

Just-in-time (JIT) inventory system an inventory system in which component parts arrive from suppliers just as they are needed at each stage of production

coordination under JIT is close proximity. Most parts suppliers for Toyota's JIT system at its Georgetown, Kentucky plant are located within 200 miles of the plant. Furthermore, parts are picked up from suppliers and delivered to Toyota as often as 16 times a day.[59] A second way to promote close coordination under JIT is to have a shared information system that allows a manufacturer and its suppliers to know the quantity and kinds of parts inventory the other has in stock. Generally, factories and suppliers facilitate information sharing by using the same part numbers and names.

Manufacturing operations and their parts suppliers can also facilitate close coordination by using the Japanese system of kanban. **Kanban,** which is Japanese for "sign," is a simple ticket-based system that indicates when it is time to reorder inventory. Suppliers attach kanban cards to batches of parts. Then, when an assembly-line worker uses the first part out of a batch, the kanban card is removed. The cards are then collected, sorted, and quickly returned to the supplier, who begins resupplying the factory with parts that match the order information on the kanban cards. And, because prices and batch sizes are typically agreed to ahead of time, kanban tickets greatly reduce paperwork and ordering costs.[60]

A third method for managing inventory is **materials requirement planning (MRP).** MRP is a production and inventory system that, from beginning to end, precisely determines the production schedule, production batch sizes, and inventories needed to complete final products. The three key parts of MRP systems are the master production schedule, the bill of materials, and inventory records. The *master production schedule* is a detailed schedule that indicates the quantity of each item to be produced, the planned delivery dates for those items, and the time by which each step of the production process must be completed in order to meet those delivery dates. Based on the quantity and kind of products set forth in the master production schedule, the *bill of materials* identifies all the necessary parts and inventory, the quantity or volume of inventory to be ordered, and the order in which the parts and inventory should be assembled. *Inventory records* indicate the kind, quantity, and location of inventory that is on hand or that has been ordered. When inventory records are combined with the bill of materials, the resulting report indicates what to buy, when to buy it, and what it will cost to order. Today, nearly all MRP systems are available in the form of powerful, flexible computer software.[61]

Which inventory management system should you use? EOQ formulas are intended for use with **independent demand systems,** in which the level of one kind of inventory does not depend on another. For example, because inventory levels for automobile tires are unrelated to the inventory levels of women's dresses, Sears could use EOQ formulas to calculate separate optimal order quantities for dresses and tires. By contrast, JIT and MRP are used with **dependent demand systems,** in which the level of inventory depends on the number of finished units to be produced. For example, if Yamaha makes 1,000 motorcycles a day, then it will need 1,000 seats, 1,000 gas tanks, and 2,000 wheels and tires each day. So, when optimal inventory levels depend on the number of products to be produced, use a JIT or MRP management system.

Kanban a ticket-based JIT system that indicates when to reorder inventory

Materials requirement planning (MRP) a production and inventory system that determines the production schedule, production batch sizes, and inventory needed to complete final products

Independent demand system an inventory system in which the level of one kind of inventory does not depend on another

Dependent demand system an inventory system in which the level of inventory depends on the number of finished units to be produced

By the Numbers

166 average number of seconds it takes to go through the Burger King drive-through

$2,000 fee small businesses pay to apply for the Baldrige Award

3.4 number of nonstandard parts per million when a company reaches Six Sigma

20% average yearly customer attrition rate

$94,917 sticker price for Mercedes-Benz G-Class

REVIEW card/

LEARNING OUTCOMES

Review 1: Management Is . . .

> Good management is working through others to accomplish tasks that help fulfill organizational objectives as efficiently as possible.

Review 2: Management Functions

> Henri Fayol's classic management functions are known today as planning, organizing, leading, and controlling. Planning is determining organizational goals and a means for achieving them. Organizing is deciding where decisions will be made, who will do what jobs and tasks, and who will work for whom. Leading is inspiring and motivating workers to work hard to achieve organizational goals. Controlling is monitoring progress toward goal achievement and taking corrective action when needed. Studies show that performing the management functions well leads to better managerial performance.

Review 3: Kinds of Managers

> There are four different kinds of managers. Top managers are responsible for creating a context for change, developing attitudes of commitment and ownership, creating a positive organizational culture through words and actions, and monitoring their company's business environments. Middle managers are responsible for planning and allocating resources, coordinating and linking groups and departments, monitoring and managing the performance of subunits and managers, and implementing the changes or strategies generated by top managers. First-line managers are responsible for managing the performance of nonmanagerial employees, teaching direct reports how to do their jobs, and making detailed schedules and operating plans based on middle management's intermediate-range plans. Team leaders are responsible for facilitating team performance, fostering good relationships among team members, and managing external relationships.

Review 4: Managerial Roles

> Managers perform interpersonal, informational, and decisional roles in their jobs. In fulfilling the interpersonal role, managers act as figureheads by performing ceremonial duties, as leaders by motivating and encouraging workers, and as liaisons by dealing with people outside their units. In performing their informational role, managers act as monitors by scanning their environment for information, as disseminators by sharing information with others in the company, and as spokespeople by sharing information with people outside their departments or companies. In fulfilling decisional roles, managers act as entrepreneurs by adapting their units to incremental change, as disturbance handlers by responding to larger problems that demand immediate action, as resource allocators by deciding resource recipients and amounts, and as negotiators by bargaining with others about schedules, projects, goals, outcomes, and resources.

KEY TERMS

Management getting work done through others

Efficiency getting work done with a minimum of effort, expense, or waste

Effectiveness accomplishing tasks that help fulfill organizational objectives

Planning (management functions) determining organizational goals and a means for achieving them

Organizing deciding where decisions will be made, who will do what jobs and tasks, and who will work for whom

Leading inspiring and motivating workers to work hard to achieve organizational goals

Controlling monitoring progress toward goal achievement and taking corrective action when needed

Top managers executives responsible for the overall direction of the organization

Middle managers managers responsible for setting objectives consistent with top management's goals and for planning and implementing subunit strategies for achieving these objectives

First-line managers managers who train and supervise the performance of nonmanagerial employees who are directly responsible for producing the company's products or services

Team leaders managers responsible for facilitating team activities toward accomplishing a goal

Figurehead role the interpersonal role managers play when they perform ceremonial duties

Leader role the interpersonal role managers play when they motivate and encourage workers to accomplish organizational objectives

Liaison role the interpersonal role managers play when they deal with people outside their units

Monitor role the informational role managers play when they scan their environment for information

Disseminator role the informational role managers play when they share information with others in their departments or companies

Spokesperson role the informational role managers play when they share information with people outside their departments or companies

Entrepreneur role the decisional role managers play when they adapt themselves, their subordinates, and their units to change

Disturbance handler role the decisional role managers play when they respond to severe problems that demand immediate action

Resource allocator role the decisional role managers play when they decide who gets what resources

Negotiator role the decisional role managers play when they negotiate schedules, projects, goals, outcomes, resources, and employee raises

Technical skills the specialized procedures, techniques, and knowledge required to get the job done

Human skills the ability to work well with others

Conceptual skills the ability to see the organization as a whole, understand how the different parts affect each other, and recognize how the company fits into or is affected by its environment

Motivation to manage an assessment of how enthusiastic employees are about managing the work of others

How to Use the Card:

1. Look over the card to preview the new concepts you'll be introduced to in the chapter.

2. Read the chapter to fully understand the material.

3. Go to class (and pay attention).

4. Review the card one more time to make sure you've registered the key concepts.

5. Don't forget, this card is only one of many MGMT learning tools available to help you succeed in your management course.

Review 5: What Companies Look for in Managers

> Companies do not want one-dimensional managers. They want managers with a balance of skills. Managers need the knowledge and abilities to get the job done (technical skills), must be able to work effectively in groups and be good listeners and communicators (human skills), must be able to assess the relationships between the different parts of the company and the external environment and position their companies for success (conceptual skills), and should want to assume positions of leadership and power (motivation to manage). Technical skills are most important for lower-level managers, human skills are equally important at all levels of management, and conceptual skills and motivation to manage increase in importance as managers rise through the managerial ranks.

Review 6: Mistakes Managers Make

> Another way to understand what it takes to be a manager is to look at the top mistakes managers make. Five of the most important mistakes made by managers are being abrasive and intimidating; being cold, aloof, or arrogant; betraying trust; being overly ambitious; and failing to deal with specific performance problems of the business.

Review 7: The Transition to Management: The First Year

> Managers often begin their jobs by using more formal authority and less people management skill. However, most managers find that being a manager has little to do with "bossing" their subordinates. After six months on the job, the managers were surprised at the fast pace and heavy workload and that "helping" their subordinates was viewed as interference. After a year on the job, most of the managers had come to think of themselves not as doers but as managers who get things done through others. And, because they finally realized that people management was the most important part of their job, most of them had abandoned their authoritarian approach for one based on communication, listening, and positive reinforcement.

Review 8: Competitive Advantage through People

> Why does management matter? Well-managed companies are competitive because their workforces are smarter, better trained, more motivated, and more committed. Furthermore, companies that practice good management consistently have greater sales revenues, profits, and stock market performance than companies that don't. Finally, good management matters because good management leads to satisfied employees who, in turn, provide better service to customers. Because employees tend to treat customers the same way that their managers treat them, good management can improve customer satisfaction.

4ltrpress.cengage.com/mgmt has great **review tools:** flash cards, quizzes, games, MP3 reviews, and self-assessments.

LEARNING OUTCOMES

Review 1: The Origins of Management

> Management as a field of study is just 125 years old, but management ideas and practices have actually been used since 6000 B.C.E. From the ancient Sumerians to sixteenth-century Europe, there are historical antecedents for each of the functions of management discussed in this textbook: planning, organizing, leading, and controlling. However, there was no compelling need for managers until systematic changes in the nature of work and organizations occurred during the last two centuries. As work shifted from families to factories; from skilled laborers to specialized, unskilled laborers; from small, self-organized groups to large factories employing thousands under one roof; and from unique, small batches of production to large standardized mass production; managers were needed to impose order and structure, to motivate and direct large groups of workers, and to plan and make decisions that optimized overall company performance by effectively coordinating the different parts of organizational systems.

Review 2: Scientific Management

> Scientific management involved studying and testing different work methods to identify the best, most efficient ways to complete a job. According to Frederick W. Taylor, the father of scientific management, managers should follow four scientific management principles. First, study each element of work to determine the one best way to do it. Second, scientifically select, train, teach, and develop workers to reach their full potential. Third, cooperate with employees to ensure that the scientific principles are implemented. Fourth, divide the work and the responsibility equally between management and workers. Above all, Taylor felt these principles could be used to align managers and employees by determining a fair day's work, what an average worker could produce at a reasonable pace, and a fair day's pay (what management should pay workers for that effort). Taylor felt that incentives were one of the best ways to align management and employees.

Frank and Lillian Gilbreth are best known for their use of motion studies to simplify work. Whereas Taylor used time study to determine a fair day's work based on how long it took a "first-class man" to complete each part of his job, Frank Gilbreth used film cameras and micro chronometers to conduct motion studies to improve efficiency by eliminating unnecessary or repetitive motions. Henry Gantt is best known for the Gantt chart, which graphically indicates when a series of tasks must be completed to perform a job or project, but he also developed ideas regarding pay-for-performance plans (where workers were rewarded for producing more but were not punished if they didn't) and worker training (all workers should be trained and their managers should be rewarded for training them).

Review 3: Bureaucratic and Administrative Management

> Today, we associate bureaucracy with inefficiency and red tape. Yet, German sociologist Max Weber thought that bureaucracy—that is, running organizations on the basis of knowledge, fairness, and logical rules and procedures—would accomplish organizational goals much more efficiently than monarchies and patriarchies, where decisions were based on personal or family connections, personal gain, and arbitrary decision making. Bureaucracies are characterized by seven elements: qualification-based hiring; merit-based promotion; chain of command; division of labor; impartial application of rules and procedures; recording rules, procedures, and decisions in writing; and separating managers from owners. Nonetheless, bureaucracies are often inefficient and can be highly resistant to change.

KEY TERMS

Scientific management thoroughly studying and testing different work methods to identify the best, most efficient way to complete a job

Soldiering when workers deliberately slow their pace or restrict their work outputs

Rate buster a group member whose work pace is significantly faster than the normal pace in his or her group

Time study timing how long it takes good workers to complete each part of their jobs

Motion study breaking each task or job into its separate motions and then eliminating those that are unnecessary or repetitive

Gantt chart a graphic chart that shows which tasks must be completed at which times in order to complete a project or task

Bureaucracy the exercise of control on the basis of knowledge, expertise, or experience

Integrative conflict resolution an approach to dealing with conflict in which both parties deal with the conflict by indicating their preferences and then working together to find an alternative that meets the needs of both

Organization a system of consciously coordinated activities or forces created by two or more people

System a set of interrelated elements or parts that function as a whole

Subsystems smaller systems that operate within the context of a larger system

Synergy when two or more subsystems working together can produce more than they can working apart

Closed systems systems that can sustain themselves without interacting with their environments

Open systems systems that can sustain themselves only by interacting with their environments, on which they depend for their survival

Contingency approach holds that there are no universal management theories and that the most effective management theory or idea depends on the kinds of problems or situations that managers are facing at a particular time and place

The Frenchman Henri Fayol, whose ideas were shaped by his twenty-plus years of experience as a CEO, is best known for developing five management functions (planning, organizing, coordinating, commanding, and controlling) and fourteen principles of management (division of work, authority and responsibility, discipline, unity of command, unity of direction, subordination of individual interests to the general interest, remuneration, centralization, scalar chain, order, equity, stability of tenure of personnel, initiative, and *esprit de corps*). He is also known for his belief that management could and should be taught to others.

Review 4: Human Relations Management

> Unlike most people who view conflict as bad, Mary Parker Follett believed that it should be embraced rather than avoided. Of the three ways of dealing with conflict—domination, compromise, and integration— she argued that the latter was the best because it focuses on developing creative methods for meeting conflicting parties' needs.

Elton Mayo is best known for his role in the Hawthorne Studies at the Western Electric Company. In the first stage of the Hawthorne Studies, production went up because the increased attention paid to the workers in the study and their development into a cohesive work group led to significantly higher levels of job satisfaction and productivity. In the second stage, productivity dropped because the workers had already developed strong negative norms. The Hawthorne Studies demonstrated that workers' feelings and attitudes affected their work, that financial incentives weren't necessarily the most important motivator for workers, and that group norms and behavior play a critical role in behavior at work.

Chester Barnard, president of New Jersey Bell Telephone, emphasized the critical importance of willing cooperation in organizations and said that managers could gain workers' willing cooperation through three executive functions: securing essential services from individuals (through material, nonmaterial, and associational incentives), unifying the people in the organization with a clear purpose, and providing a system of communication. Barnard maintains that it is better to induce cooperation through incentives, clearly formulated organizational objectives, and effective communication throughout the organization than to impose it using managerial authority.

Review 5: Operations, Information, Systems, and Contingency Management

> Operations management uses a quantitative or mathematical approach to find ways to increase productivity, improve quality, and manage or reduce costly inventories. The manufacture of standardized, interchangeable parts, the graphical and computerized design of parts, and the accidental discovery of just-in-time management were some of the most important historical events in operations management.

Throughout history, organizations have pushed for and quickly adopted new information technologies that reduce the cost or increase the speed with which they can acquire, store, retrieve, or communicate information. Historically, some of the most important technologies that have revolutionized information management were the creation of paper and the printing press in the fourteenth and fifteenth centuries, the manual typewriter in 1850, cash registers in 1879, the telephone in the 1880s, time clocks in the 1890s, the personal computer in the 1980s, and the Internet in the 1990s.

A system is a set of interrelated elements or parts that function as a whole. Organizational systems obtain inputs from both general and specific environments. Managers and workers then use their management knowledge and manufacturing techniques to transform those inputs into outputs which, in turn, provide feedback to the organization. Organizational systems must also address the issues of synergy, open *versus* closed systems, and entropy.

Finally, the contingency approach to management clearly states that there are no universal management theories. The most effective management theory or idea depends on the kinds of problems or situations that managers or organizations are facing at a particular time. This means that management is much harder than it looks.

LEARNING OUTCOMES

Review 1: Benefits and Pitfalls of Planning

> Planning is choosing a goal and developing a method for achieving it. Planning is one of the best ways to improve organizational and individual performance. It encourages people to work harder (intensified effort), to work hard for extended periods (persistence), to engage in behaviors directly related to goal accomplishment (directed behavior), and to think of better ways to do their jobs (task strategies). However, planning also has three potential pitfalls. Companies that are overly committed to their plans may be slow to adapt to environmental changes. Planning is based on assumptions about the future, and when those assumptions are wrong, plans can fail. Finally, planning can fail when planners are detached from the implementation of plans.

Review 2: How to Make a Plan That Works

> There are five steps to making a plan that works: (1) Set S.M.A.R.T. goals—goals that are **S**pecific, **M**easurable, **A**ttainable, **R**ealistic, and **T**imely. (2) Develop commitment to the goals. Managers can increase workers' goal commitment by encouraging worker participation in goal setting, making goals public, and getting top management to show support for workers' goals. (3) Develop action plans for goal accomplishment. (4) Track progress toward goal achievement by setting both proximal and distal goals and by providing workers with regular performance feedback. (5) Maintain flexibility by keeping options open.

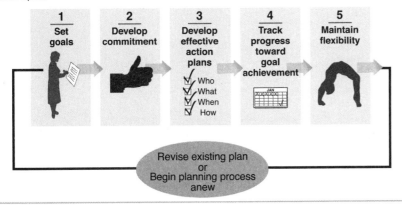

Review 3: Planning from Top to Bottom

> Proper planning requires that the goals at the bottom and middle of the organization support the objectives at the top of the organization. The goals at the top will be longer-range than those at the bottom, as shown here. Top management develops strategic plans, which start with the creation of an organizational vision and mission. Middle managers use techniques like management by objectives (MBO) to develop tactical plans that direct behavior, efforts, and priorities. Finally, lower-level managers

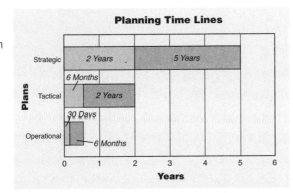

KEY TERMS

Planning choosing a goal and developing a strategy to achieve that goal

S.M.A.R.T. goals goals that are specific, measurable, attainable, realistic, and timely

Goal commitment the determination to achieve a goal

Action plan the specific steps, people, and resources needed to accomplish a goal

Proximal goals short-term goals or subgoals

Distal goals long-term or primary goals

Options-based planning maintaining flexibility by making small, simultaneous investments in many alternative plans

Slack resources a cushion of extra resources that can be used with options-based planning to adapt to unanticipated change, problems, or opportunities

Strategic plans overall company plans that clarify how the company will serve customers and position itself against competitors over the next two to five years

Vision a statement of a company's purpose or reason for existing

Mission a statement of a company's overall goal that unifies company-wide efforts toward its vision, stretches and challenges the organization, and possesses a finish line and a time frame

Tactical plans plans created and implemented by middle managers that specify how the company will use resources, budgets, and people over the next six months to two years to accomplish specific goals within its mission

Management by objectives (MBO) a four-step process in which managers and employees discuss and select goals, develop tactical plans, and meet regularly to review progress toward goal accomplishment

Operational plans day-to-day plans, developed and implemented by lower-level managers, for producing or delivering the organization's products and services over a 30-day to six-month period

Single-use plans plans that cover unique, one-time-only events

Standing plans plans used repeatedly to handle frequently recurring events

Policy a standing plan that indicates the general course of action that should be taken in response to a particular event or situation

Procedure a standing plan that indicates the specific steps that should be taken in response to a particular event

Rules and regulations standing plans that describe how a particular action should be performed or what must happen or not happen in response to a particular event

Budgeting quantitative planning through which managers decide how to allocate available money to best accomplish company goals

Decision making the process of choosing a solution from available alternatives

Rational decision making a systematic process of defining problems, evaluating alternatives, and choosing optimal solutions

Problem a gap between a desired state and an existing state

Decision criteria the standards used to guide judgments and decisions

Absolute comparisons a process in which each criterion is compared to a standard or ranked on its own merits

Relative comparisons a process in which each criterion is compared directly to every other

Maximizing choosing the best alternative

Satisficing choosing a "good enough" alternative

Groupthink a barrier to good decision making caused by pressure within a group for members to agree with each other

C-type conflict (cognitive conflict) disagreement that focuses on problem- and issue-related differences of opinion

A-type conflict (affective conflict) disagreement that focuses on individual or personal issues

Devil's advocacy a decision-making method in which an individual or a subgroup is assigned the role of a critic

Nominal group technique a decision-making method that begins and ends by having group members quietly write down and evaluate ideas to be shared with the group

Delphi technique a decision-making method in which members of a panel of experts respond to questions and to each other until reaching agreement on an issue

Brainstorming a decision-making method in which group members build on each others' ideas to generate as many alternative solutions as possible

Electronic brainstorming a decision-making method in which group members use computers to build on each others' ideas and generate many alternative solutions

Production blocking a disadvantage of face-to-face brainstorming in which a group member must wait to share an idea because another member is presenting an idea

Evaluation apprehension fear of what others will think of your ideas

develop operational plans that guide daily activities in producing or delivering an organization's products and services. There are three kinds of operational plans: single-use plans, standing plans (policies, procedures, and rules and regulations), and budgets.

Review 4: Steps and Limits to Rational Decision Making

> Rational decision making is a six-step process in which managers define problems, evaluate alternatives, and compute optimal solutions. Step 1 is identifying and defining the problem. Problems are gaps between desired and existing states. Managers won't begin the decision-making process unless they are aware of the gap, motivated to reduce it, and possess the necessary resources to fix it. Step 2 is defining the decision criteria used to judge alternatives. In Step 3, an absolute or relative comparison process is used to rate the importance of the decision criteria. Step 4 involves generating many alternative courses of action (i.e., solutions). Potential solutions are assessed in Step 5 by systematically gathering information and evaluating each alternative against each criterion. In Step 6, criterion ratings and weights are used to compute the optimal value for each alternative course of action. Rational managers then choose the alternative with the highest optimal value.

The rational decision-making model describes how decisions should be made in an ideal world without limits. However, bounded rationality recognizes that managers' limited resources, incomplete and imperfect information, and limited decision-making capabilities restrict their decision-making processes in the real world.

Review 5: Using Groups to Improve Decision Making

> When groups view problems from multiple perspectives, use more information, have a diversity of knowledge and experience, and become committed to solutions they help choose, they can produce better solutions than individual decision makers. However, group decisions can suffer from these disadvantages: groupthink, slowness, discussions dominated by just a few individuals, and unfelt responsibility for decisions. Group decisions work best when group members encourage c-type conflict. Group decisions don't work as well when groups become mired in a-type conflict. The devil's advocacy and dialectical inquiry approaches improve group decisions because they bring structured c-type (cognitive) conflict into the decision-making process. By contrast, the nominal group technique and the Delphi technique both improve decision making by reducing a-type (affective) conflict. Because it overcomes the problems of production blocking and evaluation apprehension, electronic brainstorming is more effective than face-to-face brainstorming.

LEARNING OUTCOMES

Review 1: Why Innovation Matters

> Technology cycles typically follow an S-curve pattern of innovation. Early in the cycle, technological progress is slow, and improvements in technological performance are small. As a technology matures, however, performance improves quickly. Finally, as the limits of a technology are reached, only small improvements occur. At this point, significant improvements in performance must come from new technologies. The best way to protect a competitive advantage is to create a stream of innovative ideas and products. Innovation streams begin with technological discontinuities that create significant breakthroughs in performance or function. Technological discontinuities are followed by discontinuous change, in which customers purchase new technologies and companies compete to establish the new dominant design. Dominant designs emerge because of critical mass, because they solve a practical problem, or because of the negotiations of independent standards bodies. Because technological innovation both enhances and destroys competence, companies that bet on the wrong design often struggle, while companies that bet on the eventual dominant design usually prosper. When a dominant design emerges, companies focus on incremental change, lowering costs and making small but steady improvements in the dominant design. This focus continues until the next technological discontinuity occurs.

Review 2: Managing Innovation

> To successfully manage innovation streams, companies must manage the sources of innovation and learn to manage innovation during both discontinuous and incremental change. Since innovation begins with creativity, companies can manage the sources of innovation by supporting a work environment in which creative thoughts and ideas are welcomed, valued, and encouraged. Creative work environments provide challenging work; offer organizational, supervisory, and work group encouragement; allow significant freedom; and remove organizational impediments to creativity.

Discontinuous and incremental change require different strategies, as shown below. Companies that succeed in periods of discontinuous change typically follow an experiential approach to innovation. The experiential approach assumes that intuition, flexible options, and hands-on experience can reduce uncertainty and accelerate learning and understanding. A compression approach to innovation works best during periods of incremental change. This approach assumes that innovation can be planned using a series of steps and that compressing the time it takes to complete those steps can speed up innovation.

	Experiential Approach to Innovation: Managing Innovation During Discontinuous Change	Compression Approach to Innovation: Managing Innovation During Incremental Change

Environment	Highly uncertain
	    discontinuous change - technological substitution and design competition
		Certain
		    incremental change - established technology (i.e., dominant design)

Goals	Speed Significant improvements in performance Establishment of new dominant design	Speed Lower costs Incremental improvements in performance of dominant design
Approach	Build something new, different, and substantially better	Compress time and steps needed to bring about small improvements
Steps	Design iterations Testing Milestones Multifunctional teams Powerful leaders	Planning Supplier involvement Shortening the time of individual steps Overlapping steps Multifunctional teams

KEY TERMS

Organizational innovation the successful implementation of creative ideas in organizations

Creativity the production of novel and useful ideas

Organizational change a difference in the form, quality, or condition of an organization over time

Technology cycle a cycle that begins with the birth of a new technology and ends when that technology reaches its limits and is replaced by a newer, substantially better technology

S-curve pattern of innovation a pattern of technological innovation characterized by slow initial progress, then rapid progress, and then slow progress again as a technology matures and reaches its limits

Innovation streams patterns of innovation over time that can create sustainable competitive advantage

Technological discontinuity a scientific advance or a unique combination of existing technologies creates a significant breakthrough in performance or function

Discontinuous change the phase of a technology cycle characterized by technological substitution and design competition

Technological substitution the purchase of new technologies to replace older ones

Design competition competition between old and new technologies to establish a new technological standard or dominant design

Dominant design a new technological design or process that becomes the accepted market standard

Technological lockout when a new dominant design (i.e., a significantly better technology) prevents a company from competitively selling its products or makes it difficult to do so

Incremental change the phase of a technology cycle in which companies innovate by lowering costs and improving the functioning and performance of the dominant technological design

Creative work environments workplace cultures in which workers perceive that new ideas are welcomed, valued, and encouraged

Flow a psychological state of effortlessness, in which you become completely absorbed in what you're doing and time seems to pass quickly

Experiential approach to innovation an approach to innovation that assumes a highly uncertain environment and uses intuition, flexible options, and hands-on experience to reduce uncertainty and accelerate learning and understanding

Design iteration a cycle of repetition in which a company tests a prototype of a new product or service, improves on that design, and then builds and tests the improved prototype

Product prototype a full-scale, working model that is being tested for design, function, and reliability

Testing the systematic comparison of different product designs or design iterations

Milestones formal project review points used to assess progress and performance

Multifunctional teams work teams composed of people from different departments

Compression approach to innovation an approach to innovation that assumes that incremental innovation can be planned using a series of steps and that compressing those steps can speed innovation

Generational change change based on incremental improvements to a dominant technological design such that the improved technology is fully backward compatible with the older technology

Organizational decline a large decrease in organizational performance that occurs when companies don't anticipate, recognize, neutralize, or adapt to the internal or external pressures that threaten their survival

Change forces forces that produce differences in the form, quality, or condition of an organization over time

Resistance forces forces that support the existing state of conditions in organizations

Resistance to change opposition to change resulting from self-interest, misunderstanding and distrust, and a general intolerance for change

Unfreezing getting the people affected by change to believe that change is needed

Change intervention the process used to get workers and managers to change their behavior and work practices

Review 3: Organizational Decline: The Risk of Not Changing

> The five-stage process of organizational decline begins when organizations don't recognize the need for change. In the blinded stage, managers fail to recognize the changes that threaten their organization's survival. In the inaction stage, management recognizes the need to change but doesn't act, hoping that the problems will correct themselves. In the faulty action stage, management focuses on cost cutting and efficiency rather than facing up to the fundamental changes needed to ensure survival. In the crisis stage, failure is likely unless fundamental reorganization occurs. Finally, in the dissolution stage, the company is dissolved through bankruptcy proceedings; by selling assets to pay creditors; or through the closing of stores, offices, and facilities. If companies recognize the need to change early enough, however, dissolution may be avoided.

Review 4: Managing Change

> The basic change process involves unfreezing, change, and refreezing. Resistance to change stems from self-interest, misunderstanding, and distrust as well as a general intolerance for change. It can be managed through education and communication, participation, negotiation, top management support, and coercion. Knowing what not to do is as important as knowing what to do to achieve successful change. Managers should avoid these errors when leading change: not establishing urgency, not creating a guiding coalition, lacking a vision, undercommunicating the vision, not removing obstacles to the vision, not creating short-term wins, declaring victory too soon, and not anchoring changes in the corporation's culture. Finally, managers can use a number of change techniques. Results-driven change and the GE workout reduce resistance to change by getting change efforts off to a fast start. Organizational development is a collection of planned change interventions (large system, small group, person-focused), guided by a change agent, that are designed to improve an organization's long-term health and performance.

Different Kinds of Organizational Development Interventions

LARGE SYSTEM INTERVENTIONS	
Sociotechnical systems	An intervention designed to improve how well employees use and adjust to the work technology used in an organization.
Survey feedback	An intervention that uses surveys to collect information from the members, reports the results of that survey to the members, and then uses those results to develop action plans for improvement.
SMALL GROUP INTERVENTIONS	
Team building	An intervention designed to increase the cohesion and cooperation of work group members.
Unit goal setting	An intervention designed to help a work group establish short- and long-term goals.
PERSON-FOCUSED INTERVENTIONS	
Counseling/coaching	An intervention designed so that a formal helper or coach listens to managers or employees and advises them on how to deal with work or interpersonal problems.
Training	An intervention designed to provide individuals with the knowledge, skills, or attitudes they need to become more effective at their jobs.

Source: W. J. Rothwell, R. Sullivan, & G. M. McLean, *Practicing Organizational Development: A Guide for Consultants* (San Diego: Pfeiffer & Co., 1995).

Refreezing supporting and reinforcing new changes so that they stick

Coercion using formal power and authority to force others to change

Results-driven change change created quickly by focusing on the measurement and improvement of results

General Electric workout a three-day meeting in which managers and employees from different levels and parts of an organization quickly generate and act on solutions to specific business problems

Organizational development a philosophy and collection of planned change interventions designed to improve an organization's long-term health and performance

Change agent the person formally in charge of guiding a change effort

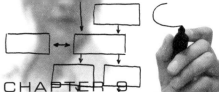

REVIEW card/

CHAPTER 9

LEARNING OUTCOMES

Review 1: Departmentalization

❯ There are five traditional departmental structures: functional, product, customer, geographic, and matrix. Functional departmentalization is based on the different business functions or types of expertise used to run a business. Product departmentalization is organized according to the different products or services a company sells. Customer departmentalization focuses its divisions on the different kinds of customers a company has. Geographic departmentalization is based on the different geographic areas or markets in which the company does business. Matrix departmentalization is a hybrid form that combines two or more forms of departmentalization, the most common being the product and functional forms. There is no single best departmental structure. Each structure has advantages and disadvantages.

Review 2: Organizational Authority

❯ Organizational authority is determined by the chain of command, line versus staff authority, delegation, and the degree of centralization in a company. The chain of command vertically connects every job in the company to higher levels of management and makes clear who reports to whom. Managers have line authority to command employees below them in the chain of command but have only staff, or advisory, authority over employees not below them in the chain of command. Managers delegate authority by transferring to subordinates the authority and responsibility needed to do a task; in exchange, subordinates become accountable for task completion. In centralized companies, most authority to make decisions lies with managers in the upper levels of the company. In decentralized companies, much of the authority is delegated to the workers closest to problems, who can then make the decisions necessary for solving the problems themselves.

Delegation: Responsibility, Authority, and Accountability

Source: C. D. Pringle, D. F. Jennings, and J. G. Longenecker, *Managing Organizations: Functions and Behaviors* © 1990. Adapted by permission of Pearson Education, Inc., Upper Saddle River, NJ.

Review 3: Job Design

❯ Companies use specialized jobs because they are economical and easy to learn and don't require highly paid workers. However, specialized jobs aren't motivating or particularly satisfying for employees. Companies have used job rotation, job enlargement, job enrichment, and the job characteristics model to make specialized jobs more interesting and motivating. The goal of the job characteristics model is to make jobs intrinsically motivating. For this to happen, jobs must be strong on five core job characteristics (skill variety, task identity, task significance, autonomy, and feedback), and workers must experience three critical psychological states (knowledge of results, responsibility for work outcomes, and meaningful work). If jobs aren't internally motivating, they can be redesigned by combining tasks, forming natural work units, establishing client relationships, vertical loading, and opening feedback channels.

KEY TERMS

Organizational structure the vertical and horizontal configuration of departments, authority, and jobs within a company

Organizational process the collection of activities that transform inputs into outputs that customers value

Departmentalization subdividing work and workers into separate organizational units responsible for completing particular tasks

Functional departmentalization organizing work and workers into separate units responsible for particular business functions or areas of expertise

Product departmentalization organizing work and workers into separate units responsible for producing particular products or services

Customer departmentalization organizing work and workers into separate units responsible for particular kinds of customers

Geographic departmentalization organizing work and workers into separate units responsible for doing business in particular geographic areas

Matrix departmentalization a hybrid organizational structure in which two or more forms of departmentalization, most often product and functional, are used together

Simple matrix a form of matrix departmentalization in which managers in different parts of the matrix negotiate conflicts and resources

Complex matrix a form of matrix departmentalization in which managers in different parts of the matrix report to matrix managers, who help them sort out conflicts and problems

Authority the right to give commands, take action, and make decisions to achieve organizational objectives

Chain of command the vertical line of authority that clarifies who reports to whom throughout the organization

Unity of command a management principle that workers should report to just one boss

Line authority the right to command immediate subordinates in the chain of command

Staff authority the right to advise, but not command, others who are not subordinates in the chain of command

Line function an activity that contributes directly to creating or selling the company's products

Staff function an activity that does not contribute directly to creating or selling the company's products, but instead supports line activities

Delegation of authority the assignment of direct authority and responsibility to a subordinate to complete tasks for which the manager is normally responsible

Centralization of authority the location of most authority at the upper levels of the organization

Decentralization the location of a significant amount of authority in the lower levels of the organization

Standardization solving problems by consistently applying the same rules, procedures, and processes

Job design the number, kind, and variety of tasks that individual workers perform in doing their jobs

Job specialization a job composed of a small part of a larger task or process

Job rotation periodically moving workers from one specialized job to another to give them more variety and the opportunity to use different skills

Job enlargement increasing the number of different tasks that a worker performs within one particular job

Job enrichment increasing the number of tasks in a particular job and giving workers the authority and control to make meaningful decisions about their work

Job characteristics model (JCM) an approach to job redesign that seeks to formulate jobs in ways that motivate workers and lead to positive work outcomes

Internal motivation motivation that comes from the job itself rather than from outside rewards

Skill variety the number of different activities performed in a job

Task identity the degree to which a job, from beginning to end, requires the completion of a whole and identifiable piece of work

Task significance the degree to which a job is perceived to have a substantial impact on others inside or outside the organization

Autonomy the degree to which a job gives workers the discretion, freedom, and independence to decide how and when to accomplish the job

Feedback the amount of information the job provides to workers about their work performance

Mechanistic organization an organization characterized by specialized jobs and responsibilities; precisely defined, unchanging roles; and a rigid chain of command based on centralized authority and vertical communication

Organic organization an organization characterized by broadly defined jobs and responsibility; loosely defined, frequently changing roles; and decentralized authority and horizontal communication based on task knowledge

Intraorganizational process the collection of activities that take place within an organization to transform inputs into outputs that customers value

Reengineering fundamental rethinking and radical redesign of business processes to achieve dramatic improvements in critical measures of performance, such as cost, quality, service, and speed

Task interdependence the extent to which collective action is required to complete an entire piece of work

Pooled interdependence work completed by having each job or department independently contribute to the whole

Sequential interdependence work completed in succession, with one group's or job's outputs becoming the inputs for the next group or job

Reciprocal interdependence work completed by different jobs or groups working together in a back-and-forth manner

Empowering workers permanently passing decision-making authority and responsibility from managers to workers by giving them the information and resources they need to make and carry out good decisions

Empowerment feelings of intrinsic motivation, in which workers perceive their work to have impact and meaning and perceive themselves to be competent and capable of self-determination

Interorganizational process a collection of activities that take place among companies to transform inputs into outputs that customers value

Modular organization an organization that outsources noncore business activities to outside companies, suppliers, specialists, or consultants

Virtual organization an organization that is part of a network in which many companies share skills, costs, capabilities, markets, and customers to collectively solve customer problems or provide specific products or services

Review 4: Intraorganizational Processes

> Today, companies are using reengineering and empowerment to change their intraorganizational processes. Reengineering changes an organization's orientation from vertical to horizontal and its work processes by decreasing sequential and pooled interdependence and by increasing reciprocal interdependence. Reengineering promises dramatic increases in productivity and customer satisfaction, but it has been criticized as simply an excuse to cut costs and lay off workers. Empowering workers means taking decision-making authority and responsibility from managers and giving it to workers. Empowered workers develop feelings of competence and self-determination and believe that their work has meaning and impact.

Pooled Interdependence

and

Sequential Interdependence

Reciprocal Interdependence

Review 5: Interorganizational Processes

> Organizations are using modular and virtual organizations to change interorganizational processes. Because modular organizations outsource all noncore activities to other businesses, they are less expensive to run than traditional companies. However, modular organizations require extremely close relationships with suppliers, may result in a loss of control, and could create new competitors if the wrong business activities are outsourced. Virtual organizations participate in a network in which they share skills, costs, capabilities, markets, and customers. Virtual organizations can reduce costs, respond quickly, and, if they can successfully coordinate their efforts, produce outstanding products and service.

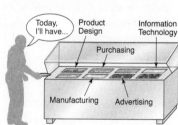

Today, I'll have... Product Design Information Technology Purchasing Manufacturing Advertising

Trivia answer: The original Mechanical Turk was an 18th-century chess playing automaton that purportedly could beat anyone at chess. The Turk was a mannequin, but the machine concealed a human chess master who would actuate the Turk with mechanical controls. The Turk beat many statesmen and luminaries, including Napoleon Bonaparte and Benjamin Franklin. Read more in Tom Standage's book *The Mechanical Turk*.

LEARNING OUTCOMES

Review 1: The Good and Bad of Using Teams

> In many industries, teams are growing in importance because they help organizations respond to specific problems and challenges. Teams have been shown to increase customer satisfaction (specific customer teams), product and service quality (direct responsibility), and employee job satisfaction (cross training, unique opportunities, and leadership responsibilities). Although teams can produce significant improvements in these areas, using teams does not guarantee these positive outcomes. Teams and teamwork have the disadvantages of initially high turnover and social loafing (especially in large groups). Teams also share many of the advantages (multiple perspectives, generation of more alternatives, and more commitment) and disadvantages (groupthink, time, poorly run meetings, domination by a few team members, and weak accountability) of group decision making. Teams should be used for a clear purpose, when the work requires that people work together, when rewards can be provided for both teamwork and team performance, when ample resources can be provided, and when teams can be given clear authority over their work.

ADVANTAGES AND DISADVANTAGES OF TEAMS

ADVANTAGES 👍	DISADVANTAGES 👎
☺ Customer satisfaction	☹ Initially high employee turnover
☺ Product and service quality	☹ Social loafing
☺ Speed and efficiency in product development	☹ Disadvantages of group decision making (groupthink, inefficient meetings, domination by a minority, lack of accountability)
☺ Employee job satisfaction	
☺ Better decision making and problem solving (multiple perspectives, more alternative solutions, increased commitment to decisions)	

Review 2: Kinds of Teams

> Companies use different kinds of teams to make themselves more competitive. Autonomy is the key dimension that makes teams different. Traditional work groups (which execute tasks) and employee involvement groups (which make suggestions) have the lowest levels of autonomy. Semi-autonomous work groups (which control major, direct tasks) have more autonomy, while self-managing teams (which control all direct tasks) and self-designing teams (which control membership and how tasks are done) have the highest levels of autonomy. Cross-functional, virtual, and project teams are common but are not easily categorized in terms of autonomy. Cross-functional teams combine employees from different functional areas to help teams attack problems from multiple perspectives and generate more ideas and solutions. Virtual teams use telecommunications and information technologies to bring coworkers together, regardless of physical location or time zone. Virtual teams reduce travel and work time, but communication may suffer since team members don't work face-to-face. Finally, project teams are used for specific, one-time projects or tasks that must be completed within a limited time. Project teams reduce communication barriers and promote flexibility; teams and team members are reassigned to their departments or new projects as old projects are completed.

KEY TERMS

Work team a small number of people with complementary skills who hold themselves mutually accountable for pursuing a common purpose, achieving performance goals, and improving interdependent work processes

Cross-training training team members to do all or most of the jobs performed by the other team members

Social loafing behavior in which team members withhold their efforts and fail to perform their share of the work

Traditional work group a group composed of two or more people who work together to achieve a shared goal

Employee involvement team team that provides advice or makes suggestions to management concerning specific issues

Semi-autonomous work group a group that has the authority to make decisions and solve problems related to the major tasks of producing a product or service

Self-managing team a team that manages and controls all of the major tasks of producing a product or service

Self-designing team a team that has the characteristics of self-managing teams but also controls team design, work tasks, and team membership

Cross-functional team a team composed of employees from different functional areas of the organization

Virtual team a team composed of geographically and/or organizationally dispersed coworkers who use telecommunication and information technologies to accomplish an organizational task

Project team a team created to complete specific, one-time projects or tasks within a limited time

Norms informally agreed-on standards that regulate team behavior

Cohesiveness the extent to which team members are attracted to a team and motivated to remain in it

Forming the first stage of team development, in which team members meet each other, form initial impressions, and begin to establish team norms

Storming the second stage of development, characterized by conflict and disagreement, in which team members disagree over what the team should do and how it should do it

Norming the third stage of team development, in which team members begin to settle into their roles, group cohesion grows, and positive team norms develop

Performing the fourth and final stage of team development, in which performance improves because the team has matured into an effective, fully functioning team

Structural accommodation the ability to change organizational structures, policies, and practices in order to meet stretch goals

Bureaucratic immunity the ability to make changes without first getting approval from managers or other parts of an organization

Individualism-collectivism the degree to which a person believes that people should be self-sufficient and that loyalty to one's self is more important than loyalty to team or company

Team level the average level of ability, experience, personality, or any other factor on a team

Team diversity the variances or differences in ability, experience, personality, or any other factor on a team

Interpersonal skills skills, such as listening, communicating, questioning, and providing feedback, that enable people to have effective working relationships with others

Skill-based pay compensation system that pays employees for learning additional skills or knowledge

Gainsharing a compensation system in which companies share the financial value of performance gains, such as productivity, cost savings, or quality, with their workers

Review 3: Work Team Characteristics

> The most important characteristics of work teams are team norms, cohesiveness, size, conflict, and development. Norms let team members know what is expected of them and can influence team behavior in positive and negative ways. Positive team norms are associated with organizational commitment, trust, and job satisfaction. Team cohesiveness helps teams retain members, promotes cooperative behavior, increases motivation, and facilitates team performance. Attending team meetings and activities, creating opportunities to work together, and engaging in non-work activities can increase cohesiveness. Team size has a curvilinear relationship with team performance: teams that are very small or very large do not perform as well as moderate-sized teams of six to nine members. Teams of this size are cohesive and small enough for team members to get to know each other and contribute in a meaningful way but are large enough to take advantage of team members' diverse skills, knowledge, and perspectives. Conflict and disagreement are inevitable in most teams. The key to dealing with team conflict is to maximize cognitive conflict, which focuses on issue-related differences, and minimize affective conflict, the emotional reactions that occur when disagreements become personal rather than professional. As teams develop and grow, they pass through four stages of development: forming, storming, norming, and performing. If a team is not managed well, its performance may decline after a period of time as the team regresses through the stages of de-norming, de-storming, and de-forming.

HOW TEAMS CAN HAVE A GOOD FIGHT

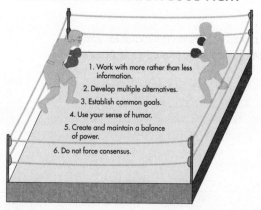

1. Work with more rather than less information.
2. Develop multiple alternatives.
3. Establish common goals.
4. Use your sense of humor.
5. Create and maintain a balance of power.
6. Do not force consensus.

Source: K. M. Eisenhardt, J. L. Kahwajy, and L. J. Bourgeois III, "How Management Teams Can Have a Good Fight," *Harvard Business Review* 75, no. 4 (July-August 1997): 77–85.

Review 4: Enhancing Work Team Effectiveness

> Companies can make teams more effective by setting team goals and managing how team members are selected, trained, and compensated. Team goals provide a clear focus and purpose, reduce the incidence of social loafing, and lead to higher team performance 93 percent of the time. Extremely difficult stretch goals can be used to motivate teams as long as teams have autonomy, control over resources, structural accommodation, and bureaucratic immunity. Not everyone is suited for teamwork. When selecting team members, companies should select people who have a preference for teamwork (individualism-collectivism) and should consider team level (average ability on a team) and team diversity (different abilities on a team). Organizations that successfully use teams provide thousands of hours of training to make sure that teams work. The most common types of team training are for interpersonal skills, decision-making and problem-solving skills, conflict resolution, technical training to help team members learn multiple jobs (i.e., cross training), and training for team leaders. Employees can be compensated for team participation and accomplishments in three ways: skill-based pay, gainsharing, and nonfinancial rewards.

LEARNING OUTCOMES

Review 1: Employment Legislation

> Human resource management is subject to numerous major federal employment laws and subject to review by several federal agencies. In general, these laws indicate that sex, age, religion, color, national origin, race, disability, and pregnancy may not be considered in employment decisions unless these factors reasonably qualify as BFOQs. Two important criteria, disparate treatment (intentional discrimination) and adverse impact (unintentional discrimination), are used to decide whether companies have wrongly discriminated against someone. The two kinds of sexual harassment are quid pro quo and hostile work environment.

Review 2: Recruiting

> Recruiting is the process of finding qualified job applicants. The first step in recruiting is to conduct a job analysis, which is used to write a job description of basic tasks, duties, and responsibilities and to write job specifications indicating the knowledge, skills, and abilities needed to perform the job. Whereas internal recruiting involves finding qualified job applicants from inside the company, external recruiting involves finding qualified job applicants from outside the company.

Importance of Job Analysis to Human Resource Management

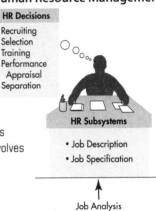

Review 3: Selection

> Selection is the process of gathering information about job applicants to decide who should be offered a job. Accurate selection procedures are valid, are legally defendable, and improve organizational performance. Application forms and résumés are the most common selection devices. Managers should check references and conduct background checks even though previous employers are often reluctant to provide such information for fear of being sued for defamation. Unfortunately, without this information, other employers are at risk of negligent hiring lawsuits. Selection tests generally do the best job of predicting applicants' future job performance. The three kinds of job interviews are unstructured, structured, and semistructured interviews.

Review 4: Training

> Training is used to give employees the job-specific skills, experience, and knowledge they need to do their jobs or improve their job performance. To make sure training dollars are well spent, companies need to determine specific training needs, select appropriate training methods, and then evaluate the training.

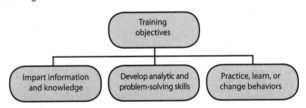

Review 5: Performance Appraisal

> The keys to successful performance appraisal are accurately measuring job performance and effectively sharing performance feedback with employees. Organizations should develop good performance appraisal scales; train raters how to accurately evaluate performance; and impress upon managers the value of providing feedback in a clear, consistent, and fair manner, as well as setting goals and monitoring progress toward those goals.

Review 6: Compensation and Employee Separation

> Compensation includes both the financial and the nonfinancial rewards that organizations give employees in exchange for their work. There are three basic kinds of compensation decisions: pay level, pay variability, and pay structure. Employee separation is the loss of an employee, which can occur voluntarily or involuntarily. Companies use downsizing and early retirement incentive programs to reduce the number of employees in the organization and lower costs. However, companies generally try to keep the rate of employee turnover low to reduce costs associated with finding and developing new employees. Functional turnover, on the other hand, can be good for organizations.

Kinds of Compensation Decisions

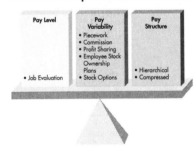

KEY TERMS

Human resource management (HRM) the process of finding, developing, and keeping the right people to form a qualified work force

Bona fide occupational qualification (BFOQ) an exception in employment law that permits sex, age, religion, and the like to be used when making employment decisions, but only if they are "reasonably necessary to the normal operation of that particular business." BFOQs are strictly monitored by the Equal Employment Opportunity Commission.

Disparate treatment intentional discrimination that occurs when people are purposely not given the same hiring, promotion, or membership opportunities because of their race, color, sex, age, ethnic group, national origin, or religious beliefs

Adverse impact unintentional discrimination that occurs when members of a particular race, sex, or ethnic group are unintentionally harmed or disadvantaged because they are hired, promoted, or trained (or any other employment decision) at substantially lower rates than others

Four-fifths (or 80 percent) rule a rule of thumb used by the courts and the EEOC to determine whether there is evidence of adverse impact. A violation of this rule occurs when the selection rate for a protected group is less than 80 percent or four-fifths of the selection rate for a nonprotected group.

Sexual harassment a form of discrimination in which unwelcome sexual advances, requests for sexual favors, or other verbal or physical conduct of a sexual nature occurs while performing one's job

Quid pro quo sexual harassment a form of sexual harassment in which employment outcomes, such as hiring, promotion, or simply keeping one's job, depend on whether an individual submits to sexual harassment

Hostile work environment a form of sexual harassment in which unwelcome and demeaning sexually related behavior creates an intimidating and offensive work environment

Recruiting the process of developing a pool of qualified job applicants

Job analysis a purposeful, systematic process for collecting information on the important work-related aspects of a job

Job description a written description of the basic tasks, duties, and responsibilities required of an employee holding a particular job

Job specifications a written summary of the qualifications needed to successfully perform a particular job

Internal recruiting the process of developing a pool of qualified job applicants from people who already work in the company

External recruiting the process of developing a pool of qualified job applicants from outside the company

Selection the process of gathering information about job applicants to decide who should be offered a job

Validation the process of determining how well a selection test or procedure predicts future job performance. The better or more accurate the prediction of future job performance, the more valid a test is said to be.

Employment references sources such as previous employers or coworkers who can provide job-related information about job candidates

Background checks procedures used to verify the truthfulness and accuracy of information that applicants provide about themselves and to uncover negative, job-related background information not provided by applicants

Specific ability tests (aptitude tests) tests that measure the extent to which an applicant possesses the particular kind of ability needed to do a job well

Cognitive ability tests tests that measure the extent to which applicants have abilities in perceptual speed, verbal comprehension, numerical aptitude, general reasoning, and spatial aptitude

Biographical data (bio-data) extensive surveys that ask applicants questions about their personal backgrounds and life experiences

Work sample tests tests that require applicants to perform tasks that are actually done on the job

Assessment centers a series of managerial simulations, graded by trained observers, that are used to determine applicants' capability for managerial work

Interviews a selection tool in which company representatives ask job applicants job-related questions to determine whether they are qualified for the job

Unstructured interviews interviews in which interviewers are free to ask the applicants anything they want

Structured interviews interviews in which all applicants are asked the same set of standardized questions, usually including situational, behavioral, background, and job-knowledge questions

Training developing the skills, experience, and knowledge employees need to perform their jobs or improve their performance

Needs assessment the process of identifying and prioritizing the learning needs of employees

Performance appraisal the process of assessing how well employees are doing their jobs

Objective performance measures measures of job performance that are easily and directly counted or quantified

Behavioral observation scales (BOSs) rating scales that indicate the frequency with which workers perform specific behaviors that are representative of the job dimensions critical to successful job performance

Rater training training performance appraisal raters in how to avoid rating errors and increase rating accuracy

360-degree feedback a performance appraisal process in which feedback is obtained from the boss, subordinates, peers and coworkers, and the employees themselves

Compensation the financial and nonfinancial rewards that organizations give employees in exchange for their work

Employee separation the voluntary or involuntary loss of an employee

Job evaluation a process that determines the worth of each job in a company by evaluating the market value of the knowledge, skills, and requirements needed to perform it

Piecework a compensation system in which employees are paid a set rate for each item they produce

Commission a compensation system in which employees earn a percentage of each sale they make

Profit sharing a compensation system in which a company pays a percentage of its profits to employees in addition to their regular compensation

Employee stock ownership plan (ESOP) a compensation system that awards employees shares of company stock in addition to their regular compensation

Stock options a compensation system that gives employees the right to purchase shares of stock at a set price, even if the value of the stock increases above that price

Wrongful discharge a legal doctrine that requires employers to have a job-related reason to terminate employees

Downsizing the planned elimination of jobs in a company

Outplacement services employment-counseling services offered to employees who are losing their jobs because of downsizing

Early retirement incentive programs (ERIPs) programs that offer financial benefits to employees to encourage them to retire early

Phased retirement employees transition to retirement by working reduced hours over a period of time before completely retiring

Employee turnover loss of employees who voluntarily choose to leave the company

Functional turnover loss of poor-performing employees who voluntarily choose to leave a company

Dysfunctional turnover loss of high-performing employees who voluntarily choose to leave a company

LEARNING OUTCOMES

Review 1: Diversity: Differences That Matter

> Diversity exists in organizations when there are demographic, cultural, and personal differences among the people who work there and the customers who do business there. A common misconception is that workplace diversity and affirmative action are the same. However, affirmative action is more narrowly focused on demographics; is required by law; and is used to punish companies that discriminate on the basis of race, color, religion, sex, or national origin. By contrast, diversity is broader in focus (going beyond demographics); voluntary; more positive in that it encourages companies to value all kinds of differences; and, at this time, substantially less controversial than affirmative action. Affirmative action and diversity thus differ in purpose, practice, and the reactions they produce. Diversity also makes good business sense in terms of cost savings (reducing turnover, decreasing absenteeism, and avoiding lawsuits), attracting and retaining talent, and driving business growth (improving marketplace understanding and promoting higher-quality problem solving).

General Purpose of Diversity Programs

To create a positive work environment where

- no one is advantaged or disadvantaged.
- "we" is everyone.
- everyone can do his or her best work.
- differences are respected and not ignored.
- everyone feels comfortable.

Source: T. Roosevelt, "From Affirmative Action to Affirming Diversity," *Harvard Business Review* 68, no. 2 (1990): 107–117.

Review 2: Surface-Level Diversity

> Age, sex, race/ethnicity, and physical and mental disabilities are dimensions of surface-level diversity. Because those dimensions are (usually) easily observed, managers and workers tend to rely on them to form initial impressions and stereotypes. Sometimes this can lead to age, sex, racial/ethnic, or disability discrimination (i.e., treating people differently) in the workplace. In general, older workers, women, people of color or different national origins, and people with disabilities are much less likely to be hired or promoted than white males. This disparity is often due to incorrect beliefs or stereotypes such as "job performance declines with age," or "women aren't willing to travel on business," or "workers with disabilities aren't as competent as able workers." To reduce discrimination, companies can determine the hiring and promotion rates for different groups, train managers to make hiring and promotion decisions on the basis of specific criteria, and make sure that everyone has equal access to training, mentors, reasonable work accommodations, and assistive technology. Finally, companies need to designate a go-to person that employees can talk to if they believe they have suffered discrimination.

KEY TERMS

Diversity a variety of demographic, cultural, and personal differences among an organization's employees and customers

Affirmative action purposeful steps taken by an organization to create employment opportunities for minorities and women

Surface-level diversity differences such as age, sex, race/ethnicity, and physical disabilities that are observable, typically unchangeable, and easy to measure

Deep-level diversity differences such as personality and attitudes that are communicated through verbal and nonverbal behaviors and are learned only through extended interaction with others

Social integration the degree to which group members are psychologically attracted to working with each other to accomplish a common objective

Age discrimination treating people differently (e.g., in hiring and firing, promotion, and compensation decisions) because of their age

Sex discrimination treating people differently because of their sex

Glass ceiling the invisible barrier that prevents women and minorities from advancing to the top jobs in organizations

Racial and ethnic discrimination treating people differently because of their race or ethnicity

Disability a mental or physical impairment that substantially limits one or more major life activities

Disability discrimination treating people differently because of their disabilities

Disposition the tendency to respond to situations and events in a predetermined manner

Personality the relatively stable set of behaviors, attitudes, and emotions displayed over time that makes people different from each other

Extraversion the degree to which someone is active, assertive, gregarious, sociable, talkative, and energized by others

Emotional stability the degree to which someone is not angry, depressed, anxious, emotional, insecure, and excitable

Agreeableness the degree to which someone is cooperative, polite, flexible, forgiving, good-natured, tolerant, and trusting

Conscientiousness the degree to which someone is organized, hardworking, responsible, persevering, thorough, and achievement oriented

Openness to experience the degree to which someone is curious, broad-minded, and open to new ideas, things, and experiences; is spontaneous; and has a high tolerance for ambiguity

Organizational plurality a work environment where (1) all members are empowered to contribute in a way that maximizes the benefits to the organization, customers, and themselves, and (2) the individuality of each member is respected by not segmenting or polarizing people on the basis of their membership in a particular group

Awareness training training that is designed to raise employees' awareness of diversity issues and to challenge the underlying assumptions or stereotypes they may have about others

Skills-based diversity training training that teaches employees the practical skills they need for managing a diverse work force, such as flexibility and adaptability, negotiation, problem solving, and conflict resolution

Diversity audits formal assessments that measure employee and management attitudes, investigate the extent to which people are advantaged or disadvantaged with respect to hiring and promotions, and review companies' diversity-related policies and procedures

Diversity pairing a mentoring program in which people of different cultural backgrounds, sexes, or races/ethnicities are paired together to get to know each other and change stereotypical beliefs and attitudes

Review 3: Deep-Level Diversity

> Deep-level diversity matters because it can reduce prejudice, discrimination, and conflict while increasing social integration. It consists of dispositional and personality differences that can be learned only through extended interaction with others. Research conducted in different cultures, settings, and languages indicates that there are five basic dimensions of personality: extraversion, emotional stability, agreeableness, conscientiousness, and openness to experience. Of these, conscientiousness is perhaps the most important because conscientious workers tend to be better performers on virtually any job. Extraversion is also related to performance in jobs that require significant interaction with others.

Review 4: Managing Diversity

> The three paradigms for managing diversity are the discrimination and fairness paradigm (equal opportunity, fair treatment, strict compliance with the law), the access and legitimacy paradigm (matching internal diversity to external diversity), and the learning and effectiveness paradigm (achieving organizational plurality by integrating deep-level diversity into the work of the organization). Unlike the other paradigms that focus on surface-level differences, the learning and effectiveness program values common ground, distinguishes between individual and group differences, minimizes conflict and divisiveness, and focuses on bringing different talents and perspectives together. What principles can companies use when managing diversity? Follow and enforce federal and state laws regarding equal employment opportunity. Treat group differences as important, but not special. Find the common ground. Tailor opportunities to individuals, not groups. Reexamine, but maintain, high standards. Solicit negative as well as positive feedback. Set high but realistic goals. The two types of diversity training are awareness training and skills-based diversity training. Companies also manage diversity through diversity audits and diversity pairing and by having top executives experience what it is like to be in the minority.

Paradigms for Managing Diversity

DIVERSITY PARADIGM	FOCUS	SUCCESS MEASURED BY	BENEFITS	LIMITATIONS
Discrimination & Fairness	Equal opportunity Fair treatment Recruitment of minorities Strict compliance with laws	Recruitment, promotion, and retention goals for underrepresented group	Fairer treatment Increased demographic diversity	Focus on surface-level diversity
Access & Legitimacy	Acceptance and celebration of differences	Diversity in company matches diversity of primary stakeholders	Establishes a clear business reason for diversity	Focus on surface-level diversity
Learning & Effectiveness	Integrating deep-level differences into organization	Valuing people on the basis of individual knowledge, skills, and abilities	Values common ground Distinction between individual and group differences Less conflict, backlash, and divisiveness Bringing different talents and perspectives together	Focus on deep-level diversity is more difficult to measure and quantify

CHAPTER 13

REVIEW card/

LEARNING OUTCOMES

Review 1: Basics of Motivation

> Motivation is the set of forces that initiates, directs, and makes people persist in their efforts over time to accomplish a goal. Managers often confuse motivation and performance, but job performance is a multiplicative function of motivation times ability times situational constraints. Needs are the physical or psychological requirements that must be met to ensure survival and well-being. Different motivational theories (Maslow's Hierarchy of Needs, Alderfer's ERG Theory, and McClelland's Learned Needs Theory) specify a number of different needs. However, studies show that there are only two general kinds of needs, lower-order needs and higher-order needs. Both extrinsic and intrinsic rewards motivate people.

MOTIVATING TO INCREASE EFFORT

- Start by asking people what their needs are.
- Satisfy lower-order needs first.
- Expect people's needs to change.
- As needs change and lower-order needs are satisfied, satisfy higher-order needs by looking for ways to allow employees to experience intrinsic rewards.

Review 2: Equity Theory

> The basic components of equity theory are inputs, outcomes, and referents. After an internal comparison in which employees compare their outcomes to their inputs, they then make an external comparison in which they compare their O/I ratio with the O/I ratio of a referent, a person who works in a similar job or is otherwise similar. When their O/I ratio is equal to the referent's O/I ratio, employees perceive that they are being treated fairly. But, when their O/I ratio is different from their referent's O/I ratio, they perceive that they have been treated inequitably or unfairly. There are two kinds of inequity: underreward and overreward. Underreward, which occurs when a referent's O/I ratio is better than the employee's O/I ratio, leads to anger or frustration. Overreward, which occurs when a referent's O/I ratio is worse than the employee's O/I ratio, can lead to guilt but only when the level of overreward is extreme.

MOTIVATING WITH EQUITY THEORY

- Look for and correct major inequities.
- Reduce employees' inputs.
- Make sure decision-making processes are fair.

Review 3: Expectancy Theory

> Expectancy theory holds that three factors affect the conscious choices people make about their motivation: valence, expectancy, and instrumentality. Expectancy theory holds that all three factors must be high for people to be highly motivated. If any one of these factors declines, overall motivation will decline too.

MOTIVATING WITH EXPECTANCY THEORY

- Systematically gather information to find out what employees want from their jobs.
- Take specific steps to link rewards to individual performance in a way that is clear and understandable to employees.
- Empower employees to make decisions if management really wants them to believe that their hard work and effort will lead to good performance.

KEY TERMS

Motivation the set of forces that initiates, directs, and makes people persist in their efforts to accomplish a goal

Needs the physical or psychological requirements that must be met to ensure survival and well-being

Extrinsic reward a reward that is tangible, visible to others, and given to employees contingent on the performance of specific tasks or behaviors

Intrinsic reward a natural reward associated with performing a task or activity for its own sake

Equity theory a theory that states that people will be motivated when they perceive that they are being treated fairly

Inputs in equity theory, the contributions employees make to the organization

Outcomes in equity theory, the rewards employees receive for their contributions to the organization

Referents in equity theory, others with whom people compare themselves to determine if they have been treated fairly

Outcome/input (O/I) ratio in equity theory, an employee's perception of how the rewards received from an organization compare with the employee's contributions to that organization

Underreward a form of inequity in which you are getting fewer outcomes relative to inputs than your referent is getting

Overreward a form of inequity in which you are getting more outcomes relative to inputs than your referent

Distributive justice the perceived degree to which outcomes and rewards are fairly distributed or allocated

Procedural justice the perceived fairness of the process used to make reward allocation decisions

Expectancy theory a theory that states that people will be motivated to the extent to which they believe that their efforts will lead to good performance, that good performance will be rewarded, and that they will be offered attractive rewards

Valence the attractiveness or desirability of a reward or outcome

Expectancy the perceived relationship between effort and preformance

Instrumentality the perceived relationship between performance and rewards

Reinforcement theory a theory that states that behavior is a function of its consequences, that behaviors followed by positive consequences will occur more frequently, and that behaviors followed by negative consequences, or not followed by positive consequences, will occur less frequently

Reinforcement the process of changing behavior by changing the consequences that follow behavior

Reinforcement contingencies cause-and-effect relationships between the performance of specific behaviors and specific consequences

Schedule of reinforcement rules that specify which behaviors will be reinforced, which consequences will follow those behaviors, and the schedule by which those consequences will be delivered

Positive reinforcement reinforcement that strengthens behavior by following behaviors with desirable consequences

Negative reinforcement reinforcement that strengthens behavior by withholding an unpleasant consequence when employees perform a specific behavior

Punishment reinforcement that weakens behavior by following behaviors with undesirable consequences

Extinction reinforcement in which a positive consequence is no longer allowed to follow a previously reinforced behavior, thus weakening the behavior

Continuous reinforcement schedule a schedule that requires a consequence to be administered following every instance of a behavior

Intermittent reinforcement schedule a schedule in which consequences are delivered after a specified or average time has elapsed or after a specified or average number of behaviors has occurred

Fixed interval reinforcement schedule an intermittent schedule in which consequences follow a behavior only after a fixed time has elapsed

Variable interval reinforcement schedule an intermittent schedule in which the time between a behavior and the following consequences varies around a specified average

Fixed ratio reinforcement schedule an intermittent schedule in which consequences are delivered following a specific number of behaviors

Review 4: Reinforcement Theory

> Reinforcement theory says that behavior is a function of its consequences. Reinforcement has two parts: reinforcement contingencies and schedules of reinforcement. The four kinds of reinforcement contingencies are positive reinforcement and negative reinforcement, which strengthen behavior, and punishment and extinction, which weaken behavior. There are two kinds of reinforcement schedules, continuous and intermittent; intermittent schedules, in turn, can be divided into fixed and variable interval schedules and fixed and variable ratio schedules.

Review 5: Goal-Setting Theory

> A goal is a target, objective, or result that someone tries to accomplish. Goal-setting theory says that people will be motivated to the extent to which they accept specific, challenging goals and receive feedback that indicates their progress toward goal achievement. The basic components of goal-setting theory are goal specificity, goal difficulty, goal acceptance, and performance feedback. Goal specificity is the extent to which goals are detailed, exact, and unambiguous. Goal difficulty is the extent to which a goal is hard or challenging to accomplish. Goal acceptance is the extent to which people consciously understand and agree to goals. Performance feedback is information about the quality or quantity of past performance and indicates whether progress is being made toward the accomplishment of a goal.

Motivating with the Integrated Model

MOTIVATING WITH	MANAGERS SHOULD . . .
THE BASICS	• Ask people what their needs are. • Satisfy lower-order needs first. • Expect people's needs to change. • As needs change and lower-order needs are satisfied, satisfy higher-order needs by looking for ways to allow employees to experience intrinsic rewards.
EQUITY THEORY	• Look for and correct major inequities. • Reduce employees' inputs. • Make sure decision-making processes are fair.
EXPECTANCY THEORY	• Systematically gather information to find out what employees want from their jobs. • Take specific steps to link rewards to individual performance in a way that is clear and understandable to employees. • Empower employees to make decisions if management really wants them to believe that their hard work and efforts will lead to good performance.
REINFORCEMENT THEORY	• Identify, measure, analyze, intervene, and evaluate critical performance-related behaviors. • Don't reinforce the wrong behaviors. • Correctly administer punishment at the appropriate time. • Choose the simplest and most effective schedules of reinforcement.
GOAL-SETTING THEORY	• Assign specific, challenging goals. • Make sure workers truly accept organizational goals. • Provide frequent, specific, performance-related feedback.

Variable ratio reinforcement schedule an intermittent schedule in which consequences are delivered following a different number of behaviors, sometimes more and sometimes less, that vary around a specified average number of behaviors

Goal a target, objective, or result that someone tries to accomplish

Goal-setting theory a theory that states that people will be motivated to the extent to which they accept specific, challenging goals and receive feedback that indicates their progress toward goal achievement

Goal specificity the extent to which goals are detailed, exact, and unambiguous

Goal difficulty the extent to which a goal is hard or challenging to accomplish

Goal acceptance the extent to which people consciously understand and agree to goals

Performance feedback information about the quality or quantity of past performance that indicates whether progress is being made toward the accomplishment of a goal

LEARNING OUTCOMES

Review 1: Leaders Versus Managers

> Management is getting work done through others; leadership is the process of influencing others to achieve group or organizational goals. Leaders are different from managers. The primary difference is that leaders are concerned with doing the right thing, while managers are concerned with doing things right. Organizations need both managers and leaders. But, in general, companies are overmanaged and underled.

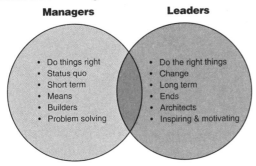

Managers
- Do things right
- Status quo
- Short term
- Means
- Builders
- Problem solving

Leaders
- Do the right things
- Change
- Long term
- Ends
- Architects
- Inspiring & motivating

Review 2: Who Leaders Are and What Leaders Do

> Trait theory says that effective leaders possess traits or characteristics that differentiate them from non-leaders. Those traits are drive, the desire to lead, honesty/integrity, self-confidence, emotional stability, cognitive ability, and knowledge of the business. These traits alone aren't enough for successful leadership; leaders who have many or all of them must also behave in ways that encourage people to achieve group or organizational goals. Two key leader behaviors are initiating structure, which improves subordinate performance, and consideration, which improves subordinate satisfaction. There is no ideal combination of these behaviors. The best leadership style depends on the situation.

Review 3: Putting Leaders in the Right Situation: Fiedler's Contingency Theory

> Fiedler's theory assumes that leaders are effective when their work groups perform well, that leaders are unable to change their leadership styles, that leadership styles must be matched to the proper situation, and that favorable situations permit leaders to influence group members. According to the Least Preferred Coworker (LPC) scale, there are two basic leadership styles. People who describe their LPC in a positive way have relationship-oriented leadership styles. By contrast, people who describe their LPC in a negative way have task-oriented leadership styles. Situational favorableness, which occurs when leaders can influence followers, is determined by leader-member relations, task structure, and position power. In general, relationship-oriented leaders with high LPC scores are better leaders under moderately favorable situations, while task-oriented leaders with low LPC scores are better leaders in highly favorable and unfavorable situations. Since Fiedler assumes that leaders are incapable of changing their leadership styles, the key is to accurately measure and match leaders to situations or to teach leaders how to change situational factors. Though matching or placing leaders in appropriate situations works well, reengineering situations to fit leadership styles doesn't because of the complexity of the model, which makes it difficult for people to understand.

KEY TERMS

Leadership the process of influencing others to achieve group or organizational goals

Trait theory a leadership theory that holds that effective leaders possess a similar set of traits or characteristics

Traits relatively stable characteristics, such as abilities, psychological motives, or consistent patterns of behavior

Initiating structure the degree to which a leader structures the roles of followers by setting goals, giving directions, setting deadlines, and assigning tasks

Consideration the extent to which a leader is friendly, approachable, and supportive and shows concern for employees

Leadership style the way a leader generally behaves toward followers

Contingency theory a leadership theory that states that in order to maximize work group performance, leaders must be matched to the situation that best fits their leadership style

Situational favorableness the degree to which a particular situation either permits or denies a leader the chance to influence the behavior of group members

Leader-member relations the degree to which followers respect, trust, and like their leaders

Task structure the degree to which the requirements of a subordinate's tasks are clearly specified

Position power the degree to which leaders are able to hire, fire, reward, and punish workers

Path-goal theory a leadership theory that states that leaders can increase subordinate satisfaction and performance by clarifying and clearing the paths to goals and by increasing the number and kinds of rewards available for goal attainment

Directive leadership a leadership style in which the leader lets employees know precisely what is expected of them, gives them specific guidelines for performing tasks, schedules work, sets standards of performance, and makes sure that people follow standard rules and regulations

Supportive leadership a leadership style in which the leader is friendly and approachable, shows concern for employees and their welfare and treats them as equals, and creates a friendly climate

Participative leadership a leadership style in which the leader consults employees for their suggestions and input before making decisions

Achievement-oriented leadership a leadership style in which the leader sets challenging goals, has high expectations of employees, and displays confidence that employees will assume responsibility and put forth extraordinary effort

Normative decision theory a theory that suggests how leaders can determine an appropriate amount of employee participation when making decisions

Strategic leadership the ability to anticipate, envision, maintain flexibility, think strategically, and work with others to initiate changes that will create a positive future for an organization

Visionary leadership leadership that creates a positive image of the future that motivates organizational members and provides direction for future planning and goal setting

Charismatic leadership the behavioral tendencies and personal characteristics of leaders that create an exceptionally strong relationship between them and their followers

Ethical charismatics charismatic leaders who provide developmental opportunities for followers, are open to positive and negative feedback, recognize others' contributions, share information, and have moral standards that emphasize the larger interests of the group, organization, or society

Unethical charismatics charismatic leaders who control and manipulate followers, do what is best for themselves instead of their organizations, want to hear only positive feedback, share only information that is beneficial to themselves, and have moral standards that put their interests before everyone else's

Transformational leadership leadership that generates awareness and acceptance of a group's purpose and mission and gets employees to see beyond their own needs and self-interests for the good of the group

Transactional leadership leadership based on an exchange process, in which followers are rewarded for good performance and punished for poor performance

---

Review 4: Adapting Leader Behavior: Path-Goal Theory

> Path-goal theory states that leaders can increase subordinate satisfaction and performance by clarifying and clearing the paths to goals and by increasing the number and kinds of rewards available for goal attainment. For this to work, however, leader behavior must be a source of immediate or future satisfaction for followers and must complement and not duplicate the characteristics of followers' work environments. In contrast to Fiedler's contingency theory, path-goal theory assumes that leaders can and do change their leadership styles (directive, supportive, participative, and achievement oriented), depending on their subordinates (experience, perceived ability and internal or external locus of control) and the environment in which those subordinates work (task structure, formal authority system, and primary work group).

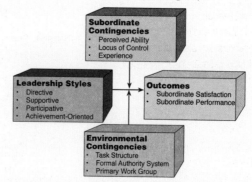

Review 5: Adapting Leader Behavior: Normative Decision Theory

> The normative decision theory helps leaders decide how much employee participation should be used when making decisions. Using the right degree of employee participation improves the quality of decisions and the extent to which employees accept and are committed to decisions. The theory specifies five different decision styles or ways of making decisions: autocratic decisions (AI or AII), consultative decisions (CI or CII), and group decisions (GII). The theory improves decision quality *via* the decision rules of quality, leader information, subordinate information, goal congruence, and problem structure. The theory improves employee commitment and acceptance *via* the decision rules of commitment probability, subordinate conflict, and commitment requirement. These decision rules help leaders improve decision quality and follower acceptance and commitment by eliminating decision styles that don't fit the decision or situation they're facing. Normative decision theory then operationalizes these decision rules in the form of yes/no questions, as shown in the decision tree displayed in Exhibit 14.8.

Review 6: Visionary Leadership

> Strategic leadership requires visionary, charismatic, and transformational leadership. Visionary leadership creates a positive image of the future that motivates organizational members and provides direction for future planning and goal setting. Charismatic leaders have strong, confident, dynamic personalities that attract followers, enable the leader to create strong bonds, and inspire followers to accomplish the leader's vision. Followers of ethical charismatic leaders work harder, are more committed and satisfied, are better performers, and are more likely to trust their leaders. Followers can be just as supportive and committed to unethical charismatics, but these leaders can pose a tremendous risk for companies. Unethical charismatics control and manipulate followers and do what is best for themselves instead of their organizations. Transformational leadership goes beyond charismatic leadership by generating awareness and acceptance of a group's purpose and mission and by getting employees to see beyond their own needs and self-interests for the good of the group. The four components of transformational leadership are charisma or idealized influence, inspirational motivation, intellectual stimulation, and individualized consideration.

LEARNING OUTCOMES

Review 1: Perception and Communication Problems

> Perception is the process by which people attend to, organize, interpret, and retain information from their environments. Perception is not a straightforward process. Because of perceptual filters such as selective perception and closure people exposed to the same information stimuli often end up with very different perceptions and understandings. Perception-based differences can also lead to differences in the attributions (internal or external) that managers and workers make when explaining workplace behavior. In general, workers are more likely to explain behavior from a defensive bias, in which they attribute problems to external causes (i.e., the situation). Managers, on the other hand, tend to commit the fundamental attribution error, attributing problems to internal causes (i.e., the worker associated with a mistake or error). Consequently, when things go wrong, it's common for managers to blame workers and for workers to blame the situation or context in which they do their jobs. Finally, this problem is compounded by a self-serving bias that leads people to attribute successes to internal causes and failures to external causes. So, when workers receive negative feedback from managers, they may become defensive and emotional and not hear what their managers have to say. In short, perceptions and attributions represent a significant challenge to effective communication and understanding in organizations.

BASIC PERCEPTION PROCESS

Stimulus · Stimulus · Stimulus

Perceptual · Attention · Filter

Perceptual · Organization · Filter

Perceptual · Interpretation · Filter

Perceptual · Retention · Filter

Perception

Review 2: Kinds of Communication

> Organizational communication depends on the communication process, formal and informal communication channels, one-on-one communication, and nonverbal communication. The major components of the communication process are the sender, the receiver, noise, and feedback. Senders often mistakenly assume that they can pipe their intended messages directly into receivers' heads with perfect clarity. Formal communication channels such as downward, upward, and horizontal communication carry organizationally approved messages and information. By contrast, the informal communication channel, called the "grapevine," arises out of curiosity and is carried out through gossip or cluster chains. There are two kinds of one-on-one communication. Coaching is used to improve on-the-job performance while counseling is used to communicate about non-job-related issues affecting job performance. Nonverbal communication, such as kinesics and paralanguage, accounts for as much as 93 percent of a message's content and understanding.

THE INTERPERSONAL COMMUNICATION PROCESS

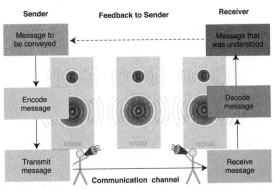

Sender · Feedback to Sender · Receiver

Message to be conveyed → Message that was understood

Encode message → Decode message

Transmit message → Receive message

Communication channel

NOISE

KEY TERMS

Communication the process of transmitting information from one person or place to another

Perception the process by which individuals attend to, organize, interpret, and retain information from their environments

Perceptual filters the personality-, psychology-, or experience-based differences that influence people to ignore or pay attention to particular stimuli

Selective perception the tendency to notice and accept objects and information consistent with our values, beliefs, and expectations while ignoring or screening out or not accepting inconsistent information

Closure the tendency to fill in gaps of missing information by assuming that what we don't know is consistent with what we already know

Attribution theory a theory that states that we all have a basic need to understand and explain the causes of other people's behavior

Defensive bias the tendency for people to perceive themselves as personally and situationally similar to someone who is having difficulty or trouble

Fundamental attribution error the tendency to ignore external causes of behavior and to attribute other people's actions to internal causes

Self-serving bias the tendency to overestimate our value by attributing successes to ourselves (internal causes) and attributing failures to others or the environment (external causes)

Encoding putting a message into a written, verbal, or symbolic form that can be recognized and understood by the receiver

Decoding the process by which the receiver translates the written, verbal, or symbolic form of a message into an understood message

Feedback to sender in the communication process, a return message to the sender that indicates the receiver's understanding of the message

Noise anything that interferes with the transmission of the intended message

Jargon vocabulary particular to a profession or group

Formal communication channel the system of official channels that carry organizationally approved messages and information

Downward communication communication that flows from higher to lower levels in an organization

Upward communication communication that flows from lower to higher levels in an organization

Horizontal communication communication that flows among managers and workers who are at the same organizational level

Informal communication channel ("grapevine") the transmission of messages from employee to employee outside of formal communication channels

Coaching communicating with someone for the direct purpose of improving the person's on-the-job performance or behavior

Counseling communicating with someone about non-job-related issues that may be affecting or interfering with the person's performance

Nonverbal communication any communication that doesn't involve words

Kinesics movements of the body and face

Paralanguage the pitch, rate, tone, volume, and speaking pattern (i.e., use of silences, pauses, or hesitations) of one's voice

Communication medium the method used to deliver an oral or written message

Hearing the act or process of perceiving sounds

Listening making a conscious effort to hear

Active listening assuming half the responsibility for successful communication by actively giving the speaker nonjudgmental feedback that shows you've accurately heard what he or she said

Empathetic listening understanding the speaker's perspective and personal frame of reference and giving feedback that conveys that understanding to the speaker

Destructive feedback feedback that disapproves without any intention of being helpful and almost always causes a negative or defensive reaction in the recipient

Constructive feedback feedback intended to be helpful, corrective, and/or encouraging

Online discussion forums the in-house equivalent of Internet newsgroups. By using Web- or software-based discussion tools that are available across the company, employees can easily ask questions and share knowledge with each other.

Televised/videotaped speeches and meetings speeches and meetings originally made to a smaller audience that are either simultaneously broadcast to other locations in the company or videotaped for subsequent distribution and viewing

Organizational silence when employees withhold information about organizational problems or issues

Company hotlines phone numbers that anyone in the company can call anonymously to leave information for upper management

Survey feedback information that is collected by surveys from organizational members and then compiled, disseminated, and used to develop action plans for improvement

Blog a personal Web site that provides personal opinions or recommendations, news summaries, and reader comments

Review 3: Managing One-on-One Communication

> One-on-one communication can be managed by choosing the right communication medium, being a good listener, and giving effective feedback. Managers generally prefer oral communication because it provides the opportunity to ask questions and assess nonverbal communication. Oral communication is best suited to complex, ambiguous, or emotionally laden topics. Written communication is best suited for delivering straightforward messages and information. Listening is important for managerial success, but most people are terrible listeners. To improve your listening skills, choose to be an active listener (clarify responses, paraphrase, and summarize) and an empathetic listener (show your desire to understand, reflect feelings). Feedback can be constructive or destructive. To be constructive, feedback must be immediate, focused on specific behaviors, and problem-oriented.

Review 4: Managing Organization-Wide Communication

> Managers need methods for managing organization-wide communication and for making themselves accessible so that they can hear what employees throughout their organizations are feeling and thinking. Email, online discussion forums, televised/videotaped speeches and conferences, and broadcast voice mail make it much easier for managers to improve message transmission and get the message out. By contrast, anonymous company hotlines, survey feedback, frequent informal meetings, and surprise visits help managers avoid organizational silence and improve reception by giving them the opportunity to hear what others in the organization feel and think. Monitoring internal and external blogs is another way to find out what people are saying and thinking about your organization.

LEARNING OUTCOMES

Review 1: The Control Process

> The control process begins by setting standards, measuring performance, and then comparing performance to the standards. The better a company's information and measurement systems, the easier it is to make these comparisons. The control process continues by identifying and analyzing performance deviations and then developing and implementing programs for corrective action. Control is a continuous, dynamic, cybernetic process, not a one-time achievement or result. Control requires frequent managerial attention. The three basic control methods are feedback control (after-the-fact performance information), concurrent control (simultaneous performance information), and feedforward control (preventive performance information). Control has regulation costs and unanticipated consequences and therefore isn't always worthwhile or possible.

Cybernetic Control Process

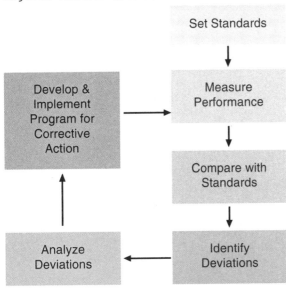

Source: H. Koontz and R. W. Bradspies, "Managing through Feedforward Control: A Future-Directed View," *Business Horizons*, June 1972, 25–36. Reprinted with permission from *Business Horizons*, © 1972 by the Trustees at Indiana University, Kelley School of Business.

Review 2: Control Methods

> There are five methods of control: bureaucratic, objective, normative, concertive, and self-control (self-management). Bureaucratic and objective controls are top-down, management-based, and measurement-based. Normative and concertive controls represent shared forms of control because they evolve from company-wide or team-based beliefs and values. Self-control, or self-management, is a control system in which managers turn much, but not all, control over to the individuals themselves.

   Bureaucratic control is based on organizational policies, rules, and procedures. Objective controls are based on reliable measures of behavior or outputs. Normative control is based on strong corporate beliefs and careful hiring practices. Concertive control is based on the development of values, beliefs, and rules in autonomous work groups. Self-control is based on individuals' setting their own goals, monitoring themselves, and rewarding or punishing themselves with respect to goal achievement.

KEY TERMS

Control a regulatory process of establishing standards to achieve organizational goals, comparing actual performance to the standards, and taking corrective action when necessary

Standards a basis of comparison for measuring the extent to which various kinds of organizational performance are satisfactory or unsatisfactory

Benchmarking the process of identifying outstanding practices, processes, and standards in other companies and adapting them to your company

Cybernetic the process of steering or keeping on course

Feedback control a mechanism for gathering information about performance deficiencies after they occur

Concurrent control a mechanism for gathering information about performance deficiencies as they occur, thereby eliminating or shortening the delay between performance and feedback

Feedforward control a mechanism for monitoring performance inputs rather than outputs to prevent or minimize performance deficiencies before they occur

Control loss the situation in which behavior and work procedures do not conform to standards

Regulation costs the costs associated with implementing or maintaining control

Cybernetic feasibility the extent to which it is possible to implement each step in the control process

Bureaucratic control the use of hierarchical authority to influence employee behavior by rewarding or punishing employees for compliance or noncompliance with organizational policies, rules, and procedures

Objective control the use of observable measures of worker behavior or outputs to assess performance and influence behavior

Behavior control the regulation of the behaviors and actions that workers perform on the job

Output control the regulation of workers' results or outputs through rewards and incentives

Normative control the regulation of workers' behavior and decisions through widely shared organizational values and beliefs

Concertive control the regulation of workers' behavior and decisions through work group values and beliefs

Self-control (self-management) a control system in which managers and workers control their own behavior by setting their own goals, monitoring their own progress, and rewarding themselves for goal achievement

Balanced scorecard measurement of organizational performance in four equally important areas: finances, customers, internal operations, and innovation and learning

Suboptimization performance improvement in one part of an organization but at the expense of decreased performance in another part

Cash flow analysis a type of analysis that predicts how changes in a business will affect its ability to take in more cash than it pays out

Balance sheets accounting statements that provide a snapshot of a company's financial position at a particular time

Income statements accounting statements, also called "profit and loss statements," that show what has happened to an organization's income, expenses, and net profit over a period of time

Financial ratios calculations typically used to track a business's liquidity (cash), efficiency, and profitability over time compared to other businesses in its industry

Budgets quantitative plans through which managers decide how to allocate available money to best accomplish company goals

Economic value added (EVA) the amount by which company profits (revenues, minus expenses, minus taxes) exceed the cost of capital in a given year

Customer defections a performance assessment in which companies identify which customers are leaving and measure the rate at which they are leaving

Value customer perception that the product quality is excellent for the price offered

When to Use Different Methods of Control

BUREAUCRATIC CONTROL	• When it is necessary to standardize operating procedures • When it is necessary to establish limits
BEHAVIOR CONTROL	• When it is easier to measure what workers do on the job than what they accomplish on the job • When cause-effect relationships are clear; that is, when companies know which behaviors will lead to success and which won't • When good measures of worker behavior can be created
OUTPUT CONTROL	• When it is easier to measure what workers accomplish on the job than what they do on the job • When good measures of worker output can be created • When it is possible to set clear goals and standards for worker output • When cause-effect relationships are unclear
NORMATIVE CONTROL	• When organizational culture, values, and beliefs are strong • When it is difficult to create good measures of worker behavior • When it is difficult to create good measures of worker output
CONCERTIVE CONTROL	• When responsibility for task accomplishment is given to autonomous work groups • When management wants workers to take ownership of their behavior and outputs • When management desires a strong form of worker-based control
SELF-CONTROL	• When workers are intrinsically motivated to do their jobs well • When it is difficult to create good measures of worker behavior • When it is difficult to create good measures of worker output • When workers have or are taught self-control and self-leadership skills

Sources: L. J. Kirsch, "The Management of Complex Tasks in Organizations: Controlling the Systems Development Process," *Organization Science* 7 (1996): 1–21; S. A. Snell, "Control Theory in Strategic Human Resource Management: The Mediating Effect of Administrative Information," *Academy of Management Journal* 35 (1992): 292–327.

We end this section by noting that each of these control methods may be more or less appropriate depending on the circumstances.

Review 3: What to Control?

> Deciding what to control is just as important as deciding whether to control or how to control. In most companies, performance is measured using financial measures alone. However, the balanced scorecard encourages managers to measure and control company performance from four perspectives: financial, customers, internal operations, and innovation and learning. Traditionally, financial control has been achieved through cash flow analysis, balance sheets, income statements, financial ratios, and budgets. (For a refresher on these traditional financial control tools, see the next card, which is a Financial Review Card.) Another way to measure and control financial performance is through economic value added (EVA). Unlike traditional financial measures, EVA helps managers assess whether they are performing well enough to pay the cost of the capital needed to run the business. Instead of using customer satisfaction surveys to measure performance, companies should pay attention to customer defectors, who are more likely to speak up about what the company is doing wrong. Performance of internal operations is often measured in terms of quality, which is defined in three ways: excellence, value, and conformance to expectations. Minimizing waste has become an important part of innovation and learning in companies. The four levels of waste minimization are waste prevention and reduction, recycling and reuse, waste treatment, and waste disposal.

Calculating Economic Value Added (EVA)

1. Calculate net operating profit after taxes (NOPAT).	$3,500,000
2. Identify how much capital the company has invested (i.e., spent).	$16,800,000
3. Determine the cost (i.e., rate) paid for capital (usually between 5 percent and 13 percent).	10%
4. Multiply capital used (Step 2) times cost of capital (Step 3).	(10% × $16,800,000) = $1,680,000
5. Subtract the total dollar cost of capital from net profit after taxes.	$3,500,000 OPTA –$1,680,000 Total cost of capital $1,820,000 Economic value added

Basic Accounting Tools for Controlling Financial Performance

STEPS FOR A BASIC CASH FLOW ANALYSIS

1. Forecast sales (steady, up, or down).
2. Project changes in anticipated cash inflows (as a result of changes).
3. Project anticipated cash outflows (as a result of changes).
4. Project net cash flows by combining anticipated cash inflows and outflows.

PARTS OF A BASIC BALANCE SHEET (ASSETS = LIABILITIES + OWNER'S EQUITY)

1. Assets
   a. Current Assets (cash, short-term investment, marketable securities, accounts receivable, etc.)
   b. Fixed Assets (land, buildings, machinery, equipment, etc.)

2. Liabilities
   a. Current Liabilities (accounts payable, notes payable, taxes payable, etc.)
   b. Long-Term Liabilities (long-term debt, deferred income taxes, etc.)

3. Owner's Equity
   a. Preferred stock and common stock
   b. Additional paid-in capital
   c. Retained earnings

BASIC INCOME STATEMENT

```
  SALES REVENUE
- sales returns and allowances
+ other income
= NET REVENUE
- cost of goods sold (beginning inventory, costs of goods purchased, ending
  inventory)
= GROSS PROFIT
- total operating expenses (selling, general, and administrative expenses)
= INCOME FROM OPERATIONS
- interest expense
= PRETAX INCOME
- income taxes
= NET INCOME
```

Common Kinds of Budgets

Revenue Budgets—used to project or forecast future sales.	• Accuracy of projection depends on economy, competitors, sales force estimates, etc. • Determined by estimating future sales volume and sales prices for all products and services.
Expense Budgets—used within departments and divisions to determine how much will be spent on various supplies, projects, or activities.	• One of the first places that companies look for cuts when trying to lower expenses.
Profit Budgets—used by profit centers, which have "profit and loss" responsibility.	• Profit budgets combine revenue and expense budgets into one budget. • Typically used in large businesses with multiple plants and divisions.
Cash Budgets—used to forecast how much cash a company will have on hand to meet expenses.	• Similar to cash flow analyses. • Used to identify cash shortfalls, which must be covered to pay bills, or cash excesses, which should be invested for a higher return.
Capital Expenditure Budgets—used to forecast large, long-lasting investments in equipment, buildings, and property.	• Help managers identify funding that will be needed to pay for future expansion or strategic moves designed to increase competitive advantage.
Variable Budgets—used to project costs across varying levels of sales and revenues.	• Important because it is difficult to accurately predict sales revenue and volume. • Lead to more accurate budgeting with respect to labor, materials, and administrative expenses, which vary with sales volume and revenues. • Build flexibility into the budgeting process.

Common Financial Ratios

RATIOS	FORMULA	WHAT IT MEANS	WHEN TO USE
LIQUIDITY RATIOS			
Current Ratio	$\dfrac{\text{Current Assets}}{\text{Current Liabilities}}$	• Whether you have enough assets on hand to pay for short-term bills and obligations. • Higher is better. • Recommended level is two times as many current assets as current liabilities.	• Track monthly and quarterly. • Basic measure of your company's health.
Quick (Acid Test) Ratio	$\dfrac{(\text{Current Assets} - \text{Inventories})}{\text{Current Liabilities}}$	• Stricter than current ratio. • Whether you have enough (i.e., cash) to pay short-term bills and obligations. • Higher is better. • Recommended level is one or higher.	• Track monthly. • Also calculate quick ratio with potential customers to evaluate whether they're likely to pay you in a timely manner.
LEVERAGE RATIOS			
Debt to Equity	$\dfrac{\text{Total Liabilities}}{\text{Total Equity}}$	• Indicates how much the company is leveraged (in debt) by comparing what is owed (liabilities) to what is owned (equity). • Lower is better. A high debt-to-equity ratio could indicate that the company has too much debt. • Recommended level depends on industry.	• Track monthly. • Lenders often use this to determine the creditworthiness of a business (i.e., whether to approve additional loans).
Debt Coverage	$\dfrac{(\text{Net Profit} + \text{Noncash Expense})}{\text{Debt}}$	• Indicates how well cash flow covers debt payments. • Higher is better.	• Track monthly. • Lenders look at this ratio to determine if there is adequate cash to make loan payments.
EFFICIENCY RATIOS			
Inventory Turnover	$\dfrac{\text{Cost of Goods Sold}}{\text{Average Value of Inventory}}$	• Whether you're making efficient use of inventory. • Higher is better, indicating that inventory (dollars) isn't purchased (spent) until needed. • Recommended level depends on industry.	• Track monthly by using a 12-month rolling average.
Average Collections Period	$\dfrac{\text{Accounts Receivable}}{(\text{Annual Net Credit Sales Divided by 365})}$	• Shows on average how quickly your customers are paying their bills. • Recommended level is no more than 15 days longer than credit terms. If credit is net 30 days, then average should not be longer than 45 days.	• Track monthly. • Use to determine how long company's money is being tied up in customer credit.
PROFITABILITY RATIOS			
Gross Profit Margin	$\dfrac{\text{Gross Profit}}{\text{Total Sales}}$	• Shows how efficiently a business is using its materials and labor in the production process. • Higher is better, indicating that a profit can be made if fixed costs are controlled.	• Track monthly. • Analyze when unsure about product or service pricing. • Low margin compared to competitors means you're underpricing.
Return on Equity	$\dfrac{\text{Net Income}}{\text{Owner's Equity}}$	• Shows what was earned on your investment in the business during a particular period. Often called "return on investment." • Higher is better.	• Track quarterly and annually. • Use to compare to what you might have earned on the stock market, bonds, or government Treasury bills during the same period.

LEARNING OUTCOMES

Review 1: Productivity

> Productivity is a measure of how many inputs it takes to produce or create an output. The greater the output from one input, or the fewer inputs it takes to create an output, the higher the productivity. Partial productivity measures how much of a single kind of input such as labor is needed to produce an output. Multifactor productivity is an overall measure of productivity that indicates how much labor, capital, materials, and energy are needed to produce an output.

$$\text{Partial Productivity} = \frac{\text{Outputs}}{\text{Single Kind of Input}}$$

$$\frac{\text{Multifactor}}{\text{Productivity}} = \frac{\text{Outputs}}{(\text{Labor} + \text{Capital} + \text{Materials} + \text{Energy})}$$

Review 2: Quality

> Quality can mean a product or service free of deficiencies or the characteristics of a product or service that satisfy customer needs. Quality products usually possess three characteristics: reliability, serviceability, and durability. Quality service means reliability, tangibles, responsiveness, assurance, and empathy. ISO 9000 is a series of five international standards for achieving consistency in quality management and quality assurance, while ISO 14000 is a set of standards for minimizing an organization's harmful effects on the environment. The Baldrige National Quality Award recognizes U.S. companies for their achievements in quality and business performance. Each year, three Baldrige Awards may be given for manufacturing, service, small business, education, and health care. Total quality management (TQM) is an integrated organization-wide strategy for improving product and service quality. TQM is based on three mutually reinforcing principles: customer focus and satisfaction, continuous improvement, and teamwork.

Review 3: Service Operations

> Services are different from goods. Goods are produced, tangible, and storable. Services are performed, intangible, and perishable. Likewise, managing service operations is different from managing production operations. The service-profit chain indicates that success begins with internal service quality, meaning how well management treats service employees. Internal service quality leads to employee satisfaction and service capability, which, in turn, lead to high-value service to customers, customer satisfaction, customer loyalty, and long-term profits and growth. Keeping existing customers is far more cost-effective than finding new ones. Consequently, to prevent disgruntled customers from leaving, some companies are empowering service employees to perform service recovery—restoring customer satisfaction to strongly

Service-Profit Chain

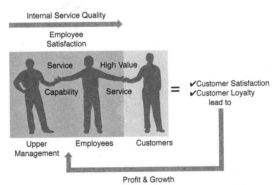

Sources: R. Hallowell, L. A. Schlesinger, and J. Zornitsky, "Internal Service Quality, Customer and Job Satisfaction: Linkages and Implications for Management," *Human Resource Planning* 19 (1996): 20–31; J. L. Heskett, T. O. Jones, G. W. Loveman, W. E. Sasser, Jr., and L. A. Schlesinger, "Putting the Service-Profit Chain to Work," *Harvard Business Review* (March–April 1994): 164–174.

KEY TERMS

Productivity a measure of performance that indicates how many inputs it takes to produce or create an output

Partial productivity a measure of performance that indicates how much of a particular kind of input it takes to produce an output

Multifactor productivity an overall measure of performance that indicates how much labor, capital, materials, and energy it takes to produce an output

Quality a product or service free of deficiencies, or the characteristics of a product or service that satisfy customer needs

ISO 9000 a series of five international standards, from ISO 9000 to ISO 9004, for achieving consistency in quality management and quality assurance in companies throughout the world

ISO 14000 a series of international standards for managing, monitoring, and minimizing an organization's harmful effects on the environment

Total quality management (TQM) an integrated, principle-based, organization-wide strategy for improving product and service quality

Customer focus an organizational goal to concentrate on meeting customers' needs at all levels of the organization

Customer satisfaction an organizational goal to provide products or services that meet or exceed customers' expectations

Continuous improvement an organization's ongoing commitment to constantly assess and improve the processes and procedures used to create products and services

Variation a deviation in the form, condition, or appearance of a product from the quality standard for that product

Teamwork collaboration between managers and nonmanagers, across business functions, and between companies, customers, and suppliers

Service recovery restoring customer satisfaction to strongly dissatisfied customers

Make-to-order operation a manufacturing operation that does not start processing or assembling products until a customer order is received

Assemble-to-order operation a manufacturing operation that divides manufacturing processes into separate parts or modules that are combined to create semicustomized products

Make-to-stock operation a manufacturing operation that orders parts and assembles standardized products before receiving customer orders

Manufacturing flexibility the degree to which manufacturing operations can easily and quickly change the number, kind, and characteristics of products they produce

Continuous-flow production a manufacturing operation that produces goods at a continuous, rather than a discrete, rate

Line-flow production manufacturing processes that are preestablished, occur in a serial or linear manner, and are dedicated to making one type of product

Batch production a manufacturing operation that produces goods in large batches in standard lot sizes

Job shops manufacturing operations that handle custom orders or small batch jobs

Inventory the amount and number of raw materials, parts, and finished products that a company has in its possession

Raw material inventories the basic inputs in a manufacturing process

Component parts inventories the basic parts used in manufacturing that are fabricated from raw materials

Work-in-process inventories partially finished goods consisting of assembled component parts

Finished goods inventories the final outputs of manufacturing operations

Average aggregate inventory average overall inventory during a particular time period

Stockout the situation when a company runs out of finished product

Inventory turnover the number of times per year that a company sells or "turns over" its average inventory

Ordering cost the costs associated with ordering inventory, including the cost of data entry, phone calls, obtaining bids, correcting mistakes, and determining when and how much inventory to order

Setup cost the costs of downtime and lost efficiency that occur when a machine is changed or adjusted to produce a different kind of inventory

Holding cost the cost of keeping inventory until it is used or sold, including storage, insurance, taxes, obsolescence, and opportunity costs

Stockout costs the costs incurred when a company runs out of a product, including transaction costs to replace inventory and the loss of customers' goodwill

Economic order quantity (EOQ) a system of formulas that minimizes ordering and holding costs and helps determine how much and how often inventory should be ordered

Just-in-time (JIT) inventory system an inventory system in which component parts arrive from suppliers just as they are needed at each stage of production

Kanban a ticket-based JIT system that indicates when to reorder inventory

Materials requirement planning (MRP) a production and inventory system that determines the production schedule, production batch sizes, and inventory needed to complete final products

Independent demand system an inventory system in which the level of one kind of inventory does not depend on another

Dependent demand system an inventory system in which the level of inventory depends on the number of finished units to be produced

dissatisfied customers—by giving them the authority and responsibility to immediately solve customer problems. The hope is that empowered service recovery will prevent customer defections.

Review 4: Manufacturing Operations

> Manufacturing operations produce physical goods. Manufacturing operations can be classified according to the amount of processing or assembly that occurs after receiving an order from a customer.

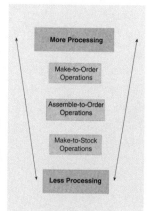

Manufacturing operations can also be classified in terms of flexibility, the degree to which the number, kind, and characteristics of products can easily and quickly be changed. Flexibility allows companies to respond quickly to competitors and customers and to reduce order lead times, but it can also lead to higher unit costs.

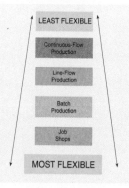

Review 5: Inventory

> There are four kinds of inventory: raw materials, component parts, work-in-process, and finished goods. Because companies incur ordering, setup, holding, and stockout costs when handling inventory, inventory costs can be enormous. To control those costs, companies measure and track inventory in three ways: average aggregate inventory, weeks of supply, and turnover. Companies meet the basic goals of inventory management (avoiding stockouts and reducing inventory without hurting daily operations) through economic order quantity (EOQ) formulas, just-in-time (JIT) inventory systems, and materials requirement planning (MRP).

$$EOQ = \sqrt{\frac{2DO}{4}}$$

Use EOQ formulas when inventory levels are independent, and use JIT and MRP when inventory levels are dependent on the number of products to be produced.